W9-DEI-077

GEORGE SAND

GEORGE SAND
Writing for Her Life

Isabelle Hoog Naginski

RUTGERS UNIVERSITY PRESS
New Brunswick and London

Library of Congress Cataloging-in-Publication Data

Naginski, Isabelle Hoog
George Sand : writing for her life / Isabelle Hoog Naginski.
p.   cm.
Includes bibliographical references and index.
ISBN 0-8135-1640-4   (cloth)   ISBN 0-8135-1674-9 (pbk.)
1. Sand, George, 1804–1876—Criticism and interpretation.
I. Title.
PQ2417.N34   1991
843'.7—dc20   90-42140
                                                                                    CIP

British Cataloging-in-Publication information available

Frontispiece: Calamatta, Portrait of George Sand,
Cliché: Musées de la Ville de Paris.
Photo copyright © 1991 by Spadem.

for Marie-Jacques and Armand,
for different reasons

Contents

Acknowledgments

My interest in George Sand was first sparked by all the allusions to her that I constantly encountered in nineteenth-century Russian literature when I was a graduate student in the mid-1970s. It intensified when I discovered the depth of her importance for Dostoevsky, both as a thinker and as a novelist. Why, I began asking myself, did this writer seem to occupy such a central position in nineteenth-century intellectual thought, when she was never mentioned or read in any of my French and Russian literature seminars at Columbia University? Finally I decided to find out for myself. I first read *Lélia*, then *Spiridion*. I was dazzled, I was entranced, and I have been reading her ever since. Joseph Frank, the eminent Dostoevsky scholar, encouraged me in that early probing period to study her further and I express my gratitude to him here.

This book might never have been written without the Friends of George Sand, an organization founded by Natalie Datlof at Hofstra University in 1976, and subsequently instrumental in putting George Sand studies on the scholarly map in this country. Their founding of two journals, the *George Sand Newsletter* and *George Sand Studies*, has also meant that serious work on Sand could be published at a time when she herself was still not considered a serious writer by the prevailing consensus. The group has been extremely supportive of all Sand scholarship and has hosted eight international George Sand conferences in the last fourteen years, providing a forum where ideas could be shared, probed, and discussed. This organization's existence has made a world of difference for me. To its founder, Natalie Datlof, and to several members of the group, Eve Sourian, David Powell, Annabelle Rea, and—especially—Marie M. Collins, I extend my heartfelt thanks.

Much of my own work has depended very directly on the remarkable work accomplished by Georges Lubin since 1964. No *Sandiste* can ever thank him enough for his exquisite erudition, his impeccable edition of *Histoire de ma vie,* and his masterly compilation of Sand's correspondence, which has been a labor of love for over twenty-five years. Above and beyond this, Georges Lubin has been a wonderful advisor and friend, patiently answering my questions, verifying certain points, and encouraging my sometimes hesitant formulations. A special personal expression of gratitude goes to him here.

I also thank many friends and colleagues who took the time to read parts of the manuscript and to offer encouragement and invaluable comments: Victor Brombert, Simone Vierne, Murray Sachs, Frank Bowman, Lucienne Frappier-Mazur, Barbara T. Cooper, Simone Balayé, Alan Clayton, Eglal Henein, Seymour Simches, Donald Fanger, and Brigitte Lane. Special gratitude goes to Henri Peyre who, sadly, is not alive today to see this book but who would have been one of the first to read it. The earliest part of the work on this project was done at Bard College, and I am grateful to a number of my former colleagues there, William Wilson, Peter Sourian, Lois Oppenheim, for their early encouragement. I also acknowledge the support of Bard's president, Leon Botstein, in connection with the Fifth George Sand Conference, held there in 1982. I am grateful for the invaluable help of my two research assistants. Erika Naginski checked footnotes, tracked down articles in the library, and cheerfully got me through the grimmer moments of revision. Janice Lamberg helped with the massive amount of translating that had to be done. I thank Leslie Mitchner, executive editor at Rutgers University Press, for her patient encouragement during the six years it took me to write this book.

Tufts University has provided continued support and encouragement in the form of a semester of research leave, a summer stipend, and extra funds for equipment and for manuscript assistants. I thank my colleagues in the Romance Languages department and, especially, the dean of the college, Mary Ella Feinleib, for believing in this book at a time when it was still in its germinal stage. My profound thanks go to the Mary Ingraham Bunting Institute of Radcliffe College for providing me with a room of my own and a serene cadre where I spent eight months in blissful retreat in 1988. I am also indebted to the Gilbert Chinard Foundation for a summer scholarship in 1986 which made possible further research at the Bibliothèque Nationale, and to the American Council of Learned Societies for a travel grant to France in the summer of 1989.

I thank Gaylord Brynolfson, who has spent many long hours pruning Gallicisms from my prose and whose invaluable encouragement during the gestation period of this book is too great to be fully measured. I am also grateful that he has put his bibliographic skill at the service of this book, and compiled the index.

My parents, Marie-Jacques Hoog and Armand Hoog, both fellow *dix-neuvièmistes*, have been inspiring models of critical imagination, careful readers, and wise critics. In gratitude for their generosity of spirit and vision, I dedicate this book to them.

Parts of the text have appeared in different form in *The George Sand Newsletter*, 4/2 (winter 1981): 38–41; the *Bulletin de la Société des Professeurs Français en Amérique*, (1983–1984): 21–36; *George Sand Studies*, 7/1–2 (1984–1985): 46–53; *Proceedings of the Seventh George Sand International Conference* (New York: University Press of America, 1991). They are reproduced with permission of the publishers.

Medford, Massachusetts   Isabelle Hoog Naginski
March 1990

List of Abbreviations

The following abbreviations and short titles have been used in this book. All pertain to works of George Sand, with the exception of the one periodical listed at the end.

Compagnon	*Le Compagnon du Tour de France* (Plan de la Tour (Var): Editions d'Aujourd'hui, 1976).
Consuelo	*Consuelo. La Comtesse de Rudolstadt*, ed. Simone Vierne and René Bourgeois, 3 vols. (Meylan: Editions de l'Aurore, 1983).
Corr.	*Correspondance*, ed. Georges Lubin, 23 vols. (Paris: Garnier, 1964–).
François le champi	*François le champi*, ed. André Fermigier (Paris: Folio, 1976).
HV	*Histoire de ma vie*, in *Oeuvres autobiographiques*, ed. Georges Lubin, 2 vols. (Paris: Pléiade, 1970–1971).
Indiana	*Indiana*, ed. Béatrice Didier (Paris: Folio, 1984).
Lélia	*Lélia*, (1833 edition) ed. Pierre Reboul (Paris: Garnier, 1960).
Lélia II	For citations from the 1839 edition of *Lélia*, I use Béatrice Didier's modern critical edition, 2 vols. (Meylan: Editions de l'Aurore, 1987).
LV	*Lettres d'un voyageur*, ed. Henri Bonnet, (Paris: Garnier-Flammarion, 1971).
La Mare	*La Mare au diable*, ed. Léon Cellier, (Paris: Folio, 1973).
Monsieur Antoine	*Le Péché de Monsieur Antoine*, ed. Jean Courrier and Jean-Hervé Donnard (Meylan: Editions de l'Aurore, 1982).
OA	*Oeuvres autobiographiques* (excluding *Histoire de ma vie* and *Lettres d'un voyageur*), ed. Georges Lubin, 2 vols. (Paris: Pléiade, 1970–1971).

"Obermann"   "Obermann," in *Questions d'art et de littérature*
                    (Paris: Calmann-Lévy, 1878).

Rêveur   *Histoire du rêveur,* presented and annotated by
                    Thierry Bodin in *Présence de George Sand,* 17, juin
                    1983.

Spiridion   *Spiridion* (Plan de la Tour, Var: Editions d'au-
                    jourd'hui, 1976), Collection "Les Introuvables."

Valentine   *Valentine,* ed. Aline Alquier (Meylan: Editions
                    de l'Aurore, 1988).

RDM   *La Revue des deux mondes*

All translations, unless indicated otherwise, are my own.

Unless stated otherwise, emphasis in the quotation is the author's.

For transliteration of the Russian, I have used the Library of Congress
system in the notes (Dostoevskii, Belinskii, Natal'ia, Lidiia). In the text,
however, I use the standard English orthography for common sur-
names (Dostoevsky, Belinsky, etc.) and first names (Natalia, Lidia).

GEORGE SAND

La liberté est le point de départ de tout acte intellectuel comme de
toute action physique.

GEORGE SAND

(Freedom is the point of departure for any intellectual act as it is
for any physical action.)

Following a visit to George Sand at Nohant in the spring of 1838,
Honoré de Balzac sent Eve Hanska a detailed account of his stay: "I
found comrade Georges [sic] Sand in her bathrobe," he writes, "smoking a cigar after dinner, sitting in front of her fireplace, in an immense
and solitary room. She was wearing pretty yellow slippers . . . and a
red pair of pants. . . . Her life is similar to mine. She goes to bed at six
in the morning and gets up at noon . . . for three days we talked from
late afternoon until five in the morning." Balzac's narration encapsulates several key elements of what has come to be known as the Sand
legend. The smoking, male attire, and nocturnal life-style noted by
Balzac conjure up a vision of the writer which is both outrageous and
unfeminine. Balzac, in fact, never ceased to consider George Sand as a
man, as a *camarade* whose first name, George, he consistently spelled
with an *s*, in the traditional French orthography: "She is masculine . . . she is an artist . . . she has the noble characteristics of a
man, *ergo* she is not a woman," he asserted in the same letter.[1] The philosopher Alain's double-edged compliment, "this great woman was a
great man," echoes Balzac's description. Both present Sand as a freak
of nature, a phenomenon *contre nature*, thereby emphasizing the image
of her as a kind of honorary man.

An equally prevalent but altogether different aspect of the Sand
legend is manifest in the notorious anecdote concerning Sand's first
meeting with Alfred de Musset at a dinner party. In this incident the
legendary Sand behaves with archetypical feminine coquettishness
and cruelty. In the version her biographer Curtis Cate recounts, Sand
"turned up for this dinner in an unusual bolero, with a little gem-
studded dagger provocatively dangling from her waist belt." When
asked by her future lover what she did with the "plaything . . . with
which she had come armed," Sand replied that she carried it around
for her own safety and as a convenient substitute for a cavalier servant.
Expressing interest in how she would use her weapon, Musset got the
reply "That is up to you."[2] Thus enthralled by Sand's clever repartee,
says the legend, Musset was ensnared in the temptress's net.

The two events recounted in the literature of the time, stressing
Sand's eccentric behavior, her mannish bearing, her provocative dress,

and her penchant for a certain sexual playfulness in her dealings with men, stand out as icons of the writer's infamous reputation. One might want to add a third vision of Sand as a cultural dilettante, lying in adulation under Chopin's piano. Today the mere mention of her name conjures up in our collective cultural consciousness a kaleidoscope of ready-made and somewhat antithetical images. A cigar-smoking young woman dressed in men's clothing. A femme fatale who devoured her lovers, one after the other. A collector of famous men whom she made into lovers, friends, or protégés. Later, her incarnation as "la bonne dame de Nohant" would depict her as a portly chatelaine, a matronly do-gooder. Not surprisingly, these aspects of Sand's spectacular career have provoked the most interest. These clichés have supplanted her rightful identity as a great nineteenth-century novelist. Instead of being studied as one of the main practitioners of the modern novel, as a major figure among male and female writers, she is most often regarded as an author of pastoral tales à l'eau de rose, the kind of books formerly given out to children as end-of-the-year school prizes, or as a sentimental lady-writer whose romantic novels have never been worthy of inclusion in the literary canon.

Vastly famous in her time, Sand and her works have languished in obscurity for much of the present century. Today most of her books are out of print, and few critical editions exist. The bulk of her oeuvre is in our day unread and unknown. Idolized in her own age, she is now an object of scorn for many critics. Her enormous fictional output may strike the amateur as an impenetrable maze of old-fashioned narratives without relevance for the modern sensibility. Yet this problematic literary figure, with her tainted reputation, around whom so many myths have crystallized, deserves another book, one that—unlike so many preceding studies—would steer attention away from the legendary cigars and sadistic daggers.

The present study, by concentrating on Sand's literary production, aims to reestablish her as one of the preeminent novelists in nineteenth-century French literature, whose work remains important both in its own right and as a force in the development of the modern novel. While a number of her contemporaries limited themselves to writing a single type of novel, Sand explored the contours of what the critic Eugène Pelletan called the novel's "maximal flexibility." Not content to establish a single style and a single formula for her fictions, she tried her hand at virtually every novelistic genre possible. Some were traditional, such as the epistolary novel, *Jacques* (1834), or the historical novel of adventure à la Walter Scott such as *L'Uscoque* (1839). Others, such as the *roman de moeurs*, the novel of the *mal du siècle*, or the novel of psychological analysis (*Indiana* and *Valentine*, both 1832; *Elle et lui*, 1859) were forms that she explored together with her fellow writers of the Romantic age. Yet other genres she helped to develop: the social novel,

Horace (1842), which deals with the Paris riots of 1832; the proletarian novel, *La Ville noire* (1861); the feminist novel of education, *Mauprat* (1837); and the political novel, *Mademoiselle la Quintinie* (1863). In other instances she was an innovator, creating new genres. Examples are the pastoral novel, or *roman champêtre* (*Jeanne*, 1844; *La Mare au diable*, 1846; *François le champi*, 1850; *La Petite Fadette*, 1849; *Les Maîtres sonneurs*, 1853); the metaphysical novel, *Spiridion* (1839), and play, *Les Sept Cordes de la lyre* (1840); the utopian socialist novel (*Le Compagnon du tour de France*, 1840; *Le Meunier d'Angibault*, 1845; *Le Péché de Monsieur Antoine*, 1845); and the female *Bildungsroman* which incorporated elements of Gothic prose and of the *roman initiatique*. *Lélia* (1833 and 1839), *Consuelo* (1842–1843) and its sequel, *La Comtesse de Rudolstadt* (1843–1844), are masterpieces belonging to this last category.

To trace the metamorphosis of the writer's name, from Aurore Dupin to Madame Casimir Dudevant, to J. Sand, to G. Sand, to Georges Sand (with an *s*), and finally to the name as we know it today, George Sand, is also to witness the astonishing transformation of a seemingly ordinary woman into a first-rate novelist. When Sand eliminated the *s* in George to sign *Lélia* in 1833, she not only anglicized her name, she also defamiliarized the traditional French spelling of the masculine name Georges with an *s*. It is tempting to speculate that, by dropping the final mute consonant from her pseudonym, Sand was also disassociating herself from the phallocentric equation of writing with the male sphere, dropping the phallus, so to speak, as a superfluous appendage for the purpose of literary enterprise. With its excised *s*, the name George Sand looks odd in French; it is not readily associated with the masculine, yet does not strike the reader as feminine in the least. It is a truly androgynous nom de plume; suggesting that for its bearer, the play with *textual* identity was necessarily also a play with *sexual* identity. And if exploding the traditional concepts of gender was a major preoccupation of many French Romantics such as Henri de Latouche, Théophile Gautier, Stendhal, and Balzac, George Sand went much farther than any of them in exploring the unknown continent of androgyny.

Not only did Sand treat this concept in her fiction, as illustrated by characters in *Gabriel*, *Lélia*, and *L'Uscoque* among others, she also transposed the need for an androgynous vision into her narrative strategies. Examples abound of narrators who are grammatically masculine: in *Indiana*, *Lettres d'un voyageur*, *Horace*, *Mauprat*, *La Mare au diable*, *François le champi*, to name just a few. Yet, since their voices express fictional complicity with the female heroines rather than with the male characters, the stance of those narrators is frequently problematic. Narrative androgyny must be understood as a striking instance of the author's gender partially going underground. As she forged her role as a nineteenth-century writer, Sand found it necessary to speak in a double-voiced discourse. And while this phenomenon may be ascribed in part to an aspect of Sand's own psychotextual identity, it also reflects certain aspects of French society in the 1830s and 1840s. The changing role of the writer in the age of mass-produced literature destined for an increasingly large and avid reading public is one significant factor. The shifting meaning of "woman" in the first half of the nineteenth century, as evidenced by the multitude of theories regarding "the woman question" from a variety of different perspectives (Saint-Simonian, Fourierist, Marxist) is another. Sand's works articulated the increasingly complex view of gender with great forcefulness as well as the yearning for an intellectual androgyny which many literary and philosophical circles of her day had begun to voice.

In tracing the development of the feminine authorial voice in French literature up to the present, we can discern on the part of women writers an increasingly uneasy awareness of the complexities of self-expression within a male-defined literary sphere. The eighteenth-century women writers—or "gynographs," as Restif de la Bretonne mockingly called them—up to and including Germaine de Staël, as we might expect, made use of a feminine narrative strategy consisting of a feminine "je" that coincided both grammatically and ideologically with their heroines. Sand's narration, however, marks a pivotal stage in the development of *l'écriture femme*.[3] It emerges from but subverts the eighteenth-century model, in which the transparency of the feminine voice revealed women's writing in what could be termed a preproblematic state, where the masculine and feminine spheres of writing were simultaneously segregated and unequal, the former considered literary, the latter marginal to the canon. And it looks forward to the twentieth-century model, in which women writers are increasingly articulating the existence of a realm of difference within a patriarchal mimetic structure. Luce Irigaray's modern view stresses disruption rather than confluence: "To engage in mimesis, therefore, is for a woman . . . to unveil the fact that, if women imitate so well, it is because they are not simply reduced to this function. *They also remain elsewhere.*"[4] If, as Sandra Gilbert and Susan Gubar suggest, the underlying plot of nineteenth-century writing by women is the "woman's quest for self-definition,"[5] we need only to expand the definition of plot to include narrative voice, in order to view Sand's "underground narration" as one of the crucial literary devices employed in this transitional stage in the development of l'écriture femme.

Like many artists whose oeuvre spans several decades, Sand's career is marked by different moments or sensibilities. Of the various items of juvenilia, works she wrote before she became George Sand, and those of collaboration with Jules Sandeau written under the pseudonym "Jules Sand," the most interesting is the posthumously published fragment entitled *Histoire du rêveur* (1830).[6] Constituting a kind of preliminary catalogue of various Sandian images, metaphors, and linguistic particularities, this work already prefigures many of Sand's most obsessive themes, and presents the earliest instance of a character's leap of faith into the depths of artistic inspiration.

George Sand's literary output as a full-fledged writer can be divided into various periods, with four clearly delineated "moments." One can identify a *période bleue* in her works, comprising the Romantic novels such as *Indiana* and *Valentine*, where the primary interest lies in delineating the "blue malady," that is, the mal du siècle in the feminine. This period is closely followed by a *période noire*, in which the somber novels of despair and suicide such as *Lélia* and *Spiridion* echo to some extent Sand's own inner crises. Then comes an antithetical *période blanche*, dominated by the vast *Consuelo* and its sequel *La Comtesse de Rudolstadt*. Sand moves away from the *roman noir* (designating both the Gothic novel and the texts of her black period) to formulate a *roman blanc*, which culminates in the blinding metaphor of whiteness to formulate a now hopeful moral universe.

In this configuration, the two very different versions of *Lélia* occupy a crucial position, hinging as they do the second and third periods of Sand's career. The 1833 version of the novel marks one of the high points of the author's *sensibilité noire*, while the 1839 rewriting already incorporates aspects of Sand's white period, in which the author proposes her version of the metaphysical sublime in the feminine. The utopian socialist novels of the 1840s (*Le Compagnon du tour de France*, *Le Meunier d'Angibault* and *Le Péché de Monsieur Antoine*), brandishing their immaculate banner of social rejuvenation and spiritual renascence, also belong to this period. Finally, Sand's fourth "moment," immediately preceding and following the events of 1848, and comprising the pastoral novels, we might call here *période verte*.[7] *Jeanne*, *La Mare au diable*, *François le champi*, *La Petite Fadette*, and *Les Maîtres sonneurs* share a common rural setting (Sand's own region, the Berry) and a peasant cast of characters. The author portrays a benevolent world through a double exploration of the charms of rustic life and the astonishing freshness of the Berrichon dialect.

In this book, I have concentrated on the first three period, limiting my consideration of the fourth to an examination of Sand's use of pastoral as a code with which to articulate a theory and apology of non-realist prose. This imbalance is intentional, motivated in part by the necessity to redress the existing critical bias, since the pastoral novels make up the only portion of Sand's oeuvre to have been consistently reedited and discussed. At the same time, it reflects my own critical view that the three other periods show Sand at her most incisive.

The present state of George Sand's published works offers discouraging proof of critical neglect, although the situation between

1984 (when I first considered writing this book) and 1990 has dramatically improved. The impeccable critical editions put out in the late 1950s and early 1960s by Garnier, of *Indiana* (ed. Pierre Salomon), *Lélia* (ed. Pierre Reboul), *Consuelo* and *La Comtesse de Rudolstadt* (ed. Léon Cellier and Léon Guichard), were out of print for years. Only in the past years have they been reissued. Likewise, Georges Lubin's scholarly masterpiece, the monumental compilation of Sand's correspondence, has been reissued by Garnier, so that all but the last two volumes (still to be published) of Sand's epistolary output—a total of twenty-four volumes—are available to scholars. Nevertheless, several of Sand's major novels are no longer in print (in English or in French), and most of the minor works are likewise unavailable. Some works, such as *Spiridion*, are available only in the expensive series appropriately called "Les Introuvables," put out by the Editions d'Aujourd'hui which reprints the original edition in offset (lacking a critical apparatus and reproducing all the imperfections of the original edition). As for a complete edition of Sand's works, our libraries can offer only the so-called *Oeuvres complètes* (an unnumbered set of 112 volumes), published by Michel Lévy (later Calmann-Lévy) between 1857 and 1890—a cheap paper edition, now hopelessly fragile, which is neither scholarly nor complete. Among other texts, the original 1833 version of *Lélia* is missing.

The present does show some signs of improvement, however. In 1982 a team of Sand scholars, under the leadership of Jean Courrier, and including Georges Lubin—the *doyen* of Sand studies—Simone Vierne, Philippe Berthier, René Bourgeois, and Pierre Salomon, began to put out *Les Oeuvres de George Sand*, from the newly founded Editions de l'Aurore, based at Meyland, near Grenoble. Courrier's intention is to publish a modern critical edition of Sand's complete works. At the rate of several volumes a year, the Aurore group has published nineteen titles to date. Thanks to their efforts, such novels as *Horace, Le Péché de Monsieur Antoine, Tamaris, Le Château des désertes,* and *Elle et lui,* long unobtainable in any form, are now available in an affordable format and with an admirable scholarly apparatus.[8]

The last few years have also witnessed a significant shift of interest among feminist theoreticians as they have moved from an "androcentric" focus to a "gynocentric" point of view, a shift which Patricia Meyer Spacks was the first to articulate in her ground-breaking *The Female Imagination* in 1975.[9] Whereas revisionary readings of male texts, such as Kate Millett's *Sexual Politics*, characterized the early years of the feminist revival of the 1970s, the last decade has increasingly seen the publication of works concentrating both on l'écriture femme, that is, the writing by women[10] and on *l'écriture féminine*, that is, the theoretical question of the feminine literary voice.[11]

This book in part reflects that shift of interest among literary scholars, insisting as it does on the examination of the fictional universe of a woman writer, just as it takes advantage of the new critical editions that the Editions de l'Aurore have been steadily making available. Chapter 1 deals with George Sand's "underground" and "androgynous" narrative strategies. Chapter 2 is concerned with the formation of the writer's voice as it is expressed in *Histoire du rêveur*, a text that prefigures Sand writing for her life. Chapters 3, 4, 5, and 6 examine a privileged selection of novels from Sand's prodigiously fertile decade, the 1830s: *Indiana, Valentine, Lélia,* and *Spiridion.* Through an examination of the utopian novels of the 1840s, Chapter 7 explores Sand's ideological passage from the Romantic and metaphysical novels to new humanitarian and mythological concerns. These issues, in full evidence in *Consuelo* and *La Comtesse de Rudolstadt,* are examined in detail in Chapter 8. Finally, Chapter 9 delineates the gynographic *ars poetica* Sand formulates in her prefaces, critical articles, and pastoral prose. The book's sequence is loosely chronological. After an initial period during which she sought to find her own voice, Sand focused upon four major issues in her novels. The first is the question of rebellion—literary, metaphysical, personal—which gives the fictional output of the 1830s a decidedly nihilistic outlook. Atheism, hopeless love, philosophical despair, suicide, and death loom over the blue and black periods. The following decade, the white period, finds Sand moving away from a poetics of destruction and toward the articulation of a personal life-affirming mythology. Her first challenge is, above all, to translate the abstract principles underlying the "social question" into a set of literary images. That is the task of the utopian novels. Then she sets out, in *Consuelo* and *La Comtesse de Rudolstadt,* to verbalize the great myths of the Romantic collective unconscious. Finally, in the green period comes her formulation of a personal poetics for fiction, a "prosaics." With a study and fuller elucidation of these texts and theoretical issues, we can begin to envisage Sand's literary rehabilitation.

Given that Sand's corpus consists of approximately eighty novels, plus numerous plays, short stories, and essays (not to mention the huge correspondence and autobiography), it is impossible to address every text here. Rather, my primary focus is on those texts that, to my mind, make up Sand's greatest achievements, the masterpieces *Lélia, Spiridion,* and *Consuelo.* Some of her early novels are also discussed in detail because they help to trace the double emergence of the woman as artist and the artist as woman. Likewise I felt that the neglected utopian novels of the 1840s merited consideration, being rich in fictional innovation and providing a privileged insight into the ferment of ideas swirling around during the last years of the July Monarchy. I regret that I could not devote more space to certain crucial texts: *Histoire de ma vie*

(1854–1855), for example, which some critics consider to be Sand's greatest work; or *Lettres d'un voyageur* (1834–1836), and the Italian novels about which much remains to be said, especially regarding the benevolent image of Venice as a countermyth to the more familiar myth of the infernal-city in the nineteenth-century novel. Lesser-known works also deserve attention: the lyrical *André* (1834), which bears comparison with Balzac's *Le Lys dans la vallée*; *Jeanne* (1844), Sand's first and perhaps greatest pastoral novel; *Le Piccinino* (1853), with its double probing of plebeian and patrician sensibilities; and especially a number of novels from the second half of Sand's career, such as the daring *Mademoiselle la Quintinie* (1863), the wonderfully abstract and philosophical *Monsieur Sylvestre* (1866), and *Nanon* (1872), a narrative tour de force, in which the events of the French Revolution are told from a peasant woman's point of view. Such works, and many others, deserve to be rediscovered and treated more fully. I can only hope that the present work will inspire others to continue the task.

My discussion of the novels I have chosen should make clear one paradoxical point—that Sand was simultaneously a writer who placed herself within the literary canon, all the while maintaining her distance from it, refusing to be completely engulfed by it. We can only marvel at the extraordinary dual nature of this writer who was truly capable of a double-gendered literary vision. On the one hand, she was a mainstream writer, as much a part of the literary scene in her lifetime as any major male writer. Her novels tended not to be limited to what has traditionally been called women's issues, although they did often privilege and highlight them. She did not shy away from subjects which have customarily been associated with masculinity, such as war, revolution, politics, philosophy, as such novels as *Nanon, Horace, Indiana, Le Péché de Monsieur Antoine, Monsieur Sylvestre,* and *Le Compagnon du tour de France* illustrate. Her topics, characters, and plots often displayed an androgynous nature. And yet, she did not, as many of her contemporaries (and some modern critics) claimed, become an honorary man. Like Jules Michelet, who maintained that he was a "complete man" because he possessed "both sexes of the mind,"[12] Sand was a "complete woman" whose mind was bisexual. Her stance resembles the one taken by Virginia Woolf, who in *A Room of One's Own* stressed the need for intellectual bisexuality: "If one is a man, still the woman part of the brain must have effect; and a woman also must have intercourse with the man in her. . . . It is when this fusion takes place that the mind is fully fertilised and uses all its faculties. Perhaps a mind that is purely masculine cannot create, any more than a mind that is purely feminine."[13] Woolf's affirmation that "a great mind is androgynous" echoes Sand's words in *Gabriel*: "L'âme n'a pas de sexe" ("The soul has no gender"). Such a remark places the French *romancière* firmly in the tradition of those writers and critics who do not ascribe to the notion of a specifically feminine arena of writing. Sand finds her company among those thinkers for whom the act of writing means transcending sexual identity and the body. All in all, Sand's generous vision of the world encouraged her at every step to break boundaries, to redefine in larger terms traditional views of the role of the sexes. That she had to don a (mostly) masculine name in order to do so was a sign of the times, a survival tactic, and in no way transformed her into a monster who betrayed her sisters by abandoning her sex. Her social and literary theories shatter the arguments in favor of strictly hermetic masculine and feminine spheres. Invariably, she sought, whenever possible, to pry open the doors between the two.

A few main ideas run through this book. The multiplicity of Sand's fictional explorations and the richness of her vision must not be equated with chaos. There is a coherence in the writer's vast fictional universe, and my readings of the different novels should emphasize that point. The most forceful unifying factor is Sand's idealist outlook and her allegiance to the abstract which mark the totality of her writings, fiction and nonfiction alike. She acknowledged time and time again that "le besoin de l'infini" was the overarching principle that structured her fictional edifice, a notion which is not unlike Balzac's "recherche de l'absolu." In *Histoire de ma vie* she articulated the fragile bond that links creation to the ideal:

> L'art me semble une aspiration éternellement impuissante et incomplète. . . . Nous avons, pour notre malheur, *le sentiment de l'infini*, et toutes nos expressions ont une limite rapidement atteinte. . . . Nous avons le désir inextinguible du beau idéal. . . . L'art est donc un effort plus ou moins heureux pour manifester des émotions qui ne peuvent jamais l'être complètement, et qui, par elles-mêmes, dépassent toute expression. (emphasis added; HV, 1: 806–807)

> (Art seems to me to be an eternally powerless and incomplete aspiration. . . . We have, for our misfortune, *an awareness of the infinite*, and all our attempts to verbalize it rapidly reach their limit. . . . We have the inextinguishable desire for the beau ideal. . . . Art is therefore a more or less successful effort to express emotions that can never be completely expressed, and that, in themselves, go beyond any expression.)

From her earliest probings of the mal du siècle in the feminine in *Indiana* to her utopian considerations in the novels of the late 1860s (such as *Monsieur Sylvestre*), Sand expressed her belief in the primordial spirituality of humankind, her faith in human perfectibility, her intense questioning of God's role in the social order, by way of an exploration of "la région du sentiment."[14] Toward the end of her career, she could confidently point to the idealistic outlook which had so intensely structured her writing when she had her hero declare: "Je suis un vieux rêveur très patient"[15] ("I am an old and very patient dreamer").

My primary allegiance throughout has been to the Sandian text itself, through which I hope to delineate the author's global vision. Since no work in English has aimed to determine the contours and boundaries of Sand's vast novelistic universe, my foremost purpose has been to deploy the appropriate critical strategies that would allow an English-speaking public to come to grips with such a huge and great fictional terra incognita. Thus, the theoretical approaches have been chosen for their capacity to illuminate the text, rather than the other way around. My methodology is at the service of the novels discussed; the primary texts have dictated the tools of their own analysis as much as possible. My critical preference has tended to be an approach that privileges the text rather than a theory that highlights theory. At various points I use the strategies of Bakhtinian, psychocritical, mythocritical, and feminist criticism. My approach to Sand is one of critical eclecticism, not restricted to any single doctrine or school. My interest lies in *l'écriture sandienne,* not theory for its own sake.

On the other hand, I have avoided the biographical approach, whether of the bio-scandal or hagiographic school. Despite critical success during her lifetime, by the end of the nineteenth century and throughout the twentieth, Sand more frequently attracted the attention of biographers than literary critics. Many critics have focused too exclusively on certain aspects of her life, displaying a obsessive fascination for what they deemed the writer's infamous affairs and scandalous behavior. My aim is to move beyond the "life and works" approach of Gustave Lanson which, in the case of Sand, has too often focused only superficially on her work by way of illustrating her notorious life. The "autobiographical fallacy," according to which a writer only and repeatedly tells his or her own story, has been blatantly abused in the critical discourse about Sand. Tainted with disdain for its subject, and at times steeped in contempt of a scatological or obscene nature, this approach has regularly been employed to reduce her novels to the saccharine and lachrymose confessions of an hysterical female of doubtful morality. We have lived long enough with the latrine insults Baudelaire hurled at Sand and with Léon Daudet's accusations that the nineteenth century and all its literary representatives were "stupid."[16] It is time to go beyond the obscenities that the likes of Henri Guillemin have passed off as a legitimate assessment of Sand and her work,[17] beyond the pathological preoccupation with her sex life, beyond the mania of the bedclothes which has dominated so much of the so-called critical discussion about her.[18]

Conversely, although potentially more fruitful than the bio-scandal approach, the hagiographic biography—which presents Sand as the ideal model of modern liberated womanhood, as a secular saint in whom twentieth-century feminists can identify a precursor of modern feminism—must also be transcended.[19] In just the three years between 1975 and 1978, for example, no less than six biographies were published, all celebrating Sand's vibrant womanhood, and mostly tending to emphasize the fabulous vita rather than the more demanding opera.[20] Those by Renee Winegarten and Francine Mallet were most successful in giving the reader a glimpse of Sand's intellectual life. But ironically the most thorough and reliable "history of the ideas of Sand" remains the old-fashioned and mammoth work undertaken by Wladimir Karénine at the end of the nineteenth century, *George Sand: Sa vie et ses oeuvres*, published in four volumes between 1899 and 1926. Despite its lack of critical sophistication, it remains the most exhaustive attempt at an assessment of Sand's prodigious *mental life*. "Clever is the one who figures out my mother," sardonically remarked Solange at her mother's death. Of all Sand biographers, Karénine is the only one who can truly claim to have nearly accomplished that feat. Needless to say, Sand still awaits the kind of biography Henry James seemed to envision when he remarked that the real story of George Sand was the story of her mind and the story of her prodigious literary output (the kind of biography that James himself was accorded by Leon Edel).[21]

The biographical obsession displayed by scholars has tacitly encouraged other nonliterary approaches to Sand. Social historians have examined her political positions and her socialist views,[22] literary historians her relationships with family members and friends,[23] and gossip-mongers her various lovers. While vindicating Sand for her extraordinary life, her avant-garde ideas, her famous friends, and her infamous love affairs may be tempting, I am convinced that her importance lies in the literary achievement of her works.

These works are now beginning to attract the serious examination they deserve. The following stand out as exceptional studies of Sand's literary production: Léon Cellier's *Parcours initiatiques*, a posthumous collection of essays, which contains three remarkable articles on Sand; Ellen Moers's *Literary Women* which includes scattered but interesting and pertinent pages on George Sand; Jean Pommier's *George Sand et le rêve monastique: Spiridion*, a short (112 pages) but first-rate examination of Sand's most mystical novel.[24] Also important are Gerald Schaeffer's *Espace et temps chez George Sand*;[25] Natalia Trapeznikova's *Romantizm Zhorzh Sand*;[26] the proceedings of the George Sand Conference held at the Centre Culturel de Cerisy in 1982, collected by Simone Vierne;[27] and, most recently, Kathryn Crecelius's study of the early novels.[28] Although distinguished, the list is astonishingly brief, considering both the scope of Sand's literary work and the central position it occupies in the development of the nine-teenth-century French novel. Significantly, these critical works repre-sent a collection of articles, a short monograph, or scattered remarks on Sand; or else they concentrate on a limited period, thus making it clear that today there is still no solid, book-length study of Sand's works in any language. This book attempts to right that wrong.

Even in studies that try to assess Sand's literary merit, a predomi-nantly biographical approach which reduces her works to transposed experience persists. Oscar Wilde's remark that "George Sand had to live her romances before she could write them" exemplifies a particu-larly offensive critical stance, which insists that love, a "soft" and femi-nine preoccupation, was the subject Sand knew the most about, only because she drew her inspiration directly from her own experience, and, subsequently, that passion was the subject that dominated her novels. Of course romance is a predominant theme in many of her works, but this is true for most novels since the etymological link be-tween *roman* and *romance* undeniably is an ideological and thematic one also. On the other hand, philosophical speculation, social thought, and utopian reflections are just as crucial themes for Sand.

André Maurois's attitude, like Wilde's remark, reveals another false track. His fascination with Sand's circle is primarily predicated on the distinguished status of her friends and lovers. While his approach in itself is not without interest, Maurois's awe before the great writers, painters, musicians, and thinkers who knew Sand gives the impres-sion that her greatness stems not from her own talent, but rather exists as a function of the genius of the men surrounding her:

> Imagine! She inspired Chopin and Musset; Delacroix had a studio at Nohant; Balzac came to ask "la camarade George Sand" for the subject of one of his most beautiful books [*Béatrix*] . . . ; Dos-toevsky saw in her a writer who was "almost unique in the vigor of her mind and her talent."[29]

Here I turn away from this kind of false adulation. Hence Sand's fa-mous friends receive no special consideration, either because they are friends, or because they are famous. The men I talk about are neither Musset (except when he comments on *Indiana*) nor Chopin, neither Delacroix nor Liszt. I do discuss, however, two men who had an piv-otal impact on Sand's literary life, the first as confrère, the second as philosophical mentor. In Chapter 4, I explore Sand's thematic affinities with Balzac, an early literary colleague and comrade. In Chapters 6 and 7, I deal with the theories of Pierre Leroux inasmuch as Sand shared his utopian socialist vision and promoted it in her novels of the forties. Studying her interaction with the novelist and the philosopher emphasizes the degree to which she collaborated as an equal participant in the overall articulation of French prose forms in the nineteenth century.

Although I discuss *Indiana* as Sand's first novel and see the hesitant gropings that characterize the writing of a first novel embedded in its underlying structure, it was not, technically speaking, Sand's first literary attempt, nor even her first published literary endeavor. *Rose et Blanche* can perhaps be considered Sand's first full-fledged novel; I have nevertheless eschewed consideration of it here, not because it is without merit—in fact it is a surprisingly readable and pleasurable text—but because the circumstances of its composition are problematic. The first version published in 1831 by B. Renault (five volumes in-12⁰) is without any doubt a joint venture with Jules Sandeau and thus cannot be studied as a text authored by Sand alone.[30] The second edition, however, published in two volumes by Dupuy and Tenré in 1833, is a much revised version, with numerous additions and deletions. Georges Lubin's lucid examination of the question shows this second redaction to be almost exclusively Sand's,[31] and his position is supported by the announcement in the *Journal des débats* that the second edition of *Rose et Blanche* was destined "to take place in the collection of the works of George Sand."[32] But however tempting it might be to examine this novel as the maiden voyage in Sand's long literary career, too much of the text is subject to speculation. Both manuscripts have been lost, thus making any attribution hazardous if educated guesswork. Here, then, my exploration of Sand's fictional universe begins with *Indiana*.

Throughout the book I quote large segments from Sand's novels in the original, since in many cases the works are not readily accessible or are not well known. Furthermore, Sand's grammatical structures tend to be complex, her sentences long, and her prose does not translate readily into English. The Sand scholar Alex Szogyi once remarked that, after Marcel Proust, Sand's sentences were the longest in the French language. Unfortunately, no translator of C. K. Scott Montcrieff's or now, Richard Howard's talent has yet appeared to render Sand's difficult prose into a flowing English equivalent. Consequently, to present her here only in translation would be a grave disservice. Therefore, even at the risk of overloading the page, I cite Sand's original prose with an accompanying translation.

If, as Jean Cassou proposes, the genius of George Sand is a metonymy for the genius of the entire nineteenth century, her literary output was not limited to the mere mimetic reflection of her age. She was not a vessel, a receptacle for the logos surrounding her, but an authentic autonomous voice, insofar as anyone can be, engaged in a constant dialogue with the voices of her age. She shared many traits with her literary contemporaries, but she also articulated brilliantly many of her differences with Flaubert, Balzac, and others. Sand herself insisted on her typicality—"mon histoire intellectuelle est celle de la génération à laquelle j'appartiens" (HV, 1:808; "the story of my intellectual life is the story of the generation to which I belong"). Her sense of belonging to a particular generation and of caring for many of the same issues as its members made her a Romantic prosateur, whose cosmology was endowed with many of the same traits found in the fictional worlds of Balzac, Hugo, or Stendhal. But she was also conscious of her anomalous situation—as the only woman writer who could dare to place herself on an equal footing with her male colleagues. Her self-appellation "Née romancier" (sic) makes her self-avowed privileged position clear (*Corr.* 5:826–827). She shared with the Romantics a triple agenda which, in the words of D. G. Charlton, can be described as the denunciation of a materialistic age and the accompanying conviction that human beings cannot live by bread alone, the exploration of the full range of social ills and the pursuit of their cures, and the elaboration of "a personal morality in a period when the traditional certainties were crumbling."[33] *Spiridion*, where the discussion centers on the French Revolution as being more than a question of basic economic rights, is Sand's most ardent denunciation of materialism. *Indiana* and *Lélia*, by exploring the feminized mal du siècle, probe the social illnesses of the age, while *Consuelo* and the utopian novels of the 1840s reflect on possible social solutions and psychological cures. Questions of personal ethos are raised in *Jacques*, *Valentine*, and *Monsieur Sylvestre*, among others. Thus Sand addressed the three crucial areas of Romanticism in her fiction, often reformulating them in the feminine. She was constantly aware that, in addition to being a member of a literary school and a generational sphere of thought, she had a particular mission as a woman writer, with a particular agenda of feminizing the literary canon. In this light, George Sand is truly a double writer—at once one of *them* and not one of *them*—contemplating a literary creation from a double perspective, with two sets of eyes and an androgynous brain.

Sand's inquiry into the of the experimental nature of the novel, of its vast possibilities in different fictional modes, is in evidence throughout her works. Her fascination with the elastic nature of the novel, on the one hand, and her exploration of the multifaceted nature of fiction, on the other, may explain why Michelet saluted her as the "greatest prose writer of the century."[34] Her dialogic imagination, her vision of the novel as a melting pot of various prose genres, and her excursion to of the outer limits of novelistic possibilities mark her, along with Balzac, Hugo, Stendhal, and Flaubert, as one of the great artisans of the modern French novel. Hippolyte Taine's insistence that Sand's oeuvre defines the "moral and philosophical history of the century" points to the breadth of her art. Undoubtedly Sand's large fictional imagination helped to transform the novel, a point which even the ill-mentioned Emile Faguet grudgingly acknowledged. Her interest in the formation of new novelistic genres can be documented from the very beginning of her literary career, when she was already incorporating into the same text such disparate elements as autobiographical fragments, philosophical treatises, Gothic tales, and discourses of initiation, thereby stretching the boundaries of the sphere of the novel.

The controversy that surrounded *Lélia* reveals the extent to which Sand was willing to take risks. Its publication marked a fall from grace in the eyes of the critics. Their reaction to the novel was no less than a "veritable furor." "Never had a novel unleashed such anathema," writes Sand in her "Préface générale" of 1842. "I was a perverse mind . . . an obscene pen, for having sketched the phantom of a woman who seeks in vain for love in the hearts of men and who retires to the desert so as to dream about the love that inflamed Saint Teresa."[35] Sainte-Beuve was one of the few critics to admire the work. Yet, even he was somewhat nonplussed by its incongruous mixture of lyricism and philosophy, its bizarre mix of "réel" and "impossible." He wrote: "this powerful and often graceful work, which however contained no nurturing breeze (zéphyr mûrissant), seemed extraordinary rather than beautiful, and it terrified rather than charmed those who admire a work according to the dictates of their hearts."[36] His remarks highlight the iconoclastic intrepidity of the author of *Lélia*, who willingly faced critical misprision in the name of literary innovation.

Many years later, another champion of Sand, Henry James, made a similarly astute remark concerning her fiction:

> Other novels seemed mediated, pondered, calculated, thought out and elaborated with a certain amount of trouble; but the narrative with Madame Sand always appears to be an invention of the moment, flowing from a mind which a constant process of quiet contemplation absorption, and reverie keeps abundantly supplied with material.[37]

Perhaps only James sensed the special quality of this "improvisatrice" when he defined her work, not as the artless product of a hasty writer, but as masterful texts revealing a superior imagination. "She has the true, the great imagination—the metaphysical imagination," he wrote in February 1876, distinguishing her from the minor French novelists of her day.[38] In his view Sand's greatest achievement was this double vision, her ability simultaneously to suffuse the real with a transcendent dimension and to anchor the spiritual in the fabric of realistic fiction.

1

Gynography and Androgyny

Est-ce un homme, une femme
Est-ce un ange, un démon?
Je suis l'être complet,
J'existe par moi-même,
Et j'ai résolu le problème
Des androgynes de Platon.

VERSES BY ETIENNE DE JOUY
ADDRESSED TO GEORGE SAND

(Is it a man, a woman
Is it an angel, a demon?
I am the complete being
I exist by myself alone
And I have resolved the problem
Of Plato's androgynes.)

When *Indiana* was published in May 1832 under the pseudonym G. Sand, no one recognized the enigmatic signature. Many critics assumed the author was a man. Some thought the hand of a woman had perhaps "feminized" the text.[1] Sand's incognito, however, was short-lived, lasting barely a year. It was still in effect in December, when Aurore Dupin Dudevant published a short story "La Marquise" in the *Revue de Paris* and signed it with the conventionally spelled Georges Sand. But by the time *Lélia* came out in July 1833, the pseudonym was completely transparent. Interestingly, it was the first time the writer signed her work George Sand, thereby establishing the permanent form of the pseudonym by which ever after she would be known.[2] Later, amusingly, George Sand would even be referred to as Madame Sand, the nom de plume now transmuted into a family name to be passed on in the "Sand" family. This almost unheard-of occurrence emphasizes that the signature "George Sand" had somehow gone beyond the boundaries of the literary sphere and had become enmeshed in the writer's nonliterary identity. Furthermore, the evolution of the name George is significant. The transition from an initial to the standard masculine French form ending in *s* and finally to a truncated, somewhat demasculinized (and perhaps even anglicized) form signals not so much the adoption of a standard male pen name as a transparent mask of identity. By her appropriation of the mostly male name of George, Sand refused to be limited to an identification as a woman writer. But conversely, by altering the name to a form neither masculine nor feminine in French, and particularly by adopting this androgynous orthography just at the time it was no longer useful as a gender disguise, Sand made clear her refusal to assume an absolute male identity. In the end, this paradoxical development constituted a series of essential steps in the complex construction of her androgynous literary persona and identity.[3]

What is the relation between identity and writing for Sand? What is the point of this pseudonym, neither quite feminine nor masculine, neither quite authentically French nor patently invented? For Aurore herself this androgynous disguise was the mask that would allow her to move freely and thrive in the Parisian literary arena of the early 1830s. In her works it points to a principle of androgyny which structures the literary materials in her narration, and it draws attention to the theme of androgyny often highlighted in the stories she recounts.

As a topos, androgyny is not new with Sand but constitutes an almost obsessive preoccupation among many French Romantic prose writers.[4] *Fragoletta* by Henri de Latouche, *Lamiel* by Stendhal, *Mademoiselle de Maupin* by Théophile Gautier, and *Séraphita* by Balzac are key examples. Séraphitus-Séraphita, the bisexual angel whose sexual character changes inversely according to the gender of the beholder, is the purest embodiment of a problematic identity explored in a literary text. Unlike the modern psychological notion of identity crisis wherein gender definition is a crucial element of the integration process, Balzac's depiction of the "syndrome" has at its core the desire for a double vision of the external world. To be both a man and a woman simultaneously guarantees a complete comprehension of the universe: "Angels are always at the most perfect point of beauty," he writes. "Their weddings are celebrated with marvelous ceremonies. In this union, which produces no children, the man has provided *understanding*, the woman has provided *will*: they become a single being, a single body here in this world."[5] As the critic Lucienne Frappier-Mazur puts it, the androgyne "can embody in one single being the harmonious and ideal fusion of matter and spirit, of body and soul, of intelligence and love, of reason and intuition etc., all characteristics that are respectively masculine or feminine in a very general and traditional framework."[6] The androgyne, Carl Jung reminds us, is an archetype of the collective unconscious. From Greek literature come several characters who plumb the androgynous nature of the psyche. The wise Tiresias, originally a man, becomes a woman in old age. The Greek philosopher Empedocles remembers having been both a girl and a boy in childhood.[7] Interestingly, the fate of George Sand's first hero, Amédée, who is at once a kind of androgyne and the first embodiment of the Sandian artist, resembles that of Empedocles (see Chapter 2). At the same time, Sand's androgyne, yearning for the infinite, represents a variant of the Romantic thirst for total knowledge, which is a fundamental impulse of the Romantic ethos articulated elsewhere, in Gautier's *Mademoiselle de Maupin*, for example. Here, the transformation of the heroine into Théodore de Sérannes reflects the search for a new way of seeing, and in this metamorphosis, we have one solution to the Stendhalian paradox of the eye that cannot see itself.[8] For the woman who has become androgyne can now see in other women her self as she once was. At the same time, to the eye of the androgyne, men appear as they really are, through the Gates of Horn rather than through the Gates of Ivory. "Women," says Madelaine de Maupin, "have only read the fiction [le roman] about man and never his true story [son histoire]." With her acquisition of the knowledge ordinarily accorded exclusively to men, she is transformed into a being who is neither man nor woman: "I belong to a separate, third gender which has yet to be named . . . I have the body and soul of a woman, the mind and strength of a man . . . my fantasy would be to become male and female in turn so as to satisfy my double nature."[9]

In Sand a variant of the androgyne—a female character disguised in men's clothing and assuming a male persona—appears in *Gabriel*, in *Lélia*, and especially in *L'Uscoque* where the troubling figure of Naam/Naama explains: "Il me semblait . . . avoir changé de sexe en changeant d'habit. Je me croyais ton frère, ton fils, ton ami"[10] ("It seemed to me . . . that I had changed my sex by changing my clothing. I thought I had become your brother, your son, your friend"). Sand of course knows whereof she speaks when she has her characters make remarks such as these. *Histoire de ma vie* recounts a number of amusing incidents concerning her own adoption of male attire and the confusion that ensued. To give but one example:

> Je dînais alors chez Pinson. . . . Un de mes amis m'ayant appelée madame devant lui, il crut devoir en faire autant. "Eh non, lui dis-je, vous étes du secret, appelez-moi monsieur." Le lendemain, je n'étais pas déguisée, il m'appelle monsieur. Je lui en fis reproche, mais ce fréquent changement de costume ne put jamais s'arranger avec les habitudes de son langage. Il ne s'était pas plutôt accoutumé à dire monsieur que je reparaissais en femme, et il n'arrivait à dire madame que le jour où je redevenais monsieur.[11]

> (I was having dinner at Pinson's. . . . One of my friends called me Madame in front of him, and he thought he ought to do the same. "No," I told him, "you are in on the secret, call me Monsieur." The next day, I was not disguised, and he called me Monsieur. I reproached him for it, but my frequent change of costume never managed to synchronize with his language habits. No sooner was he accustomed to say Monsieur than I would reappear as a woman;

and he only managed to say Madame the day I became Monsieur again.)

Much has been written about Sand and the male attire she adopted during her early years in Paris. But rather little attention has been paid to what Sand herself wrote about it in *Histoire de ma vie*. In the context of the androgynous impulse I have outlined, her own account deserves careful reading. When she moved to Paris from her native region of Berry, she found herself in an unfamiliar position of inequality vis-à-vis the young men in her circle.

> Je voyais mes jeunes amis berrichons . . . vivre à Paris avec aussi peu que moi et se tenir au courant de tout ce qui intéresse la jeunesse intelligente. Les évènements littéraires et politiques, les émotions des théâtres et des musées, des clubs et de la rue, ils voyaient tout, ils étaient partout. *J'avais d'aussi bonnes jambes qu'eux et de ces bons petits pieds du Berry qui ont appris à marcher dans les mauvais chemins.*   (emphasis added; HV, 2:116–117).

> (I saw my young male friends from the Berry . . . living in Paris with as little as I had, and keeping up-to-date with everything that interests intelligent young people. Literary and political events, the excitement of the theaters and the museums, the clubs and the streets, they saw everything, they were everywhere. *I had legs to match theirs and good little country feet that had learned to walk on rough paths.*)

The reason for her feeling of insecurity, she goes on to say, had to do with her female dress, which, literally and figuratively, spelled vulnerability, confinement, defeat:

> Sur le pavé de Paris, j'étais comme un bateau sur la glace. Les fines chaussures craquaient en deux jours, les socques me faisaient tomber, je ne savais pas relever ma robe. J'étais crottée, fatiguée, enrhumée, et je voyais chaussures et vêtements . . . s'en aller en ruine avec une effrayante rapidité.   (HV, 2:117)

> (On the cobblestone streets of Paris, I was like a boat on ice. Fancy shoes would crack in two days, clogs made me fall, and I didn't know how to lift up my dress. I was covered with mud, exhausted, constantly catching colds, and I could see that my shoes and clothes were getting ruined at a frightening rate.)

Her woman's attire was ill suited to her life in the capital among the *bohème*. And, as her friend Balzac reminded her, the expense of dressing properly was markedly greater for a woman.

But even more than its cost or discomfort, Sand realized that her female clothes per se imposed limitations on her movements in the social and intellectual sphere, limitations that did not apply to someone in male attire.[12] Far from being a simple emblem of sexual inversion, male dress for Sand meant a release from financial constraints and, more important, freedom of movement, both physical and intellectual.

In her frock coat, Sand the woman became invisible. No longer the object of men's scrutiny, escaping the reification of woman in the male glance, Sand in her male dress joined the observers, became the subject whose eyes define what is seen.[13] Liberated from her skirts, Sand was free to go to the theater alone and to move about at will in the world of artists and intellectuals.

> Je courais par tous les temps, je revenais à toutes les heures, j'allais au parterre de tous les théâtres. Personne ne faisait attention à moi et ne se doutait de mon déguisement. Outre que je le portais avec aisance, l'absence de coquetterie du costume et de la physionomie écartait tout soupçon. J'étais trop mal vêtue et j'avais l'air trop simple . . . pour attirer ou fixer les regards.   (HV, 2:117–118)

> (I went out whatever the weather, I came home at all hours, I sat in orchestra seats in all the theaters. No one paid attention to me, or suspected my disguise. Not only did I wear it with ease, but the absence of coquettishness in my attire and in my face removed all suspicion. I was too poorly dressed and I looked too unsophisticated . . . to attract or hold anyone's stares).

Having discovered her "invisibility," Sand found the autonomy of the subject vis-à-vis the outside world. She now could occupy the place of the one who observes. This was already to assume the role of the writer. Clearly from the account of these events in *Histoire de ma vie*, Sand associates the emergence of her literary identity with the newly found freedom she acquired in her male attire. Freed from being the (feminine) focus of observation and discourse, she was at liberty to become the (masculine) subject that observes and determines that discourse. If, as Lacanian theory has suggested, the constituting of the self is effected through the construction of one's body image, Sand was here undergoing a kind of second "mirror phase." Her dressing in male clothing effectively allowed her to construct a new identity, a new self, that of the writer who would shortly become George Sand.

In her autobiography, then, she prepares her reader for the sudden metamorphosis of Mme Dudevant, young chatelaine and mother, into a famous writer through the use of images denoting a change of sexual character. By intimating that her identity had never been entirely circumscribed by conventional definitions of femininity, Sand was seeking to explain her odd and eccentric destiny. Her education, her natural indifference toward clothes, and the complete lack of co-quetry in her behavior, she informs us, had already set her apart even before she ever wrote a single line:

> Je voyais bien qu'une éducation rendue un peu différente de celle des autres femmes par des circonstances fortuites *avait modifié mon être*. . . . Je sentais bien aussi que la stupide vanité des parures, pas plus que l'impur désir de plaire à tous les hommes, n'avaient de prise sur mon esprit. . . . *Je n'étais donc pas tout à fait une femme* . . . j'avais dans l'âme l'enthousiasme du beau, la soif du vrai, *et pourtant j'étais bien une femme* comme toutes les autres, souffreteuse, nerveuse, dominée par l'imagination, puérilement accessible aux attendrissements et aux inquiétudes de la maternité. (emphasis added; HV, 2:126–127)

> (I could see that my education, because of fortuitous circumstances, had been somewhat different from that of other women, and *had modified my being*. . . . I was also well aware that the stupid frivolity of fineries, and the impure desire to please all men, had no hold on my spirit. . . . *I was therefore not entirely a woman* . . . my soul possessed an enthusiasm for the beautiful, a thirst for truth, *and yet I was a woman* like all the others, weak, irritable, dominated by imagination, easily prone to the soft-hearted feelings and anxieties of motherhood.)

That her sexual ambiguity predisposes Sand to the vocation of writer is exemplified in the famous letter of July 1832 addressed to Laure Decerfz, in which her discussion of the critical reception of *Indiana* ends with the triumphant statement: "A Paris Mme Dudevant est morte. Mais Georges Sand est connu pour un vigoureux gaillard" (emphasis added; *Corr.*, 2:120; "In Paris, Mme Dudevant is dead. But Georges Sand is known to be a vigorous fellow").

This formation of a new self did not take place entirely without anxiety. Since to become a subject is to mark the gap between the observer and the observed, Sand's account of becoming a subject is also a tale about watching herself, sometimes anxiously, as object. Although a tone of bravado generally permeates the chronicle of her metamorphosis in both *Histoire de ma vie* and the correspondence, a revealing exception involves a dream she recounts from her Italian trip of December 1833: "La nuit, je rêvais que je devenais mosaïque, et je comptais attentivement mes petits carrés de lapis et de jaspe" (HV, 2:206; "At night, I dreamed that I had become a mosaic, and I was counting very carefully my little squares of lapis lazuli and jasper."). This anguish of the fragmented body—heightened by Sand's use of the iterative imperfect tense—clearly spells out that a sense of corporeal unity is the result of a long process of psychic integration. Sand's phantasm of bodily fragmentation is an indication that, as late as December 1833, the fashioning of her new identity was not yet complete.

This decisive transformation of identity in her personal life was reproduced in the analogous disguises embedded in the narrative structures of her novels. While the fables the androgynous characters recount may to a degree be reworkings of the familiar stock of traditional stories, the double-gendered vision that Sand created in the narration of her fables is quite exceptional. Her fiction is rife with narrators grammatically defined as male. And when these voices develop into fully embodied characters in the text, they appear in male costume, with the physical traits and the traditional occupations of nineteenth-century middle- and upper-class men. Even so, Sand's handling frequently complicates our sense of these seemingly male personae and renders them problematic.

The sympathetic involvement of the male narrator of *Indiana*, *Valentine*, or *Mauprat* with the heroine's situation goes beyond the usual objective and distant interest evinced by a narrator for his female characters and suggests a kind of sororal complicity distinctly different from the norm. A palpable gap exists between the gender indicated by the grammar and the language of the text as a whole on the one hand, and the gender of the author and her ideology on the other. This seeming contradiction, in which we can see one of the inherent characteristics of nineteenth-century feminine writing is, no doubt, an instance of the author's working within the established literary arena, all the while "subverting patriarchal literary standards."[14] But in addition, in the case of Sand, the ambiguity of gender imbedded in her alias, her characters, and her narrators suggests an original literary solution; it is more than an inverted reflection, more than a weaker polarity of the patriarchal mode.

Sand adopted the strategies of androgynous writing in an effort to escape the restrictive sphere traditionally assigned to the female word. Anticipating Virginia Woolf's advice that "women . . . must cultivate . . . their masculine side,"[15] in order to transcend the limits of their sex in the act of writing, she discovered, in the words of Patricia Spacks, that "the intellectual can be a sphere of freedom."[16] She understood that the woman writer must attempt to transcend gender in order to escape a female ghetto of the imagination which is not of her own making, and to which men have relegated her. It is not surprising, then, to see the male narrator of a Sandian text associated with metaphors of escape. The frequent positioning of the narrator in an open space demonstrates the way her androgynous narratives represent access to a larger geographic sphere which in turn symbolizes a breaking down the narrow confines of the feminine arena.

A network of images—associating open space, unfettered narrator, and literary inspiration—links the narration and narrators of two Sand novels, *La Mare au diable* and *François le champi*. In both the pastoral setting has an identical ideological function. In *La Mare au diable* the expansive natural landscape becomes a sort of *tableau vivant*. The male narrator is walking through the fields, deep in the contemplation of the opposite roles of artist and laborer. By chance he becomes the spectator of a lyrical plowing scene, and this prompts him to relate a story about one of the plowers. Thus the spatial theme—the landscape wherein the narrator can let his gaze and meditation rove freely—functions as the impulse for the writing.

In the preface to *François le champi*, the narrator is out walking in the "paths [of] the darkened countryside" (40) with "his" friend R . . . (the scene is based on a real exchange between Sand and her friend, François Rollinat). Although no physical description of the narrator is provided, all references to "him" in the text are masculine ("toi, romancier"). Again the open space that is the setting of their conversation assumes an active, determining role in the production of the text. To conclude the conversation about "la vie factice" and "la vie primitive," and to illustrate the workings of the pastoral imagination, the narrator proposes to relate a story. The open-space technique empowers the author to launch into the tale.

The semiautobiographical travelogue, *Lettres d'un voyageur*, is another central text for understanding Sand's artistic itinerary. The narrator's masculine identity is already established in the title itself. This *voyageur*, suffering from a Romantic malady of the soul, becomes a "promeneur contemplatif" in the Italian Alps, seeking an antidote to his melancholy in his aimless hiking. Traveling, when fixed in writing, constitutes the narrator's real cure. The introduction to the *Lettres d'un voyageur* asserts the possibility of restored health for those who seek escape and who at the same time are able to write through their cure. The affirmation of health and salvation is conveyed by the progression in the verbs of motion "ceux qui *errent* avec des pieds sanglants et qui *appellent* avec des plaintes amères, *retrouveront* le chemin de la terre promise et ils *verront luire* le soleil" (emphasis added; LV, 40; "Those who *wander* with bleeding feet and *call out* with bitter complaints *will find* the path of the promised land and they *will see* the sun *shine*").

In the "Première lettre" a walk through open spaces expresses the liberation of the writer's imagination and, as a result, functions as a curative pharmakon. The first-person narrator, grammatically defined as masculine but semantically marked as feminine, has embarked on this tramping through the Italian Alps in search of religious and senti-

mental solace. After wandering about for two days, the "solitaire ré-
signé" ends up by chance in Oliero and falls asleep in the late afternoon
at the mouth of the grotto. Upon awakening, "he" seems transported
into a nocturnal setting. "He" enters the grotto, only to encounter a
mirrorlike reflection of the Other that provokes terror. Looking out
from an underground pool, a ghostly face returns the narrator's gaze,
emphasizing that the voyageur has reached the "stade du miroir":

> Je vis au fond [de la source] une figure pâle dont le calme me fit
> peur. J'essayai de lui sourire, et elle me rendit mon sourire avec
> tant de froideur et d'amertume, que les larmes me vinrent aux
> yeux.   (LV, 56–57)

> (I saw at the bottom [of the spring] a pale face of such stillness that
> it frightened me. I tried to smile at it, and it smiled back at me so
> coldly and with such bitterness that tears came to my eyes.)

This meditation associates the phenomenon of *dédoublement* with the
theme of frigidity with which Sand often depicts spleen. Curiously, the
discovery of the Other coincides with a growing sense of paralysis:

> Je restai debout sur la roche. Le froid me gagna peu à peu. Il me
> sembla que moi aussi je me pétrifiais. Il me revint à la mémoire je
> ne sais quel fragment d'un livre inédit [son propre roman intitulé
> *Jacques*]. "Toi aussi, vieux Jacques, tu fus un marbre solide et
> pur. . . . Tant d'orages ont terni ton éclat que ceux qui passent . . .
> ne savent plus si tu es d'albâtre ou d'argile sous ce crêpe mor-
> tuaire. . . . Tu te glorifiais jadis d'être une matière dure et inatta-
> quable. . . . Mais la gelée fend les marbres. Le froid te
> détruira . . ."   (LV, 57)

> (I remained standing on the rock. The cold gradually spread
> through my body. It seemed that I also was becoming petrified.
> Heaven only knows what fragment from an unpublished book
> came to my mind [her own novel, *Jacques*]: "You also, old Jacques,
> once were like a solid slab of pure marble. . . . So many storms
> have tarnished your sheen that those who pass by . . . no longer
> know if you are made of alabaster or of clay underneath the
> mourning crepe. . . . You used to take pride in being made of hard
> and indestructible matter. . . . But the frost cracks marble. The
> cold will destroy you . . .")

Spelling emotional emptiness, poetic sterility, and a paralysis of the intellect and the senses, the trope of *froideur* is double-gendered. Used
here to define the *voyageur* and to associate "him" with a Sandian masculine character, it is also exploited to define the marble souls of Valen-

tine and Lélia. That the same theme of petrification should describe the masculine hero of *Jacques*, the heroine of *Valentine*, the feminine anti-hero of *Lélia*, and the androgynous traveler illustrates Sand's determination to undermine clear single-gender identities. Lélia, Jacques, and the voyageur are all androgynous narrator-characters, united by a common moral malady and a common disposition.

But as the traveler emerges from the grotto of Oliero, "accablé d'une épouvantable tristesse" (emphasis added), the nocturnal decor brings about a moment of psychological mutation, a life-affirming epiphany:

> Un dernier rayon du couchant venait frapper la voûte de la grotte. . . . Une hirondelle sortit du fond de la grotte et traversa le ciel. . . . Elle prit son vol magnifique vers le grand rocher de l'horizon.   (LV, 57)

> (A last ray of the sun struck the vault of the grotto. . . . A swallow came out of the depth of the grotto and crossed the sky. . . . It flew off in its magnificent flight toward the great rock on the horizon.)

The passage signals the change from sterility to rebirth, creativity, and writing. The host of positive elements, the setting sun and the bird especially, are witness to the voyageur's initiation into spiritual renascence, and literary inspiration. The frozen stillness of the grotto gives way to a fertile landscape. The swallow's flight, symbolically figuring the traveler's soul, marks the narrator's existential and poetic rebirth.

From a Bakhtinian point of view, we could speak of the essential presence in these texts of a pastoral chronotope, the term that designates the organizing unity of time and space in a literary text. Sand's pastoral chronotope strongly resembles the idyllic time frame of a Rousseau's pastoral works. As Bakhtin defines it: "the major protagonists [of the idyll] are the author's contemporaries . . . people with an interior perspective. They heal themselves through contact with nature and the life of simple people, learning from them the wisdom to deal with life and death."[17] But in Sand the pastoral chronotope is associated more with the narrator than with the protagonist. Not only does rural life possess curative power for the narrator, it makes "his" liberation from confinement possible and facilitates the passage to the threshold of writing. Sand's text in fact presents a double-faced construct in which "the worker in the field" designates not only the laborer but the writer as well.

What sets the narrators apart from the authorial figure in these three fictions is sexual identity. Narrator and author are nearly identical in all respects except that of gender. The male narrator of *François le champi* has written books signed George Sand. The young man of the

Lettres d'un voyageur has spent his childhood in the "Vallée noire" (the private name Sand used in her works to designate her native region of the Berry province); he speaks of his children, named Maurice and Solange and refers to a novel that he has written entitled *Lélia*. Even the height of this young man—4 feet 10 inches—corresponds exactly to Aurore Dupin's. Phallocentric critics have been quick to castigate the invasive autobiographical presence in woman's writing announced by just such a close congruity between author and narrative persona.[18] But in the case of Sand, the distance between the two, however narrow, demonstrates to what extent the narrative voice in her works is a strategic and intentional construction.

Sand's male narrators, then, are marked by a fundamental paradox. They represent not so much a covert attempt to camouflage the author's identity as a veritable and open "commitment to disguise."[19] The social determination of place, in Western culture at least, has traditionally been based upon gender, with women confined to interiors and men allowed the large expanse of the wide world out-of-doors. Sand felt an ineluctable need to escape from the limitations of this paradigm. She did not hate being a woman and long to be man, but she bridled at functioning under the restricted conditions imposed on the women of her time. Hence the paradoxical imperative that gives birth to Sand's androgynous vision: to appropriate for herself, with the adoption of male dress, an unconfined artistic perspective and yet to preserve her native female sympathy for traditional feminine preoccupations and values. Sand's use of male narrators does not constitute treason against her own sex. On the contrary, it is an enabling strategy that allows her to reclaim a unified human vision beyond gender-imposed restrictions. In the fusion of masculine and feminine elements, Sand invented a new voice.

Such a distinctive narrative voice incorporating both genders, a graphic instance of what Elaine Showalter calls "doubled-voice discourse," is in evidence throughout Sand's oeuvre. Her correspondence offers numerous examples, such as this letter to Adolphe Guéroult of 12 April 1835: "Il me semble que je m'appelle Georges et que je suis votre ami, ou votre amie, comme vous voudrez. . . . Ainsi appelez-moi comme il vous plaira" (*Corr.*, 2:852–853; "It seems to me that my name is Georges and that I am your male friend, or your female friend, as you wish. . . . So address me as you like"). Or again to Guéroult on 6 May 1835:

> Si j'étais garçon, je ferais volontiers le coup d'épée par-ci, par-là, et des lettres le reste du temps. N'étant pas garçon je me passerai de l'épée et garderai la plume, dont je me servirai le plus innocemment du monde. . . . Je n'ambitionne pas la dignité de l'homme. . . . Mais je prétends posséder aujourd'hui et à jamais la

superbe et entière indépendance dont vous seuls croyez avoir le droit de jouir. . . . Prenez-moi donc pour un homme ou pour une femme, comme vous voudrez. Duteil dit que je ne suis ni l'un ni l'autre, mais que [je] suis un *être*.   (*Corr.*, 2:879–880)

(If I were a young man, I would happily engage in sword play from time to time, and in writing the rest of the time. As I am not a young man, I will do without the sword and keep the pen, which I will use with the greatest innocence in the world. . . . I do not covet the dignity of a man's position. . . . But I do claim to have, today and forever more, the glorious and unconditional independence that all you men believe is your right alone to enjoy. . . . So take me for a man or a woman, as you wish. Duteil says that I am neither one or the other, but that I am a *being*.)

In clear and uncompromising terms, this letter announces Sand's lifelong position of defiant nonaggression vis-à-vis the male literary establishment. Using the sexual image of the "coup d'épée," which could be construed to refer to the all-powerful phallus both in and out of the world of letters, Sand makes several notable points in this letter. First, she insists that one does not need a phallus in order to write ("n'étant pas garçon . . ."). Second, she makes it clear that, for her, the act of writing constitutes a declaration of independence from the established social norms. Finally, she openly avows that, because of her equation of writing with freedom, she has somehow changed sex, not becoming a male, but some kind of androgynous being. The paradigm she proposes can be reformulated as follows. For men, writing has traditionally been nonproblematic inasmuch as it has been defined as a manly act, directly parallel to sexual potency, to the thrust of the penis ("le coup d'épée . . . des lettres"). But women who write must chose between two antithetical models, each of which is reductive. In the first choice, women lose their femininity; in the second, they lose all credibility in the serious literary world. They can either pretend to be men (the obvious male pseudonym) or relegate themselves to the sphere of woman's writing. But if they refuse, as Sand did, to work within the confines of either model, if they reject both phallocentrism and the feminine ghetto, they become creatures of a strange sex, neither male nor female. A George without an *s*.

Béatrice Didier notes that "George Sand herself loses track" since in her correspondence she frequently employs the masculine and the feminine when referring to herself.[20] A letter to Franz Liszt, dated October 1835, for example, has references to the author in both the feminine and the masculine: ". . . *décidée* à vivre agricolement, philosophiquement . . . je serai parfaitement *heureux* et je mourrai *content* . . . *occupée* à soigner le vieux républicain malade" (emphasis added; *Corr.*, 3:65; ". . . *having decided* [participle with feminine ending] to live in a pastoral, philosophic fashion . . . I will be perfectly *happy* [masculine form] and I will die *content* [again masculine] . . . *busy* [another feminine participle] caring for the old sick republican"). No specific activities are associated here with a particular gender. In Sand's usage, gender is chaotic, not linked to occupation, and not bipolar.

These examples of epistolary androgyny are matched by frequent instances of multivoiced discourse in Sand's critical writings. In *Autour de la table* (1856) she relates a literary discussion at the Montfeuilly household, among the grandmother Louise de Montfeuilly, "chef ac-tuel de la famille," the oldest son Théodore, the neighbor's daughter named Julie, and a male "I." The fission of the author into four markedly distinct characters is striking in itself. Yet this work offers a further surprise, incorporating, as it turns out, two different and possi-bly contradictory initiatives. One is a straightforward defense of Victor Hugo's *Contemplations* against the negative criticism it provoked upon its appearance. The second is an experiment in dialogic criticism, a fas-cinating example of polyphonic writing employed to create a frame-work in which differing points of view can compete and confront one another. Wladimir Karénine (usually one of the more reliable commen-tators on Sand) evidently failed to appreciate this aspect of the text when she criticized the work for being a "hybrid genre," "neither a true work of the imagination, nor a truly critical one."[21] But surely Sand's experimental use of a multivoiced nonhierarchical dialogue here is part of her innovative narrative strategy. By splitting herself into several characters, all on an equal plane, the author gains an un-limited field of action. *Autour de la table* constitutes the search for max-imal expression in a maximal field of possibilities.

Sand's metaphorically expressed need to break out of the nar-rative confines of the literary models available to her is the polar op-posite of the claustro*philia* which Stendhal associated with the writer's true nature: "Have you ever seen, kind reader, a silkworm who has eaten enough mulberry tree leaves? The comparison is not noble, but it is accurate! This ugly creature no longer wants to eat, it needs to climb and build its silk prison. Such is the animal named writer."[22] Instead of this image of the writer as silkworm that wraps itself up in the cocoon of its own text, Sand proposes a vision of the writer as a bird, the meta-phorical creature of freedom. Early on in *Histoire de ma vie* the author speaks of her "particular affinities" with birds, those "mysterious pa-trons" (HV, 1:16). The passage continues with an overview of the phys-ical and moral resemblances between humans and beasts (inspired, perhaps by the ideas of Cuvier or Geoffroy Saint-Hilaire): "Are there not among us foxes, wolves, lions, eagles, cockchafers, beetles, flies?" (HV, 1:17). Her bestiary confirms Balzac's remark in the well-known 1842 "Avant-Propos" to *La Comédie humaine* that there have always existed social species, just as there are zoological species.[23] Sand's text quickly proceeds from the general to focus exclusively on the bird, the animal she considers to be "l'être supérieur de la création." The avian species has a privileged place in Sand's cosmogony through its identification in her mind with the world of the artist. Sand concludes this passage with a striking formula: "l'homme-oiseau, c'est l'artiste" (HV, 1:18; "the artist is a bird-man"). The bird is an animal of liberation, of migration, of travel; a creature whose passage to maturity offers one of our most dramatic images of freedom, whose very mode of locomotion has become for us a metaphor for escape. It exists in almost perfect antithesis to the silkworm who, for its part, constructs a prison in which it can enclose itself.

Significantly, Sand also recognizes in the bird an androgynous being, combining qualities that have been allocated, among humans, to the masculine or feminine gender: "Dans la race canine si vantée, la femelle seule a l'amour de la progéniture, ce qui la rend supérieure au mâle; chez l'oiseau, les deux sexes, *doués d'égales vertus,* offrent l'exemple de l'idéal de l'hyménée" (emphasis added; HV, 1:18, "In the much vaunted canine race, only the female shows love for the offspring, which makes her superior to the male; with birds, where both sexes are *endowed with the same virtues,* we have the example of marriage in its ideal form"). Sand locates the superiority of both genders of birds in their maternalism. since birds share certain traits regardless of gender, the poet-bird is a fitting metaphor for the androgynous writer Sand invented.

In her autobiographical oeuvre, Sand continued to view her double nature as a fundamental aspect of her becoming a writer. In *Histoire de ma vie* (pt. 4, ch. 12) she chronicles her first stay in Paris and, by describing the reactions of her friends, documents the emergence of her androgyny. According to Béatrice Didier the enterprise of autobiography often leads to the artist's discovery of his or her own bisexual imagination.[24] Sand's realization of this coincides with her efforts to forge an androgynous narrative voice in her fictions. Several friends who knew her both before and after she metamorphosed into a novelist began to sense, as early as 1833, that another different person from the one they knew existed within her. This other being, whom they encountered in her writing, struck them as an distinctly unfeminine presence. Significantly, Sand links her friends' troubled responses with the publication of her two most abstract novels, *Lélia* and *Spiridion,* the two texts in which she perhaps experimented the most with narrative voice:

> quand . . . j'eus écrit *Lélia* et *Spiridion,* deux ouvrages qui résument pour moi beaucoup d'agitations morales, mes plus intimes amis se demandaient avec stupeur en quels jours, à quelles heures

de ma vie, j'avais passé par ces âpres chemins entre les cimes de la
foi et les abîmes de l'épouvante.   (HV, 2:96)

(when . . . I had written *Lélia* and *Spiridion*, two works that epito-
mize a great deal of moral agitation for me, my closest friends won-
dered in astonishment at what time, in what period of my life I had
traveled these bitter paths between the summits of faith and the
depths of desperation.)

Sand also records in her autobiography a remembered conversation with Everard[25] in 1835 in which he articulated his difficulty in rec-
onciling his conflicting impressions of two Sands, the "male" author
and his female friend. She quotes him as saying:

"I have made a discovery . . . that souls have a gender and that
you are a woman. . . . When I read *Lélia* and your *Premières lettres
d'un voyageur*, I always saw you in the guise of a young boy, of a
child-poet whom I took for my son. . . . When I saw you in person
for the first time, I was . . . surprised . . . that in real life you wear
a dress and that you have a woman's name. . . . I wanted to keep
my dream, to call you simply George, to address you in familiar
terms. . . . I have always spoken to you as to a young man. . . .
Now I see . . . that you have the ambitions and the insistence . . .
of those beings of pure sentiment and imagination, in a word, of a
woman."   (HV, 2:335–336)

Everard's remark makes clear to what an extent Aurore had been su-
perceded by George even in the writer's everyday life. We see that
Sand's authorial persona increasingly came to inhabit the world and
that her pseudonym was less and less restricted to the literary sphere.
But these words also point to a fundamental hesitation on the part of
members of her circle as to her "real" gender. In the process of becoming a writer, Sand had become an Other.

In Sand's fiction her Otherness projects itself with the greatest
vigor in the form of a masculine persona. *Spiridion* clearly illustrates
this phenomenon. The narrator is a young man, a novice named Angel, whose very name puts into question his gender since, as the Romantics liked to remind their readers, angels are bisexual. The novel
opens with his account of himself in the form of a confession. His first
words read: "Lorsque j'entrai . . . au couvent des Bénédictins, j'étais à
peine âgé de seize ans" ("When I entered the Benedictine monastery I
was just barely sixteen"). This opening sentence establishes in the text
two levels of reading—one fictional and masculine, the other autobiographical and feminine. The word convent, with its two coexisting
meanings—a religious dwelling for nuns or monks and, by extension,

a boarding house for young girls run by nuns—has a double resonance here that leads the modern reader to suspect that *Spiridion*, an austere and abstract novel in which a masculine world of religious meditation and mystical vision is portrayed, is thematically linked to another text by Sand, *Histoire de ma vie*. With their descriptions of convent life in the "Couvent des Anglaises," her memoirs curiously echo numerous monastery scenes in *Spiridion*. The two works offer some stunning parallels which will be studied at greater length in Chapter 6. Since we are not accustomed to the phenomenon of gender crossing in autobiography, Sand's insistence that *Spiridion* is perhaps the most autobiographical of her novels strikes us as odd. In *Histoire de ma vie* she went so far as to say:

> On n'a pas manqué de dire qu'*Indiana* était ma personne et mon histoire. Il n'en est rien. . . . Si j'avais voulu montrer le fond sérieux [de mon caractère], j'aurais raconté une vie qui jusqu'alors avait plus ressemblé à celle du moine *Alexis* (dans le roman . . . *Spiridion*) qu'à celle d'Indiana la créole passionnée. (HV, 2:160)

> (Naturally, people said that *Indiana* was my person and my story. It is absolutely not so. . . . If I had wanted to show the serious depth [of my character], I would have portrayed a life which up until then resembled more closely that of the monk *Alexis* (in the novel . . . *Spiridion*) than that of Indiana, the impassioned Creole.)

Alexis, an autobiographical projection of George Sand? Should we read this as a jest? a paradox? or a revealing confession? Sand's statement once again questions the conventional view of the "autobiographical fallacy," which automatically equates female author with heroine. If the description that Sand gives of her spiritual itinerary in *Histoire de ma vie* can be seen as an intertext for the novel, then we might better understand Alexis as a kind of authorial double that is more "autopsychological," to use Lidia Ginzburg's formula, than properly autobiographical, that is to say, it refers more to mental life than to daily existence.[26]

Lélia, probably Sand's most experimental novel, was recognized by its author as "l'action la plus hardie et la plus loyale de ma vie" (LV, 140; "the most audacious and loyal act of my life"). The novel relies on a double strategy: the heroine Lélia is both a character, a partial autobiographical projection in the feminine, and one of the main narrators, one of the voices which articulates the text. As a result, the novel is doubly polyphonic, in both story line and narration. Writing in her private diary, however, Sand emphasizes the polyvalent connection between herself and her characters, thereby controverting any simplistic or absolute identification of her with any one of them:

> Quelques uns diront que je suis Lélia, mais d'autres pourraient se
> souvenir que je fus jadis Sténio. J'ai eu aussi des jours de dévotion
> peureuse, de désir passionné, de combat violent et d'austérité
> timorée où j'ai été Magnus. Je puis être Trenmor aussi. Magnus,
> c'est mon enfance, Sténio, ma jeunesse, Lélia est mon âge mûr;
> Trenmor sera ma vieillesse peut-être. Tous ces types ont été en
> moi.   ("Sketches and Hints," OA, 2:615)

> (Some will say that I am Lélia, but others might remember that I
> was once Sténio. I also had days of timid devotion, of passionate
> desire, of violent struggle, and timorous austerity when I was
> Magnus. I can be Trenmor as well. Magnus is my childhood, Sté-
> nio, my youth, Lélia is my mature self; Trenmor will perhaps be
> my old age. All these types have been a part of me.)

Furthermore, Lélia as an authorial self-projection may have her origin equally in a masculine and purely literary model: the pale and disillusioned Romantic hero. Beginning with Werther, continuing with the Byronic clan, and on to their French cousins, René, Obermann, Octave de Malivert, and culminating with Musset's "enfant du siècle," these heroes constitute a brotherhood from which Lélia can be excluded only because of her sex. Significantly, the formula "enfant du siècle," which gave Musset his well-known title, was Sand's to begin with and appears several times in *Lélia* and in the *Lettres à Marcie*.

We may suppose from Chateaubriand's response to *Lélia* that he recognized the Romantic masculine hero at the center of the novel; after finishing the book, he wrote to Sand in August 1833: "You will be the Byron of France."[27] Gustave Planche saw a similar analogy, pointing out parallels between Lélia and Manfred. George Sand, for her part, was not reticent about identifying the texts that had inspired her. In *Histoire de ma vie* she writes about taking herself for René or Obermann (eponymous heroes of Chateaubriand and Senancour novels) and attributing to herself "une sensibilité exceptionnelle" (HV, 2:195). Significantly, up until the mid-thirties Sand responded more readily to masculine than to feminine characters created by other writers. Not until 1837, when she read Sainte-Beuve's reedition of *Corinne*, did Staël's heroine have an impact on Sand's imagination, an impact that played a measurable role in the rewriting of *Lélia*.[28]

What interested Sand in the case of Obermann was precisely the gap between sensibility and intelligence, between desire and the will to act, a gap she probed more fully in the character of Lélia. In the psychological analysis of Senancour's hero which she wrote for *La Revue des deux mondes*, a feminization of the Romantic type can already be discerned:

> Obermann . . . c'est la rêverie dans l'impuissance, la perpétuité du désir ébauché. . . . C'est un chant triste et incessant sur lui-même . . . sur sa perpétuelle oisiveté. C'est une mâle poitrine avec de faibles bras. . . . Obermann est cet oiseau des récifs à qui la nature a refusé des ailes, et qui exhale sa plainte calme et mélancolique sur les grèves *d'où partent les navires et où reviennent les débris.* ("Obermann," 29)

> (Obermann . . . represents dream made impotent, the perpetual glimmer of desire. . . . He sings a sad and incessant song about himself . . . about his endless idleness. He has a male chest with weak arms. . . . Obermann is that bird of the reefs to whom nature has refused wings, and who calls out his calm and melancholic complaint from the shores *where the ships leave and the wreckage returns.*)

This character who sings his melancholy on the edge of life ("sur les grèves"), who observes but does not act, is a kind of male double of Lélia. In Lélia's soliloquy about her century, where she opposes Balzac's categories of *savoir* and *pouvoir*, she discerns an inertia, a paralysis of being among her contemporaries which describes perfectly that other "enfant du siècle," Obermann. The bonds that link Obermann and Lélia will be studied in Chapter 5. For now, let us remember the profoundly androgynous character of Lélia, by virtue of the literary models on which she is based, the male dress she sometimes dons, and the kinship she shares with some of Sand's own heroes.

How then are we to understand this statement in Sand's autobiography denying any authorial projection in her heroines?

> J'ai présenté beaucoup de types de femmes, et je crois que quand on aura lu cet exposé des impressions et des réflexions de ma vie, on verra bien que *je ne me suis jamais mise en scène sous des traits féminins.* Je suis trop romanesque pour avoir vu une héroïne de roman dans mon miroir.   (emphasis added; HV, 2:160)

> (I have described many female types, and I think that when the reader has finished this account of the impressions and reflections of my life, the reader will see that *I have never depicted myself in any of my books in a female guise.* I am too much a dreamer to have taken what I saw in my mirror for the heroine of a novel.)

Sand is not so much deliberately stating a paradox as much as she is affirming yet once again her need, when constructing either her characters or her narrators, to create them as fundamentally androgynous because such a double vision at once enlarges the polarized male or female perspective and allows the breaking of the barriers for the woman writer. Her opinion, already stated in an early short story, "La Fille d'Albano" (1831), that genius has no gender ("Le génie n'a pas de sexe") would not change throughout her long career.[29]

Another revealing item of juvenilia, published only in 1875, entitled "Nuit d'hiver" (1829), proposes an enigma to the reader. Sand, disguised as a young man, her face hidden behind a mask, visits a working-class ball incognito and enthusiastically takes part in the dancing. Her mask falls off but none of her acquaintances recognize her. She herself, as she explains it, does not recognize herself:

> Mon masque tombe. Je continue sans m'en apercevoir, mais personne ne me reconnaît. Ils sont tous si loin de penser à moi. . . . Et moi-même, personnage grave en dedans, et en possession d'un sang froid souvent mis à l'épreuve, je ne pense pas que ce soit moi. Non, ce n'est pas moi, *c'est l'autre*. C'est le petit qui s'amuse.[30]

> (My mask falls. I continue without noticing it, but nobody recognizes me. They are all so far from thinking of me. . . . And I myself, inwardly such a serious person, and possessing an oft-tested cold-bloodedness, don't think it is I. No, it isn't I, *it's the Other*. It's the youngster having some fun.)

It is this Other, wearing the mask of a transparent pseudonym, dressed up as a gamin, who becomes George Sand the writer. Can this Other, who will soon write for "her" life, be unmasked?

2

Histoire du rêveur:
The Dreamer's Plot

George Sand, fille du feu et fille des ténèbres
JEAN CASSOU

(George Sand, daughter of fire and daughter of the shadows)

The Empedocles Complex

Histoire du rêveur is one of Sand's earliest manuscripts, a forty-five-page fragment written in all likelihood in the early part of 1830, though not published until 1924 in the *Revue des deux mondes*.[1] It is obviously the work of a novice, fragmentary and marked by extravagant rhetoric and awkwardness. Yet for all its youthful faults, it reveals some of the writer's earliest efforts to organize her fictional universe and it already prefigures many of the thematic concerns that come to dominate Sand's novels of the 1830s and 1840s. Among these we can identify the budding writer's attempt to probe the dreams and intellectual longings of her generation. Her exploration of the Romantic topos of nature is effected through the depiction of a sublime landscape in two very specific and interrelated modes, in mountainous and nocturnal scenes, and through the deforming lens of dream. The fascination for Italy as a benevolent space, the privileging of music as the most sacred of all the arts, and the flight of the imagination that constitutes the poet's obsessive occupation are all expressed here for the first time. The text gives life to the first of the voyageur-poets. Most important, a major metaphor for poetic inspiration is constructed, so that behind the story of the protagonist unfolds another story in which Sand traces the itinerary of her own creative gropings.[2]

Using an inserted narrative technique, the young author constructs a tale in which several layers of discourse are imbedded within one another. The nameless first-person narrator (whom we might call Aurore, as Thierry Bodin suggests, *Rêveur*, 5), asks her friend, the magician Tricket,[3] to entertain her with a story. As the second narrator, he proposes to take his interlocutor to the Sicilian *regione piemontese* surrounding Mount Etna. Amédée, the young hero of Tricket's story, intends to visit the highest active volcano in Europe, which has traditionally fascinated poetic sensibilities. Symbolically stripping himself of all earthly possessions, he leaves his horse and belongings in a nearby village, rents a mule to help him on his climb, and sets off in the late afternoon. His plan is to walk a good part of the night, so as to arrive at the edge of the crater at sunrise.

Traveling to exotic sites for the sole purpose of contemplating a sublime landscape in solitary splendor has been on every fashionable young man's agenda since *René*, Chateaubriand's novel of 1802, provided the inspiration.[4] German and English landscape painters, such as Caspar David Friedrich and J. M. W. Turner, also traveled to the Alps in search of the sublime. Many English Romantic poets described their sense of poetic epiphany when crossing the Alps.[5] Amédée's excursion to "contemplate the most magnificent spectacle in the universe" (*Rêveur*, 10) is contemporaneous with René's departure for the New World and with the wanderings of Byronic heroes through mountainous regions. As a proponent of the new sensibility, Amédée would concur with Childe Harold's dictum: "To me high mountains are a feeling." The spiritual ancestry of Sand's protagonist is both multinational and masculine, as if to suggest that this early literary enterprise could be attempted only in the masculine mode. The author emphasizes here the maleness of her literary repertoire, although she will soon dare to propose a series of artists *au féminin*.

As Sand's hero climbs, he congratulates himself for traveling alone and anticipates with pleasure the violent exhaltation he is about to experience: "seul au terme de ce désert terrible et majestueux . . . je veux pouvoir enfin abandonner mon âme au désordre de ces éléments fougueux qui règnent en maîtres absolus sur une terre déchirée et bouleversée" (*Rêveur*, 10; "alone on the edge of this terrible and majestic desert . . . I want a last to be able to surrender my soul to the disorder of these impetuous elements that rule like tyrants over a torn and tormented land"). Amédée's sense of the sublime is constructed with a mixture of the sinister and the enthralling. His Gothic vocabulary ("âme abandonnée au désordre," "éléments fougueux," "terre déchirée et bouleversée") and oxymoronic description ("désert terrible et majestueux") reflect the categories of Edmund Burke's aesthetics, as expressed in his *Philosophical Enquiry into the Origin of Our Ideas of the Sublime and the Beautiful*.[6] These ideas are echoed a few pages later when Sand equates sublimity with terror in her depiction of the Italian volcano, an "admirable spectacle dans toutes ses horreurs" (*Rêveur*, 12). In her earlier "Voyage en Auvergne" (written circa 1829, discovered in 1888), Sand had already admired "cette horreur du silence et de la solitude qui pénètre l'âme de terreur et l'absorbe de rêverie"[7] ("this horror of silence and solitude which fills the soul with terror and plunges it into reverie"). The need for the senses to be moved, both literally and figuratively, expresses the writer's poetics of vertigo. *Histoire du rêveur* demonstrates how early Sand became interested in probing the literary possibilities of the sublime for her own poetic ends.

In addition to Chateaubriand, Byron, and Burke, Rousseau's *La*

Nouvelle Héloïse and Senancour's *Obermann* should be mentioned as two likely sources of *Histoire du rêveur*. Both preromantic texts exploit mountain descriptions to elaborate an emotive ideology. St. Preux's outings in the Valais and Obermann's intoxicating ascent to La Dent du Midi explore the metaphysical dimensions of an elevated landscape. Senancour's "liberté alpestre"[8] echoes Rousseau's "enchantement du paysage" St. Preux's description of the "ethereal realm" expresses an "aesthetics of the infinite" which is echoed in Sand's *Rêveur*.[9] The mountain as locus of poetic *déclenchement* remained for Sand, to a greater degree than for her contemporary fellow-novelists, the optimal expression of vertiginous isolation. The rarified atmosphere of the heights allows the writer to express metaphorically and succintly a character's discovery of his or her most profound moods—poetic, life affirming, or morbid.

Sand thus exploits the stratified geological structure of Mount Etna symbolically. When wandering in the lower regions, her hero Amédée presents a mundane frame of mind. He resembles a fashionable tourist who has set off on an ordinary if somewhat foppish sightseeing excursion. As he reaches the highest portion of the wooded concentric layer, however, the mood changes and the tale takes on a decidedly fantasmagorical tone. Amédée's delirium increases in direct proportion to his climb (*Rêveur*, 16). At the point where he transcends the level of ordinary human life to enter the "life of phantoms," (*Rêveur*, 17), the young man's solitary hike is interrupted by the melancholic song of an unknown intruder. The voice Amédée hears is curiously disconcerting. At once androgynous[10] and otherworldly, it provokes the young traveler to exclaim: "qui que tu sois, homme ou femme, ange ou démon, sylphide ou nécroman, viens à moi, que je rende hommage au talent sublime que tu possèdes" (*Rêveur*, 13; "whoever you are, man or woman, angel or devil, sylphid or seer, come to me, that I might pay tribute to the sublime talent with which you are endowed"). Amédée anticipates here Sténio's opening words to Lélia: "Qui es-tu? . . . Tu es un ange ou un démon, mais tu n'es pas une créature humaine" (Who are you? . . . You are an angel or a devil but you are not a human creature"). Compared at first to a child, then to a girl in disguise, the enigmatic *ragazzo* is a "bizarre companion" whose wide coat tails are likened to an angel's wings. In the phraseology of rites of passage, this strange creature might represent an intermediary, whose function is to guide the dreamer to a higher realm. From what we know of Sand's fictional universe, we recognize here yet one more example of the androgyne. Sustained by the flame of inspiration, his raw poetry displays a "caractère de l'improvisation" (*Rêveur*, 13), thus making him the prototype of Sand's numerous improvisators. He joins the company of a long series of singer-visionaries of both sexes, from Lélio in *La Dernière Aldini*, to Albert de Rudolstadt in *Consuelo*, Hélène in *Les Sept cordes de la lyre*, and Teverino, to name just a few. As a gifted singer and delirious intercessor between the ordinary and the visionary, his claim to a superior understanding seems justified. His talent is also heightened by privileged proximity to the volcano, which has provided him with what could be termed a baptism of vertigo.[11] The great Sandian theme of music finds its first expression here.

The young artist's reference to the volcano's "elevated regions" has a double meaning, referring to not only the physical climb of the two travelers, but also the willful exploration of pleasure of the void as expressed by the abyss. The volcano reconciles the extremes ("cette neige éternelle du sein de laquelle s'exhalent des feux souterrains"; "this eternal snow, from the bosom of which the subterranean fires rise up") and represents the entrance to the surreal realm. Amédée pleads with the young singer's to initiate him into this second life so as not to let him vegetate in "this real life" (*Rêveur*, 17). In his meeting with the strange singer, it now becomes clear that Sand's traveler has been promoted to the status of a would-be poet in search of the secret of Art itself. The Word is inscribed in the mouth of the crater in "hieroglyphic symbols" that the "furrows of fire" make for the hero to decipher.

From the *regione silvosa* the two young men continue to the very top. Like the concentric circles of Dante's hell, the successive arenas surrounding the crater draw the characters closer to their intended goal. As the two come to the last circle before the mouth of the volcano itself, the moonlit atmosphere reaches oneiric intensity, and the tale takes on an openly fantastic aura. The young singer is metamorphosed into a spirit. Instructing his pupil to abandon the life of humans and to follow him into a phantom realm, he transports Amédée through the air up to the mouth of the crater by holding him by the hair, another detail from Dante. As they are hovering over the terrifying chasm, their bodies are consumed by lava. Just as the biblical fire is linked to the word of God, so here the burning crater is likened to the vessel of a sacred revelation. The hero takes a lustful plunge when the spirit becomes a diabolically beautiful woman who will then then lead Amédée into the very heart of the crater itself: "Dans l'intérieur du volcan, il éprouvait l'ardeur de la flamme non comme une douleur cuisante, mais comme une indicible volupté" (*Rêveur*, 18; "Inside the volcano, he endured the ardent flames, not as a smarting pain, but as an inexpressible rapture"). In this archetypical scene of a baptism of fire, the sorceress promises Amédée the revelation of "a magical life." She invites him to follow her into the heart of the furnace, for "c'est là que mon palais enchanté et mon premier baiser accueilleront mon fiancé" (*Rêveur*, 18; "there my enchanted palace and my first kiss will welcome my betrothed"). The hero finds himself on a "bed of fire" in the sorceress's "arms of snow" where he experiences a "violent electrical shock," thereby sinking into unconsciousness.

Sand's feminine sylphlike creature might be taken as a prefiguration of Nerval's queen whose burning kiss leaves a red mark on the poet's cheek.[12] And indeed we know that Nerval felt a special kinship to Sand, as evidenced by the sonnet he dedicated to her and the friendly allusions to her in his correspondence.[13] But, more crucial, this text points to the primordial image Sand uses to express the death-defying nature of poetic enterprise. By using the image of a journey into the very heart of a volcano in search of some primordial fire of revelation, the writer communicates metaphorically to the reader what she judges to be a forbidden desire to palpate the unknown, to scale unknown heights, and to plunge into hidden depths. The volcano as a metaphor for Art is a constant motif in Sand's works of the early 1830s. The short story "La Fille d'Albano," for example, in which a woman artist is carried away by her brother's improvisation, celebrates: "L'ivresse de l'artiste, l'exaltation fougueuse d'un délire sublime, la brulante sensation du plaisir intellectuel! la débauche du génie, l'invasion du feu céleste!"[14] ("The intoxication of the artist! The fiery exaltation of a sublime ecstasy, the burning sensation of intellectual pleasure! The orgy of genius, the penetration of celestial fire!") While these words convince a talented young woman to refuse marriage in exchange for the free life of the artist, the bizarre mixed metaphors link artistic inspiration and erotic pleasure. By weaving together a double vocabulary of mental ecstasy and corporeal delight, both texts emphasize the affinity between the passion of creation and the creation of passion.

Undoubtedly, Amédée's nocturnal and fantastical excursion, in the company of a person of ambiguous gender, can be read as a metaphor for Sand's own literary journey. *Histoire du rêveur* confirms her fascination for destruction by fire, the urge to live dangerously at the risk of being consumed. Gaston Bachelard's examination of this text prompted him to see in Sand what he called an Empedocles complex, constituting a kind of inverted pyromania. She did not so much express the desire to set things afire as she affirmed the impulse to be ecstatically consumed.[15] In *Histoire du rêveur*, Sand designated herself as a female Empedocles in search of the sacred fire that denotes poetic creativity. The artistic endeavor was evoked as an act of transgression for which the artist might well be punished. Several years later, the character of Lélia in her long lyrical improvisations would formulate the idea of art as simultaneously a curse and a blessing. Whereas her illustrious predecessor, Germaine de Staël, had privileged the figure of Sappho to designate the woman artist, Sand chose to portray a modern incarnation of Empedocles. Significantly, in the two myths, both the

Greek woman poet and the male philosopher plunge to their deaths, but the first does so by jumping off a cliff into the sea, while the second hurls himself down into the volcano. To Staël's baptism by water Sand preferred a baptism by fire.

The exploration of the artist's soul in this early piece delineates the impending metamorphosis of Aurore as a dreamer-about-to-become-a-writer. *Histoire du rêveur* is also *Histoire de la rêveuse*. Amédée is a budding poet whose ascent represents the entrance of the artist into a second, transcendent life out of which art emerges. In this rarified sphere the character of the initiator can proclaim his artistic manifesto: "Ma voix, c'est ma vie" (*Rêveur*, 14), a statement that Sand was about to appropriate for her own. While the entire episode of Etna unfolds under the sign of the nocturnal, it also ends in the fiery brilliance of the volcano. Beginning as an ascension to the summit, the hero's itinerary plunges downward toward the bowels of the mountain. Sand thus creates a powerful synthesis of diurnal elements (the mountain, flight, wings) with nocturnal images (shadows, descent, chasm). At the same time, the hero's descent into the crater can be understood as representing the author's movement into her own psyche. In this way Sand fuses the archetypal image of transcendent flight, which so powerfully delineated the poet's lyrical outbursts for her admired predecessors, Rousseau and Chateaubriand, with the no less powerful counterimage of the descent into the entrails of the earth, thereby constructing a master image to represent the Romantic itinerant writer and Sand's own groping for literary coming-into-being. *Histoire du rêveur* can be read as a prelude to *Lettres d'un voyageur*, to *Lélia*, and to later works, as a reflection on poetic initiation, a reverie on reverie itself.

The image of Amédée willingly *plumbing the depths* of the volcano has both Gothic and Romantic resonances. Sand's text seems to effect a transition between Burke's Gothic aesthetic of the sublime, which privileges depth over height to achieve the greatest *dérèglement* of the senses,[16] and the sensibility of a Romantic poet such as Hugo who links the poet's "deep-seeing eye" with the need to descend into the entrails of the earth so as to unearth literally the truth. A long meditative poem in Victor Hugo's *Contemplations*, entitled "Ce que dit la Bouche d'ombre," deals with preoccupations similar to Sand's and uses many of the same poetic elements—the image of the sacred abyss and the spirit who leads the poet to unknown spheres.[17] Rather than suggest any instance of literary "influence" here, all the more unlikely as *Histoire du rêveur* remained unpublished throughout Hugo's life, I emphasize the striking kinship between the young woman's hesitant prose text and the poet's later lyrical composition to stress the fundamental lyricism of Sand's text and intertextual engagement with the Romantic ethos as a whole. Her story shares with Hugo's work an allegiance to a hyperbolic landscape, the exploitation of spatial images, a belief in the artist's mission as prophet, and a view of humankind's incessant and insatiable desire to transcend the quotidian so as to decipher the hidden meanings beneath the mundane surface of existence. The analogy of *Histoire du rêveur* and "Ce que dit la Bouche d'ombre" also reveals to what extent Sand's early prose style was informed by poetry. She wrote little poetry (there is only one poetic composition in "Sketches and Hints"), but her prose, as much by its lyricism as by its choice of devices, clearly resonates with a poetic sensibility. Before Baudelaire, one might even say, and on the heels of Chateaubriand and Rousseau, Sand invented the prose poem.

Appropriately Sand refers at length to Byron in her early years and her work bears the Byronic stamp. And it is fitting that Chateaubriand recognized her talent, that Musset was haunted by the lyrical intensity of certain scenes in *Indiana*, that Baudelaire was deeply impressed by the poetic prose in *Lélia*, which prefigured his subsequent "poèmes en prose."[18] Sand's poeticized fiction occupies an exceptional position in French Romanticism where lyric poetry and drama tended to dominate the literary scene. Since many of her pages are situated halfway between preromantic lyrical novels and Baudelaire's prose poems, poets of her generation rightly responded to her writing with particular fervor.

Sand's modern Empedocles, Amédée, reveals himself to be the prototype of the traveler in Sand's works. The wanderings of the narrator in *Lettres d'un voyageur*, Consuelo's itineraries throughout Europe, Teverino's excursions into Italy, and the hero's travels in the *Compagnon du tour de France* comprise a series of adventures whose main purpose is inevitably the search for the sublime, the Ideal, Art, or Brotherhood. These wanderers all articulate the author's own personal quest and the intoxication of travel for travel's sake.[19] Throughout her memoirs, for instance, the image of the mountain is associated with her discovery of a benevolent and fertile space that liberates her capacity to dream. In *Histoire de ma vie* she notes the impact on her adolescent imagination of Mme de Genlis's *Les Battuécas*, where a small tribe lives in a valley "encircled by inaccessible mountains" (HV, 1:627). To live in a place separated from the rest of the world by mountains is identified as an eighteenth-century dream (expressed by Voltaire and many others) that aroused in her the first glimmers of her utopianism (HV, 1:629). She uses the mountainous landscape as the focus of her articulation of the poet's never-ending search for transcendent meaning. Whether it is called a longing for the ideal, a thirst for the infinite, or a search for the absolute, the psychic phenomenon is the same. The desire of the voyageur to extract information that a privileged landscape seems ready to divulge is a particularly Sandian form of intellectual quest. *Jacques*, the *Lélia* of 1839, *Spiridion*, *Consuelo*, *Le Marquis de Villemer* (1861) all end in the mountainous heights.

Sand's thirst for the infinite presents the feminized version of a quest traditionally thought to be the exclusive domain of the male. This longing, stated repeatedly throughout her literary career, is expressed as early as 1833: "Combien je me suis laissée dévorer par cette soif de *l'irréalisable* que n'ont pas encore daigné éteindre les saintes rosées du ciel" ("Sketches and Hints," OA, 2:616; "How I have allowed myself to be devoured by this thirst for *the unattainable* which the holy dews from heaven have not yet deigned to quench"). In *Histoire de ma vie* the author traces this longing back to her childhood: "Me voilà donc, enfant rêveur . . . *lancée à la recherche d'un idéal*, et ne pouvant pas rêver un monde, une humanité idéalisée, sans placer au faîte un Dieu, l'idéal même" (emphasis added; HV, 1:810–811; "Here I was a dreamy child . . . *embarked on a quest for an ideal*, unable to dream of a universe, an idealized humanity, without crowning it with a God, the idea itself"). Much later, in a preface she wrote for her son Maurice's *Monde des papillons* (1867), this same thirst for the infinite is associated with height: "Pour monter, non pas jusqu'au sublime architecte, mais . . . vers le foyer de sa pensée . . . il nous faut graviter le long des spirales de *l'infini*" ("In order to rise, not up to the level of the sublime architect himself, but . . . within reach of his innermost thought . . . we must gravitate along the spirals of the *infinite*").[20] Sand's attachment to "la recherche de l'absolu" is as dominant a theme in her work as it is in Balzac's philosophical novels, and in the pages of many of her Romantic predecessors and contemporaries. The mountain, preferably in a nocturnal aspect is the preferred image for that search, and the exploration of that topos coincides with the early stages of her career when she was only beginning to define the outlines of her literary cosmology.

The Attraction of the Void

The desire to throw oneself into a volcano so as to be consumed by fire, the dominant theme in *Histoire du rêveur*, points to a larger configuration in Sand's future fictional universe. The human leap will always remain a sign of superiority, a mark of sainthood or poetic fervor, a gestural symbol expressing a mystical longing for union with the ideal. But, underlying this craving for the infinite, there sometimes lurks a death wish. In Sand's epistolary novel, *Jacques*, the hero seeks permanent escape from public and domestic life in the isolation of the Tyrol. His death wish finds it echo in the "brutal and enormous magic"[21] of mountainous heights. His suicide note, written while he is wandering alone in the Swiss glacier of Runs, is a declaration of faith which affirms his sacred right to exercise total power over his own life: "Je monterai sur la cime des glaciers, et je prierai du fond de mon coeur . . . je m'élancerai dans l'abîme en levant les mains vers le ciel et en criant avec ferveur: 'O justice! justice de Dieu!' " ("I shall climb up to the glaciers' peaks, there I shall pray from the bottom of my heart . . . I shall hurl myself into the abyss with my hands raised toward heaven, and fervently crying: 'Oh justice! oh divine justice!' ")[22] These last ,words of Jacques end the epistolary portion of the novel. Only an Editor's Note is added on somewhat artificially to confirm the hero's dramatic death:

> on n'entendit plus parler de lui; et les montagnards chez qui il avait logé firent savoir aux autorités du canton qu'un étranger avait disparu. . . . On l'avait vu prendre le sentier des glaciers, et s'enfoncer très-avant dans les neiges; on présuma qu'il était tombé dans une de ces fissures qui se rencontrent parmi les blocs de glace, et qui ont parfois plusieurs centaines de pieds de profondeur.[23]

> (nothing more was heard of him; and the mountaineers who had put him up reported a missing foreigner to the authorities of the canton. . . . He had been seen taking the trail leading up the glaciers, and venturing quite far out into the snow; it was presumed that he had fallen into one of those crevasses one finds among the blocks of ice, and which sometimes are several hundred feet deep.)

Suicide has long been a prominent literary topos. The neoclassical tragedians regarded it as the best strategy for transforming Pascal's "moi haïssable" into a "moi admirable." For the preromantics, it was seen as the natural if extreme solution for a morbid sensibility. Even a rationalist and "homme des lumières" such as Diderot had one of his characters, Saint-Alban, posit the existence of a double instinct of self-preservation and self-destructon. Thus, in the works of George Sand (as in other Romantic texts), self-inflicted death, deployed as a metaphor for the apotheosis of the individual, is a predominantly literary theme. It is not so much connected to the Sand's own life as it is the *mise en écriture* in the feminine of a certain intellectual obsession. Even in the two letters on suicide in *Lettres d'un voyageur* her "attrait du suicide" (LV, 138) is more the exploration of a literary rather than an autopsychological impulse.

While historical documents of the time show that suicide was rampant in the cities, especially among the lower middle classes, literature tells a different story. The literary setting of suicide is a lonely landscape—a mountain, a glen, a lake. Typically, Sand's suicidal characters choose to end their days in a majestic natural landscape that echoes the sublimity of their inner world. The heroes and heroines who kill themselves in these novels verify the comment of writer and politician Saint-Marc Girardin, for whom suicide "is not the disease of the simple-hearted and simple-minded, but the disease of the refined and the philosophers."[24] This remark rings especially true for *Lélia* and *Jacques*, novels that highlight the suicides of two young aristocrats, one a refined poet, the other a philosopher. Both Sténio and Jacques justify suicide philosophically—the first through the double apology of despair and vertigo (*Lélia*, 290), the other as an integral part of his ideology which includes the philanthropic desire to give his wife the freedom to love another. Jacques puts his act into a "philosophical" framework: "Quand la vie d'un homme est nuisible à quelques-uns, à charge à lui-même, inutile à tous, le suicide est un acte légitime et qu'il peut accomplir, sinon sans regret d'avoir manqué sa vie, du moins sans remords d'y mettre un terme" (347; "When a man's life is harmful to someone, a burden to himself, useless to all, suicide is a legitimate act, which he can carry out, if not without regret for having missed out on life, at least without remorse for putting an end to it"). He commits what one might call an invisible suicide, executing his plan secretly, preferring to "disappear" from society so as to give free reign to his project in the solitude of the mountains.[25]

But suicide is not a monolithic entity with a monological significance in Sand's fictional universe. Suicide is polysemic, or at the very least, bipartite. On the one hand, the author portrays a strong suicide that expresses itself in a leap into nothingness, a form of rebirth, a baptism, an act of initiation.[26] Amédée's leap into the volcano is merely the first in a long line of this kind of Sandian suicide. Ralph and Indiana jump into the Bernica Falls. Jacques leaps into the glacier. In the pastoral novel *Jeanne* the peasant heroine throws herself out the window to protect her virginity. Jeanne is presented not as a simple but rather as a naive folk philosopher whose act of defiance is also an act of heroism. The topos of the suicidal plunge is an obsessive variation of Sand's "Empedocles complex."

On the other hand, Sand presents suicide by drowning in sharp contrast to this active, willful, esthetic suicide. The suicides of Noun in *Indiana* and of Sténio in *Lélia* are both described through metaphors of passivity. These two characters are portrayed as weak, their passivity specifically contrasted to the resilience and strong-mindedness of Indiana and Lélia. Béatrice Didier, in an article on the Ophelia complex argues, unsuccessfully to my mind, that the recurrent theme of passive suicide in Sand's early novels reveals the author's own "dreams of passivity." But Didier neglects to mention the more dominant presence of strong suicides in those same novels. Ophelia loses out to Empedocles, all the more since the leap remains an important figuration of suicide in later texts. Traditionally each form of suicide highlighted by Sand has been linked to a specific gender. Self-destruction by drowning presents itself as passive and "feminine"; leaping to one's death is considered daring and "masculine." But once again, Sand is playing with the categories of gender, since she constructs a fictional model that assigns both types of suicide to both sexes. And I wonder if, when she reread *Corinne* around 1837, this time more attentively, along with Sainte-Beuve's flattering introduction to it, her "shock of recognition" was not associated in some way with the propensity of Staël's heroine for the Sapphic leap.

The Discovery of the Visual

Sand's decision to situate *Histoire du rêveur* on Mount Etna can almost surely be ascribed to her literary temperament which initially privileged the visual. Years later, the author traveled again to the same site in her imagination to compose a novel entitled *Le Piccinino* (1847). In it one of her characters explains that Etna is "le plus grand spectacle que la nature puisse offrir *à un peintre*" ("the greatest spectacle that nature can present to a painter").[27] Although Sand does not name a particular painter, a clue is provided by the "Notice" of *Le Piccinino*. She chose Sicily for the site for the novel, she writes, because she was looking at an album of fine engravings at the time. As early as 1822, Aurore had in her possession Gigault de la Salle's work, *Voyage pittoresque en Sicile*,[28] which contained engravings of many of the sites mentioned in *Le Piccinino* and *Histoire du rêveur*, particularly the "grotte aux chèvres" where Amédée spends part of the night and the inside of the crater.[29]

Sand's real discovery was not the mountains per se, whether the Alps, the Pyrenees, or Etna, but the fertile interaction which she found between what she *saw* and the way it inspired her. When she wrote, "Je rêve donc je *vois*" ("I dream therefore I *see*"), in her private journal, "Sketches and Hints," she might well have added: ". . . *donc je compose*" ("*. . . therefore I write*").[30] She knew the Italian landscapes through reproductions, and certain images "excited her imagination."[31] As a result, they had an enormous visual impact on the author's literary imagination. She started to write as if she were drawing; her early prose took on a decidedly pictorial style. The narrator of *Le Piccinino* describes Etna as a painting, immobilizing the scene as if the landscape were posing for the artist. Any allusion to sound, smell, or movement is excluded from the description. Only the pictorial is valorized:

> C'était un *spectacle* étrange et magnifique. Tout était vague dans cette *perspective infinie*, et la région *piedimonta* se distinguait à peine de la zone supérieure. . . . Mais, tandis que l'aube . . . glissait en *lueurs pâles* et confuses sur le bas du *tableau*, la cime du mont *dessinait* avec netteté ses déchirures grandioses et ses neiges imaculées sur l'air *transparent* de la nuit.   (emphasis added; I:143)

> (It was a strange and magnificent *spectacle*. Everything in that *infinite perspective* was vague, and the Piedmont region could barely be

distinguished from the upper zone. . . . But, while the *pale* and indistinct *glimmers* of dawn . . . crept into the lower half of the *picture*, the grandiose and jagged outlines on top of the mount and its immaculate snows were clearly *outlined* against the night's *transparent* air.)

Sand's painterly imagination evident in this novel confirms her affinity for the poetic voice rather than the prosaic. Her particular attention to landscape descriptions and to the devices which promote the visual sense link her with the French and English Romantic poets of her age. More important, Sand highlights this allegiance to the visual when she attempts to articulate the birth of her vocation. As she describes it in *Histoire de ma vie*, in spite of four years of "tâtonnements" with various mostly nonliterary enterprises—translations, sewing, dressmaking, and painting knick-knacks—she felt herself to be an artist at heart. Her fragile sense of a vocation coincided exactly with the discovery, not of her writing talent, but of her receptivity to visual inspiration. The initial discovery of the artist within her took place, not as might be expected at a writing desk, but in a museum:

> malgré moi, je me sentais artiste, sans avoir jamais songé à me dire que je pouvais l'être. Dans un de mes courts séjours à Paris, j'étais entrée un jour au musée de peinture. Ce n'était sans doute pas la première fois, mais j'avais toujours regardé sans voir, persuadée que je ne m'y connaissais pas, et ne sachant pas tout ce qu'on peut sentir sans comprendre. Je commençai à m'émouvoir singulièrement. J'y retournai le lendemain, puis le surlendemain; et, à mon voyage suivant . . . je m'en allai mystérieusement toute seule, dès que le musée était ouvert, et j'y restais jusqu'à ce qu'il fermât. J'étais comme enivrée, comme clouée devant les Titien, les Tintoret, les Rubens.   (HV, 2:105–106)

> (in spite of myself, I felt I was an artist, without ever having acknowledged consciously that I could become one. One day, during one of my short stays in Paris, I visited an art museum. It was not the first time, but I had always looked at painting without really seeing it before, convinced that I knew nothing about it, and not knowing all that one can feel without understanding. Remarkably, I began to be very moved. I went back the following day, then the next; and, during my next stay . . . I started going, by myself, not letting anyone know what I was doing. I would get there as soon as the doors of the museum opened, and stay until it closed. I was intoxicated, transfixed before the Titians, the Tintorettos, the Rubens.)

The visual is defined as the privileged path of inspiration. Through the contemplation of paintings, another world ("un monde nouveau") emerged for her. The visual arts unleashed her dormant writing talents. According to Georges Lubin, Aurore Dupin Dudevant haunted the arts exhibits and museums in May and June of 1830, on the threshold of her transformation into George Sand.[32] Significantly, *Histoire de ma vie* dwells on her "literary projects" and her resolution to go to Paris to seek her literary fortune immediately after this museum episode.

Sand also insists on the strange fact that she did not simply admire the paintings then and there; somewhat later she would be haunted again by all the pictorial sensations experienced during the day. This veritable artistic re-creation occurred at night:

> La nuit, je voyais passer devant moi toutes ces grandes figures qui, sous la main des maîtres, ont pris un cachet de puissance morale. . . . C'est dans la belle peinture qu'on sent ce que c'est que la vie: c'est comme un résumé splendide de la forme et de l'expression des êtres et des choses, trop souvent voilées ou flottantes dans le mouvement de la réalité et dans l'appréciation de celui qui les contemple; c'est le spectacle de la nature et de l'humanité vu à travers le sentiment du génie qui l'a composé.   (HV, 2:106)

> (At night, I would see pass before me all those great figures who, at the hand of masters, had been marked with a stamp of moral strength. . . . It is through great painting that one senses the real meaning of life: it presents a splendid summing up of the forms and expressions of beings and things, too often veiled or floating in the swirl of reality and in the observer's appreciation; it presents the spectacle of nature and humanity as interpreted by the spirit of genius which has composed it.)

This episode sets up a time frame that would soon mark the writer's optimal writing time. We know from *Histoire de ma vie* that her first attempts at writing took place at night. And throughout her long career, Sand's nocturnal sessions would produce book after book.

The desire to write became apparent, then, not as a direct result of experience, nor as an artless autobiographical urge, but through the contemplation of art. As she examined the paintings, she became aware of various artistic movements and she *internalized* this awareness:

> L'univers se révélait à moi. Je voyais à la fois dans le présent et dans le passé, *je devenais classique et romantique* en même temps. . . . Je voyais le monde du vrai surgir à travers tous les fantômes de ma fantaisie et toutes les hésitations de mon regard. Il me semblait avoir conquis je ne sais quel trésor d'infini dont j'avais ignoré l'existence.   (emphasis added; HV, 2:107)

(The universe was revealing itself to me. I could see in both the present and the past, *I was becoming classic and romantic* at the same time. . . . I could see the real world emerge through all the phantoms of my fantasy and all the hesitations of my observations. I felt as though I had secured infinity's treasure trove, the very existence of which I had not even suspected.)

"Phantoms of her fantasy," "infinity's treasure trove"—are so many metaphors for poetic inspiration. Discovery of the visual leads her to recognize within herself a previously suspected passion to write:

> Je n'aurais pu dire quoi, je ne savais pas de nom pour ce que je sentais se presser dans mon esprit rechauffé et comme dilaté; mais j'avais la fièvre, et je m'en revenais du musée, me perdant de rue en rue, ne sachant où j'allais, oubliant de manger.   (HV, 2:107)

(I could not have said what it was, I could not have given a name to what I was feeling, pressing in on my inflamed and inspired spirit; but I was feverish as I returned from the museum, losing my way through the streets, forgetting my destination, forgetting to eat.)

Disoriented, feverish, her mind elsewhere, she was possessed by a force she did not recognize, and could not name. She knew she had been transported to an unknown realm. Her sense of physical disorientation only intensified her spiritual distraction. By suggesting that she might attempt to transpose her own inner vision into an artistic form of her own choosing, painting had worked a miracle on her imagination. The writer was about to be born.

The contemplation of art as a mysterious catalyst for Sand's impulse to write never ceased to inform her work. Throughout her literary career, individual paintings, illustrations, or engravings were at the genesis of various novels. During her brief period as J. Sand, for example, a painting was the initial inspiration for "La Fille d'Albano." *Indiana*, according to Marie-Jacques Hoog, was inspired in part by a portrait by Antoine Gros which the budding writer discovered at the Louvre.[33] The inspiration for *Jeanne* comes from a Holbein painting representing a "virgin of the golden age,"[34] just as *La Mare au diable* has its origin in the contemplation of the same artist's *Simulachres de la mort*: "une gravure d'Holbein, qui m'avait frappé . . . m'a poussé à écrire cette histoire modeste" ("Notice," *La Mare*, 28; "an engraving by Holbein, which had had a strong impression on me . . . prompted me to write this modest story"). In the "Notice" to *Le Meunier d'Angibault*, Sand described in a generalized way this creative process of crystalization, when the writer encountered by chance a source of inspiration from the outside world: "Tous ceux qui ont écrit . . . des ouvrages d'imagination . . . savent que la vision des choses intellectuelles part souvent de celle des choses matérielles" ("All those who have written . . . works of the imagination . . . know that the envisioning of intellectual things often proceeds from material things.)

"The Literature of Images"

Natural landscapes likewise functioned for Sand as a springboard for poetic inspiration, and consequently descriptions of the physical world figured prominently in her works. In *Histoire du rêveur*, as we have just seen, the looming presence of Etna was an early manifestation of her predilection for landscape, which she used to figure a character's mental state symbolically and to convey a visual embodiment of the sublime as part of her allegiance to an "aesthetics of the infinite." As Sand's fictional geography began to form, *paysage* emerged as a privileged means of symbolic presentation. Landscape is a much more salient theme in her novels than in those of Balzac and Stendhal, her most prominent literary contemporaries. Not only does this reinforce our sense of Sand as a Romantic poet, for whom the visual is the chosen route to the visionary, it also suggests that the crucial role played by landscape in her fiction sets her apart from the male novelists of the day, and, as such, helps formulate a distinctive aspect of her self-identification as a woman writer.

In the early period of Sand's writing, this particular aspect of her literary temperament corresponds most closely to what Balzac called "la littérature des images." In an article in praise of Stendhal, the creator of *La Comédie humaine* suggested that three tendencies could be distinguished in contemporary literature. He opposed "la littérature des idées"—with its emphasis on action, events, dialogue, and on nonvisible manifestations of the world—to "la littérature des images"—with its focus on nature descriptions, lyricism, and the contemplation of the outside world. While Stendhal was the representative of the literature of ideas, Victor Hugo represented the imagist tendency described in this way: "In every generation, in every people, there are elegiac, meditative, contemplative souls, who, more that others, are obsessed by *the great images, the vast spectacles of nature*, and who carry them in their hearts. Hence a school, which I would designate *the Literature of Images*."[35] In Hugo's camp, Balzac placed poets and lyrical novelists, such as Lamartine, Chateaubriand, Ballanche, Senancour, and Vigny. He identified their illustrious predecessors as Rousseau and Bernardin de Saint-Pierre. This category, however, admirably suits the sensibility that dominates in *Histoire du rêveur* and many of Sand's pastoral novels.

But significantly Balzac situated George Sand in the third category of writers—along with other novelists like himself whose work achieved a synthesis of the literature of images and that of ideas.

Possessing what he called "a bifrontal intelligence" ("une intelligence *bifrons*"), these writers were capable of expressing both lyricism and action, "l'idée dans l'image ou l'image dans l'idée." Balzac labeled this third tendency *l'Eclectisme littéraire*. What is remarkable about Balzac's configuration of writers and their conflicting sensibilities is how accurately he sensed Sand's double allegiance to idea and image, and the degree to which he was able to understand the profoundly dual nature of Sand's art. Interestingly, among the handful of writers who make up his third category of "literary eclecticism," two are Germaine de Staël and George Sand. Whether Balzac was conscious of placing himself next to the most illustrious woman writers of his age is open to speculation. But the article hints that the nature of the "bifrontal writer" is associated with a "bisexual" or androgynous literary persona, that "eclectic" novelists have a complete understanding of the world. They are, as he puts it, "whole beings . . . [who] embrace everything, who must have both lyricism and action . . . in the belief that perfection requires a total vision of things."[36]

In Sand's fictional world, the opposing tendencies of the "littérature des images" and the "littérature des idées" typically dominate in different novels. Whereas Balzac's world synthesized the two opposing sensibilities, Sand most often kept them distinct by highlighting each in turn. Balzac's knowledge retained its integrity in synthesis in *La Comédie humaine*; with some notable exceptions, Sand's knowledge preserved its integrity in multiplicity. Throughout the 1830s, Sand would at times privilege the one, at others, the second. It is striking how rapidly in that fertile decade Sand developed from the "literature of images" to the "literature of ideas." In *Histoire du rêveur*, and in her first and second novels, *Indiana* and *Valentine* (1832), imaging predominated. But within a year, Sand was already exploring the concept of the abstract, constructing a fictional universe that was entirely in the domain of Idea. *Lélia* (1833) and *Spiridion* (1839) are her purest novels of ideas. In the 1840s, however, several texts offered a synthesis of "the idea in the image and the image in the idea." Of all her novels, *Consuelo* and *La Comtesse de Rudolstadt* most effectively achieved a synthesis of idea and image. At the same time, the utopian novels tended to underscore the ideational by figuring it in images.

Although writers of the same "eclectic school," Balzac and Sand nevertheless tended to exploit different settings in their novels. Balzac is above all a city novelist, whose "Scènes de la vie privée" and "Scènes de la vie parisienne" take place for the most part in an urban environment. Conversely, the natural world dominates much of Sand's fiction. When Baudelaire opposed Balzac, whom he called the king of modernity, to Hugo, the representative of "the forces of nature and their harmonious struggle," his comment regarding the poet could just as easily have applied to Sand.[37] If Balzac is the poet of Paris, as Dickens is the poet of London and Dostoevsky of Saint Petersburg, then Sand is the poet of the Berry. True, *Consuelo* takes place in Venice, Vienna, and Berlin, parts of *Indiana* occur in Parisian salons, and *Horace* and *La Ville noire* are urban narratives, but many more of her novels, and not only the *romans champêtres*, have a rural setting. As a result, Sand's lyricism often manifests itself in nature descriptions. When Balzac leaves Paris, he is more likely to focus on a provincial town than on the countryside. Where he lovingly describes the traveler's walk through the cobblestoned streets of Saumur (in the beginning of *Eugénie Grandet*, for example), Sand expends the same energy on a traveler's approach to the rustic decor of the Vallée noire (in *Valentine*). Her insistence on the importance of landscape is a clear indication of her allegiance to a certain visual and poetic sensibility.

Sand's memoirs emphasize to what an extent her imagination was a constructor of visual panoramas. Her form of "making real" was not so much being "realistic" as it was "making visible." *Histoire de ma vie* reveals the author's preference for images that are elaborated whenever possible to illustrate or flesh out the arid world of ideas. For example, as Sand describes the impact her mother's reading had on her childish imagination—Sophie is reading a novel by Mme de Genlis out loud—she articulates the dialect between "literature of ideas" and "literature of images":

> J'écoutais d'abord attentivement . . . peu à peu je perdais le sens des phrases que me lisait ma mère; sa voix me jetait dans une sorte d'assoupissement moral, où il m'était impossible de suivre une *idée*. Des *images* se dessinaient devant moi et venaient se fixer sur l'écran vert.   (emphasis added: HV, 1:630)

> (At first I listened attentively . . . little by little, I lost track of the sense of what my mother was reading; her voice would put me in a kind of moral drowsiness, in which I simply could not concentrate on a single *idea*. *Images* would outline themselves before my eyes, and come to rest on the green screen.)

The "images" she created in her mind are imaginary landscapes. We see the child Aurore transform the auditory into complex visual images in the detailed landscape description that follows:

> C'était des bois, des prairies, des rivières, des villes d'une architecture bizarre et gigantesque . . . des palais enchantés avec des jardins . . . des milliers d'oiseaux d'azur, d'or et de pourpre, qui voltigaient sur les fleurs. . . . Il y avait des roses vertes, noires, violettes, des roses bleues surtout.   (HV, I, 630)

> (There were woods, meadows, rivers, cities of a strange and gigan-
> tic design . . . enchanted palaces with gardens . . . thousands of
> azure, gold, and purple birds, which fluttered above the
> flowers. . . . There were green, black, purple and most of all blue
> roses.)

Significantly Sand insists on the power of creating images, specifically
in reference to her childhood. Indeed, *Histoire du rêveur* can be read as
an early literary manifestation of the very same power of transforming
ideas into images demonstrated so vividly by the child Aurore.

Years later, the great "visuel," Baudelaire, would express his regret that the paysagists of his generation were no longer painting what
he called "the Romantic landscape." His "Salon de 1859" ends with the
following melancholic remark:

> I miss those great lakes that symbolize the immobility of despair, I
> miss the immense mountains, the staircases from this planet to the
> sky, from whose heights all that once appeared large now seems
> small . . . the gigantic bridges, the ruins of Nineveh which inspire
> vertigo, in short everything that would have to be invented, if all of
> it did not already exist.[38]

If no longer in evidence in the painting of Baudelaire's time, such exag-
gerated landscapes of were still to be found in the writing of his contemporary, George Sand. She displayed an energy of imagination
which counteracted what Baudelaire terms with contempt "a very
great laziness of the imagination" among the "overly herbivorous"
nature painters of his day.[39] If the symbolist poet was able to recognize
Hugo as "roi des paysagistes" (a talent displayed both in the ink drawings and the poetry), his misogynist lenses blinded him to Sand's remarkable ability to paint "Romantic landscapes" with words. By
providing in *Histoire du rêveur* a vertiginous poetic decor to depict the
mental landscape of artistic creation, Sand had already established her
aesthetic vocabulary. She was now ready to embark on the enduring
task of writing for her life.

3

Indiana or the Creation of a Literary Voice

"Un Début dans la vie"

The embryonic *Histoire du rêveur* was abandoned and remained unfinished, never to be published in Sand's lifetime. It was the earliest manifestation of her exploration of the nocturnal landscape and her first articulation of a hero in search of artistic integration. Nevertheless, its fragmented form revealed that Aurore Dupin, the *rêveuse*, was still a long way away from George Sand, the *écrivaine*. And although after *Histoire du rêveur* she published a full-length novel and several short stories in collaboration with Jules Sandeau and under the truncated pseudonym J. Sand, it was not until the publication of *Indiana*, on 19 May 1832 that G. Sand burst upon the literary scene in her own "write." The event precipitated its anonymous and unknown author (whose enigmatic signature Gustave Planche deciphered as denoting a certain "Georgina Sand") into immediate celebrity. The book was proclaimed the literary event of the year by almost all the critics of the time. The writer and journalist H. de Latouche, who had been Sand's mentor when she first came to Paris, wrote to his young protégée that *Indiana* placed her "in one leap, at the head of contemporary writers" (*Corr.*, 2:88n). An anonymous article in the June issue of *La France littéraire* announced that the novel was "worthy of being included among the best novels of our time" (*Corr.*, 2:115n). In the July 9 feuilleton of the *Journal des débats*, Jules Janin declared that *Indiana* was "the most splendid *roman de moeurs* that has been published in France in the last twenty years" (*Corr.*, 2:119). Certain intrinsic qualities of *Indiana* and the particular situation of the novel in France in the beginning of the 1830s combined to make the work's publication a sensation.

The French novel found itself in a period of rapid expansion around 1832. The years 1832 to 1834 represent the culminating point in an ascending curve of published novels. From 179 novels published in 1831, the number jumped to 282 for 1832 and reached 345 for 1834.[1] This fertile period witnessed the emergence of three young novelists: Stendhal (*Le Rouge et le noir* came out only two months before *Indiana* which was favorably compared with it); Balzac (Sand was constantly compared to him); and Sand. This period also coincided with a "prise de conscience" on the part of the critics concerning the possibilities of the novel.[2] Since there existed remarkably little theory of the novel before 1830 and almost no *ars poetica* for fiction, the Romantic generation saw itself increasingly associated with the valorization of fictional forms.

This is not to say that suddenly, in the critical discourse concerning the novel, opposition or antagonism or disparagement ceased to be heard. The novel continued to be defined by its adversaries as marginal literature, the pulp genre of the day. As late as 1821, for instance, the table of contents of the literary journal *L'Abeille* (formerly *La Minerve Littéraire*) did not include the category "novels" under the general rubric of "literature."[3] By 1832, however, the opinions of such a critic as Louis-Simon Auger—for whom the novelistic genre was "a kind of monster, born of the adulterous coupling of Falsehood and Truth,"[4] and writing novels a feminine occupation barely superior to sewing ("We must let women have . . . the tasks best suited to their physical and moral constitutions. . . . I am therefore of the opinion that they should be allowed to scribble their novels as they do their needlework")[5]—were on the way out. The novel, now worthy of men's attention, was being taken more and more seriously. Its lack of imposed formal conventions was now valued for its potential, seen as a sign of maximal flexibility, rather than as a defect. Eugène Pelletan, in a review of Sand's *Le Meunier d'Angibault* (1845) for example, praised the novel genre for being "the most complete, the most comprehensive": "What constitutes the superiority of the novel in our era is its triple universality. It deals with all subjects, addresses all readers, and encompasses all literary forms. The novel has no limits, no barriers, no fixed path."[6] The novel was increasingly being considered as the great reservoir of endless possibilities, one that could accommodate all forms, all subjects, all styles. When in our day Mikhail Bakhtin claims that "it is only in the novel that discourse can reveal all its specific potential and achieve its true depth,"[7] he also is asserting the genre's unlimited range of possibilities.

But, whether the novel was considered a sign of literary decadence[8] or of literary renewal[9] (both opinions can be found in the press of the time), it was invading the entire literary domain. And with examples such as Sand making her literary début in 1832 with a novel, the genre's respectability seemed increasingly secure. Before the 1830s in France, a young writer who sought to become established in the sacred realm of literature, was obliged to display his or her talents in a tragedy. After 1830, increasingly, a young writer's debut tended to be in the form of a novel.

The dazzling success of Sand's *Indiana* derived in part from the critics' perception of the work as the "prototype of the new novel."[10] The press of 1832 judged it, with its blend of history, poetry, drama, and politics, to be profoundly modern. *Indiana* represented "the official chronicle of the passions of our time";[11] it contributed to the elaboration of "the charter (la charte) of what is going to become the modern novel";[12] it was a sign of the author's "original and independent mind."[13] It also prefigured *Lélia*, which would be defined as "the most innovative and revolutionary novel that our civilization has produced".[14]

Today this ascription of modernity may seem somewhat excessive. In fact, the word modernity in the critical usage of 1832 was used to convey two main concepts. First, it alluded to Romanticism. *Indiana* represented the story of a "modern passion," said the *Figaro* of May 31, the drama of an "enfant du siècle." It was a study, among other things, of the almost pathological hypersensitivity of the time, which the comparatist Paul Van Tieghem has called Romanticism's "hypertrophy of the imagination and sensibility."[15] The novel probed Indiana's sickly sensibility as she succumbed to "l'instinct du malheur," and "[le] magnétisme de la souffrance" (*Indiana*, 227). As a chronicle of the splenetic ideal of the day, *Indiana* appeared modern. Sand's even more innovative transposition of the Romantic hero into a feminine incarnation only accentuates *our* impression of newness.

Second, and paradoxically, modernity was also used as a synonym for realism. And in this sense as well *Indiana* was modern. It could readily be seen as belonging to the fashionable category of the "études de moeurs," which characterized many novels of the 1830s. Stendhal's subtitle for *Le Rouge et le noir*, "Chronique de 1830," could apply just as easily to *Indiana*. In fact, a variant of the first edition referred to the text as "cette chronique" (*Indiana*, 380). The subtitle of another Stendhal novel, *Armance*, "Quelques scènes d'un salon de Paris en 1827," could be slightly altered to read "Scenes from a Parisian and a provincial salon in 1830" and would fit *Indiana* equally well. Sand's novel could be read as another illustration of Balzac's "Scènes de la vie privée." *Indiana* also integrated contemporary historical events into the fiction, specifically the political crisis that led to the three frenetic days—"les Trois Glorieuses"—of the July revolution of 1830.[16] But, although one should not neglect this "documentary" aspect of *Indiana*, critics traditionally have been overly concerned with the mimetic aspect of the text and with the role that historical events play in it. The historical dimension, it is true, documents a given moment in French society in precise fashion, but above all it serves to illustrate symbolically the central subject of the novel, which is not so much History as the Word. It is this symbolic subject that ensures the true and lasting modernity of the novel.

Indiana is remarkable in that it does not appear to be a first novel, but rather the product of an already mature talent. Numerous critics were surprised by this quasi-miraculous birth of George Sand the novelist. As far as the reading public was concerned, the young novelist, like Athena emerging in adult form from Zeus's thigh or head, had suddenly appeared out of nowhere, with a fully-formed voice and a fully-developed talent. Even Henry James, years later, was to comment upon this brilliant literary "début dans la vie," marveling at the unexpected plenitude of the author's talent and voice:

> About this sudden entrance into literature, into philosophy, into rebellion . . . there are various different things to be said. Very remarkable, indeed, was the immediate development of the literary faculty in this needy young woman who lived in cheap lodgings and looked for "employment." She wrote as a bird sings; but unlike most birds, she found it unnecessary to indulge, by way of prelude, in twitterings and vocal exercises; she broke out at once with her full volume of expression.[16]

Three points need to be made here in reference to the unusual virtuosity of this literary début. First, *Indiana*, at least in the early pages, contains clear indications of being written by a reader of Chateaubriand. The novel opens with a brilliantly constructed scene evoking Romantic spleen, a subject that inevitably conjures up the author of *René* as Sand's literary forefather. Second, Henry James expressed his regret that the author if *Indiana* had not shed more light on its gestation when he writes: "[there is] no account of how she learned to write, no record of effort or apprenticeship . . . the thing about which she had least to say was the writer's, the inventor's, the romancer's art. She possessed it by the gift of God, but she seems never to have felt the temptation to examine the pulse of the machine."[17] Yet *Histoire de ma vie* does contain several passages that James seems to have skimmed over too quickly or not read at all which offer some insight into the "pulse of the machine." Third, while many readers and critics considered Sand's bursting onto the literary scene as a kind of artistic parthenogenesis, *Indiana*, in an unusual way, is very much a work of apprenticeship. The novel can be seen as a series of narrative experimentations which culminates in the writer's acquisition of a voice to match her point of view. Embedded within the novel, the story of Ralph recapitulates the writer's progress from initial uncertainty and hesitation to ultimate assurance and eloquence. The deep structure of *Indiana*, which contains a reflection on the genesis of Sand's literary voice, will be examined in this chapter.

A Feminized mal du siècle

Indiana opens with a tableau of the heroine, her cousin Ralph, and her husband Delmare sitting in silence, immediately conveying the characters' dominant mood of melancholic gloom:

> Par une soirée d'automne pluvieuse et fraîche, trois personnes rêveuses étaient gravement occupées, au fond d'un petit castel de la

Brie, à regarder brûler les tisons du foyer et cheminer lentement l'aiguille de la pendule. Deux de ces hôtes silencieux semblaient s'abandonner en toute soumission au vague ennui qui pesait sur eux; mais le troisième donnait des marques de rébellion ouverte: il s'agitait sur son siège, étouffait à demi haut quelques bâillements mélancoliques, et frappait la pincette sur les bûches pétillantes.   (*Indiana*, 49)

(On a rainy and cool autumn evening, three pensive people in a small chateau in Brie were solemnly watching the embers burning in the hearth and the slow rotation of the clock hand. Two of these silent inhabitants seemed submissively resigned to the vague boredom that weighed down on them; but the third gave signs of open rebellion: he fidgeted in his chair, he half-stifled several melancholic yawns, and hit the tongs against the smoldering logs.)

Sand frames her characters in an atmosphere of mal du siècle, placing *Indiana* in the tradition of *René*, with its reference to the gloomy "paternal castle" in "a remote province," home to the hero's sickly and hypersensitive soul. Chateaubriand's "château gothique" like Sand's, is described in its autumnal incarnation. Clearly *René* was important to Sand, as we see from several allusions in *Histoire de ma vie*. Sand's first reading of the novel in adolescence prompted her to identify with the hero ("it seemed to me that *René* was myself"; HV, 1:1092). And of her decision to live the bohemian life in Paris, she wrote: "Cela valait mieux qu'une cellule et j'aurais pu dire avec *René* . . . que je me promenais dans le *désert des hommes*" (HV, 2:135; "It was preferable to a cell and I could have said, as in *René*, . . . that I was wandering in the *desert of men*"). But if at first René was a character to emulate in her own life, he was quickly transformed into an exemplar for her first authentic literary heroine.

Inclined to be more inspired by male rather than female literary models, Sand expressed this fascination for Chateaubriand's splenetic character in *Indiana*. Her heroine, therefore, was modeled on René rather than on his sister, Amélie, too peripheral a character with too simplistic a mental life. Indiana possessed "comme René, le coeur mort avant d'avoir vécu" (HV, 1:1093; "like René, a dead heart even before having lived"). Like him she was prey to the "goût du siècle," attributing to herself an exceptional sensibility and wallowing in self-absorbed suffering (HV, 2:195):

[Indiana] avait dix-neuf ans, et, si vous l'eussiez vue enfoncée sous le manteau de cette vaste cheminée de marbre blanc incrusté de cuivre doré; si vous l'eussiez vue, toute fluette, toute pâle, toute triste, le coude appuyé sur son genou, elle toute jeune . . . à côté de ce vieux mari, semblable à une fleur née d'hier qu'on fait éclore dans un vase gothique, vous eussiez plaint la femme du colonel Delmare. (*Indiana*, 50)

([Indiana] was nineteen years old, and if you had seen her huddled beneath the mantelpiece of that vast, white marble fireplace encrusted with brass; if you had seen her, so thin, pale, sad, her elbow propped up on her knee, she who was so young . . . next to this old husband, she who resembled a fresh, budding flower made to bloom in a Gothic vase, you would have pitied Colonel Delmare's wife.)

This elaborate portrait highlights the character of Indiana and focuses the reader's attention on the author's main reason for using *René* as a model. Sand wished to elaborate on the theme of a feminized agony. Chateaubriand's text served not so much to guide the young writer stylistically as much as to offer a model to emulate and subvert simultaneously. Chateaubriand had articulated the mal du siècle in its heretofore unambiguously masculine form—as a metaphysical malady so poetic and sophisticated that it could only be suffered by men. Sand's hidden agenda was to cross the boundaries of gender-defined moral ailments. By identifying her heroine from the first as a kind of female René, Sand was attempting, in her first novel, to feminize the mal du siécle.[18]

From *Rêveuse* to *Ecrivaine*

Sand's correspondence for 1832 is a good source of information about the period encompassing the writing and publication of *Indiana*. But, surprisingly, what is singularly missing in these letters is much information on Sand's apprenticeship as a writer and on the gestation of her first novel. Between 1832 and 1837 only a very few letters discuss the book's impact, its subject matter, or her intentions when composing it. Most references discuss it as an object, a consumer product. Her most pressing problems are the reedition, the sale price, the number of copies sent out and sold.

To make matters more difficult, even when Sand does touch on her writing and literary life in her correspondence from this early period, she most often does so in an offhand manner and with a lightness of tone which seem intended to discourage taking the subject entirely seriously. Talking about her pseudonym, for instance, in a letter of May 1832 to Charles Duvernet, she writes: "Les commerçants littéraires nous [disent] prenez un nom. Un nom vous le savez c'est une marchandise, une denrée, un fonds de commerce" (*Corr.*, 2:90; "Literary merchants tell us to take a name. A name, as you know, is a kind of merchandise, a commodity, a business"). Such passages clearly convey

Sand's characteristic stance of not taking herself seriously as a writer, at least in her public statements. The tone of self-mockery which shows through in her correspondence is frequently reinforced by a profound ambivalence in *Histoire de ma vie* when the discussion turns to the birth of her literary career. She writes, for example: "quand je parlais d'écrire, c'était en riant et en me moquant de la chose et de moi-même. Une sorte de destinée me poussait cependant . . . une destinée de liberté morale et d'isolement poétique" (HV, 2:133; "when I spoke of writing, it was in jest and I joked about it and about myself. Something like destiny was pushing me in spite of it all . . . a destiny of moral freedom and poetic isolation"). Here the tone is less playful, but the self-deprecation remains, as Sand ennobles the writer's vocation on which she is embarking, while undermining her own literary ambitions through ironic juxtaposition.

In the last chapters of Part 4, Sand refers to what she called her "vie d'écolier littéraire" or "vie de gamin" (HV, 2:132) to describe the period of her life when she had just come to Paris to become a writer. She uses a playful, lighthearted tone that belies the seriousness of her subject. For example, she chats amusingly about the Ecole Frénétique, the Romantic school that took as its model English Gothic prose and was the height of fashion in the 1830s:

> On cherchait des titres impossibles, des sujets dégoûtants, et, dans cette course au clocher d'affiches ébouriffantes, des gens de talent eux-mêmes subissaient la mode, et, couverts d'oripeaux bizarres, se précipitaient dans la mêlée. J'étais bien tentée de faire comme les autres écoliers, puisque les maîtres donnaient le mauvais exemple, et je cherchais des bizarreries que je n'eusse jamais pu exécuter.   (HV, 2:159)

> ([Writers] went in pursuit of impossible titles, revolting subjects, and in this obstacle race in search of shocking placards; even talented people were enslaved by fashion, and dressed in bizarre and flashy costumes, they rushed into the fray. I was tempted to act like the other schoolboys, since the masters were setting a bad example, and I searched for oddities that I would never have been able to carry off.)

Thanks to the guidance of Latouche, she informs us, she did not let herself be carried along down the slippery path of frenetic literature, in imitation of Pétrus Borel or Charles Lassailly. At the same time, by his repeated insults and mockery of her as a "cerveau creux," Latouche discouraged her from further literary endeavors. Downhearted, she returned to Nohant, ready to abandon literature. Then, as she presents it, unexpectedly the subject of *Indiana* surged up ex nihilo, haunting her, invading her entire being. She started to write "sans projet, sans espoir, sans aucun plan . . . et ne fouillant ni dans la matière des autres ni dans ma propre individualité pour le sujet et les types" (HV, 2:160; "without a preliminary design, without hope, without a plan . . . and delving neither into the material of others nor into my own individuality for the subject and the characters"). The abrupt passage from discouragement to euphoria is noted, but not elucidated. Nothing in Sand's description clarifies for the reader the nature of the literary miracle. One moment she is still a hollow brain; the next she has been metamorphosed into a fertile one. This transformation is presented as instantaneous and mysterious. Furthermore, in her description of the way she composed *Indiana*, the negative aspects of writing are stressed: the need to start afresh, to make a clean slate. She empties her mind of any apprenticeship, any influence, any acquired technique: "mettant résolument à la porte de mon souvenir tout ce qui m'avait été posé en précepte ou en exemple" (HV, 2:160; "resolutely putting out of my mind the memory of everything that had been set before me as a precept or as an example"). Highlighting inspiration rather than methodology, she eludes any discussion of genesis, of gestation, of development. She presents herself as possessed by a "powerful emotion," which sustains her during a prolonged period of creative hallucination. As Sand explains it in *Histoire de ma vie*, the text of *Indiana* suddenly emerged, fully formed, as she found herself fully a writer overnight:

> J'écrivis tout d'un jet, sans plan . . . et littéralement sans savoir où j'allais. . . . J'avais en moi seulement, comme un sentiment bien net et bien ardent, l'horreur de l'esclavage brutal et bête. . . . J'écrivis donc ce livre sous l'empire d'une émotion et non d'un système.   (HV, 2:164)

> (I wrote in one stroke, without a plan . . . and literally without knowing where I was going. . . . I had only a very distinct and vehement feeling, and this was the horror of brutal and stupid enslavement. . . . I therefore wrote this book in the grip of an emotion and not according to a system.)

Any notion of effort, labor, correction, hesitation, or groping is absent from this lyrical description of the creation of *Indiana*. The reader is not given any view of the writing process—but only the finished product on the table. Sand's persona remains hidden.

Whether Sand's version about the composition of *Indiana* represents the "truth" or not matters little. What is important is how faithfully it coincides with the image she draws of herself as a writer who depended on improvisation and the inspiration of the moment. Her sense that she did not write *Indiana*, but that in some way it wrote itself may well be a self-protective device, but such an attitude served her public persona well. So we will not find sufficient information about this literary period of experimentation which so intrigued James, either in her autobiography or in her correspondence. We have to look for it elsewhere, inscribed metaphorically in another text. It is in *Indiana* itself, where the embedded theme of the search for a literary voice emerges as a crucial structural element, that we can read about it.

The Search for a Literary Voice

Indiana is a novel about writing a first novel. Sand inscribes this theme into her text through an examination of each character's language system. Some characters are already eloquent, such as Raymon. Others are resolutely dull in their speech, as in the case of Delmare. Finally, some such as Ralph, come to master a certain elegance of expression in the course of the novel. To listen to these three men discuss politics in the early pages of the novel is to get a sense of the importance the author accords each individual's phraseology. As critics have already noted, these male characters represent the three main political tendencies in the last years of the Restoration. On the right, the "Ultras," "plus royalistes que le roi," in Louis XVIII's own words. Against them, the liberal opposition, in two factions: the heirs of the eighteenth-century *philosophes,* those whom Napoleon called the "idéologues"; and the mass of Bonapartist ex-soldiers and ex-officers, unemployed and dissatisfied, who remained faithful to the emperor's memory.[19] Colonel Delmare is the old Bonapartist whose dreams have been broken. He has retreated into moodiness and glumness as a way of life and as a way of talking politics. Ralph Brown, Indiana's phlegmatic cousin, is a democrat who argues for the return of a republic. Raymon de la Ramière, whom Gustave Planche defined as the representative of corruption in the nineteenth century, is politically to the right, attached to the "Charte," walking a fine line between "l'abus du pouvoir et celui de la licence" (*Indiana*, 129). As for the women, they do not discuss politics.

The text, however, does more than simply present a spectrum of political positions. It allows the reader to glimpse the author's search for a language that is at once powerful and authentic. Each man is not so much defined as an emblematic representative of the political realities of the day as identified with a specific mode of speech, which in turn is linked inextricably with a particular political position.

Colonel Delmare's language is fossilized. He interminably rehashes the same stale formulas, the same ready-made ideas, the same refrains: "treason," "motherland betrayed." Unlike Balzac's positive portrayal of Colonel Chabert or Goguelat (in *Le Médecin de campagne*), both of whom, like Delmare, have their ideological roots in the good old days of the Empire, Sand's depiction of her character as a man who has become petrified in the old ideas is drawn with no sympathy: "Il n'avait pas fait un pas depuis 1815. C'était un vieux stationnaire encroûté" (*Indiana*, 168; "He hadn't moved forward since 1815. He was an old fossil set in his ways"). Since the narrator expresses his belief that "l'opinion politique d'un homme, c'est l'homme tout entier" (166; "a man's entire identity is to be found in his political opinions"). We are prompted to see Delmare's reactionary political stance the index of his reactionism in all aspects of life. In this light, the reader can begin to understand the importance of each character's political world view. It stands as a metonymy for temperament. Politics provide a privileged insight into each protagonist's psychological makeup. Delmare's political vocabulary is the expression of his mummified character.

The opposing political views of the two protagonists, Raymon and Ralph, are exemplified in their antithetical rhetorical talents. The first is a "champion of the existing society"; the second attacks the "edifice on all points" (166). Their confrontation on the political front in fact conceals the latent hostility they feel for each other in private life: "On n'eût pas osé se traiter de fourbe, d'imbécile, d'ambitieux et de poltron. On enferme les mêmes idées sous le nom de jésuite, de royaliste, de révolutionnaire . . ." (171; "They would not have dared to call each other rogue, imbecile, upstart, or coward. So the same ideas were couched in different terms: Jesuit, Royalist, Revolutionary . . ."). The confrontation of ideologies is at the same time a confrontation of antithetical rhetorics.

Ralph's power of speech, as the narrator reminds us more than once, is almost nonexistent: "[il] avait si peu le talent de la persuasion, il était si candide, si maladroit . . . sa franchise était si raboteuse, sa logique si aride, ses principes si absolus! Il ne ménageait personne, il n'adoucissait aucune vérité" (167; "He so completely lacked the ability to be persuasive, he was so naive, so awkward. . . . His candor was so unpolished, his logic so dry, his principles so absolute! He humoured no one, and never softened the truth"). The more he tries to convince his opponent, the more he gets tangled up in his arguments. This "maladresse d'élocution" (184), a veritable existential handicap, prevents him from expressing fully his inner feelings. More serious still, it prevents him from recognizing the entire scope of his sentiments and thoughts. Ralph is a stranger unto himself. This drama of the spoken word embodied in Ralph, a kind of paralysis of the tongue which the text defines as "impotence" (304), finds its opposition in Raymon's triumphant discourse. He speaks "skillfully," uses "vicious arguments," "a flowered rhetoric" that always guarantees that he will be surrounded by a group of admiring listeners. He has at his disposal "all the subtleties of language, all the small-minded treacheries of civilization" (170). As a partisan of the dominating ideology, Raymon is politically and linguistically identified with a rhetoric of falsehood which is proficient in manipulating the truth. The regime Raymon approves of is characterized, in the narrator's view, by a distortion of truth accompanied by a certain degradation of speech. The entire phraseology of this regime is, in the narrator's words,

> une reine prostituée qui descend et s'élève à tous les rôles, qui se déguise, se pare, se dissimule et s'efface . . . le plus honnête des hommes est celui qui pense et qui agit le mieux, mais *le plus puissant est celui qui sait le mieux écrire et parler.* (emphasis added; *Indiana*, 130)

> (a prostituted queen who is ready to assume all roles, be they noble or lowly, who disguises, adorns, conceals, and effaces herself . . . the most honest man is the one who thinks and acts in the best manner, but *the most powerful is the one who knows best how to write and speak.*)

To learn how to talk and how to write, that is the issue at the heart of Sand's first novel. The author's insistence on the supremacy of the word and of the signifier in the construction of her fictional universe makes for the modernity of *Indiana*. She strives to capture the various individualized languages of her milieu and to embody them in the different characters. Unlike Stendhal's mirror novel, whose fortune is to travel along a road in order to refract the outside world, *Indiana* can be considered as a recording machine. Stendhal articulates mimesis in terms of images, while Sand expresses the mimetic act through verbal reduplication. The precise manner by which Sand inscribes her initiation into writing metaphorically into her text deserves further elucidation.

The Coining of a Literary Vernacular

A lot of talking goes on in *Indiana*—long pronouncements, monologues, declarations of love, confessions, tirades, verbal seductions. To give one notable example, toward the end of the novel Ralph talks for some fifteen pages without a break. Much writing goes on as well, with many of these missives transcribed verbatim for the reader. I will return to one of them, from Indiana, later in the chapter. Clearly verbal expression is a major element of the text. Furthermore, each of the principal characters speaks a language that embodies the role he or she plays.

Colonel Delmare wants to exercise fully the rights conferred upon him by his marital status. He believes in the absolute power of husbands. Their right is to govern: the wives' duty is to submit. He says to the heroine: "Qui donc est le maître ici, de vous ou de moi? Qui donc porte une jupe et doit filer une quenouille? Prétendez-vous m'ôter la barbe du menton? . . . femmelette" (*Indiana*, 232; "Who is the master here, you or I? Who wears a skirt and must spin the yarn? Do you dare take the beard from my chin? . . . weakling"). He formulates his contempt for women as a group in generalized declarations where all the clichés of misogyny are reiterated: "[les femmes sont] toutes menteuses et rusées pour le plaisir de l'être" (122; "[Women are] all liars and cunning simply for the pleasure of it"); or "Les femmes sont faites pour obéir" (204; "Women are meant to obey"). Finally, he often has recourse to violence, occasionaly in his actions— we see him beat Indiana and her pet dog (a female, the text carefully specifies)—and habitually in his speech: "Ses épigrammes favorites roulaient toujours sur des coups de bâton à donner et des affaires d'honneur à vider." (133; "His favorite epigrams always revolved around beatings to be administered and matters of honor to be settled"). Delmare, occupying the role of the overbearing husband, incarnates in his speech the brutalizing idiom of the master.

Noun, the maid, is almost without speech. As a woman, as a servant, and as a Creole, she is triply disempowered of her right to speak. Nearly mute, she is also barely literate. When, fearing that Raymon may have abandoned her, she commits the grave mistake of writing him a letter in which the "rules of grammar" are not respected, its style and orthography make the seducer blush. This letter, significantly not transcribed in the novel, but described by the narrator as a "chef-d'oeuvre de passion naïve et gracieuse" (77; "masterpiece of naive and graceful passion"), is the prologue to the definitive silence that Noun will seek in suicide, leaving behind no word of explanation to clarify the motive of her act. Noun speaks and writes in the language of female subjection. Her brief act of revolt against the system of masters and slaves reveals all the more starkly her fundamental powerlessness. Her suicide through drowning, an expression of her Ophelia complex, signifies passive acquiescence. Not surprisingly, her ultimate language is silence.

Laure de Nangy, the woman who finally marries Raymon, occupies only a small place in the novel, but she nevertheless fits into Sand's spectrum of speech types. She is first presented to the reader in the following symbolic situation:

> Dans le grand salon, à la place où madame Delmare se tenait d'ordinaire pour travailler, une jeune personne grande et svelte, au long regard à la fois doux et malicieux, caressant et moqueur, était

assise devant un chevalet et s'amusait à copier à l'aquarelle les bizarres lambris de la muraille. C'était une chose charmante que cette copie, une fine moquerie tout empreinte du caractère railleur et poli de l'artiste. . . . A coté de cette oeuvre . . . elle avait écrit le mot *pastiche*. (*Indiana*, 285–286)

(In the main drawing room, at the place madame Delmare usually occupied when she was at work, sat a tall, svelte, young woman with a gaze that was both gentle and malicious, caressing and mocking. She was sitting before an easel, amusing herself by making a watercolor copy of the wall's bizarre ornamentation. It was a charming thing, this copy, a delicate mockery stamped with the artist's satirical and polite mark. . . . Next to this work . . . she had written the word *pastiche*.)

The obvious point here is that Laure has no authentic speech of her own. She imitates, makes a pastiche of, the language of her class, with a self-aware touch of irony. Her language is uncreative, only a parody of preexisting forms. She is also, as critics have remarked before, a kind of Balzacian character.[20] The author, then, presents a double pastiche. Laure drawing a pastiche of an original is analogous to Sand writing a pastiche of Balzac. In so doing she exorcizes the influence of her young fellow writer. As such, this little scene is not without mischief.[21]

Meanwhile, within the novel itself, a different kind of parallelism is evident in the rhetorical fortunes of Raymon and Ralph. Raymon makes his debut in the novel as a skillful manipulator of a semantic system of lies. He ends up reduced to silence. Ralph, on the other hand, is depicted throughout as an awkward conversationalist, as a man who prefers silence to speech. But he dominates the conclusion with a fully articulated confession. *Indiana* ends with his voice, which at first glance may appear to be startling considering the novel's title and its underlying ideology of sympathy for woman's plight. But, as we shall see, Ralph's voice is androgynous, an echo of the author's own search for authorhood, a working model for the author's double-gendered voice. Ralph's and Raymon's destinies are antithetical and can be studied as mirror images of one another. This antithesis transcends the distinction of noble versus ignoble character, since Ralph represents a male projection of the author's own search for an authentically poetic voice, while Raymon stands for the artful but dangerously seductive voice of the literary establishment. The poet versus the political pamphleteer.

Undeniably, Raymon speaks the language of the seducer. His rhetoric manipulates people, notably women, and events. His letters are masterpieces of falsehood. As an aristocrat and a sometime political journalist, he has mastered the idiom of high society and power.

> Raymon avait une incroyable puissance sur tout ce qui l'entou-
> rait . . . c'était . . . un homme supérieur dans la société . . . vous
> avez été entraîné, en lisant les journaux du temps, par le charme
> irrésistible de son style, et les grâces de sa logique courtoise et
> mondaine. (*Indiana*, 128)

> (Raymon had tremendous influence over everything that sur-
> rounded him . . . he was . . . a superior man in society . . . you
> have been carried away, while reading the newspapers of the day,
> by the irresistible charm of his style, and the grace of his courteous
> and worldly logic.)

In his first seduction scene with Indiana, this French Lovelace appropriates all the clichés of the fashionable rhetoric of the time which
depicts woman as sylph, spirit, nymph, ethereal creature of men's
desire:

> "Tu es la femme que j'avais rêvée, la pureté que j'adorais; la
> chimère qui m'avait toujours fui, l'étoile brillante qui luisait devant
> moi. . . . De tout temps, tu m'étais destinée, ton âme était fiancée
> à la mienne, Indiana! . . . tu m'appartiens, tu es la moitié de mon
> âme, qui cherchait depuis longtemps à rejoindre l'autre. . . . Ne
> t'ai-je pas reconnu, ange, lorsque tu étanchais mon sang avec ton
> voile . . ." (*Indiana*, 95–96)

> ("You are the woman I have dreamed of, the pure soul I have
> adored, the chimera who has always escaped me, the brilliant star
> that shone before me. . . . You were always destined for me, your
> soul was betrothed to mine, Indiana! . . . You belong to me, you
> are the other half of my soul, which has been searching for its part-
> ner for so long. . . . Did I not recognize you, angel, as you
> stanched my blood with your veil . . .")

A master in the art of turning any situation to his advantage with
words he excuses his brutality when a love scene turns violent by
blaming it on the victim: "Pardon, Indiana, pardon! Si je t'effraye *c'est
ta faute;* tu m'as fait tant souffrir que j'ai perdu la raison" (emphasiss
added; *Indiana*, 195; "Forgive me, Indiana, forgive me! If I frighten you,
it is your fault; you have made me suffer so much that I have lost all
reason"). Sometimes he acts out his passion with so much verisimilitude, he is so "puissant dans son langage" (220) that he allows
himself to be persuaded by his own rhetoric. He then comes to feel
emotions that are not authentic.

Finally, he is an odious liar, without any concern for the relation
between truth and the spoken word. In Raymon, Sand reveals the
complicity between language and power. The stylized eloquence of his

speech expresses his privileged status in the symbolic order. His powerful and haughty voice duplicates the discourse of the established newspapers in power at the time. The fascination Raymon exerts on both heroines of the novel also affected its young author. Raymon's rhetoric was fashioned by Sand so as to be exorcized, and transcended.

Ralph will exemplify this transcendence. Originally lacking both skill or elegance in his manner of speaking, laconic and lackluster in his correspondence, he undergoes a linguistic metamorphosis that constitutes the crucial episode of the book. Significantly, Ralph's transformation into a poet-philosopher is as brusque and unexplained in the novel as Sand's own transmutation into a novelist, a parallel that helps shed light on his key role in the novel as the figure around whom so much of the plot crystallizes.

Ralph's linguistic metamorphosis occurs during the initiatory voyage that brings him, accompanied by Indiana, back to the "désert" (read "wilderness") of the Ile Bourbon:

> Son âme, longtemps roidie contre la douleur, s'amollit à la chaleur vivifiante de l'espérance. Le ciel descendit aussi dans ce coeur amer et froissé. Ses paroles prirent l'empreinte de ses sentiments. (*Indiana*, 309)

> (His soul, long hardened against pain, softened with the revitalizing warmth of hope. Heaven penetrated this injured and bitter heart. His words began to express his feelings.)

The scene in which Ralph finally begins to speak echoes the biblical episode in which the Apostles are touched by grace and start to communicate in many tongues. If, as she asserted in *Histoire de ma vie*, inspiration is "for artists what grace is for Christians" (HV, 2:163), Ralph becomes in these pages the supreme Sandian artist. His newly found but already secure eloquence ensures that he can never again be reduced to silence.

The language he will use is the vernacular of poets. Here is an example of the lyricism of his prose:

> "le baptême du malheur a bien assez purifié nos âmes: rendons-les à celui qui nous les a données. . . . Pour nous *l'univers est le temple* où nous adorons Dieu. C'est au sein d'une nature grande et vierge qu'on retrouve le sentiment de sa puissance, pure de toute profanation humaine. Retournons donc au désert, afin de pouvoir prier . . ." (emphasis added; *Indiana*, 307)

> ("The baptism of misfortune has purified our souls well enough: let us return them to the One who gave them to us. . . . For us, *the*

> *universe is the temple* in which we worship God. It is in the bosom of
> a great and pure nature that one rediscovers the feeling of His
> power, pure of any human profanation. Let us return to the desert,
> so that we can pray . . .")

Ralph's striking image in the phrase "l'univers est le temple" presages
the well-known line in Baudelaire's sonnet "Correspondances," "la
nature est un temple."[22]

For Sand the spoken word, *la parole,* is the privileged path of
thought. From a "crétin sans intelligence et sans voix" (324), Ralph is
transformed into a prophet (the one who announces a revelation). Because in Sand's cosmogony the creation of one's own authentic language is synonymous with self-knowledge, Ralph's tale, as he tells it to
Indiana, with all its detailed information about his inner life, his affective and moral world view, is likened to "un moment d'ivresse intellectuelle, [un moment] d'exaltation et d'extase où [les] pensées s'épurent,
se subtilisent, s'éthèrent" (313; "a moment of intellectual intoxication,
of exaltation and ecstasy in which thoughts become purified, refined,
ethereal"). The result of Ralph's confession is true self-discovery. His
long speech constitutes a veritable talking cure. But this treatment goes
beyond the purely psychological realm, since his passage from silence
to the spoken word is also the decisive step in his life as an artist. The
figure of Ralph has now come to symbolize the young author's metamorphosis from *cerveau creux* to *cerveau fertile.* In his confession scene,
which takes place *in extremis,* on the verge of death, he translates his
inner dreamworld into speech. In so doing, Ralph also articulates the
writer's discovery of her own vernacular.

Ralph's confession dominates Part Four of *Indiana,* and leads directly to the culminating suicide pact between the two characters:
"Alors Ralph prit sa fiancée dans ses bras, et l'emporta pour la précipiter avec lui dans le torrent" (330; "Ralph then took his fiancée in his
arms, and carried her away in order to hurl her down into the torrent
with him"). This scene, however, is not the end of the novel, although,
according to Sand's biographer Wladimir Karénine, it was so in the author's original plan.[23] All editions of the novel, including the first,[24]
contain a concluding chapter, an epilogue, which depicts Indiana and
Ralph living the ideal life in a "chaumière indienne," an eighteenth-
century dream reminiscent of both l'Abbé Laugier's "primitive hut"[25]
and Bernardin de Saint-Pierre's paradisiac Ile de France.

This double ending—suicides, an idyll—has always bothered
the critics for its implausibility. But there is a legitimate reason for the
false suicide to be transmuted into a happy ending. The heroes' flight
to a paradise lost—far from society, far from history, into a circular
mythological time—can be understood only in light of the meta-

morphosis that Indiana and Ralph undergo in this most poetic of scenes. Ralph's confession results in true self-discovery and thus the desire to live.

The paradox, of course, is that Sand's first novel is at the same time about suicide and survival. She plays with the powerful literary motif of suicide but recasts it in a symbolic system of her own coining. Ralph's cry "Mourons ensemble" ("Let us die together") is a leitmotif of Sand's imagination reappearing in *Valentine* and also in the fourth of the *Lettres d'un voyageur*, where the narrator imagines that her children are saying to her: "Oui, la vie est insupportable dans un monde ainsi fait; mourons ensemble! Montrez-nous le chemin de Bernica, ou le lac de Sténio, ou les glaciers de Jacques!" (LV, 133; "Yes, life is unbearable in the world such as it is; let us die together! Show us the path to Bernica or Stenio's lake, or the glaciers where Jacques chose to end his life"). Here this cry is transformed into "Vivons ensemble." Ralph articulates his life-affirming credo to the "voyageur"[26] in the Epilogue: "nos jours . . . passent rapides et purs comme ceux de notre enfance. Chaque soir, nous bénissons le ciel; nous l'implorons chaque matin, nous lui demandons le soleil et les ombrages de la veille" (342; "our days . . . pass swiftly and innocently like those of our childhood. Each evening, we bless heaven; we turn to Him every morning, and we ask Him to provide again the sun and the shade of the day before"). *Indiana*, opening with a gloomy description evoking René's Gothic castle, begins under the sign of Chateaubriand, but it ends under the sign of Bernardin de Saint-Pierre. Between these two poles of inspiration the author's own double meditation on suicide—in its active and passive versions—constitutes a privileged insight into her imagination.

Sand in her autobiography clearly offers a parallel between the emotion she encountered in the remarkably short period of the novel's composition and the feelings Ralph experiences when discovering the miracle of speech:

> Cette émotion, lentement amassée dans le cours d'une vie de ré-flexions, déborda très impétueuse dès que le cadre d'une situation quelconque s'ouvrit pour la contenir; mais elle s'y trouva fort à l'étroit, et cette sorte de combat entre l'émotion et l'exécution me soutint pendant six semaines dans un état de volonté tout nouveau pour moi   (HV, II, 164–165).

> (This emotion, built up slowly during the course of a life of meditation, overflowed quite impetuously as soon as some situation offered a framework to contain it; but this emotion was very confined, and the struggle between emotion and implementation kept me for six weeks in a sustained state of will power which was entirely new to me.)

During the composition of *Indiana*, two inner events took place. First, Sand discovered her true literary vocation, which marked *Indiana* off from all her preceding literary efforts: "Je sentis en commençant à écrire *Indiana* une émotion très vive et très particulière, ne ressemblant à rien de ce que j'avais éprouvé dans mes précédents essais . . ." (HV, 2:164; "When I began to write *Indiana*, I experienced a very powerful and distinctive emotion, totally different from what I had felt during my previous writing attempts . . ."). This event Sand incorporated in the novel in the form of Ralph's transformation. Second, she realized that the elaborate mythical world that she had created in her childhood and that had nourished her imagination up to that time had suddenly ceased to exist. Ever since she had been a child, the binary helix of Aurore's intellectual preoccupations had been religion and literature: "Religion and novel grew side by side in my soul," she wrote in *Histoire de ma vie* (1:810). Sand's instinctive rapprochement of literature and religion led her to express Ralph's poetic inspiration in theological terms, to equate the grace conferred on him by mystical ecstasy with a poetic state. At the center of her childhood mythical world, at once pagan and Christian, was Corambé, a private deity she had invented. The pacifist Corambé was androgynous, with a woman's face but referred to as "il" by the author.[27] This creation now receded. The writing of *Indiana* had somehow brought about the disappearance of double-gendered Corambé and his or her world. Sand relates the episode in *Histoire de ma vie*:

> A peine eus-je fini mon livre, que je voulus retrouver le vague ordinaire de mes rêveries. Impossible! . . . j'espérai en vain voir reparaître . . . ces figures à moitié nettes, ces voix à moitié distinctes, qui flottaient autour de moi comme un tableau animé derrière un voile transparent. Ces chères visions n'étaient que les précurseurs de l'inspiration.   (HV, 2:165)

> (I had barely finished my book and I longed to return to the usual vagueness of my reveries. It was no longer possible! . . . I hoped in vain for the reemergence of . . . those half-discernable figures, half-distinct voices, which floated around me like an animated painting behind a transparent veil. Those precious visions had been nothing but the precursors of inspiration.)

This strange phenomenon can be understood as a very specific passage in Sand's mental life from an inexpressible but vividly present system of reveries (at the center of which stood Corambé) to an intellectualized and verbalized system of storytelling. From *rêveuse*, Sand had indeed become a full-fledged *écrivaine*. Sand's formulations—"le vague des rêveries," "figures à moitié nettes," "voix à moitié distinctes," "tableau derrière un voile"—are all metaphors for a preverbal language, for a prelinguistic state Julia Kristeva calls the semiotic.[28] The composition of *Indiana* and the sudden dissipation of this "phénomène de demi-hallucination" which until that point Sand had experienced regularly in her life, marks an exceptional moment—Aurore's re-creation of herself as George Sand the writer.

If Ralph's coining of a personal phraseology coincides with the birth of Sand's specifically literary voice, what are we to make of the character of Indiana and the symbolic function of her language? More complex than either Raymon or Ralph, Indiana at first speaks very little. In the course of the novel she employs three main forms of discourse. The most forceful of these she uses in a moment of heightened epiphany, when she becomes an impassioned letter writer. After her flawed suicide and in the novel's final pages, she falls silent. Of all the characters, she alone presents an enigma, since her linguistic evolution does not parallel her personal development. Whereas Ralph's loosened tongue signifies the author's own poetic unleashing of language, Indiana can be eloquent only in protest—against her tyrannical and exploitative husband, or the injustice of marriage. The moment she finds a solution to her mal du siècle she is overcome by contentment which results in silence.

First of all, she articulates a language of resistance, which she reserves for her husband. Her speeches condemning the patriarchal arbitrariness of power and its violence are perhaps the most famous passages of the novel. Contemporary critics drew great attention to them and went on to proclaim Sand as a champion of women's rights. This eloquent tirade of Indiana, often cited, is addressed to Delmare:

> "Je sais que je suis l'esclave et vous le seigneur. La loi de ce pays vous a fait mon maître. Vous pouvez lier mon corps, garotter mes mains, gouverner mes actions. Vous avez le droit du plus fort, et la société vous le confirme; mais sur ma volonté, monsieur, vous ne pouvez rien, Dieu seul peut la courber et la réduire. Cherchez donc une loi, un cachot, un instrument de supplice qui vous donne prise sur moi! C'est comme si vous vouliez manier l'air et saisir le vide." (*Indiana*, 232)

> ("I know that I am the slave and you are the lord. The laws of this land have made you my master. You can tie up my body, bind my hands, govern my actions. You have the right of the strongest, and society confirms it; but over my will, monsieur, you have no hold, only God can curb and abate it. Search if you will a law, a prison, an instrument of torture that could give you a hold over me! It's as if you wanted to touch air and grasp nothingness.")

Many critics have used this passage to make of Indiana a double of the author and to accentuate Sand's feminism above all. Of course Sand was very much interested in denouncing the marital rights of men and in proclaiming women's rights both within and outside of marriage.[29] Her hatred of physical brutality, whether the violence of husbands against their wives, of governments against political opposition, or of any majority's use of violence against any minority, was frequently a motivating force in her writing. Several years after *Indiana*, she was still fighting for the inclusion of women in what she called the social and moral order. In a letter written in the spring of 1837 to Frédéric Girerd [sic], for example, she wrote:

> le monde trouve fort naturel et fort excusable qu'on se joue avec les femmes de ce qu'il y a de plus sacré: les femmes ne comptent ni dans l'ordre social, ni dans l'ordre moral. Oh! J'en fais le serment, et voici la première lueur de courage et d'ambition de ma vie! Je relèverai le femme de son abjection, et dans ma personne et dans mes écrits.   (*Corr.*, 4:18)

> (society finds it quite natural and quite excusable to treat contemptuously what is most sacred about women: women have no status in the social order, or in the moral order. Oh! I make an oath of this, and here is the first glimmer of courage and ambition in my life! I will lift women out of their abjection, both in my person and in my writings.)

In spite of such statements and Indiana's demonstrated resistance to her husband's authority, it is somewhat shortsighted to equate heroine with author, or indeed to use Indiana's words as unequivocal proof of Sand's feminism. Sand's position was more complicated and more contradictory.[30] Nor does Indiana herself always express a militant feminist view. In fact her language of resistance is counterbalanced by a second antithetical code, what we might call submissive discourse, the discourse she reserves for her lover Raymon:

> "je viens pour te donner du bonheur, pour être tout ce que tu voudras, ta compagne, ta servante ou ta maitresse . . . je n'ai plus le droit de te refuser aucun sacrifice. Dispose de moi, de mon sang, de ma vie; je suis à toi corps et âme. J'ai fait trois mille lieues pour t'appartenir, pour te dire cela; prends-moi, je suis ton bien, tu es mon maître."   (*Indiana*, 296–297)

> ("I come to offer you happiness, to be everything you wish, your companion, your servant or your mistress . . . I no longer have the right to refuse you any sacrifice. Dispose of me, of my blood, of my life; I am yours, body and soul. I have traveled three thousand leagues to belong to you, to say this to you; take me, I am your property, you are my master.")

This is a shocking text when viewed from a modern feminist perspective. It is also a passage not often quoted. But Indiana's words here translate the inherent subservient relationship of the woman-as-object to the male creator of a false rhetoric. It expresses a moment of weakness in which the heroine is attracted to the master code which the male embodies.

How can Indiana's two antithetical vocabularies be reconciled? The author illustrates in these two verbal systems the only two linguistic solutions available to a woman who finds herself in a position of inequality with a man. Her linguistic range can be only reactive—either in revolt or in resignation. The passages quoted are less examples of an authentic language than of an idiom made up of contradictions, an idiom common to all women living in a similar situation of dependence.

Indiana begins to fashion an authentic discourse for herself late in the novel (almost as late as does Ralph); in a letter addressed to Raymon she finally sees the seducer for what he really is. Here the heroine ceases to speak in reaction to another's word and takes the initiative to speak in her own right. This third language puts forward her claims; it articulates another law, another reality:

> "je ne sers pas le même Dieu [que vous]. . . . Le vôtre, c'est *le dieu des hommes*, c'est le roi, le fondateur et l'appui de votre race; le mien, c'est le Dieu de l'univers, le créateur, le soutien et l'espoir de toutes les créatures. Le vôtre a tout fait pour vous seuls; le mien a fait toutes les espèces les unes pour les autres. Vous vous croyez *les maîtres du monde;* je crois que vous n'en êtes que les tyrans. Vous pensez que Dieu vous protège et vous autorise à usurper l'empire de la terre; moi je pense qu'il le souffre pour un peu de temps, et qu'un jour viendra où, comme des grains de sable, son souffle vous dispersera . . . la religion que vous avez inventée, je la repousse; toute votre morale, tous vos principes, ce sont les intérêts de votre société que vous avez érigés en lois et que vous prétendez faire émaner de Dieu . . . mais tout cela est mensonge et impiété." (emphases added; *Indiana*, 248–249)

> ("I do not serve the same God [as you]. . . . Yours is *the god of men,* he is the king, the founder and pillar of your race; mine is the God of the universe, the creator, support, and hope of all creatures. Yours has made everything for men alone; mine has made all creatures for each other. You believe yourselves to be *the masters of the world;* I believe you are nothing but its tyrants. You think that God protects you and authorizes you to usurp the earth; I think He endures it for a while, and the day will come when, like grains of sand, his breath will scatter you. . . . I reject the religion you have invented; your morals, your principles have been erected as law in

the interest of your society, and you pretend that they emanate from God . . . but all this is nothing but lies and blasphemy.")

Through her heroine Sand denounces the absolute equation of language with masculine power. She replaces the passage through language into the symbolic phallocratic order with a feminine utopia—a structure that is both social and linguistic. The double *si* (if/yes) of Woman replaces the double *nom/non* (name/no) of the Father:

> "Si [Dieu] daignait descendre jusqu'à intervenir dans nos chétifs intérêts, il briserait le fort et relèverait le faible; il passerait sa grande main sur nos têtes inégales et les nivellerait . . . il dirait à l'esclave: "Jette ta chaîne . . ." Il dirait aux rois: "Jetez la pourpre . . ." Il dirait aux puissants: "Courbez le genou . . ." Oui, *voilà mes rêves; ils sont tous d'une autre vie, d'un autre monde où la loi du brutal n'aura point passé sur la tête du pacifique . . .*"   (emphasis added; *Indiana*, 249–250)

> ("Yes, if [God] deigned to take an interest in our paltry affairs, He would break the strong and uplift the weak; He would pass His great hand over our unequal heads and make them equal . . . He would say to the slave: "Cast your chain aside . . ." He would say to the kings: "Relinquish the scarlet robes . . ." He would say to the powerful: "Kneel down . . ." Yes, *these are my dreams: they are of another life, of another world in which the law of brutality will have no precedence over pacifism . . .*")

To denounce the "law of brutality", that is Indiana's definitive role. After having fallen prey to the passive reactive behavior that identifies her with regard to both husband and lover, Indiana finally comes into her own, articulating a utopian position of such force as to make this first of Sand's heroines authentically subversive and a fitting older sister of Lélia.

After the forceful tone of Indiana's letter, it is disappointing, if not incomprehensible, to witness her silence at the novel's conclusion. But it can be explained when examined in relation to the two male principal's patterns of speech. Dispelling once and for all the temptation to identify Indiana with Sand, the reader can clearly sense that the equilibrium of the book defines itself through the three main characters of the novel Indiana, Ralph, and Raymon. Significantly Indiana is placed in a position where she must choose between the two discourses represented by Raymon and Ralph. First she chooses Raymon's code, seduced by skillful rhetoric; subsequently she will reduce him to silence. Then, when she decides to follow Ralph on his journey, she makes his awakening into language possible. The astonishing scene of Ralph's confession follows, taking place symbolically at Bernica Falls, "les gorges de Bernica." The word "gorge" can be read in two ways here, as a geological and a physiological term—gorges/falls and throat. In this desert, this other world from which "la loi du brutal" is banished, the poetic word appears. Sand certainly shares common traits with her heroine; she even perhaps shares certain faults with Raymon. But at the end it is with Ralph the poet, whose speech closes the book, that the writer finds the closest identification.

New ways of considering the characters of *Indiana* suggest themselves. The old theory, the search for the real-life models for any given character, needs to be transcended. In this naive perspective which has been so much abused, Indiana and Noun are the double transposition of George Sand; Colonel Delmare, a portrait of the hateful Casimir; Raymon, a combination of Aurélien de Sèze and Stéphane de Grandsagne;[31] Ralph, Jules Néraud, nicknamed Le Malgache; and so on. A second approach, according to which a given character is the incarnation of a type, allows us to see in the novel the elaboration of a Romantic cast of characters fixed in a modern commedia dell'arte. In this interpretation Indiana is a romantic heroine; Ralph, a suffering Byronic hero; Raymon, a Lovelace; Laure, a woman of the world; Delmare, the brutal husband; Noun, the woman-slave. Yet a third approach is possible in *Indiana*, one where the character is the incarnation of a certain mode of being of the author. Each character symbolizes a possible solution to the central dilemma, the creation of a literary voice. From this perspective the six characters represent six possible solutions, ranging from the patriarchal code (in Delmare), on to false journalistic rhetoric (Raymon), through silence (Noun) and parody (Laure), to arrive at the language of protest (Indiana) and poetic discourse (Ralph).

The novel's double ending, which has always bothered the critics for its implausibility now finds its true significance. I do not agree with Planche that the novel should have ended with Raymon's marriage and Indiana's abandonment.[32] There is a legitimate reason for the false suicide to be transmuted into a happy ending, a logic behind the two heroes' flight to a paradise lost, as they engulf themselves in a circular mythological time. The solution reached in the novel regarding the creation of an authentic language system is represented metaphorically in the novel's ending. Indiana can finally realize her dream of a voyage initiatique: "Si j'écoutais la voix que Dieu a mise au fond de mon coeur, je fuirais au désert" (*Indiana*, 250; "If I listened to the voice that God has placed at the bottom of my heart, I would escape to the desert"). Ralph, taking her back to Ile Bourbon, can finally express the plenitude of his being.

Paradoxically, the exile motif at the close of the novel is also an expression of the underhanded way in which Sand enters as a full-fledged member into the masculine world of literature. In the desert of Ile Bourbon a new system of communication has been hammered out, through Ralph. The author can now return to Paris, with a finished

novel under her arm. Sand leaves Indiana and Ralph in their "chau-
miére indienne" (a direct allusion to Bernardin de Saint-Pierre's text of
1790), but she herself comes back from exile and into the world of
letters.

In conclusion, Sand's fictional text is less the story of unrequited
love than the triumph of the spoken (and written) word, the triumph
of the text. The conclusion does not so much advocate recourse to solitude and the renunciation of society, or the stopgap measure of friendship at the expense of true love, as it proclaims the triumph of
language, the discovery of the power of the word, and the transfigura-
tion of silence into speech. As a novel of apprenticeship, then, *Indiana*
is an instance of what Henry James called the breaking of a spell of silence. Through the character of Ralph—in whom the critic Eugène
Morisseau (read Balzac) correctly saw "la grande figure du livre"[33]—
Sand expressed her own coming into language. When the narrator
says of Ralph, "c'était la première fois, peut-être, depuis qu'il était né,
que sa pensée tout entière venait se placer sur ses lèvres" (312; "it was
maybe the first time since he had been born that all his thought managed to form itself whole on his lips"), this observation equally refers to
Sand's discovery and articulation of a "parole bienfaisante." All evidence in the novel points to the equation of spoken and written discourse with healing.

Sand will mention this unleashing of verbal power again, with
emotion, in her 1832 preface to *Indiana*. There, not surprisingly, she expresses the twin themes of freedom and verbal expression:

> Liberté de la pensée, liberté d'écrire et de parler, sainte conquête
> de l'esprit humain! Que sont les petites souffrances et les soucis
> éphémères engendrés par tes erreurs ou tes abus, au prix des bien-
> faits infinis que tu prépares au monde.   (*Indiana*, 47)

> (Freedom of thought, freedom to write and to speak, sacred con-
> quest of the human spirit! The small sufferings and the ephemeral
> worries engendered by your mistakes or your excesses are mean-
> ingless, when compared to the infinite benefits that you bestow
> upon the world.)

Every woman who writes, Julia Kristeva has remarked, is "an
eternal disident in relation to the social and political consensus, *exiled
in relation to power*, and therefore always eccentric, fragmented."[34]
Fragmentation and exile: Sand experienced them both cruelly. *Indiana*
is at the same time the locus of her psychic integration and the expression of her return from exile. Here she started in actuality writing
for her life.

4

Valentine and the Theory of Spheres

Chaque monde avait un centre où tendaient tous les points de sa sphère.

Balzac

(Each world had a center toward which all the points of its sphere tended.)

The year of Sand's first literary success, 1832 was also the year of *Valentine*. This second novel appeared so quickly after the first (less than six months) that the two were often reviewed together in the press of the day.[1] In *Valentine* three tendencies already germinating in *Indiana* found a fuller development: the symbolic use of landscape, the principle of spheres, and the presence of a two-gendered autopsychological persona.

Indiana had contrasted the provincial to the urban landscape as a comment on human ennui and social corruption. Its heroine had abandoned the familiar temperate climes of France for the exotic lushness of the tropics in search of an oasis of serenity and artistic integration. The primary physical setting of *Valentine*, by contrast, was the writer's province of Berry (with Paris, it is true, as the backdrop for the hero's disillusionment). With so much of the novel set in the country, *Valentine* is the first extended display of Sand's pastoral imagination which would figure so prominently in the novels of the 1840s and 1850s. In order to exploit effectively the symbolic resonances of the many places in her novel, she deployed a spatial strategy erected on the principles of spheres. While the concept of sphere in *Indiana* operated at the linguistic level, to distinguish the various "languages" spoken by the six main characters, *Valentine* depicts different social spheres largely through spatial deployment. This concept may well have been inspired by the author's friendship with Balzac. Finally, the two protagonists, Bénédict and Valentine, are in a similar relationship to the author as were Ralph and Indiana. Sand expresses her ideological complicity with the female characters, but tends to voice her own intellectual and creative yearnings through the male characters. Ralph had represented Sand's own search for a literary voice; Bénédict would portray Sand's own mal du siècle in the form we might call her "complexe de la mansarde bleue," the "blue garret" referring to her apartment on the Quai Malaquais.

Balzac and George Sand: An Exceptional Friendship

During her first stay in Paris, from January to April 1831, George Sand made the acquaintance of Balzac and established a very close though nonamorous friendship with him. The two writers exchanged conversations, books, and confidences about their literary ambitions. Five years Sand's elder, Balzac became something of a literary counselor for her. While it is not my intention here to trace the chronology of their friendship,[2] I would suggest that a certain cross-fertilization of ideas, concepts, and character types is manifest in the early works of the two writers and that it is pertinent to Sand's development as a novelist. This is especially evident in her second novel, *Valentine*.

Pierre Reboul, in his edition of *Lélia*, remarks that "the debt contracted by Sand towards the early Balzac has never been fully and exactly established."[3] Reboul himself tries to delineate the impact of *La Peau de chagrin* on *Lélia*. But, since his vision of literary influence is strictly reductionist, it conforms to his unfortunate underlying assumptions about Sand—that she is a parasitical and imitative writer who regurgitated badly digested versions of what she had assimilated through superficial reading. Bakhtin's theory of the fundamentally dialogic nature of all literary enterprise helps to debunk Reboul's shortsighted opinions. In fact, Balzac and Sand's literary relationship is perhaps one of the most perfect illustrations of literary dialogism, both intertextually (as seen in their novels) and intersubjectively (as evident in their friendly exchanges). Both within and outside their novels the two Romantic realists engaged in one of the great literary dialogues of the century.[4] That dialogue highlights the many fictional concepts and devices the two had in common: the use of spheres, the probing of the *mal romantique*, the psychic disharmony that could ensue from an overdevelopment of mental faculties.

One of the most whimsical episodes of *Histoire de ma vie*, in the section entitled "Du mysticisme à l'indépendance," gives the reader a sense of their relationship. Sand recounts a strange dinner in Balzac's newly redecorated apartment on the rue Cassini, near the Observatoire—an apartment, Sand comments wryly, which the author of *La Peau de chagrin* had transformed into "un assemblage de boudoirs de marquise" (HV, 2:155). After a meal of melon, boiled beef, and champagne, Balzac unaccountably decided to show off his newly acquired cashmere bathrobe. Enthralled by his new purchase, he decided to accompany Aurore (who was with Jules Sandeau) as far as the gate to the Luxembourg gardens. Taken aback by his eccentricity, Sand remarks:

> It was late, the place deserted, and I pointed out to him that he might well be murdered on his way home. "Not at all," he said to me; "if I should meet up with thieves, they will take me for a mad-

man, and will be afraid of me, or else they'll take me for a prince and will respect me." . . . He accompanied us in this fashion, carrying his lighted candle in a lovely, engraved vermeil candlestick. . . . He would have walked us all the way to the other end of Paris, if we had let him.   (HV, 2:157)

Her social interaction with the literati of the day was not always so casual. Her meeting with Senancour, two years later, makes it clear that she could be shy in the presence of literary masters. In that particular episode, which was a fiasco, neither the budding young novelist and admirer of *Obermann* nor the grand old man of letters was able to break the silence. After a pause lasting several minutes, during which an excruciatingly awkward silence reigned in Senancour's living room, Sand rose, nodded her head as a sign of farewell, and left. Neither had uttered a single word.[5]

But with Balzac, things were decidedly different. His was an extroverted personality, with a marked tendency to vent his expansiveness on his surrounding acquaintances. Sand, a good listener, was an ideal foil for her fellow novelist:

> [Balzac] loved to speak about his writings, to talk through the stories before they were written, to create them as he went along, to read them aloud in draft form or from the proofs. Naive and *bon enfant* in the extreme, he would ask for one's opinion . . . but he would not listen to the answer. . . . He would never give advice, he spoke of himself and of himself alone.[6]

Balzac, Sand insists, was the only "celebrity" she knew at the time. Her comment "a literary conversation with a stranger would have have horribly intimidated me" (HV, 2:157) points to the exceptionally informal and relaxed nature of her relationship with the future architect of *La Comédie humaine*. Balzac's verbal exuberance contrasts sharply with Senancour's stony sense of decorum. Dialogues between the two young writers tended inevitably to become lopsided, Sand reported, since they talked much more about Balzac's own projects than her own:

> I spoke very little of my literary projects with Balzac. . . . His company was very pleasant, though the talk was somewhat tiring for me, because I didn't know how to intervene so as to diversify the topics of conversation. . . . With his huge belly, he would climb up to the top floor of the house on the Quai Saint-Michel and arrive panting, laughing, and telling stories without even catching his breath . . . and immediately, thinking about the book he was writing at the time, he would begin running through it.   (HV, 2:156)

Since neither writer recorded them, we can only speculate on those conversations and on Balzac's logorrheic monologues. 1831, the year of their acquaintance, was a watershed for the future creator of *La Comédie humaine*. He began to devote his time and energy exclusively to writing novels under his own name (no more Lord R'Hoone or Horace de Saint-Aubin). It was also the period of Balzac's immersion in his philosophical fictions, the year of *La Peau de chagrin*, "Les Proscrits," and "Le Chef-d'oeuvre inconnu." His first "Contes philosophiques"— "Les Deux Rêves" and "L'Elixir de longue vie"—had come out the year before. The publication of *Louis Lambert* would follow in 1832. Like Sand, he had a huge capacity for work, the ability to write without interruption for up to sixteen hours at a time, and a voracious appetite for reading. This was the epoch of Balzac's growing interest in mystical theories. His affinity for the theories of the Gnostic heresiarchs and mystical thinkers must have greatly increased the interest of his conversation for Sand, all the more since she was probably not well versed in those writers at the time. What specific writers Balzac discussed and which of their works he chose to comment on is speculation for us. But we can be reasonably sure that he talked about Emanuel Swedenborg (whose name appears in his works in 1831),[7] the eschatological theories of Charles Nodier,[8] and the plots of *La Peau de chagrin* and *Louis Lambert*—the two mystical precursor texts to the great *Séraphita*. Since there is no Balzac–Sand correspondence comparable in size and scope to the Flaubert–Sand letters, much of their dialogue will remain forever unknown. We can only attempt to trace its effects weaving themselves through some of their novels.

Throughout their very different careers, in spite of many quarrels and periods of *refroidissement*, political disagreements, and different life-styles, Balzac and Sand would over and over refer with wonderment to the enduring affinity between them and their lasting mutual sympathy. Balzac's letter to Dr. Boulland in 1842 stresses the noble goal the two writers shared of examining the century's "pensée motrice";[9] Balzac dedicated *Les Mémoires de deux jeunes mariées* to Sand to thank for her role as literary confidante.[10] And in a letter to Flaubert, years after Balzac's death, Sand fondly remembered their work sessions, thereby formulating her version of an ideal literary entente:

> ça ne fait pas qu'on se change l'un l'autre, au contraire, car en général on s'obstine davantage dans son *moi*. Mais, en s'obstinant dans son moi, on le complète, on l'explique mieux, on le développe tout à fait, et c'est pour cela que l'amitié est bonne, même en littérature, où la première condition d'une valeur quelconque est d'être soi.[11]
>
> (this does not mean that we change one another, on the contrary; for in general each of us insists all the more on the *individual I*. But,

in so doing, each one completes it, explains it better, develops it fully, and this is why friendship is good, even in the realm of literature, where the first requirement for producing anything of worth is to be oneself.)

The importance of dialogue in the affirmation of one's own personality represents a crucial aspect of literary friendship for Sand. During such a dialogue, where the two novelists discussed and shared certain readings, certain novels in gestation, and certain key ideas for their works, the concept of spheres may well have been analyzed. Originally a philosophical and spiritual concept, the theory of spheres was transmuted into a literary device in the hands of Sand and Balzac. Sand's own application of this theory would allow her to put this concept of mystical origin in the service of her androgynous vision.

The Theory of Spheres Explained

Sphere was a buzzword in the 1830s, a fashionable concept in both literature and mystical philosophy. It was already part of the preromantic repertoire, as Chateaubriand's expression, *"la sphère des merveilles,"* to designate the glories of the universe, exemplifies.[12] Senancour contrasted the "unlimited sphere" of the imagination to the "narrow sphere" in which a person is circumscribed.[13] Ballanche, in turn, in his brooding text, *La Ville des expiations,* used the term repeatedly, opposing the concrete institutions of social life, the "civil and political sphere" and the purely cerebral realm of the "religious and philosophical sphere."[14] Conversely, he united the antithetical "sphere of reality" and "sphere of ideality"[15] in his terrifying dystopian vision of the City of Expiation. Nodier, a disciple of Ballanche and a writer whom both Sand and Balzac admired, linked the notion of sphere to that of mal du siècle in his controversial article of 1832, "De la palingénésie humaine." It is, he explained, because humankind feels its sphere to be limited that it revolts against the human condition: "no species has more impatiently hurled itself toward the limits of its *sphere* [than humankind] in order to exceed them."[16]

The concept of sphere came to these French Romantics from two main sources. "Sphere" belonged to the vocabulary of such mystographers as Swedenborg, for whom the idea of two worlds, one visible, the other invisible, opposed the material to the spiritual realm; "sphere" was also a key word in the writings of the Gnostics, a collection of which was published in French in 1828.[17] Both Balzac and George Sand inherited this tradition. Although the concept of sphere has been studied by such Balzac scholars as Per Nykrog and Henri Gauthier as a crucial element in the elaboration of Balzac's novelistic universe, it has been entirely ignored in Sand studies.

Documenting Balzac's intellectual interests and his readings is relatively easy. He enlists Louis Lambert and Séraphita as his *porte-paroles* to expound on Swedenborgism and Gnostic philosophy; his letters are full of references to his various readings. But in Sand's case, very little is known of her apprenticeship years in terms of her intellectual formation and the books that shaped her world view. It is particularly frustrating that the author provides even less information about the composition of *Valentine* than *Indiana*. Virtually nothing is known of the circumstances in which this novel was written or of its possible sources of inspiration. Sand's text, then, must speak for itself. In it, as in Balzac's philosophical tales, the theory of spheres is a structuring device. We know that Sand either read or listened to readings of Balzac's early novels. But how much of an impact did a particular text such as *Louis Lambert* have? We can only speculate, although it is certain that some aspects of Balzac's world view as expressed by his philosopher-herald were transmitted to Sand.[18] We can further assume that Sand also read books Balzac recommended. A charming scene from *Béatrix*—which depicts Camille Maupin, Balzac's version of the "femme auteur" based on George Sand, and her admirer, the young Calyste—emblematizes the "reading relationship" of the two authors. The two characters are engaged in reading—Camille, "books about mystical theology" and Calyste, *Indiana*.[19] Can we not see in this tableau a portrayal of Sand and Balzac reading each other's novels or each other's recommended books? Thierry Bodin speculates that Balzac must have seen Sand engaged in such readings when she was working on *Spiridion* and the *Lélia* of 1839.[20] But it is equally likely that she was reading these books several years earlier, at about the time she was listening to Balzac read *Louis Lambert*.

Outlining the theory of spheres in Balzac is a prerequisite to examining its workings in the novels of Sand. Balzac exploited the concept in two very different ways: as a philosophical concept with which his heroes articulated their vision of a world divided up into various social, intellectual, or geographic strata and as a structuring device whereby Balzac organize the various facets of his *Comédie humaine*. Sand used the notion of sphere primarily in the second way.

In his penetrating analysis of the Balzac novel, Per Nykrog proposes that the theory of spheres constitutes a powerful organizing principle in the novelist's fictional universe. The term is used repeatedly by a host of Balzac's characters, many of whom make up the dramatis personae of *Le Livre mystique*. Dr. Sigier and Louis Lambert, for example, classify human intellect into different categories that make up distinct spheres.[21] As a concept counteracting the centrifugal forces of *La Comédie humaine*, it functions to give coherence to Balzac's vast collection of novels. As Nykrog puts it: "The structure in spheres for Balzac encompasses the whole of the universe, both human and non-human, and he finds or thinks he finds the same types of relationships, oppositions, conflicts everywhere, in the systems of astronomy as well as in groups of a few tightly bound human atoms."[22] At first, Balzac used spheres as a fictional structure to articulate a binary world view, the basic opposition being the superior versus the inferior sphere. But, in his philosophical tales, *Louis Lambert* and *Séraphita*, with the discovery of Swedenborg's sphere of Speciality, he switched to a trinary structure, creating what he called a hierarchy of spheres.[23] Because "spheres" incorporate the notion of correspondences so cherished by the Romantics, these two novels are cogent examples of the way in which Swedenborg and mystical literature nourished Balzac's imagination.

If the early Balzac used spheres as a mystical principle, later novels transformed the theory into a literary device to organize the fictional geography of *La Comédie humaine*. Sphere, no longer a philosophical term expressed by his characters, became a structural ploy in the text. In *La Fille aux yeux d'or*, for example, the narrator divided Paris into various spheres, each identified with a social stratum. The organizing center of the Parisian sphere was the aristocracy, just as the center of the sphere of France was Paris. Henceforth, each novel would use the notion of sphere to construct plot and to delineate the private worlds of certain key characters.[24] It is this particular application of the theory in *La Comédie humaine* that operates with uncanny success in many of Sand's novels, but especially in *Valentine*.

Sand's Spheres

As early as *Histoire du rêveur* Sand used space symbolically. The crater of Etna and the concentric circles surrounding it served as a spatial metaphor for the attainment of artistic expression. Space was again exploited in *Indiana* where the gorges of Bernica provided out the locus of Sand's coming into language, and the "*chaumière* on the Ile Bourbon expressed the author's dream for an oasislike retreat of one's own." In *Valentine* Sand once again deploys spatial strategies for symbolic purposes. Using the concept of spheres she organizes the novel's geography and architecture even more systematically. In the fictional universe of *Valentine*, stripped of all fantastic or exotic color, space is associated with both class and gender. A binary opposition is constructed between the château de Raimbault, which is both aristocratic and primarily feminine, and the Lhéry farmstead, which represents the peasant sphere and is dominated by the masculine character, Bénédict. Throughout, the text presents various nongendered or double-gendered spaces where the different classes can interact.

Sand is less interested here in figuring her own coming into writing than she is in probing the great Romantic dream of the reconciliation of opposites. This major new theme in her fiction will manifest itself in an exploration of the social and cultural gap that separates two young people of two different classes when they fall in love. Valentine and Bénédict prefigure here a host of future Sandian lovers who all attempt to effect the synthesis of two opposing spheres. Many fail in their attempts, especially in the early novels; two examples are André de Morand and the grisette, Geneviève (in *André*, 1834), and Yseult de Villepreux and Pierre Huguenin (*Le Compagnon du tour de France*, 1840). In the utopian novels of the 1840s and later, other couples succeed: Emile Cardonnet and Gilberte de Châteaubrun (*Le Péché de Monsieur Antoine*, 1845); Marcelle de Blanchemont and Henri Lémor (*Le Meunier d'Angibault*, 1845); Nanon and Emilien de Franqueville (*Nanon*, 1871). The love store between the aristocratic heroine and the peasant hero which *Valentine* relates is depicted as a clash of spheres. We first encounter Valentine through Bénédict's eyes. What we are given is a surface impression which already suggests latent antagonisms. Bénédict's initial negative reaction to Valentine's beauty seems to be a purely aesthetic assessment, but in fact it conceals a conflict between two social, ideological, and spatial spheres:

> Elle ne lui plut pas. Il s'était fait un type de femme brune, pâle, ardente, espagnole, mobile, dont il ne voulait pas se départir. Mademoiselle Valentine ne réalisait point son idéal; elle était blanche, blonde, calme, grande, fraîche, admirablement belle de tous points.   (*Valentine*, 45)

> (She didn't appeal to him. He favored the type of woman who was dark-haired, pale, fiery, Spanish looking, changeable, and he wasn't about the change his taste. Mademoiselle Valentine did not embody his ideal at all; she was fair, blond, calm, tall, cool, admirably beautiful in every respect.)

At first, we might think that Bénédict bases his negative judgment on the standard masculinist opposition of blonde versus brunette—a stereotypical opposition that a writer popular in Sand's day such as Walter Scott used as a shortcut to contrast the pliant and passive wife with the passionate and intrepid mistress,[25] that Balzac would soon exploit in *Le Lys dans la vallée*, and that Flaubert would later inscribe in his *Dictionnaire des idées reçues*. But Sand uses the same physical traits for other purposes. Her intention is no so much to reiterate the traditional theory of a double female nature in general—hot versus cold, frigid versus passionate—as to set up a contrast between the two main characters. That Valentine is Sand's first blond heroine suggests that her physical appearance is at the service of a structural device. What counts in *Valentine* is not so much that the heroine herself is blond while her sister,

Louise, and her rival, Athénaïs, are dark haired, but rather that Valentine is presented in strong contrast to Bénédict himself (his dark and brooding good looks make him a kind of brother of Julien Sorel), just as Indiana had been contrasted to Ralph.[26] In her exploration of doubles, Sand constructed a two-gendered system in *Valentine* and *Indiana*, while in *Lélia* she would contrast the two sisters more directly, the intellectual and dark Lélia versus the blond courtisan, Pulchérie.

Valentine's fair good looks, furthermore, combined with a regal air of composure, place her in a long line of fictional heroines: she is at once a modern Iseut la Blonde, as Kathryn Crecelius has suggested, and a Romantic Princesse de Clèves.[27] This distinguished literary ancestry serves to accentuate her archaism. Valentine appears fundamentally out of place; she is not of her time. As the rest of the novel demonstrates, she belongs to neither her geographic nor her social sphere. To Bénédict she appears outmoded, her sphere the epitome of an aristocratic ideal become antiquated:

> Dans la courbe de son profil, dans la finesse de ses cheveux, dans la grâce de son cou, dans la largeur de ses blanches épaules, il y avait mille souvenirs de la cour de Louis XIV. On sentait qu'il avait fallu toute une race de preux pour produire cette combinaison de traits purs et nobles, toutes ces grâces presque royales, qui se révélaient lentement, comme celles du cygne jouant au soleil avec une langueur majestueuse.   (*Valentine*, 46)

> (In the line of her soft profile, in the delicacy of her hair, in the gracefulness of her neck, in the breadth of her white shoulders, there lingered countless memories of the court of Louis XIV. One sensed that a long line of nobles had been necessary to produce this combination of pure and aristocratic features, all those almost regal graces, which revealed themselves slowly, like those of a swan playing majestically and langorously in the sunlight.)

This first scene unfolds in a *terra media*. The public ball is a space where two social spheres can come into contact, "depuis le sous-préfet du département jusqu'à la jolie grisette . . . depuis la noble châtelaine jusqu'au petit *patour*" (*Valentine*, 32; "from the local functionary to the pretty grisette . . . from the lady of the manor to the little shepherd boy"). In the future fictional universe of Sand's pastoral novels, the *bal champêtre* will increasingly designate a privileged locus of social intermingling, where aristocrats and peasants are able to interact freely. The "Romantic festival," where commoners and the local gentry can dance together, is highlighted in many of Sand's novels which deal with love between two social spheres, such as *Le Compagnon du tour de France*, *Le Meunier d'Angibault*, and *André*.

The bal champêtre is identified as a zone where the usual social hierarchies are destabilized, amorous alliances between different classes are made, even gender-associated occupations are deconstructed. In this initial scene, for example, as the *bourrée* is about to begin, lowly Bénédict has been paired with Mlle Valentine de Raimbault. This state of affairs puts Valentine's mother in a state of fury. Seeing the mismatch, the *vielle* player mischievously takes advantage of the situation by giving the musical signal for the new dancer to kiss his partner. A champion of a rigid social structure, Mme de Raimbault, pale with rage, cannot bear to witness a commoner kissing her aristocratic daughter. She also is vaguely aware that the rustic locus and the bal champêtre are responsible for the impropriety. She scolds her mother-in-law for having insisted on attending: "Voilà une jolie fête, une charmante partie de plaisir. . . . C'est vous qui l'avez voulu; vous m'avez amenée ici à mon corps défendant. Vous aimez la canaille, vous; mais moi, je la déteste!" (*Valentine*, 49; "Here's a pretty picture for you, a simply charming occasion. . . . You're the one who asked for it; you brought me here against my will. You, for your part, like the rabble, but I detest it!"). In this scene, Sand, amusingly, has constructed an inversion of the droit du seigneur topos.

The mother's outburst lays bare Sand's tendency to depict places where such interaction is made possible. A typology of such places includes public events such as country dances; popular festivities and weddings that allow the mingling of different groups;[28] and natural settings—the road, the river, a pastoral landscape where different classes may encounter each other by chance. In such instances, conventions are subverted so that a destabilized social universe is created. While Mme de Raimbault is merely outraged by the lack of "comme il faut," and the two young people simply embarrassed by the incident, the reader senses that the fictional dice have been thrown. Bénédict and Valentine have sealed their fate by one ritualistic kiss.[29]

In *Valentine* spatial identifications replace the linguistic peculiarities seen in *Indiana*. Whereas in Sand's first novel each character was defined by a particular language and that language functioned as a linguistic sphere, here spheres are determined spatially. Not that Sand lost interest in delineating linguistic spheres, as throughout her pastoral fictions she would continue to raise the problems encountered by the conflict between different social spheres as exemplified by the clashing of hermetic linguistic systems. In the *Compagnon du tour de France*, for example, a long dialogue between two artisans, Amaury and Pierre Huguenin, would provoke the narrator to comment:

> lecteur bénévole . . . sois indulgent pour le traducteur impuissant qui te transmet la parole de l'ouvrier. *Cet homme ne parle pas la même langue que toi*, et le narrateur qui lui sert d'interprète est forcé d'al-

térer la beauté abrupte, le tour original et l'abondance poétique de son texte, pour te communiquer ses pensées. (emphasis added; *Compagnon*, 93)

(gentle reader . . . do not condemn the powerless translator who is simply relaying the worker's idiom to you. *This man does not speak the same language as you*, and the narrator, who acts as his interpreter, is obliged to alter the raw beauty, the peculiar turn of phrase, and the poetic richness of his text, in order to communicate his thoughts to you.)

As a novel of the 1840s, *Le Compagnon du tour de France* shows not only Sand's continued attention to linguistic spheres, but also her increasing interest in delineating the parameters of a literary version of a peasant vernacular.[30]

The linguistic spheres of *Indiana* were differentiated only on the level of style and rhetoric, since the characters ostensibly used a common linguistic register, denoting the same cultural class. Even the servant Noun spoke a language that was not distinguishable from the idiom of the bourgeoisie on linguistic grounds alone. Similarly, in *Valentine*, when Sand introduces authentic *berrichon* characters into her fictional universe, peasants as well as local landowners, the different social groups nevertheless speak the same idiom; no patois (save a "je vas" once or twice), no provincialisms, no linguistic markers of social stratification.

Sand uses the theory of spheres to define and contrast the different strata she wishes to explore in *Valentine*. The very restricted and stylized spatial layout in the first half of the novel points to a polar construction in which the château de Raimbault stands in opposition to the Lhéry farmstead. Interestingly, these two contrasting *loci* give way to a second oppositional set in the second half of the text, where Bénédict's cottage and Valentine's pavilion exemplify the couple's desperate attempt to create a middle ground, a shared space of their own, free of class and gender definitions.[31]

The Raimbault Sphere

As seen from the outside, Valentine's world appears a hermetically sealed and indivisible aristocratic sphere. Examined from within, however, the social space Valentine inhabits breaks down into three subspheres. Each centers on a different idol—in turn glorifying money, social superiority, or propriety—and each competing for Valentine's soul.[32] Valentine's grandmother and mother embody the antithetical spheres of the Emigration and the Empire. The elderly Marquise de

Raimbault represents the old nobility of the Ancien Régime, with her main attention fixed on questions of etiquette. She has adopted an attitude of benevolent but patronizing condescension vis-à-vis the lower classes. Addicted to luxury, contemptuous of all social groups outside her own, Valentine's grandmother is basically a woman of superficial morals and world view. The few scenes in which she dominates the fictional canvas depict a weak-willed, snobbish, and selfish character whose entire raison d'être is her own *bien-être*. On her deathbed, her final words, resonating with the hubris characteristic of her class, express begrudging gratitude to Valentine's lower-born mother for having cared for her: "Pour une femme sans naissance, après tout, elle s'est conduite assez bien envers moi. Je n'attendais pas tant, je l'avoue, de la part de mademoiselle Chignon" (*Valentine*, 188; "For a woman of lowly birth, after all, she treated me rather well. I did not expect as much, I must admit, from mademoiselle Chignon").

Valentine's mother portrays the new aristocracy, the nouveaux riches of the Empire and the Restoration. Daughter of a rich merchant, Mlle Chignon lays bare the consumerism and materialistic obsession of the bourgeois monarchy. Her hatred for the *noblesse d'épée* whose privileges and titles she nevertheless covets is matched only by her fear and hostility toward the plebeians. Careful above all to maintain the social barriers between her parvenu circle and those less fortunate, she embodies the ambitious aspirations of the new aristocracy of bankers and merchants. Significantly, and for the first time, Sand deploys the social repertoire in *Valentine* through strong figures of women. In *Indiana* the three political spheres had been represented by men; in *Valentine* it is the women almost exclusively who incarnate the social Ideas that form the backbone of the novel. The novel thus offers a counterpoise not only to her first work but also to Balzac's fictional cosmology, where the embodiments of capitalism and old-time aristocracy figure most prominently in the masculine: Rastignac, the emblem of ambition, and père Grandet, of greed incarnate. Sand depicts a similar struggle, now transposed to the feminine; there is no mention of the old marquise's husband, and Valentine's father has been conveniently disposed of before the novel begins.

The only male representative of the aristocratic sphere is Monsieur de Lansac, a peripheral character. Too weak, too passionless to attract much attention on the part of the narrator, he is a direct descendant of *Indiana*'s Raymon, but far less talented and far less prominently displayed. At first, he seems entirely composed of surfaces. His exquisite politeness to Valentine and her mother on the one hand and to Bénédict on the other initially conceals his fundamental contempt for human values. But soon, his lurking greed and profound amorality emerge more prominently. His letters to Valentine are "obscure, empty, and pretentious" (107), his epistolary style echoing his character which lacks content and consists primarily in attention to form. His lacquered surface serves him well. Lansac presents a rapacious nature in the Balzacian mode, and the roughness of his name, which ends in a harsh guttural, is a Sandian echo of Gobseck, a character created by Balzac in 1830.[33] Gobseck is a usurer—"as much of a banker as the executioner of Paris is a doctor . . . [he is] a financial guillotine";[34] Lansac represents the usurer's necessary companion, the young man in need of money. The two go hand in hand, Balzac's "négociant" swallowing people and their fortunes whole ("gobe sec"), while Sand's dandy, M. de Lansac, ransacks his wife's inheritance (his name an anagram of "dans le sac"). Lansac is a character who illustrates the increasing visibility of money in early capitalist France. With his entire discourse rooted in financial considerations, his fundamentally unpoetic nature reveals itself. The narrator's remark that Lansac "never dreams" (90) is a devastating marker of character in Sand's fictional universe and points to a total lack of imagination. A worthy successor of Indiana's husband, Lansac behaves as a petty domestic tyrant once he has obtained Valentine's hand. Appearances for Lansac are the fitting substitute of authenticity. In the personal sphere, for instance, marital fidelity counts far less than the semblance of faithfulness. His maxim regarding the confession a wife's remorse for adulterous actions might bring about—"une femme ne doit jamais prendre son mari pour son confesseur" (185; "a woman must never attribute the role of confessor to her husband")—clearly subordinates true remorse to etiquette.[35] His fanatic respect for *le paraître* echoes the attitude of the old marquise whose precept regarding extramarital affairs—"ne prends jamais un amant qui ne soit pas de ton rang" (188; "never take a lover who is not of the same rank as you")[36]—ensures the strict maintenance of the social hierarchy.

Valentine's Sphere

In contrast to these characters, each of whom has a clearly delimited social and spatial sphere, Valentine seems strangely outside of any sphere. Brought up on aristocratic soil, she is like a plant struggling to grow in unfertile ground. Her entire education is described in the negative, as a rejection in turn of the two spheres her mother and grandmother represent. Each, by offering a competing world view, has also provided an antimodel:

> [Valentine] se promettait d'échapper à ces inclinations ardentes qui faisaient sous ses yeux le malheur des autres; à l'amour du luxe, auquel sa grand-mère sacrifiait toute dignité; à l'ambition, dont les espérances déçues torturaient sa mère. (*Valentine*, 52)

([Valentine] promised herself not to fall prey to those passionate inclinations that had brought about the misfortune of others before her very eyes: the love of luxury, for which her grandmother had sacrificed all dignity; ambition, whose dashed hopes tormented her mother.)

Valentine becomes increasingly alienated from her grandmother's emigration philosophy and her mother's adulation for the Empire's era of ambition. Pulled between two forces, Valentine experiences severe dislocation: "[elle] était entre elles comme un rocher battu de deux courants contraires" (81; "she was, between the two of them, like a rock battered by two opposing currents"). The image of the rock situated at the *confluence*, where two currents meet conjures up a similar remark in *Mémoires d'outre tombe* where Chateaubriand expresses his sense of not belonging to either the Ancien Régime or the new society.[37] But the river metaphor denoting alienation from a given milieu does not need a literary source in Sand's case. Later in her memoirs she will describe her childhood as a period during which she also was torn between her "two mothers."[38]

Left to her own devices, Valentine, very much like the child portrayed in *Histoire de ma vie*, fabricates for herself a world of meditation and solitary study as protection from her family's conflicting ideational spheres: "Elle s'était faite elle-même ce qu'elle était, et, faute de trouver des sympathies bien réelles dans sa famille, elle avait pris le goût de l'étude et de la rêverie" (51; "She had made herself what she was, and, for want of real understanding in her family, she had taken to studying and to daydreaming"). Her natural inclinations draw her closer to Bénédict and make her a stranger in the aristocratic sphere she inhabits. Significantly, her first serious discussion with Bénédict reveals what she thinks about the anachronistic educational principles espoused by her social class, especially as they relate to women:

"dans le temps où nous vivons, il faut une spécialité. Notre rang, notre fortune, ne tiennent à rien. . . . L'éducation que nous recevons est misérable; on nous donne les éléments de tout, et l'on ne nous permet pas de rien approfondir. . . . On nous élève toujours pour être riches, jamais pour être pauvres." (*Valentine*, 56)

("in the times we live in, one needs a specialization. Our social rank, our wealth are without consequence. . . . The education we receive is worthless: we are given the basics of everything, but then we are not permitted to deepen our knowledge of anything. . . . We are always raised to be rich, never to be poor.")

The desire for self-sufficiency, expressed by many of Sand's heroines, is echoed in the author's correspondence during the 1830s and gives deeper meaning to many of her remarks regarding the financial considerations that led her to write for her life. Such comments do not spell a lack of seriousness so much as they express pride in achieving financial independence through one's own efforts, an accomplishment that normally at the time was reserved only for men. Valentine prefigures the heroine of *Le Meunier d'Angibault* who, upon learning that she is *ruinée*, experiences an extraordinary sense of relief that from now on she must earn her own keep and thereby deserve her fate.

Valentine's assertion that she needs to master a trade—"une personne qui fait très bien une chose se soutient toujours dans la société" (57; "a person who excels at something always holds his or her own in society")—because nothing ensures the stability of her social standing, is prophetic of the novel's dénouement. In the final chapters, she will be stripped of all financial advantage by her predator husband and evicted from the spatial sphere where she had always felt out of place. At the same time, her point of view is remarkably farsighted for a provincial young aristocrat who has been sheltered from the world. In the novel Valentine's desire for financial independence is linked to her pursuit of painting and music. The sphere she creates in the pavilion contains all the accouterments of her artistic endeavors. Non-hierarchical space and artistic production are thus connected and valorized.

Valentine's attitudes are broad-minded, and in keeping with this, her social interaction with the peasant class does not depend on a pre-fabricated code of behavior such as the marquise and the countess rely upon. She seemingly shares none of her mother's instinctive dislike. She associates freely with the farmer's daughter, Athénaïs, and cheerfully goes to live with the Lhérys when she is dispossessed. In contrast to her grandmother's despising joviality or her mother's haughty distance, Valentine treats Bénédict as another human being on an equal footing: "[Bénédict] trouva qu'elle était fille noble de bonne foi, sans morgue et sans fausse humilité. Elle était comme le terme moyen entre sa mère et sa grand-mère; elle savait se faire respecter sans offenser jamais" (55; "[Bénédict] found her to be noble in good faith, without pride and false modesty. She was like the golden mean between her grandmother and her mother; she knew how to command respect, but without ever offending anyone"). In fact, Valentine feels more in sympathy with Bénédict and Athénaïs than with her own family, as a visit to the Lhéry farm attests: "Jamais Valentine ne s'était sentie si heureuse; loin des regards de sa mère, loin de la roideur glaciale qui pesait sur tous ses pas, il lui semblait respirer un air plus libre, et, pour la première fois depuis qu'elle était née, vivre de toute sa vie" (86; "Never had Valentine felt so happy; far from her mother's supervision, far from the frozen stiffness that weighed on her every step, she felt she was breathing a freer air, and, for the first time ever, that she was living life to the fullest").

In this crucial scene Valentine's usual uneasiness is finally articulated in spatial terms. The young woman fantasizes that she is a farm girl for an afternoon. As she feeds the animals and plays about the farm, Sand's narrator uses the Balzacian key word: "il lui sembla être là dans la *sphère* pour laquelle elle était créée" (emphasis added; 87; "she felt she was there in the *sphere* she had been born to occupy"). Although Valentine's idyll is but a fleeting epiphanic moment, she nevertheless seems to be more aware than the other characters that the social architecture is subject to permutations. In a statement that prefigures some of Sand's utopian declarations of the 1840s, Valentine denies that substantial differences exist between her sphere and the one the Lhéry family represents: "Au temps où nous vivons . . . il n'y a plus de paysans. Ne recevons-nous pas la même éducation dans presque toutes les classes?" (95; "Nowadays . . . there are no more peasants. Do we not receive the very same education in almost all classes of society?"). The gradual collapsing of different social groups—which she links, interestingly, with the expansion of educational possibilities—has not eliminated a persistent inequality of opportunity according to gender, however. Valentine emphasizes that a young man such as Bénédict is much better educated than she can ever hope to be. Although the novel does not explore this difference further, many of Sand's later writings address the issues of women's literacy and education at greater length, one of the most notable being *Nanon*.

Bénédict's Sphere

Just as Valentine is cruelly uncomfortable in the glacial life-style of her ancestral home, Bénédict is estranged from his own peasant origins. Sent to Paris by the wealthy Lhérys, he has received an education on a par with a young bourgeois. By his education and intelligence he is as out of place in his social sphere as Valentine is in hers.

> "[Les Lhéry] m'on recueilli, adopté, et, au lieu de me mettre à la charrue, comme l'ordre social semblait m'y destiner, ils m'ont envoyé à Paris . . . ils m'ont fait faire des études, ils m'ont métamorphosé en bourgeois, en étudiant." (*Valentine*, 36)

> ("[The Lhérys] took me in, adopted me, and instead of setting me to the plow, as the social order seemed to destine me, they sent me to Paris . . . they had me educated, they transformed me into a bourgeois, a student.")

Bénédict concludes with the pessimistic remark: "Maudite soit la manie de prétendre plus haut qu'on ne peut atteindre!" ("Cursed be the mania of aspiring higher than one can every reach!"). For Sand,

Bénédict is typical of an intermediary generation—one that articulates the painful transition between an Ancien Régime society in which individual destinies are fixed and the new society where obtaining a proper education and acquiring money replace titles of nobility and privilege.

> Le mal était . . . grand chez Bénédict. Au lieu d'engourdir ses sentiments généreux, l'éducation les avait développés outre mesure. . . . Ce caractère ardent . . . aurait eu besoin d'un ordre d'idées calmantes, de principes repressifs. . . . Les lumières de la civilisation qui ont développé tant de qualités précieuses, en ont vicié peut-être autant. C'est *un malheur des générations placées entre celles qui ne savent rien et celles qui sauront assez:* elles savent trop. (emphasis added; *Valentine*, 40)

> (The extent of the illness in Bénédict's case was considerable. Instead of numbing his generous sentiments, education had developed them beyond measure. . . . Such an ardent temperament . . . would have benefited more from a tranquilizing set of ideas, and constraining principles. . . . The advances of civilization, which have developed so many valuable qualities, may well have spoiled just as many. It is *a misfortune of those generations, situated between those who know nothing and those who will know enough;* they know too much.)

Sand had a deep interest in what she conceived to be a modern phenomenon: the multiplicity of moral ailments which could result from an overly active mental life. Within a year, in an article on Obermann, she would be musing on the as yet undiscovered maladies of the soul which were to provide a major subjects of discourse for the nineteenth-century novelist. The notion that thought could atrophy the vital faculties also has been Balzacian resonances with *Louis Lambert*, *Les Martyrs ignorés*, and *Gobseck*, to name just a few texts that provide ample reflection on the topic.[39]

As one of the first men of French Romanticism out of place (for this concept Russian has invented the wonderful word *raznochinets*, meaning, literally, a man of various ranks) Bénédict reveals the dangers of a cerebral life. With no physical labor to counteract its effect, Bénédict becomes prone to spleen:

> L'ennui, ce mal horrible qui s'est attaché à la génération présente plus qu'à toute autre époque de l'histoire sociale, avait envahi la destinée de Bénédict dans sa fleur; il s'étendait comme un nuage noir sur tout son avenir. Il avait déjà flétri la plus précieuse faculté de son âge, l'espérance. (*Valentine*, 40)

(Boredom, that terrible sickness that has struck the present generation more than at any other time in history, had invaded Bénédict's
destiny in the bloom of youth; it was spreading like a black cloud
over his entire future. It had already stricken the most precious faculty of his youth, hope.)

What distinguishes Bénédict from his preromantic brothers, René,
Obermann, and Werther, is his lowly class. Breaking down the invisible literary codes that routinely restricted the fictional arena to upper-
class heroes, Sand here was doing for the category of class what she
had done for her gender in *Indiana*, refusing to write according to the
rules of the male literary order. By stressing that Valentine and Bénédict, although at opposite ends of the social spectrum, shared the same
sensibility and intelligence, Sand was able to denounce the arbitrary
codes of "class" and "gender."

When the reader first encounters Bénédict, he is wearing the
black costume of a civil servant or legal clerk, and boots instead of peasant clogs. His rival clearly identifies his dress as setting him off from
the young men of his class.[40] Pale and dark, easily offended, with
ironic look on his face, Bénédict represents Sand's inverted version of
Stendhal's social climber. The term "singulier" (as in "singulier caractère") with which Sand describes her hero clearly establishes the link
between the two fictional characters, it being a favorite descriptive ad-
jective in Stendhal's repertoire.

What ails Bénédict is a new and social form of the mal du siècle.
While Sand plumbed its feminine variant in *Indiana*, here the author
explores its masculine and provincial incarnation.

> Bénédict . . . tomba dans une rêverie profonde . . . un jeune
> homme trop riche d'imagination et de connaissance pour goûter le
> repos de l'esprit. . . . A Paris . . . il avait travaillé beaucoup; mais il
> s'était arrêté lorsque la pratique devenait nécessaire. Il avait senti le
> dégoût au moment où les autres recueillent le fruit de leurs
> peines.   (*Valentine*, 39)

> (Bénédict . . . fell into a deep reverie . . . a young man too en-
> dowed in imagination and knowledge to allow him to enjoy peace
> of mind. . . . In Paris . . . he had worked hard; but he had stopped
> when it became necessary to apply his knowledge. At the very mo-
> ment when others reap the fruit of their labors, he had experienced
> disgust.)

Several months later, Sand's third novel, *Lélia*, will highlight to an even
greater degree the gap between knowledge and realization, between
desire and praxis. Bénédict's Romantic sister, Lélia, will pick up where

the young student left off and display the full-blown effects of an overly intellectualized existence.

The Complex of the "Mansarde bleue"

By exploring alienation from one's social sphere in both the feminine and the masculine, Sand created in Valentine and Bénédict two protagonists who found themselves truly on an equal footing. At the same time, both characters have autopsychological links to the author—Valentine, by her reactions to her difficult childhood, and Bénédict, by the pathological intensity of his brilliant intellect. Bénédict's student days in Paris can be seen as a fictional transposition of Sand's own desire for access to the higher education reserved for men. The number of young heroes in her works—in *Simon*, *Horace*, *Isidora*, and *La Daniella*—who are students, preferably of law, is significant. Sand wanted to be a law student like Balzac, Sandeau, and others among her Berrichon friends. She would have liked to attend lectures at the Sorbonne. Who knows, perhaps, disguised in her boots and frock coat, she did sneak into an amphitheater in the early 1830s to hear the celebrated philosopher, Victor Cousin, discuss his views of "le beau idéal." Her assimilation with Bénédict expresses her wistful desire to partake of this exciting intellectual existence so many of her comrades had. In the same way that Aurore had projected herself into Amédée (in *Histoire du rêveur*), Sand continued to explore via male characters the abstract intellectual questions that haunted her. Through Ralph she sought a poetic language (*Indiana*); through Jacques she exorcized the temptation of suicide (*Jacques*); in Alexis she probed the mystical ruminations of a religious temperament (*Spiridion*); in Bénédict she examined her own melancholic temperament.

One could speak of a veritable double life of George Sand, which manifested itself in acute form in the early thirties. On the one hand, her public and social life portrayed a carefree existence, filled with friends, brimming over with activity—travel, festivities, gatherings, dinners, excursions, the theater, endless discussions. On the other hand, her private, inner life was characterized by mal du siècle. References to her "accès de spleen épouvantable" (*Corr.*, 2:721) and to her "moments d'irritation bilieuse" (2:879) are almost constant in her correspondence between 1832 and 1835. "I have the spleen," she writes in August 1832 to her friend François Rollinat (*Corr.*, 2:128). She blames her "disposition splenétique," her "noire disposition" on "fatigue, disgust, a bad temper and ennui."[41] "I am really suffering from a kind of cerebral fever," she writes Emile Regnault several months later, "which is more moral than physical" (*Corr.*, 2:106). Her suffering is "purely intellectual," a result of reflection, study, and "a philosophical examination of life in general."[42] She scribbles away ("je noircis du papier") so as to relieve her spleen "which is metamorphosed into ink" ("qui s'en va en encre").[43] Expressed throughout the letters of the time, in which she candidly pours out her inner feelings, is a heightened sense of moral solitude. With the creation of this private persona in her *Correspondance* and such other autobiographical texts as "Sketches and Hints" and with its re-creation in *Histoire de ma vie*, the public figure recedes into the background, and Sand's resemblance to such fictional characters as Bénédict becomes clear.

Her "obsessive tendency to analyze" ("manie d'analyse", HV, 2:128) echoes Bénédict's "esprit qui examine et déprécie tout" (*Valentine*, 37; "mind that examines and denigrates everything"). This ailment is a kind of hypertrophy of the brain, connected to mental labor, a sickness of intellectuals, in which the critical faculties are overdeveloped and tend to overshadow feeling. Sand insists on the vocabulary of pathology to describe this psychological state. She describes herself as "a leper of misfortune" (*Corr.*, 2:823) and in a letter to Sainte-Beuve compares herself to an invalid consulting her doctor (2:863). Bénédict's case illustrates one of those "illnesses in the moral order" she alludes to in *Histoire de ma vie* "which are analogous to physical ones in that they leave us crippled and forever disabled" (2:199).

Lost Illusions

Bénédict also shares many traits with a character being fashioned by Balzac during the same months that the young berrichon was emerging from Sand's pen, Benassis of *Le Médecin de campagne*. The crucial chapter, bearing the Rousseau title "La Confession du médecin de campagne," highlights the hero's student days in Paris. In these pages Benassis bears a striking resemblance to Bénédict. Bernard Guyon's very careful analysis of the genesis of Balzac's novel assures us that this central narrative in its final form was not composed until the later part of June 1833, thus superceding the earlier so-called "Confession inédite," composed in September 1832.[44] The second version of the "Confession" expounds on "one of the major themes of the great Balzacian symphony,"[45] the young man from the provinces arriving in Paris, a theme left completely unexplored in the original version. The dates of composition of the later text leave open the possibility that Balzac's reading of *Valentine* at approximately this time might have had an effect on the second redaction of the "Confession." We know that, in February of that year, Balzac had been sent a copy of *Valentine*, as a letter of Sand's attests.[46] No documentation is available of any direct influence of Sand's novel on the "Confession" (although the possibility is cer-

tainly there). But remarkable similarities make it clear that we are dealing here, not just with the elaboration of a Balzac character, but with
the consolidation of a more general literary type in the early 1830s. The
dialogic relationship of Sand and Balzac and the evidence for a genuine
literary exchange between the two make it likely at the very least that
they discussed their elaboration of the *enfant du siècle* in its various
embodiments.

What links the two characters is an archetypal plot element structuring many nineteenth-century novels, in which the narrator charts
the psychology of lost illusions in the protagonist, as he discovers the
capital and becomes revulsed by the "moral sewer of Paris."[47] Whether
of a noble family or of modest origins, Balzac's and Sand's young Parisian students suffer from alienation, lack of funds, unhappy love affairs, and filthy lodgings. Most destructive of all is a kind of inner fire
that burns everything in its path:

> A Paris, la solitude . . . avait rebuté [Bénédict]. Toute préférable à
> la société qu'elle lui semblait, il l'avait trouvée, au fond de sa petite
> chambre d'étudiant, trop solennelle, trop dangereuse pour des
> facultés aussi actives que l'étaient les siennes. Sa santé en avait
> souffert. (*Valentine*, 40)

> (In Paris, solitude disheartened [Bénédict]. Although it seemed to
> him far preferable to the company of others, still he had found it,
> all alone in his small student's room, too solemn, too perilous for
> faculties as active as his. His health had suffered from it.)

Like Bénédict, Benassis suffers from disillusion. Like Bénédict,
he charts his own aimless wandering through the chaotic city, denouncing the "Parisian lack of sensitivity . . . where the most gracious
frivolity conceals either politics or money."[48] Leading an "uncertain
life," he confronts the rupture of his identity with a triple result. First
comes scepticism—he cannot see the relationship between knowledge
and work, desire and will: "I fancied myself intellectually superior
simply because I had the potential to become so; and, without a
thought either to the patience necessary to produce great works or to
the doing wherein are manifest all the inherent difficulties, I counted
on every kind of glory" (251). Second is profound discouragement—he
walks the streets of the capital: "Like all those young men, disgusted
with their chosen profession, and without any fixed plans . . . so too I
aimlessly wandered for days at a time through the streets" (251). The
spatial symbolism here emphasizes that such a character as Benassis,
much like Bénédict, has no allotted space that belongs to him. Therefore he wanders through the public spaces of the city, with no sphere of

his own. Third, his heart shrinks. He is metamorphosed into one of those insensitive young men who populate Balzac's Parisian sphere:

> In the midst of the endless struggle of ambitions, desires and hatreds, it is impossible not to be either the victim or the accomplice of this general agitation; imperceptibly, the continuous spectacle of vice rewarded and virtue ridiculed trips up a young man. Parisian life soon removes the velvety softness of his conscience; then begins the infernal process of his demoralization, destined not to stop. . . . This struggle drains and shrinks the heart while stimulating the life of the intellect, and thus produces that famous Parisian insensibility. (252–253)

Both Benassis and Bénédict are characterized by short phrases reminiscent of René. The latter's "too rich imagination" matches the former's "vague des passions" (253). Like René, Benassis experiences the temptation of paralyzing melancholia, the desire for inaction and retreat, and the ultimate solution of suicide. But unlike Bénédict who succumbs to the Romantic glorification of suicide, Benassis triumphs over his malady to become a positive hero, fashioning for himself a positive life. Benassis ends up being "fatigué de malheur"[49] while Bénédict remains true to what the critic Louis de Loménie called Sand's "moralité du malheur."[50]

Despite the connections between these two characters, the different fates they undergo highlight the dissimilarities between the artistic temperaments of Sand and Balzac. Whereas Balzac choses to trace the mental itinerary of a young man from moral illness to spiritual rebirth, Sand prefers to embody each state in a different character. Thus, in this respect the architecture of *Valentine* places the two male protagonists, Lansac and Bénédict, in almost perfect opposition, with the latter in the *beau rôle*. While Lansac has embraced what the narrator contemptuously designates as "une vie positive," Bénédict refuses to "establish his place in society" and engages in a mirror-life, which functions as "une vie négative." In a bitter denunciation of *embourgeoisement*, Bénédict condemns the "positive man's" credo for its exclusive attention to the maximal acquisition of creature comforts:

> "C'est vous qui m'invitez à dépenser mon énergie en fumée, quand vous me dites de travailler pour être un homme comme les autres, de consacrer ma jeunesse . . . à gagner de quoi mourir de vieillesse commodément, les pieds dans la fourrure et la tête sur un coussin de duvet. Voilà pourtant le but de tous ceux qu'on appelle de bons sujets à mon âge, et *des hommes positifs* à quarante ans." (emphasis added; *Valentine*, 105)

("Are you really the one who encourages me to spend my energy in trifles when you advise me to work so as to be like everyone else, to devote my youth . . . to earning enough money to die of old age in comfort, my feet wrapped in fur and my head on a down cushion. Such in any case is the goal of all those who are called sensible fellows at my age and *positive men* at forty.")

Bénédict describes with contempt and a pre-Flaubertian irony the life that such an active man of ambition as Lansac leads:

"Laissez-les aspirer de tous leurs efforts vers ce but sublime: être électeurs du grand collège, ou conseillers municipaux, ou secrétaires de préfecture . . . voilà *la vie positive* qui se déroule dans toute sa splendeur autour de moi! Voilà la glorieuse condition d'homme vers laquelle aspirent tous mes contemporains d'étude." (emphasis added; *Valentine*, 105)

("Let them strive with all their might to this elevated goal: to be voters in the electoral college, or municipal counselors, or district clerks . . . that is the *positive life* that unfolds in all its splendor around me! That is the glorious condition of man to which our generation of students aspires.")

Sand is putting her own words into Bénédict's mouth. When discussing her own period of youthful disillusionment in *Histoire de ma vie* quite a few years later, she would use the same expression and entitled a chapter "Aversion pour la vie positive" (HV, 2:32).

The negativity of Sand's hero and his subsequent refusal to engage in a struggle with what he estimates to be beneath his contempt stand in stark contrast to the Balzac hero's energetic and life-giving rage as symbolized by Rastignac's defiant challenge to Parisian society in *Le Père Goriot*: "A nous deux, maintenant!" Whereas he is intent on attacking what he despises both figuratively in speech and literally through his seduction of high and influential social circles, Bénédict only seeks to retreat immediately from what he attacks so vigorously through words. For him his condemnation constitutes a valid enough pretext for nonparticipation in the social sphere. He rejects the active solution by renouncing his social identity as exemplified by his citizenship:

"Mais ici, sur le sol de la France, où, quoi qu'on en dise, la terre manque de bras, où chaque profession regorge d'aspirants, où l'espèce humaine, hideusement agglomérée autour des palais, rampe et lèche la trace des pas du riche, où d'énormes capitaux, rassemblés . . . dans les mains de quelques hommes, servent

d'enjeu à une continuelle loterie entre l'avarice, l'immoralité et l'in-
eptie, dans ce pays d'impudeur et de misère, de vice et de désolation; dans cette civilisation pourrie jusqu'à sa racine, vous voulez
que je sois *citoyen?*" (*Valentine*, 106)

("But here, on French soil, where, in spite of what one may say, the
land needs more helping hands, where every profession is glutted
with ready candidates, where the human species, grotesquely
concentrated around palaces, fawns and licks the footsteps of the
rich, where enormous fortunes, concentrated . . . in the hands of
a few men, serve as the stakes in the endless lottery among greed,
immorality, and stupidity, in this country of immodesty and poverty, of vice and desolation; in this civilization rotten to the core
you want me to be a *citizen?*")

Bénédict's analysis of restoration France is expressed in negative terms
only. His nihilistic diagnosis brings a sense of powerlessness in its
wake. The image of France as a society rotten through and through
suggests also that its disease is terminal. By contrast, Benassis's
appraisal of the "large town near La Grande Chartreuse" includes
negative aspects only as a preamble for envisaging potential improve-
ments. For the Balzacian doctor, society may be sick but it is eminently
curable. Illness does not reach the core of the societal body; the sores
covering its surface can be treated. Instead of a strategic retreat,
Benassis proposes a strategy of action, "une prière active" (*Le Médecin
de campagne*, 290).

It is significant that the doctor's social class is different from Bénédict's. As the son of a rich provincial from Languedoc, he is like many
of the young heroes of *La Comédie humaine*, whose social origins are either the old landed gentry, albeit impoverished, or the modest but still
respectable middle class. This fact alone does not fully explain the differences in character between Benassis and Bénédict. It does however
accentuate the fact that the estrangement of Sand's character is more
firmly defined by the social fabric, while Balzac's hero undergoes only
a temporary period of distancing from the social world in which he naturally belongs. Balzac, says the Marxist critic Pierre Barbéris ap-
provingly, "needed Benassis so as to signify his constructive and
responsible vision of life."[51] In this perspective, the Balzacian character
mirrors the vitality and life-affirming world view of Balzac. For Barbéris, Benassis is a remarkable hero precisely because his message
"L'avenir, c'est l'homme social" (102) transcends Romanticism's tendency to glorify the individual at the expense of the social: "Benassis
accomplished what the other heroes of the mal du siècle had never
done: he progressed from concentrating on himself to concentrating
on others and on history."[52] Not surprisingly, in order to make this
claim, Barbéris conveniently overlooks the good doctor's conservative

and authoritarian social theories. Benassis's allegiance to *praxis* is reason enough in his view to warrant our admiration. But Sand's indictment of a society in which social dislocation rendered so many individual destinies intolerable, is more poignant than Balzac's, which advocates a paternalistic solution to social ills. Sand sees in Bénédict a tragic figure, caught between two worlds, neither of which he could completely accept. He could only retreat to his cottage and become a dreamer. In this light, the main character of *Valentine* reformulates some of the issues of *Histoire du rêveur*.

The Theory of Spheres and the Romantic "Trilogy"

In the works examined thus far, *Histoire du rêveur*, *Indiana*, and *Valentine*, Sand paid special attention in her fictional world to both landscape and character types, with *Valentine* representing a kind of synthesis of the two, where character is largely defined through spacial means. In this first stage of Sand's literary output, the principle of "la littérature des images" dominates in the structuring of the fictional material. With the writing of *Valentine*, Sand's accelerated period as apprentice extraordinaire comes to an end. Having produced two novels in rapid succession, she was now ready to embark upon the writing of her masterpiece, *Lélia*. In it the fictional dialogue with Balzac continued. The second stage of Sand's literary career, exemplifying "la littérature des idées," was about to begin.

The creation of character types, already apparent in the three works examined, continued to interest Sand. Years later, when she wrote a preface to Balzac's *La Comédie humaine* (for the posthumous Houssiaux edition of 1855), one of the delineating characteristics of Balzac's genius that she highlighted was his fashioning of a multitude of types. She refers to Armand Baschet's biography of the novelist and quotes his definition of a type[53] and then muses admiringly on the "innumerable characters" created by her fellow novelist in what the critic Roger Shattuck calls his "flood novel."[54] The following comment obviously demonstrates her envy at this formidable talent "competing with the état civil" so brilliantly:

> voilà la grande et la vraie puissance de l'artiste. Personne ne l'a encore possédée avec l'universalité de Balzac. *Personne n'a autant créé de types complets,* et c'est là ce qui donne tant de valeur et d'importance aux innombrables détails de la vie privée, qui lasseraient chez un autre, mais qui, chez lui, sont empreints de la vie même de ses personnages et, par là, indispensables.[55]

(This is the great and true power of the artist. No one has yet possessed it with the universality that Balzac has. *No one has created*

complete types as much as he has, and this is what gives so much
worth and importance to the innumerable details of private life,
which would be tiresome in the works of another, but which, in his
novels, are marked with the very life of his characters and are, consequently, indispensable.)

Clearly the type for Sand, as it was for Balzac, was a vehicle for ideology, an incarnation of a dominant psychological temperament, a key
to the sensibility of an age. Like the architect of *La Comédie humaine*, she
was intent on loading her characters with as much ideological, psychological, and historical weight as possible.

While Sand did not employ Balzac's device of recurring characters, certain kinships can be established among many of her fictional
creations. As will become clear in the next chapter, Indiana, Valentine, and Lélia are from the same family of minds. Indiana and Lélia
are linked by their basically splenetic temperaments, by the lyrical
outbursts in their epistolary writing, and by their common denunciation of the institution of marriage as a slave market for women. Valentine and Lélia share many physical and psychic attributes. Though
one is blond and the other dark, allusions to Valentine as "a frigid
statue" (132) or "a marble statue" (181) prefigure references to Lélia's
marble soul.

Histoire du rêveur, Indiana, Valentine, and, as we are about to see,
Lélia, can be read as the elaboration of a cast of female and male types,
which make up a kind of Sandian *commedia dell'arte*, from the splenetic
"femme du siècle," disillusioned *intellectuelle*, overly sensitive ingé-
nue, cynical dowager, cruel mother, innocent servant girl, pleasure-
loving courtesan to the convulsive dreamer, brutal husband, Don
Juanesque lover, Romantic poet, atheistic priest, stoic sage, ambitious
fiancé, amorous parvenu, and awkward would-be poet.

In the two novels of 1832 (and, to a lesser degree, in the fragmentary *Rêveur* of 1830), Sand exploits the theory of spheres as a privileged
device to create a multitude of character types. In *Indiana* each character type is predominantly characterized by a particular speech and
epistolary style. The device works in two ways. As Sand invents the
character's linguistic sphere, she also makes a value judgment about
each one and clarifies for herself which language systems she will val-
orize in her own search for a literary voice.

In *Valentine*, spheres are spatially identified. Sand appropriates
some of Balzac's ideas about the opposition between the Parisian and
the provincial spheres. In this light, Bénédict can easily be defined as a
provincial who has been corrupted by the capital and so brings tragedy
to his life and to Valentine's. In the first half of the novel the reader
constantly watches Valentine and Bénédict cross over from one socially
loaded sphere (the château de Raimbault) to the other (the Lhéry farm-

stead). Then, in the second half, these polarities are replaced by two self-contained spaces—Bénédict's cottage mirrors Valentine's pavilion. Each protagonist thus hopes to create his or her own sphere free of any social determinism, tinged with poetry, and dedicated to artistic pursuit. Against the aristocratic and peasant spheres the two lovers try to erect the dreamer's and the artist's spheres.

Nancy Miller has written convincingly about the meaning of the pavilion in *Valentine*.[56] I should like to situate this structure as an image in the larger framework of Sand's fiction. Since it also appears in *Le Meunier d'Angibault*, as the meeting place for the aristocratic Marcelle and her lower-class lover, Henri Lémor, the building functions as the locus where different spheres can meet without conflict and outside accepted social intercourse. A sanctuary for those caught between two spheres, the pavilion's counterimage is the patriarchal castle: "au château, tous les ennuis, toutes les servitudes, toutes les tristesses . . . au pavillon, tous les bonheurs, tous les amis, tous les doux rêves, l'oubli des terreurs, et les joies pures d'un amour chaste" (*Valentine*, 187; "in the castle, nothing but boredom, servitude, sadness . . . in the pavilion, nothing but happiness, friendship, sweet dreams, terrors forgotten, and the pure joys of a chaste love"). Concealed from sight, the pavilion becomes a "rêveuse and mystérieuse retraite" ("a dreamy and mysterious retreat"), "un lieu de repos et de délices" (185; "a place of rest and delight"), "l'Elysée, le monde poétique, la vie dorée de Valentine" (187; "Valentine's elysium, her poetic realm, her golden life"). Sand uses the exotic synonym, oasis, already a key word in *Indiana*, to express its power: "C'était comme une île enchantée au milieu de la vie réelle, comme une oasis dans le désert" (187; "It was like an enchanted island in the midst of ordinary life, like an oasis in the desert"). The need for a place of retreat, escape, exile—an oasis of safety and pleasure—for the female imagination, which the ending of *Indiana* had already prefigured, becomes a powerful generator of the plot in *Valentine*. The pavilion, ridiculed by Lansac as a "fairy-tale palace" and judged worthless by Lansac's financial advisor, does not survive as a retreat. Sold and destined to be torn down, it no longer can offer asylum to its heroine. The fall of Valentine coincides with the brutal cessation of "les mystères du pavillon" (189). As for the cottage, its status is ambiguous, neither altogether rustic nor quite civilized. Having belonged to Bénédict's parents who farmed the land surrounding it and used it as a farmhouse, it passes to the young heir, who has no such intentions for it. Rather, like the pavilion, it becomes a poetic retreat and a place of study and reflection.

The ending of the book can be seen as a total redistribution of space and as a dislocating of spheres. Valentine loses her fortune and is evicted from her aristocratic sphere, while Athénaïs moves into the chateau to become the new countess of Raimbault.[57] This type of novel, because it focuses on the interaction of separate spheres, depicts a society in flux. Sand constructs a world that is the vivid expression of her world view, her vision of nineteenth-century French society in which nothing was permanent, in spite of the encumberance of opinion and mores. She shows us a society in transition, which can survive only by the exploration of alien spheres, only by the tearing down of the various artificial barriers between classes. The very Rousseau-like ending of *Le Meunier d'Angibault*, in which she will propose her version of Clarens some twelve years later, functions as a broader development of *Valentine*. With no patriarchal power dominating, it is a woman's perspective of a community in which everything is non-hierarchical and shared, where all spheres have merged harmoniously into one. In this novel of 1844 Sand will finally have achieved the reconciliation of opposites.

In turning to *Lélia*, we shall see that the theory of spheres continues to operate, but not so much on a linguistic or spatial level. This most abstract and philosophical of Sand's early novels will isolate five contemporary character types: the splenetic female, the Romantic poet, the stoic gambler, the corrupt priest, and the courtesan. Each character will represent an ideological sphere, each will embody a philosophical position elaborated in the pages of the novel. Gustave Planche, in his "Autopsie de *Lélia*," included in the pages of "Sketches and Hints," was one of the first to recognize and articulate the basic configuration of the various characters. Lélia represents doubt, Trenmor "expiation and stoicism," Sténio "poetry and credulity," Magnus "superstition and repressed desire," Pulchérie "the senses, opposed to Psyche." In the letter where Planche talks about *Lélia* as a duel, he opposes "l'idée Lélia" and "l'idée Sténio": "Lélia stands for disappointment, suffering, a defiant and hardened heart, despair; Sténio stands for hope, trust in the future, love."[58] The two main characters thus become "two personified ideas." In her third novel, Sand plunges further into an extensive analysis of her century's intellectual and religious spheres.

5

Lélia: Novel of the Invisible

A Privileged Novel

Much evidence supports the claim that *Lélia* holds a special place in Sand's oeuvre. To begin with, it is the first novel she signs with her pseudonym as we know it today. With the publication of *Lélia* the writer and the nom de plume "George Sand" merge. To be sure, to her mother and a few early friends, she remained Aurore; and to the French government she was still Aurore Dupin épouse Dudevant. But otherwise, from *Lélia* on, and especially to the author herself, there was only George Sand. Borrowing for a moment the Jungian concept of integration to denote a harmonious personality, and applying it to a case of literary identity, one could say that *Lélia* coincided with the integration of Sand's pseudonymous personality.

Second, *Lélia* represents a high point in an exceptional cycle of works—which includes *Spiridion, Lettres d'un voyageur, Les Sept Cordes de la Lyre,* and *Consuelo*—all of which could be loosely classified as "metaphysical fictions." The nineteenth century, "graced with imagination," as Jean Cassou reminds us,[1] was marked by a richness of new prose genres. Among others, it gave birth to the novel of initiation or, more generally, the "mystical novel," a fictional construct in which the spiritual itinerary of the human mind supplants the more prosaic plot structure based on external events. The abstract quality of *Lélia* is of direct relevance here. Sand herself, in need of a defining category for her novel, called it "a poetic essay," "a fantastic novel."[2] In *Histoire de ma vie* she acknowledged that the novel's dreamlike quality placed it, as she says, in "l'école de Corambé" (2:196). Indeed, the novel was seen by hostile critics as belonging to a new brand of "mystical literature," which, in the words of Alfred Desessarts, was an unhealthy hybrid of *angélisme* and Voltairianism, of the sacred and the sacrilegious: "After a "littérature d'agrément" . . . comes this mystical literature, entirely based on sensations. . . . The body is reduced to a primitive machine. . . . That is the animistic genre."[3] We shall see that the genre of Sand's novel was a major cause for various critical attacks.

Third, the historical record shows that *Lélia* preoccupied its author to an exceptional degree. Ordinarily, to cite Baudelaire, Sand "throws her masterpieces in the mail like letters."[4] And while she had a predilection for making dismissive comments regarding her work, such remarks are curiously absent in reference to *Lélia*. Not only does she discuss it at length, in *Histoire de ma vie*, in *Lettres d'un voyageur*, and in her correspondence, but the usual bantering tone has been replaced by one of deep seriousness. In a letter to François Buloz, dated June 1837, for example, she claims: "Je ne traîterai jamais, *quoi qu'on en die*, cet ouvrage aussi lestement que les autres . . . c'est le seul ouvrage auquel je m'intéresse" (*Corr.*, 4:121; "I will never treat this work, *whatever one may say*, as lightly as the others. . . . It is the only work I take an interest in"). In another letter Sand called *Lélia* "ma meilleure [sic] ouvrage" (3:363; 14 May 1836). Sand's atypical concern for this novel, then, is an invitation to attempt to define its position in her literary corpus. This is all the more so if we remember that, in the few Sand novels existing in two versions (*Indiana, Leone Leoni, Mauprat, Spiridion* are the major examples) only the denouements have been altered. *Lélia* is the only novel to have undergone a complete textual reworking.

Fourth, it is a novel of estrangement, to use a word from the formalist repertoire. That is to say, the novel expresses or reveals a discrepancy between the familiar—in this instance the authorial voice of *Indiana* and *Valentine*—and the quite unknown—the voice/voices of *Lélia*. In this new novel, the narrative voice is one many of Sand's friends did not recognize. It is as if the author of *Indiana* had undergone a metamorphosis. Jules Néraud, among others, expressed astonishment at finding a stranger behind the heroine's narrative voice in *Lélia* instead of his familiar friend:

> "What in the devil is this? . . . Why have you written this book? . . . I knew you to be a dreamer, I *thought* that basically *you were a believer*; but I would never have suspected that you could give such importance to fathoming the secrets of the great *unknown*. . . . Who, then, is the author of *Lélia*? Is it you? No. This character type is a fantasy. It doesn't resemble you. You are cheerful, you dance the bourrée, you appreciate the lepidopteran. . . . You even sew fairly well, and make wonderful jam! It may be . . . That we didn't really know you, and that you cunningly hid your reveries. But is it possible that you could have thought about so many things, pondered so many questions . . . without anyone ever being aware of it?"   (HV, 2:96–97)

Even Pierre Reboul, editor of the standard Garnier edition of *Lélia*, whose introduction to and commentary on *Lélia* is a remarkable demonstration of bad faith and an attempt to dismantle and sabotage Sand's text from within,[5] nevertheless senses a new voice here. Groping for a paradigm to express this, he remarks that *Indiana* and *Valentine* are novels of the heart, while *Lélia* is a novel of the head.[6]

Finally, this is a novel many critics have called "illisible." This accusation of incomprehensibility runs throughout the commentaries of

Lélia. Sainte-Beuve, for instance, who admired the work, nonetheless felt uneasy, puzzled, frightened by it: "There is a side of you (permit me to say this) that I don't know and don't understand very well; that side of you which forces Sténio to say: *Lélia, you frighten me*, [and] which forced me to say the same thing after one evening of reading this: *it's terrifying*."[7] Even Sand did not completely understand her creation: "*Lélia* is a book that is quite obscure, even to me," she writes to the notary N.-H. Cellier-Dufayel, an amateur of literature (*Corr.*, 3:93).

Revealing authorial integration, displaying metaphysical and highly serious qualities, eliciting accusations of estrangement and unintelligibility, *Lélia* is a problematic text deserving of further scrutiny. It is crucial to see *Lélia* as an experimental novel, a novel that introduces new formal strategies—an invisible plot, a labyrinthine structure, a polyphonic narrative—and also as a novel that extends the exploration of new thematic elements of Romantic prose—unheroic heroism and "heroinism," to use Ellen Moers's term, the moral maladies of the century. The novel's exceptional and often strange tone and style are signs of Sand's profoundly innovative theory of fiction. *Lélia* reveals Sand striving toward the formation of a new kind of novel genre, incorporating elements of autobiography or autopsychology, philosophical meditation, confession, Gothic tale, and Bildungsroman. No doubt, this striving in part reflects her awareness of the new hybrid fictional form, the *roman-feuilleton* (the serialized novel). But it also demonstrates Sand's intense intellectual involvement with, and innovative response to, issues that increasingly determined the shape of the nineteenth-century novel. *Lélia*, the most poetic of Sand's novels, then, is also one of the most theoretical in its efforts to articulate a new kind of prose. The critical focus of this chapter is the cerebral character of *Lélia*. The novel's narrative structure is imbedded in the delineation of a theory of the novel, and its subject matter reveals Sand struggling to create a new type of heroine.

Theory of the Invisible Novel

Twenty-five years before Flaubert attempted to write "a novel about nothing," and several years before Stendhal investigated the novel of growing silence in *La Chartreuse de Parme*, George Sand was setting forth the existence of a new type of fiction, whose main quality would not be nothingness or inaudibleness as much as invisibility. In a remarkable article on Senancour's *Obermann* which she published just a few months before *Lélia*, Sand announced the coming of a "new literature," a literature that would replace "le récit des guerres, des entreprises et des passions" ("the narration of wars, historical events, and romances") in favor of narratives about "les intimes souffrances de l'âme humaine dégagées . . . des évènements extérieurs" ("Obermann," 25; "the intimate suffering of the human soul unhampered . . . by exterior events"). Sand is obviously thinking of her own novel when she writes of *Obermann*:

> Le mouvement des intelligences entraînera dans l'oubli la littérature réelle, qui ne convient déjà plus à notre époque. Une autre littérature se prépare et s'avance à grand pas, idéale, intérieure, ne relevant que de la conscience humaine, n'empruntant au monde des sens que la forme et le vêtement de ses inspirations, dédaigneuse . . . de la puérile complication des épisodes, ne se souciant guère de divertir et de distraire les imaginations oisives, parlant peu aux yeux mais à l'âme constamment.   ("Obermann," 42)

> (The direction that creative minds are taking will sweep realistic literature into oblivion, because it is already no longer appropriate for our time. Another kind of literature is imminent and advancing with great strides, ideal, internal, depending only on human conscious, borrowing only from the realm of the senses the form and the cloak of its inspirations, disdainful . . . of childish plot complications, concerned but little to divert or entertain idle imaginations, speaking little to the eyes, but constantly to the soul.)

Indeed, when *Lélia* was first announced in the *Revue des deux mondes*, this essentially invisible subject matter was seen as a revolutionary blow directed at several types of fiction: novels of adventure, with their thick plotting; historical novels à la Walter Scott, with their emphasis on the picturesque (props, costumes, pageantry); and the psychological novel (*Adolphe*, for example), with its exclusive interest in sentiment without regard to the subtler modulations of abstract, mental reflections. The editorial board of the *Revue des deux mondes*, announcing the publication in its pages of a "fragment" of *Lélia*, referred to these prose forms I just mentioned as "poésie purement visible," in opposition to Sand's text of poetic invisibility:

> [In *Lélia*], exterior events are unimportant. The unfolding of events, the complications, the peripeteia, and the unraveling of this mysterious drama are formed and resolved in the folds of human conscious. *Lélia*, we are confident, will provoke a dazzling revolution in contemporary literature and will deal the final blow to purely *visible* poetry.   (*RDM*, 15 May 1833, 2:460)

In the critical debate that followed, those in favor of the work stressed its importance as the manifesto for a new kind of novel. Sainte-Beuve, for example, spoke of *Lélia* as a "lyrical and philosophical novel"; he applauded the "impressive dazzle" of its "new form," and yet added: "This mixture of the real and the impossible, although almost inevitable in a lyrical novel, is somewhat disconcerting."[8]

As early as 1830, Sainte-Beuve had praised E.T.A. Hoffmann for replacing the visible in fiction with the visionary. In his review of *Les Contes nocturnes* for *Le Globe*, he defined Hoffmann's prose as reaching "the limits of perceivable things [up to] the border of the tangible universe."[9] Sand makes frequent references to Hoffmann in the 1830s herself, and it is likely that she had read her friend's review. Sainte-Beuve's remark points to a growing awareness on the part of the critics of the complexities of the contemporary novel and their efforts as a result to formulate new critical concepts and categories to describe the novel's widening sphere better.

Musset, also, in a letter to François Buloz, emphasized the revolutionary impact of *Lélia* on the literary world and presented Sand's novel as the highest and purest representative of the "new literary school":

> *Lélia* is . . . the most important work of the new school. It distinguishes itself by an outstanding quality, the purity of its style, and the originality of its form. . . . None of the thickish threads that bind the plots of modern drama have slipped into the weave of this beautiful fabric.

Musset, however, was reluctant to rally to the cause of the invisible novel. With a characteristically ironic tone, he dismissed such a theory:

> Certain coteries have suggested that *Lélia* was the banner of a mass uprising against realistic literature and that we were dealing with nothing less than *the destruction of the visible novel* [il ne s'agissait de rien moins que de *faire crouler tous les romans visibles*]. . . . We are obliged, in this matter, to declare that we absolutely do not understand questions of this nature.[10]

This "new school" is Musset's shorthand way of referring to the young generation: Hugo, Balzac, Sainte-Beuve, Musset himself, Gautier, Mérimée. But his reference to "certain coteries" specifically designates the group of critics at the *Revue des deux mondes*. In hindsight we have no sense of a "school" beyond the vague appellation of the "Romantic generation," no sense, certainly, of a literary school whose program included the crumbling of so-called visible novels. An important article by Hippolyte Fortoul,[11] however, published in the *Revue encyclopédique* of 1833, helps to lay bare some of the alignments in effect among the young writers of the day. Fortoul identifies two critical camps, one grouped around the *Revue des deux mondes*, a veritable "petite république," as he says;[12] the other assembled at *L'Europe littéraire*. Fortoul takes the word visible as a springboard for his whole discussion of the warfare between these two influential literary journals: "The epithet *visible* came from the *Revue des deux mondes*. It was thrown in the enemy camp like a challenge and a victory" ("De l'art actuel," 127).

The group at *L'Europe littéraire* represents what Fortoul calls "la poésie visible" (here and throughout Fortoul uses the word "poésie" as synonymous with "littérature," including "roman"). It finds its champions in two novelists—Victor Hugo and Prosper Mérimée. Hugo's "formule hiérophantique" in an article for *L'Europe littéraire* of 28 May 1833—"The line drawing, the line drawing! It's the first law of all art!"—provoked Fortoul to comment on Hugo's preference for dressing up his characters rather than probing their psychological depths: "Hugo sees only the change of costumes, and he believes in the fixed identity of passions" ("De l'art actuel," 129).

The critic points to this unrestrained dependence on the visual, to the school's excessive love of pageantry—what we might call their painterly quality—as the Achilles heel of the visible school: "You amuse yourself by describing the costumes of past civilizations . . . by draping fabric over phantoms" ("De l'art actuel," 151).

In the other school of "la poésie intime" at the *Revue des deux mondes*, Sainte-Beuve, Senancour, George Sand, and Musset are concentrating on the depiction of solitary, socially indifferent but spiritually active characters. Their novels do not so much paint a colorful world of costumes and objects; rather they insist on probing the intangible states of being and moral maladies of their contemporaries through the themes of reverie and solitude. Taking as his two primary illustrations *Obermann* and *Lélia* (his discussion of Musset and Sainte-Beuve is extremely scanty), Fortoul criticizes the school's excessive glorification of their characters' individualism and social irresponsibility even as he praises its original and complex insights:

> *Intimist* poetry lacks sociability; it dreams; it does not know how to set anything into action; it fixes its eyes toward heaven or hell; it proceeds in abstractions; it falls asleep in its solitude; it possesses a jealous and rebellious nature.   ("De l'art actuel," 151)

Whereas Fortoul accused the visible school of emphasizing surfaces at the expense of depths, he accuses the "intime" poets of an almost morbid attraction to the ailments of their society, which manifests itself in excessive diagnosis and complete lack of attention to possible remedies. He says to the intimist writers: "You exaggerate the spleen of our time; you lose yourselves in deserts, in ruins, in lakes, and in glaciers" ("De l'art actuel," 151).

Stendhal's *Racine et Shakespeare*; Hugo's "Préface de Cromwell" and the riotous opening night of *Hernani*; Théophile Gautier's "Légende du gilet rouge"; Musset's *Lettres de Dupuis et Cotonet*: these are some of the texts and emblematic events that articulate the ideological positions of French Romanticism for us today and spell out the quarrel between the *anciens*—the classicists, the "Philistines" (Gautier's term)—and the *modernes*—the Romantics, the "Jeune-France"—in the early part of the nineteenth century. We tend to think of Romanticism as a single unified movement. In fact, as Fortoul's article makes quite clear, Romanticism was made up of many small factions that came to be considered as one large and homogeneous literary tendency, even as they were warring against each other. The profound duality of Romanticism articulated by Fortoul seems to be in part ascribed to its English heritage. Like Janus, Fortoul explains, the French Romantic school has two faces—one turned toward Walter Scott, the other toward Byron. The split in this new literary movement needs to be mended, he goes on. Visible poetry lacks soul; intimist poetry needs action. Reconciled, they can produce great works:

> The visible school doesn't have a sense of the present; the intimist school doesn't have the sense of the future. . . . Between those two art forms, and above them, there is room for a more complete art form, one that will affirm the future against the past. . . . Today, prophecy is necessary for all great poetry. ("De l'art actuel," 151)

Remarkably the publication of *Lélia* in late July 1833 precipitated, in a very real sense, the open expression of the simmering hostility between the two groups. The emblematic event of this feud was the duel between Capo de Feuillide, critic for *L'Europe littéraire*, and Gustave Planche of *La Revue des deux mondes*. In August 1833 Capo de Feuillide published two articles containing injurious remarks about *Lélia* and its author.[13] Planche, an habitué of the *mansarde bleue*, found Feuillide's articles to be personally offensive. In a letter of August 25, he challenged him to a duel which took place two days later at the Bois de Boulogne. Neither party was hurt.[14] In his article Fortoul specifically refers to this somewhat ridiculous event and situates it at the heart of the feud between the two literary journals:

> Art today has two different critical schools, *L'Europe litteraire* and *La Revue des deux mondes*; two types that are once again rivals, Walter Scott and Byron; two distinct manifestations of poetry, visible poetry and intimist poetry. You know very well that *these two types of poetry met recently in the Bois de Boulogne, and fired at each other.* (emphasis added; "De l'art actuel," 127)

The appearance of *Lélia*, then—provoking attacks, praise, even a duel—crystallized the literary loyalties of the day. On one side was an imagist school, on the other, an abstract school, now epitomized by Sand herself. We may marvel at Sand's precipitous transformation from a "writer of images" (as apparent in *Histoire du rêveur, Indiana*, and *Valentine*) to a "writer of ideas," as manifest in *Lélia*. To a very real extent she shared this intense concern for formal innovations in prose with Balzac. Interestingly enough, Fortoul does not mention him in his article, perhaps because he was hard pressed to decide in which camp Balzac belonged. On the one hand, 1833 was the year of publication of two of Balzac's important "visible" novels, *Eugénie Grandet* and *Le Médecin de campagne*; on the other, the two preceding years had seen the appearance of two "intime" novels, *La Peau de chagrin* and *Louis Lambert*. In fact, Balzac's philosophical tales, especially *La Peau de chagrin, Louis Lambert*, and *Séraphita*, correspond quite closely to Sand's "Invisible novel," being prose works in which ideas predominate, plots are minimalized, and the characters are ciphers through which certain philosophies can be expressed. Balzac, of course, was too preoccupied with the creation of his mammoth "roman déluge" to take much interest in all this talk about different factions in the Romantic school. But it is worth referring back to his laudatory review of Stendhal's *La Chartreuse de Parme* in the *Revue parisienne* of 1840, in which he also classified the literature of his time into several categories. Although these categories do not quite coincide with those proposed by Fortoul, Balzac did define a predominantly visual and static kind of literature and a predominantly abstract and kinetic school. The writers were classified by Balzac somewhat differently than in Fortoul's scheme. But Balzac's third category of "literary eclecticism" corresponds quite well to Fortoul's call for a synthetic and complete poetry.[15]

Séraphita, begun in 1833 significantly—the same year *Lélia* was published, seems to have been perceived by author and contemporary critics alike as a kind of invisible fiction, revealing some of the same virtues and faults as *Lélia*: use of a poetic prose, literary innovation, an abstract topic almost impossible to translate into fictional form, lack of clarity of expression,[16] an exception work in the corpus of the writer.[17] For Albert Béguin, the eminent Romanticist, *Séraphita* is an exceptional work whose composition represented for its author a literary challenge of the greatest magnitude. Like *Lélia*, which sets standards for the rest of Sand's corpus (Sainte-Beuve wrote to her: "all your novels will be illuminated from above by it"[18]), *Séraphita* marked a watershed: "[*Séraphita* is] the work in which [Balzac] boldly attempted to depict the figure of the human angel. . . . He made a supernatural creature come to life. . . . This creation was . . . a decisive test of his own creative power."[19] Balzac himself described his novel as a transparent work: "It will be the book of souls which seek to lose themselves in infinite images."[20] Elsewhere he compared his effort to translating the immaterial into praxis: "To put meditative poetry into action."[21]

Balzac's three novels and Sand's *Lélia* were sufficiently important to establish a tradition of the nineteenth-century nonrealist novel, subsequently discernible in such works as Nerval's *Aurélia* and Gautier's *Spirite*,[22] and as one of the currents feeding symbolism. Clearly, however, no formal school emerged with the publication of *Lélia*. Sand, like Balzac, was essentially a creator, a searcher after forms and meanings, not a group leader or a founder of literary coteries. Furthermore, both writers went on almost immediately to develop more "visible" novels, in which the real made its reappearance—Balzac with *Goriot*, and Sand with *Quintilia* (a novel, she explained to Sainte-Beuve, "closer to the genre practiced by Walter Scott").[23]

The invisible novel, then, is significant not so much because it spawned a literary school in the formal sense (it did not), nor because it proved to be a dominant prose form (it was not), nor indeed because it articulated a programmatic manifesto for fiction in the manner that Hugo's preface to *Cromwell* did for the theater. Rather, its significance lies in its insistence on the growing seriousness of the novel, on its capacity to be more than pure entertainment, on its ability to compete on an equal basis with philosophical and lyrical forms for subtlety of meaning and complexity of argumentation, and, finally, on its right to demand a new and more sophisticated kind of reader. Gustave Planche's review of *Lélia* stressed all these points:

> *Lélia* is not the ingenious account of an adventure, nor does it describe the dramatic development of a passion. It is the reflection of the present century upon itself, it is the lament of a society in agony. . . . It is therefore not an ordinary novel or poem, and one must not seek episodes in it which excite an idle imagination, or traits of exterior reality which anyone can locate in one's personal life.   (*RDM*, 15 Aug. 1833, 3:353)

Thus the novel's difficulty is deliberately woven into its fictional texture. The incorporeality of the characters and the plotlessness are deliberate stratagems employed to achieve a fiction of the invisible. The critics who supported *Lélia* understood this and concentrated their discussions on the work's form. Those in opposition to the novel, on the other hand, insisted on its moral bankruptcy. "A work displaying shamelessness and cynicism," ranted a critic writing for *Le Petit Poucet*. "*Lélia* is destroying our moral edifice. . . . This book seems dangerous to me," observed Desessarts in *La France littéraire*. "Disgraceful consequence of Saint-Simonianism," wrote Ballanche. Capo de Feuillide's attacks stressed the book's profound immorality ("it is prostitution of the

body and the soul"[24]) and its potential for the spreading of moral disease: "The day you open the pages of *Lélia*, lock yourself up in your
study, so as not to contaminate anyone. If you have a daughter whose
soul you wish to keep virginal and innocent, send her out to play."[25]
While *Lélia*'s significance in the development of the nineteenth-
century French novel has still not been fully established, it obviously
served as a model for a certain type of prose form, based on a new sensibility and a new reader. As Jean Pommier reminds us: "The banner of
literary regeneration in this age of Saint-Simonianism was brandished
by a woman."[26]

It remains to be seen what, in a plotless novel such as *Lélia*, replaced the peripeteia and the denouement. With the usual sequence of
events banished from the fictional space of the novel, what material
did Sand choose to put in its place?

The Character as Abstract Type

Since there is no dominating plot in *Lélia*, the emphasis shifts to the
characters as embodiments of the various ideas that structure the
novel. Thus the book proceeds by abstraction, with each character's
spiritual itinerary presented as the progression of a soul from one abstract state to another. In one of the prefaces, Sand defines her heroines
and heroes as exceptional beings:

> qui passent du désabusement au désespoir, du désespoir au
> doute, du doute à l'ironie, de l'ironie à la pitié et de la pitié à la rés-
> ignation sereine et impassible, au dédain religieux et grave de tout
> ce qui n'est pas Dieu ou la Pensée.[27]

> (who pass from disillusionment to despair, from despair to doubt,
> from doubt to irony, from irony to pity, and from pity to a serene
> and unperturbed resignation, to a religious and solemn disdain of
> everything that is not God or Thought.)

Similarly, the characters, who are neither completely realistic nor
completely allegorical, as Sand notes in the 1839 preface, stand halfway between abstractions and types. In this perspective, the author
convincingly argues that the autobiographical resonances of the novel
are fallacious and irrelevant: "Lélia n'est pas moi et Pulchérie encore
moins. L'une et l'autre sont des passions à l'état abstrait que j'ai essayé
de revêtir de formes humaines" ("I am not Lélia, and I am even less
Pulchérie. [Both are] passions in an abstract state which I have attempted to dress in human form" *Corr.*, 4:345). We are here urged most
vehemently to reject the autobiographical fallacy, according to which a
woman's novel is routinely reduced to an artless transposition of auto-

biographical materials. When Flaubert flatly asserts his identity with his heroine (Madame Bovary, c'est moi"), we automatically resist the possibility. But when Sand just as flatly denies any identity between herself and her heroine (Lélia, ce n'est pas moi"), we are equally loath to accept her disclaimer.[28]

In fact, Sand's multivoiced narrative ceases to appear unstructured or chaotic when apprehended as a polyphonic dialogue between the various dominant tendencies of her generation. As she explains:

> les personnages . . . représentent une fraction de l'intelligence philosophique du 19e siècle: Pulchérie, l'épicuréisme . . . Sténio, l'enthousiasme et la faiblesse d'un temps où l'intelligence monte très haut . . . et tombe très bas, écrasée par une réalité sans poésie . . . Magnus, le débris d'un clergé corrompu ou abruti. . . . Quant à Lélia, . . . [j'ai voulu] en faire la personnification . . . du spiritualisme de ce temps-ci. ("Préface de 1839," *Lélia*, 350)

> (The characters . . . represent a segment of the philosophical intelligence of the nineteenth century: Pulchérie is epicureanism . . . Sténio, the enthusiasm and the weakness of a time when intelligence climbs very high . . . and falls very low, crushed by a reality without poetry . . . Magnus, the remains of a corrupt or stupefied clergy. . . . As for Lélia, . . . [I wanted to] make her the personification . . . of the spiritualism of our age.)

The last sentence is significant. Lélia does not personify spiritualism in general, but the particular brand of her own age. In the text she claims to be telling the "story of an entire generation" (*Lélia*, 167). Thus is revealed Sand's other major intention in the creation of *Lélia*: to invent a fiction whose main character would personify a contemporaneous type. Lélia is an "enfant du siècle" (the formula, as we know, is Sand's); she is a heroine of her time, a character who acutely displays all the symptoms of a new malady, a new specimen of the mal du siècle.

In her article on *Obermann* where she discusses the ailments of the Romantic heroes—Werther, René and Obermann—Sand makes clear that such maladies of the soul, as they pervade society, are also capable of "introducing the germ of a new poetry." ("Obermann," 39) Chateaubriand had already linked illness and literature in his 1805 preface to *Atala*, when he examined the connections between *le vague des passions* and the growing poetic nature of humankind.[29] In the ever-widening "field of observed and poeticized distress," Sand speculates on the appearance of new moral illnesses. One such ailment is a prefiguration of "le mal Lélia":

> Le mal de Werther, celui de René, celui d'Obermann, ne sont pas les seuls que la civilisation nous ait apportés, et le livre où Dieu a

inscrit le compte de ces fléaux n'est peut-être encore ouvert qu'à la première page. Il en est un qu'on ne nous a pas encore officielle-ment signalé . . . c'est la souffrance de la volupté dépourvue de puissance . . . c'est la souffrance énergique, colère, impie, de l'âme qui veut réaliser une destinée, et devant qui toute destinée s'enfuit comme un rêve. . . . C'est l'épuisement et la contrition de la passion désappointée.   ("Obermann," 40)

(The illnesses of Werther, of René, and Obermann are not the only ills that civilization has brought us, and the book where God has inscribed these calamities is perhaps open only to the first page. There is one more that has not been officially reported . . . it is the suffering of voluptuousness deprived of power . . . it is an ener-getic, angry, impious suffering of a soul that wants to realize a des-tiny, and in front of which destiny flees like a dream. . . . It is the exhaustion and contrition of disappointed passion.)

Sand's commentaries about Obermann foreshadow Lélia's pathol-ogy—she is characterized as sexually frigid and spiritually powerless. Her intellectual and sensual impotence are metaphors for the pro-found splenetic basis of her temperament.

Part 3 of the novel, which constitutes Lélia's confession to her sis-ter Pulchérie, spells out in painful detail "la volupté dépourvue de puissance" and "la passion désappointée." Lélia admits that she is re-counting "l'histoire d'un coeur malheureux, égaré par une vaine richesse de facultés, flétri avant d'avoir vécu, usé par l'espérance et rendu *impuissant* par trop de puissance peut-être" (emphasis added; *Lélia*, 163; "the story of an unhappy heart, distracted by a superior yet useless richness of faculties, withered before having lived, worn down by hope, and rendered *powerless* perhaps by too much power"). When Pulchérie reproaches her for not trying to "poeticize things," for apply-ing her superior intelligence to the repudiation of the world and its ac-cepted wisdom, for not concentrating on enjoying life ("jouir"), Lélia responds with a medical diagnosis for an entire generation:

"Et vous avez raison, cruelle . . . c'est mon travers, *c'est mon mal, c'est ma fatalité.* . . . Je . . . m'afflige d'être un type si trivial et si commun de *la souffrance de toute une génération maladive et fai-ble.*"   (emphasis added; *Lélia*, 164)

("You are only too right, cruel sister . . . it is my flaw, *it is my illness, my fatality.* . . . I . . . am distressed to be such a common and trivial representative of *the suffering of an entire sickly and weak generation.*")

Lélia denounces the gap between intellect and action, or, to cite the opposing categories set up in Sand's *Obermann* article, the gap between "energetic . . . impious suffering" and "destiny [that] flees like a dream". In the following passage Lélia lucidly articulates the basic contradiction of her character: on the one hand the power to criticize and to destroy, on the other, a failure to find in herself a life-giving force. About God, she says:

> Ce qui m'indigne et m'irrite contre [Dieu], c'est qu'il m'ait donné *tant de vigueur* pour le combattre et qu'il se tienne si loin de moi; c'est qu'il m'ait départi la *gigantesque puissance* de m'attaquer à lui et qu'il se tienne . . . au-dessus de tous les efforts de ma pensée. (emphasis added; *Lélia*, 164)

> (What makes me indignant and irritated about [God] is that he gave me *so much vigor* with which to combat him, and he holds himself so far from me; that he bestowed on me *gigantic power* to grapple with him and that he holds himself . . . beyond all the efforts of my thought.)

In fact, the main concepts in this confession revolve around illness and powerlessness. The words *puissance* and *impuissance* are the keystones of Lélia's world view: "le désir chez moi était une ardeur de l'âme qui paralysait *la puissance* des sens avant de l'avoir éveillé" (emphasis added; 174; "desire, in me, was an ardor of the soul that paralyzed *the power* of the senses before having aroused it"); "Mon sang se glaçait, *impuissant* et pauvre . . ." (ibid.; "My blood froze, *powerless* and impoverished . . ."); "je m'identifiais avec ces images d'une lutte éternelle entre la douleur et la nécessité, entre la rage et *l'impuissance*" (182; emphasis added; "I identified with those images of an eternal struggle between pain and necessity, between rage and *powerlessness*"); "je ressentis tous les aiguillons de l'inquiétude, des désirs vagues et *impuissants*" (emphasis added; 184; "I felt all the stings of anguish, vague and *powerless* desires"). Lélia's spleen, then, is not so much an expression of what Pierre Reboul calls sarcastically her "spiritual autophagy" (*Lélia*, 185n); rather, it reveals the kinship between Sand's heroine and the world of suffering beings of which Obermann is a privileged example.

More crucial than Senancour's novel for George Sand was the phenomenon of crystallization resulting from her reading which in turn brought about her own commentary on *Obermann*. In her article she not only presented a work she greatly admired to the public, but transcended the model at hand and leaped forward in anticipation of her own novel. Thus this article on Senancour—using *Obermann* as a literary point of departure—can also be seen as a critical reflection on her own novel in progress. Lélia the character is the feminization of a type first presented in *Obermann*. *Lélia* the work represents the feminized study of the moral pathology of the age. Will devoid of power defines what Gustave Planche called Lélia's "noopathologie" [sic], a kind of disfunction of her capacity to come to grips with the realm of knowledge.

This difficult novel, then, articulated a style that is simultaneously *at* the service and *in* the image of a new subject, the delineation of the newest mal de siècle in the feminine. "La maladie fait le livre," Sand will remark when rewriting *Lélia* (*Corr.*, 3:474; "The illness makes the book"). Subject and form in this novel are intimately linked. To the illness of the soul, as abstract and elusive as a subject can be, correspond Sand's theories of a fiction of the invisible. Reconsidered in this new light, *Lélia* becomes a properly readerly (*lisible*) text.[30]

An Enterprise in Polyphony

"voilà qu'un lien sacré est établi entre nous . . . que je n'ai plus le droit de dénouer"

LÉLIA

("a sacred bond has now been established between us . . . which I no longer have the right to untie.")

A close scrutiny of the narrative structure of *Lélia* reveals to what extent it differs fundamentally from Sand's two preceding novels and *Histoire du rêveur*. As we saw in Chapter 3, *Indiana* begins *in medias res*, with a tableau vivant depicting the heroine, Delmare, and Ralph in a moment of sullen repose. The reader's entrance into this fictional world is made secure on at least two counts. First, a traditional masculine third-person narrator clearly sets up the temporal and spatial framework of the text at the outset and in the very first page introduces three of the five main characters. Second, this initial scene, by virtue of its thematic link with and stylistic similarity to Chateaubriand's fictions of the *mal-du-siècle*, places the reader on familiar ground. She or he encounters a familiar, recognizable cast of actors evolving in a specific, apprehendable chronotope.

The beginning of *Valentine* follows a different but just as distinctive model. An anonymous traveler-narrator (grammatically defined as "il") gradually identifies the site and time of the novel. Like a camera zoom lens, his eyes focus on an increasingly restricted and detailed sphere: from a broad landscape, the southeastern region of the Berry, to a smaller portion of it, the Vallée noire, and then to the smallest part of all, the Lhérys' farm, Grangeneuve. The reader knows precisely where and when the story begins, and quickly is ushered into a room of the farm to encounter two of the four main characters—Athénaïs and Bénédict—suspended in an emblematic fragment of time. By depicting each of the heroes in a characteristic gestural and psychological state, the tableau vivant expresses each character's private world in microcosm. Athénaïs is primping in front of the mirror, the epitome of a silly, vain, and empty-headed girl; her fiancé, slouching negligently on the couch, watches her with a sardonic look on his face. The coquettish airs of the one and the ironic position of the other provide a clue to the calamitous denouement of their engagement and starts the novel off on a *note grinçante*. The scene also anchors the reader firmly to a fictional world, easy to visualize.

The topos of the narrator-traveler who introduces a fictional world by walking his reader through the landscapes of the text is a common device of the nineteenth-century novel. Balzac often begins this way, as in *Eugénie Grandet* or *Le Médecin de campagne*, for example. In Stendhal's *La Rouge et le noir*, the approach to Verrières is effected by a narrator-traveler who drops out of sight as soon as the reader has been introduced to all the significant facts and inhabitants of the small town. Even much later in the century, Zola uses the device in *Germinal*.

The case of *Lélia*, however, is anomalous. Sand's third novel breaks radically with the fictional forms of her two preceding novels. Its narrative structure seems to have no literary model, nor does it participate very actively in any narrative tradition either before or after 1833. As a result, the novel's opening strikes the reader as a troubling terra incognita. No third-person narrator (male or female) starts off the tale; no tableau vivant informs the reader; no clearly delineated time and space component is provided. With respect to its narrative form, its chronotopic specificity, and its character presentation, *Lélia* presents a baffling enigma to the reader.

The novel begins with a disembodied and unidentified voice asking a question to an unknown interlocutor:

> "Qui es-tu? et pourquoi ton amour fait-il tant de mal? Il doit y avoir en toi quelque affreux mystère inconnu aux hommes. A coup sûr tu n'es pas un être pétri du même limon et animé de la même vie que nous! Tu es un ange ou un démon, mais tu n'es pas une créature humaine." (*Lélia*, 7)

> ("Who are you? And why does your love hurt so much? There must be in you some horrible mystery unknown to men. Surely you are not a being molded from the same clay and animated with the same life-force as we are! You are an angel or a demon, but you are not a human creature.")

Only in the tenth sentence of the text is the "tu" identified as feminine ("Toi si belle et si pure!" "You, so beautiful and pure!"); only in the second paragraph is the feminine "tu" identified as Lélia ("Et, cependant, Lélia, il y a en toi quelque chose d'infernal"; "And yet, Lélia, there is

something infernal in you"). Some six pages later another voice inter-
venes, addressing a "jeune poète"; and only four pages after that is the
young poet given the name of Sténio. These floating texts are letters,
the reader comes to realize, and they continue for nearly thirty pages,
comprising twelve short chapters to form what Gustave Planche called
the duel between Sténio and Lélia. There is no attempt in the text at
localization—the reader does not know who the people are, or where
and when they are writing to each other. The content of their letters
does not offer information as much as lyrical exclamations and dreamlike meditations.

The epistolary form of these early pages is used deliberately to
obscure the typology of characters and the setting of the novel. With
no dates, no place names, no addresses, the letters constitute a free-
floating dialogue between an elusive enigmatic heroine and her enthusiastic and naive admirer. Unlike the eighteenth-century epistolary
model, in which all efforts are made to help the reader make sense of
the situation, these pages exploit the form but subvert any attempt at
elucidation.

Chapter 13 abruptly terminates the epistolary mode by providing
the baffled reader with two paragraphs of third-person narration and a
fixed locale and time: a lake and the last hours of the day. "Le lac était
calme ce soir-là, calme comme les derniers jours de l'automne" (*Lélia*,
37; "The lake was calm that evening, as calm as on the last days of
autumn"). Rather than provide a clearly identified time/space component, the sentence emphasizes the Romantic charge of such a chronotope. The lake is a favorite site of Romantic reveries—a metaphor for
the rhythm of the reverie itself. Beginning with Rousseau and continuing on with Lamartine's poetry and Stendhal's prose, the lake represents the site of solitary meditation, or of amorous discourse. The end
of the day and its comparison to the last days of autumn conjure up
images of Chateaubriand's *René* and *Mémoires d'outre-tombe*, where autumn and evening are designated as the Romantics' preferred season
and time of day. Thus the narrator's clue points to a thematic link with
Sand's Romantic predecessors more than it provides specific information on the novel's time and place. The lake's exact location is not given;
we do not know what year this is taking place. The third-person narration, here, does little to assist in the reader's orientation. Furthermore,
the text quickly plunges back into dialogue, this time between the poet
and a new character, the ex-gambler and ex-convict Trenmor. Dialogue
rapidly develops into monologue, with Trenmor's confession dominating the rest of the chapter.

Chapter 14 contains a few lines of third-person narration, but is
overpowered by a dialogue between Sténio and Trenmor. This episode
contains the famous emblematic scene where the heroine, dressed in
male attire and seen through the eyes of the two male protagonists,

comes down an elegant and majestic staircase. This is the only time in the novel when the reader is given a full-length portrait of Lélia. Replacing the juxtaposition of invisible and fragmented instances of the characters' mental lives which the novel thus far has offered, a visible tableau at last is painted for the reader to contemplate:

> elle avait le vêtement austère et pourtant recherché, la pâleur, la gravité, la regard profond d'un jeune poète d'autrefois. . . . Les cheveux noirs de Lélia . . . laissaient à découvert ce front où le doigt de Dieu semblait avoir imprimé le sceau d'une mystérieuse infortune. . . . Le manteau de Lélia était moins noir, moins velouté que ses grands yeux couronnés d'un sourcil mobile. La blancheur mate de son visage et de son cou se perdait dans celle de sa vaste fraise et la froide respiration de son sein impénétrable ne soulevait pas même le satin noir de son pourpoint et les triples rangs de sa chaîne d'or.[31]

> (She had the austere and yet refined clothing, the palor, the solemnity, the deep gaze of a young poet from bygone days. . . . Lélia's dark hair . . . left uncovered that forehead where God's touch seemed to have imprinted the seal of a mysterious ill-fated destiny. . . . Lélia's coat was less black, less velvety than her large eyes, crowned by expressive brows. The mat pallor of her face and neck was lost in the whiteness of her large ruff, and the calm breathing of her impenetrable breast did not even stir the black satin of her doublet and the triple rows of her gold chain.)

The dominant impression is one of austerity and regal composure. Lélia is painted here in black and white, in coldness and silence. She seems fixed in her immobility, frozen, inhuman. She neither speaks nor moves. There is no visible sign of emotion on her face. The objective and direct surface portrait of the heroine is probed by Trenmor. He penetrates the opaque image of Lélia and provides the reader with a perplexing interpretation:

> "Regardez Lélia . . . Peut-on imaginer quelque chose de plus complet que Lélia vêtue, posée et rêvant ainsi? C'est le marbre sans tache de Galatée, avec le regard céleste du Tasse, avec le sourire sombre d'Alighieri. C'est l'attitude aisée et chevaleresque des jeunes héros de Shakespeare: c'est Roméo . . . c'est Hamlet . . . c'est Juliette . . . Le jeune Raphaël devait tomber dans cette contemplation extatique, lorsque Dieu lui faisait apparaître une virginale idéalité de femme. Corinne mourante devait être plongée dans cette morne attention lorsqu'elle écoutait ses derniers vers déclamés au Capitole par une jeune fille. Le page muet et mystérieux de Lara se renfermait dans cet isolement dédaigneux de la foule. Oui, Lélia réunit toutes ces idéalités, parce qu'elle réunit le

génie de tous les poètes, la grandeur de tous les héroïsmes. Vous pouvez donner tous ces noms à Lélia . . ."   (*Lélia*, 45–46)

("Look at Lélia . . . Can one imagine anything more complete than Lélia dressed, posed, and dreaming in this way? She is Galatea's spotless marble, with Tasso's divine gaze, and Alighieri's somber smile. She has the carefree, chivalrous attitude of Shakespeare's young heroes: she is Romeo . . . she is Hamlet . . . she is Juliet . . . The young Raphael must have fallen into such an ec-static contemplation, when God made a virginal, ideal woman ap-pear before him. The dying Corinne must have been plunged into this bleak state, as she heard her last verses being recited at the Capitol by a young girl. Lara's silent and mysterious page must have locked himself in such a disdainful isolation from the crowd. Yes, Lélia brings together all these idealities, because she brings to-gether the genius of all poets, and the grandeur of all heroism. You can give all these names to Lélia . . .")

Thus the portrait of Lélia, fixed in its specificity for the first time, is im-mediately dismantled in favor of a kaleidoscopic series of changing identities. Lélia is not Lélia, she is in turn a Greek statue, a heroine from Tasso and Dante, both Romeo and Juliet, Hamlet, the painter Raphael himself, Mme de Staël's heroine, a Byronic hero. She under-goes not only a change of face but several gender transformations. The result is that the reader cannot *visualize* such a diversity of faces as be-longing to a single character. What can a character who simultaneously resembles Romeo *and* Juliet possibly look like? The reader's inability to fix Lélia's face in spite of the description of her poised at the top of the staircase points to another instance of the author's deliberate disrup-tion of the reader's normal expectations when encountering a fictional world. Although two sites have been described—a lake (in Italy, no doubt) and an Italian ball (site unknown), although three characters have been introduced, the reader is still unsure about the shape of this novel.

Chapters 15 to 20 return to the epistolary form with letters being written and sent three ways. Lélia writes to both Sténio and Trenmor, they both write to her but not to each other. Once again, these letters are less concerned with events than with impressions about a char-acter—in this case, Sténio. Just as before Lélia was fragmented into several identities, so now Sténio is described through the eyes of Lélia and then Trenmor, thus constructing a highly incongruous character. Again, the reader senses the author's subversion of expectations, in the uncertain plot, the imprecise chronotope, and the problematic identity of the heroes.

The final section of Part 1—Chapters 21 and 22—presents a

change of narration once again. Some interventions are made by a third-person narrator, but dialogue makes up most of the text. Lélia, dying of cholera,[32] is deep in conversation with four characters—Trenmor, Sténio, doctor Kreyssneifetter, and the priest Magnus. The scene's lack of verisimilitude points to the author's indifference to the mimetic aspect of her text; something else preoccupies her here. The scene categorically avoids depicting a case of cholera realistically. Reboul, in his commentary, is only too glad to pick up the "invraisemblances," but he misses the point. Lélia is blue, the diagnosis is "choléra-morbus," and everyone expects her to die, and yet in the philosophical dialogue that ensues, Lélia probes the moral bankruptcy of medicine and the church, as embodied in Kreyssneifetter and Magnus. In spite of her color and convulsions followed by catalepsy, Lélia is seemingly well enough to mock the two helpless aides at her side; neither the medical man nor the Christian can save her:

> "Voilà donc . . . à quoi tient votre force? La faiblesse d'autrui fait votre puissance; mais dès qu'on vous résiste, vous reculez et vous avouez en riant que vous jouez un faux rôle parmi les hommes, charlatans et imposteurs que vous êtes. Hélas, Trenmor, où en sommes-nous? Où en est le siècle? Le savant nie, le prêtre doute. Voyons si le poète existe encore." (*Lélia*, 67)

> ("Is this where your strength lies? The weakness of others gives you your power; but when someone resists you, you retreat and laughingly admit that you are acting out a false role among men, charlatans and imposters that you are. Alas, Trenmor, what has become of us? What has become of our century? The scientist denies, the priest doubts. Let us see if the poet still exists.")

Lélia's challenge to Sténio provokes him into making a poetic declaration that turns out to be the best remedy of all. Lélia sends Trenmor away: "ton calme m'attriste et me décourage" (68; "your self-composure saddens and discourages me"), and the scene ends in a dialogue between the poet and the invalid. "Sténio," remarks Lélia, "a relevé mon âme" ("Sténio has uplifted my soul").

The scene thus describes a confrontation of four ideologies offered to and judged by the central female character. Lélia, whose blue illness is a metaphor for her despair, is paralyzed by her incapacity to act in the world, to participate in society. She asks each bearer of a given philosophy or discipline to provide her with answers about life. She rejects Trenmor's stoicism along with Kreyssneifetter's scientific rationalism and Magnus's intolerant religious fanaticism, however, in favor of Sténio's apology of poetry. The five voices of the five characters come together and wage a battle in this most polyphonic of Sand's scenes. Poetry's seeming victory suggests that literature may be the solution to Lélia's spleen. Might we have here a clue to Lélia's malady? Might she be a character who is an author in search of a voice?

Thus ends Part 1 of this novel. I have chosen to dwell on its narrative construction because it is indicative of the rest of the text. What we find throughout, although more pronounced in this early portion of the book, is a text predominantly shaped into dialogues, monologues, epistolary missives, confessions, poetic outbursts, philosophical statements, with a minimum of third-person narrative control. Sand's here-to-fore familiar (male) narrator, who shaped the raw materials of the fabula in *Indiana* and *Valentine*, has disappeared in *Lélia*, and is not replaced by a unique, dominant, controlling narrative voice. The reader is hard pressed to identify the novel's major narrator. The evidence suggests that in this novel Sand was searching for an innovative narrative structure.

As I established in Chapter 2, Sand's narrators tend to be male and to use a standard third-person narration. All the novels immediately preceding and following *Lélia* follow this pattern, with the exception of *Lettres d'un voyageur* and *Leone Leoni* (with first-person male narrators) and *Jacques* (an epistolary novel).

As a text dominated by several voices, both feminine (Lélia and Pulchérie) and masculine (Sténio, Trenmor, Magnus), *Lélia* appears to be a singular exception in Sand's corpus. Furthermore, the (disembodied) third-person narrator occupies very little textual space: almost none, as we saw, in Part 1; somewhat more in Part 2 (21 out of approximately 85 pages of the edition cited); none in Part 3 (which consists of Lélia's confession to Pulchérie); approximately 4 out of 31 pages in Part 4. Only Part 5 is a more traditional form with a controlling narrator introducing the action, directing the events, and concluding the story. Thus, *Lélia* can be said to be a particularly apt instance of what Bakhtin called a polyphonic novel, a fiction that can be "broken down into a series of disparate, contradictory philosophical stances, each defended by one or another character." Such a multiplicity of points of view leaves the reader with the impression that "one is dealing not with a *single* author-artist . . . but with a number of philosophical statements by *several* author-thinkers."[33] Although Bakhtin's words are meant to describe the specificity of Dostoevsky's novels, his commentary admirably suits *Lélia* (a text which, as I have discovered, inspired Dostoevsky, as did *Spiridion*).

Lélia, with its quadruple confession and profession of faith, with its multiple narrators, with its lack of a monologic superstructure, is a brilliant precursor to the nineteenth-century novel of ideas, epitomized by the Russian novelists of the second half of the century. Trenmor's spiritual itinerary, from an overpowering passion for gambling to a philosophy halfway between pagan stoicism and Christian quietism, competes with Sténio's passionate allegiance first to the poetic realm, and then to epicureanism. Pulchérie's philosophy of the flesh is counterbalanced by Lélia's espousal of frigidity both as a sexual and existential code. The four "author-thinkers" confront, wage battle, and at times overpower each other, in a state of relative narrative equilibrium, although, in all fairness, Lélia's discourse—as the synthesizer—occupies the most textual space. Bakhtin claimed that Dostoevsky was the first to articulate the full range of polyglossia, of multivoicedness. I would suggest that Sand, with *Lélia*, is an admirably fitting precursor and foremother.

The Ideological Core of Lélia

An experimental novel, a polyphonic novel, *Lélia* also articulates an ideological testament through the heroic-heraldic main character.[34] Chapter 28 of Part 2, entitled "Dans le désert," and Chapter 29 "Solitude," are central for the expression of Lélia's world view.

> "Je vous ai amenée dans cette vallée déserte que le pied des troupeaux ne foule jamais, que la sandale du chasseur n'a point souillée. Je vous y ai conduite, Lélia, à travers les précipices. Vous avez affronté sans peur tous les dangers de ce voyage." (*Lélia*, 102)

> ("I have brought you to this deserted valley where flocks have never tread, where the hunter's sandal has never trespassed. I have brought you here, Lélia, across precipices. You have confronted all the dangers of this journey without fear.")

Thus begins the chapter in which Sténio and Lélia pursue their verbal duel. The narrative insists on a spatial break with the preceding chapters; the action now unfolds in a deserted place. To get here, the heroes have had to cross waterfalls and pass over "des gouffres qui vomissent l'écume à pleins bords" (103; "chasms overflowing with foam"). Here is a curious echo of Indiana and Ralph's dilemma. But while the latter speak parallel languages and discover together the same desire for life, Sténio and Lélia are locked in a dialogue of opposites which does not lead to harmony but rather confirms for the reader the unbridgeable ideological gap between them. Still, Sand often sends her heroes away from society on symbolic journeys to secluded landscapes so that spiritual rejuvenation can take place.

The motif of the desert—a standard topos of hagiographic writing—emphasizes here Lélia's removal from the world and presents itself as a privileged locus of meditation. This is the heroine's second retreat into the desert, where she once again willingly endures a "claustration volontaire" and gives herself over to the furors of her imagination (118, 119). In this episode Lélia at first turns outward and, like a prophet, offers a prognosis of her century; then, turning inward, she examines and verbalizes the rich dream world generated by her sickly brain ("cerveau malade," 203). The notion of virgin territory defines the Romantic landscape par excellence. It expresses the Romantic predilection for wilderness (a nonexistent word in French; the closest approximation is, significantly, *désert*), just as it offers the promise of possible new vistas of understanding. Finally, the desert metonymically expresses Lélia's isolation from the world. In the chapter entitled "Solitude," Lélia is left behind to ponder and to dream. She apprehends solitude as a lightness of being: "A mesure que Sténio s'éloignait, je sentais le poids de la vie s'alléger sur mes épaules" (122; "As Sténio withdrew, I felt the weight of life being lifted from my shoulders"). The heroine's euphoria at finding herself entirely alone in an open place constitutes what one might call a case of agoraphilia. As she confesses to Trenmor:

> "Tout ce que vous m'avez dit du calme enchanteur révélé à vous après les orages de votre vie, je l'ai senti en me trouvant seule enfin, absolument seule entre la terre et le ciel. Pas une figure humaine dans cette immensité; pas un être vivant dans l'air ni sur les monts." (*Lélia*, 124)

> ("I recognized the validity of everything that you had told me about the entrancing calm revealed to you after the storms of your life, when I finally found myself alone, absolutely alone between the earth and the sky. Not a single human figure in this immensity; not one living being in the air or in the mountains.")

Lélia represents the epitome of the solitary woman. As much as her frank avowal of sexual frigidity and her declaration that marriage makes women into slaves, this fact of Lélia's life was shocking for the period. The solitary woman represented the antithesis of the chaperoned woman, the antithesis of the protected female, under the guardianship of a parent or a husband. Since Rousseau, literature had provided numerous portraits of the solitary hero as *promeneur*, traveler, recluse. But Lélia is the first female character (with the possible exception of Corinne) to embody successfully the Romantic urge for solitude. For the critic Fortoul, *Lélia* is the culmination of Sand's study of the solitary woman initiated in *Indiana* and continued in *Valentine*. Commenting on *Obermann* in relation to Sand's work, he says:

> A solitary man is an anomaly, but a possible one. . . . I understand therefore the abstract concept of a man situated outside society; I

absolutely cannot grasp what a woman outside of society en-
tails. . . . A solitary woman, this concept makes no sense.   ("De
l'art actuel," 138)

But here is a writer who has accomplished the impossible. Where Senancour had failed, in the character of Isabelle, to create a kind of female
Obermann, Sand has invented a heroine who plausibly embodies
many of the Romantic characteristics here-to-fore reserved for male
characters. By fashioning the first convincing portrait of "une pro-
meneuse solitaire," Sand takes up where Senancour left off: "We can
suppose that Mme Dudevant wanted primarily to add her observations to the notion of the couple in the Obermann manner. Lélia, this
poor, disembodied soul, has effectively resolved the problem of the
solitary woman" ("De l'art actuel," 144). The "désert," then, has a triple significance—religious, Romantic, and emblematic, expressing
Lélia's situation in the world.

Lélia's Night Thoughts

Lélia is a case study of Romantic hagiography in which the novel's arid
landscape, rather than symbolizing a holy retreat to the desert leading
to revelation, echoes instead the heroine's inner aridity. Because no fertile soil nourishes the character, because no life-giving light and water
bathe the text, the landscape sketches the mental gloom and despair of
its heroine. In the chapter entitled "Contemplation," first published in
the *Revue des deux mondes* (1 Dec. 1836) and added to the version of
1839, Lélia uses the metaphor of a bleak landscape to express her own
sense of metaphysical frustration:

> Autrefois il n'était pas de caverne assez inaccessible, pas de lande
> assez inculte, pas de place assez stérile pour exercer la force de mes
> pieds et l'avidité de mon cerveau. . . . Je guettais l'avalanche et ne
> trouvais jamais qu'elle eût assez labouré de neige, assez balayé de
> sapins, assez retenti sur les échos effrayés des glaciers. L'orage ne
> venait jamais assez vite et ne grondait jamais assez haut. J'eusse
> voulu pousser de la main les sombres nuées et les déchirer avec
> fracas. J'aurais voulu assister à quelque déluge nouveau, à la chute
> d'une étoile, à un cataclysme universel.   (*Lélia* II, 2:106)

> (In the past, there was no cave inaccessible enough, no moor wild
> enough, no place sufficiently barren for me to exercise the strength
> in my feet and the boundless thirst in my brain. . . . I waited for
> the great avalanche in vain: I never felt that the snow crashed
> down as it should have, that it mowed down enough pine trees,
> that it resounded enough, echo upon frightening echo, over the
> glaciers. The tempest never came swiftly enough, and never

roared loud enough. I wanted to push apart the somber clouds with my hand and rend them violently asunder. I longed to witness a new flood, or a falling star, or a universal cataclysm.)

In this description the biblical resonance of the heroine's imagery and vocabulary is at the service of a secular mal du siècle rather than a sign of Lélia's religiosity. The tropes of sterility and the eschatological desire for an apocalypse are expressions of the character's death instincts. The controlling feature is an aggressive sense of barrenness whereby Lélia's rageful sterility is expressed.

In the 1833 version of *Lélia*, Part 3 constitutes Lélia's confession to Pulchérie, in which she describes her retreat in an abandoned monastery. In this novel perhaps more than in any other, the nocturnal landscape (familiar to Sand's readers since *Histoire du rêveur*) is depicted as the antithesis of the pastoral. Lélia focuses her attention on the nights of her retreat, thus encouraging the reader to subtitle this portion of the novel "Les Nuits de Lélia." Her meditations, framed by sunsets and sunrises, unfold entirely under "le régime nocturne" of the imagination:

"Quand [le soleil] avait disparu lentement derrière les insaisissables limites de l'horizon, des brumes bleuâtres, légèrement pourprées, montaient dans le ciel et la plaine noire ressemblait à un immense linceul étendu sous mes pieds . . . il n'y avait d'autre bruit, dans cette profondeur sans bornes, que celui d'un ruisseau frémissant parmi les grès, le croassement des oiseaux de proie et la voix des brises enfermées et plaintives sous les cintres du cloître." (182)

("When [the sun] had finally disappeared beyond the elusive limits of the horizon, bluish, faintly purple mists rose in the sky and the black plain resembled a gigantic shroud stretched out at my feet . . . there was no other sound in that limitless depth than the sound of a brook gurgling among the sandstone, the croaking of predatory birds, and the voice of the breezes trapped and plaintive beneath the arches of the cloister.")

Lélia's words point to the devastating effects that nocturnal solitude exercises on her mind. The image of the shroud, the bird of prey, the sinister black plain are metonymic markers of her despair. Her delirious descent into a personal hell and the "dérèglement" (193) of her mental faculties are the very antithesis of the nocturnal epiphanies that crown *Histoire du rêveur* and *Indiana*. The former had culminated with the dreamer's discovery of the nocturnal word. In the latter the Bernica Falls provided a nocturnal decor symbolic of the characters' rejuvenation, so that the darkness at the beginning of the initiation scene made possible their entrance into the light. But the Gothic phase emblematized by *Lélia* and *Spiridion*, in which the night desert constitutes the privileged place of meditation, emphasizes only the nightmarish terror that emerges from a character's confrontation with the nocturnal. During the second winter, Lélia again measures time by the nights she spends in mental agony:

> "Assise dans l'embrasure de ma fenêtre, je voyais la lune s'élever lentement . . . et reluire sur les aiguilles de glace qui pendaient aux sculptures dentelées des cloîtres. Ces nuits froides et brillantes avaient un caractère de désolation, dont rien ne saurait donner l'idée. Quand le vent se taisait, un silence de mort planait sur l'abbaye. . . . On eût pu secouer toutes les ronces desséchées qui garnissaient les cours, sans y éveiller un seul être animé, sans entendre siffler une couleuvre ou ramper un insecte." (192)

> ("Sitting in the casement of my window, I saw the moon rise slowly . . . and begin to gleam on the icicles hanging from the intricate sculptures of the cloister. Those bright cold nights had a desolate character such as nothing else could begin to suggest. As the wind subsided, a deathly silence reigned over the abbey. . . . One could have shaken all the dried-up thorn bushes that decorated the courtyards and not wake a single living being, or hear the hiss of any serpent or the stirring of any insect.")

The scene is filtered through a prism of negativity—the animate is a snake or an insect; the wind is described only through its opposite—a deathlike stillness; the only plants mentioned are thorns. The entire landscape is a harbinger of desolation and profound melancholy. In keeping with the nocturnal structure Lélia gives to her confession, her final night in the desert is circumscribed by a brutal spring storm. But whereas, before, the nocturnal terror was mirrored in Lélia's soul, here nature creates a violent, even passionate mood that contrasts with the heroine's inner numbness and cynical indifference:

> "tout semblait contristé, fatigué, brisé; moi seule j'étais paisiblement assise au milieu de mes livres, occupée de temps en temps à suivre d'un oeil nonchalant la lutte terrible des grands ifs contre la tempête et les ravages de la grêle sur les jeunes bourgeons des sureaux sauvages." (197)

> ("Everything seemed saddened, exhausted, broken; I alone sat there calmly, among my books, from time to time observing with an indifferent eye the violent struggle of the great yew trees against the storm and the ravages of the hail on the young wild elder shoots.")

This description stresses Lélia's pessimistic and rigidly binary world view: the antithesis of violent spleen is not a sense of harmonious inner serenity, but a feeling of deathlike lethargy, a parody of the sought-for religious sense of peace. Violence in this case can only be counteracted by apathy. While in this instance, inner and outer landscape are contrasted, the contrast is between two negative poles: "Ceci . . . est l'image de ma destinée, le calme au fond de ma cellule, l'orage et la destruction au-dehors" (197; "This . . . is the image of my destiny; serenity in the depth of my cell, destruction outside").

Although the symbolic resonance of Lélia's nocturnal ruminations is strongly hagiographic—the desert is the locus of mystical retreat just as the night is the preferred hour for religious meditation— the result of her pilgrimage to the desert presents a total reworking of the hagiographic motif. Sand's heroine emerges from her monastery more dissatisfied and more splenetic than ever before. When, at the end of Chapter 29, the heroine renounces her retreat in favor of a return to society, it is with the double realization that solitude is an inner state of being, "pour moi la solitude est partout et c'est folie que de la chercher au désert plus qu'ailleurs" (132; "for me solitude is everywhere, and it is madness to seek it in the desert as opposed to anywhere else"), and that she needs the sensation of suffering, like a drug, in order to feel alive. The "peaceful desert" offers no final solution to Lélia's spleen:

> "J'ai découvert . . . ce qui me soutient encore dans cette vie de désenchantement et de lassitude: c'est la souffrance. La souffrance excite, ranime, irrite les nerfs; elle fait saigner le coeur, elle abrège l'agonie. C'est la convulsion violente, terrible, qui nous relève de terre et nous donne la force de nous dresser vers le ciel pour maudire et crier."   (132)

> ("I have discovered . . . what sustains me in this life of disenchantment and lassitude: it is suffering. Suffering excites, revives, irritates the nerves; it causes the heart to bleed, it shortens agony. It is the violent and terrible convulsion that lifts us up from the earth and gives us the strength to turn toward the sky with curses and cries.")

In her speech, with its frenetic overtones, Lélia renounces quietism in favor of a convulsive delirium. Like her spiritual pre-romantic brothers, René, Obermann, and Werther, Lélia finds no cure for her metaphysical ailment. Whereas the retreat was beneficial for Ralph and Indiana, the desert here only marks a period of hallucinatory repose in Lélia's fruitless quest. She laments in her epistolary monologue to

Trenmor: "Pour moi, rien au désert, rien parmi les hommes, rien dans la nuit, rien dans la vie" (125–126; "For me, nothing in the desert, nothing among men, nothing in the night, nothing in life"). This nihilism, with its nocturnal emphasis, echoes a passage of "Sketches and Hints," in which Sand, talking about herself in the masculine, exclaims: "Rien, rien! pas la face [d'un] ange, pas un rêve du ciel durant nos tristes nuits, pas une voix, pas une ombre dans ces ténèbres" (OA, 2:604; "Nothing, nothing! not the face [of an] angel, not a dream from heaven during our sad nights, not a voice, not a shadow in this darkness"). Lélia's negative language also links her to Bénédict and his refusal to *be* anything in French society ("Je ne veux *rien* être dans cette belle France").[35] If Lélia can be said to be a psychological double of the author, this negative discourse is a most significant link.

The Novel of a Generation

In Chapter 28, "Dans le désert," Lélia, like Count Altamira of *Le Rouge et le noir*, sets out to define the dominating characteristics of her society. In her meditations on the nineteenth century, she sees first and foremost an age of inertia: "L'inertie, Sténio! c'est le mal de nos coeurs, c'est le grand fléau de cet âge du monde" (*Lélia*, 103; "Inertia, Sténio, is the illness of our hearts, the great curse of our time"). Stendhal depicted restoration France as a society drained of its energy; so Lélia, uncovering the same symptoms, points to the emblematic event of the duel as "un spectacle fait pour constater l'apathie du siècle" ("a spectacle that records the apathy of the century").[36] Psychic inertia leads inexorably to moral indifference: "nous ne sommes plus ni bons ni méchants, nous ne sommes même plus lâches, nous sommes inertes" (104; "we are no longer good or bad, we are not even cowards, we are inert").

For Lélia, the apathy of her age is symptomatic of an old, decrepit world on the verge of collapse: "le colosse [i.e. le monde] vieillit et s'affaisse; il chancelle maintenant comme une ruine qui va crouler pour jamais" (115; "the colossus [i.e. the world] is getting old and is on the verge of collapsing: it now staggers, like a wreck that will soon crumble for good"). Anthropomorphism gives force to her analysis. The mal du siècle is seen as a direct reflection of the age of the world. Against Sténio's optimistic view of the progressive march of history, Lélia sees only the great law of time which dictates that everything is headed for an apocalypse: "Ne voyez-vous pas Sténio, que le soleil se retire de nous? La terre fatiguée dans sa marche ne dérive-t-elle pas sensiblement vers l'ombre et le chaos" (120; "Don't you see, Sténio, that the sun is pulling away from us? The earth, tired in its course, is perceptibly drifting toward shadow and chaos"). In a powerful passage on the end of the world, Sand uses the metaphor of frigidity to express simultaneously the slowing of time, the paralysis of body and soul, the increasing impotence of men and women in the world:

> "Oh le froid! ce mal pénétrant qui enfonce des aiguilles acérées dans tous les pores . . . ce mal à la fois physique et moral qui envahit l'âme et le corps, qui pénètre jusqu'aux profondeurs de la pensée et paralyse l'esprit et le sang; le froid, ce démon sinistre, qui rase l'univers de son aile humide et souffle la peste sur les nations consternées! . . . Le froid qui décolore tout dans le monde matériel comme dans le monde intellectuel . . . Vous voyez bien que tout se civilise, c'est à dire que tout se refroidit. . . . L'âme s'exalte et quitte la terre . . . pour dérober au ciel le feu de Prométhée; mais perdue au milieu des ténèbres, elle s'arrête dans son vol et tombe; car Dieu, voyant son audace, étend la main et lui ôte le soleil." (*Lélia*, 120–121)

> ("Oh the cold! This penetrating pain which thrusts sharp needles in all the pores . . . this pain, at once physical and moral, which invades body and soul, which penetrates the depths of thought and paralyzes the mind and the blood; the cold, this sinister demon, which brushes the universe with its humid wing and blows pestilence on alarmed nations! . . . The cold that discolors everything both in the material world and in the intellectual world . . . You can see that everything is becoming more civilized, that is to say, everything is becoming colder. . . . The soul is exalted and leaves the earth . . . in order to steal Prometheus's fire from the heavens; but lost in darkness, it stops its flight and falls; for God, seeing its audacity, stretches out his hand and takes the sun away.")

Like her Romantic colleagues, Chateaubriand, Nodier, Senancour, and Balzac, Sand expresses here the growing dissatisfaction of the individual for the world in which he or she lives; she denounces God's readiness to mete out punishment; and she foresees civilization's imminent catastrophic end. But the polysemic image of frigidity is hers, shaping the entire novel, defining as it does the heroine's sexuality, her beauty, psyche, illness, world view, and eschatology. These pages, with their extravagant rhetoric and emotive outbursts, function to make Lélia the powerful figure she is. By comparison with her violent pessimism and strident nihilism, Sténio's declarations on the beauty and youthfulness of the world seem silly and naive. In this dialogical confrontation, Lélia definitely has the best role.

After Lélia *la solitaire*, here is Lélia the thinker. Her spleen derives directly from intellectual hypertrophy, as Sténio remarks: "Ne personnifiez-vous pas, avec votre beauté et votre tristesse, avec votre ennui et votre scepticisme, l'excès de douleur produit par l'abus de la pensée?" (117–118; "Don't you personify, with your beauty and sadness, with your sorrow and scepticism, the excess of pain resulting from the abuse of thinking?"). Like René, Obermann, and Raphaël de Valentin in *La Peau de chagrin*, Lélia defines the mal du siècle as a gap, a disfunction, between ideals and the world, echoing Pascal's notion (Romantic before its time) of a disproportion between two infinites:

> "Hélas, pourquoi Dieu s'est-il plu à mettre une telle *disproportion* entre les illusions de l'homme et la réalité? Pourquoi faut-il souffrir toujours d'un désir de bien-être qui se révèle sous la forme du beau et qui plane dans tous nos rêves, sans se poser jamais à terre?" (emphasis added; *Lélia*, 109)

> ("Alas, why did God choose to create such a *discrepancy* between men's illusions and reality? Why do we always yearn for happiness which is revealed to us in the form of the beautiful and soars in all our dreams, without ever touching the earth?")

Using the same categories of "savoir" and "pouvoir" with which Balzac had structured the drama of *La Peau de chagrin*, Sand has her heroine describe the gap between the two concepts as another instance of mal du siècle:

> *"Savoir*, ce n'est pas *pouvoir*. . . . Rapprendre, ce n'est pas avancer; voir, ce n'est pas vivre. Qui nous rendra la puissance d'agir et surtout l'art de jouir et de conserver? . . . Ce qui fut le repos pour les civilisations éclipsées sera la mort pour notre civilisation éreintée." (*Lélia*, 120)

> (*"Knowing* is not the same as *being able to act*. . . . Relearning is not advancing; seeing is not living. Who will give us the capacity to act, and more important, the art of enjoying and preserving? . . . What spelled serenity for eclipsed civilizations will be the death knell of our worn-out civilization.")

As an inversion of the aphorism the eighteenth-century rationalists liked to cite—"Knowledge is power" ("Nam et ipsa scientia potesta est")[37]—Lélia's words represent the ultimate realization that in the nineteenth century knowledge is synonymous with paralysis.

Not surprisingly, Píerre Reboul's notes for these pages are particularly copious and openly contemptuous of the author's efforts: "Hasty reading," he comments; "Sand did not completely understand all that she read; she quickly annexed portions of thought which remained opaque to her" ("Introduction," *Lélia*, lxiii). That the critic is here particularly intent on dismantling the text by interpreting Lélia's testament as a sign of Sand's undigested and unassimilated regurgitation of hasty and badly understood readings indicates how central these pages are to the thrust of the novel. In general, the copiousness of Reboul's commentary is in direct proportion to the importance of a given passage. Foremost among sources for Sand he places Senancour, Nodier, and, to a lesser extent, Balzac.[38]

Sand's article on *Obermann* suggests not only that she had read the work carefully and with appreciation but that she, along with Sainte-Beuve, was one of the few writers of the 1830s to appreciate fully the richness and significance of this work as a precursor of the Romantic ethos. The themes in *Obermann* of the individual's powerlessness vis-à-vis the world, the disproportion between desire and reality, the loss of illusions, and, most crucially, the negative effect of thought on the human psyche are all present in *Lélia*. About the conjunction of Sand's novel with *Obermann*, several points need to be made however.

These themes, first of all, are not restricted to Senancour's works. Personal impotence is already one of the controlling or motivating forces in such texts as *René, Armance*, or *Olivier* by Mme de Duras. The disproportion between desire and reality finds its expression throughout the period and is a key element of the ideological unemployment of a generation who came of age with the fall of the Empire and the social stagnation of the Restoration. Musset, Stendhal, and Vigny among others commented on its impact on their contemporaries.[39] The Romantics were the first in a sense to identify what we today call burnout. Furthermore, the motifs of lost illusions and the danger of excessive thought are also crucial aspects of Balzac's world view manifest especially in *La Peau de chagrin*, which had come out just two years before *Lélia*.

All these themes are really ideas the Romantics articulated for their generation. As such, they were part of the artistic and cultural air that the literati of the day breathed. When Dostoevsky, many years later, commented on his *Crime and Punishment*, "Ideas go flying about the air, but certainly in accordance with laws: ideas are alive and spread according to laws that are too difficult for us to perceive; ideas are infectious,"[40] he was referring to this very phenomenon of timely ideas permeating the cultural landscape at a given moment.

Sand was a kind of super reader who voraciously consumed her contemporaries' works and responded to the issues of the day in her letters, critical essays, and literary works. But to say, as some critics have claimed, that she read uncritically and without understanding is simply not borne out in her novels. On the contrary, Sand was a masterful assimilator of "those ideas that go flying about the air," and she entered into dialogue with them in her works. In fact, to use a Bakhtinian concept for a moment, Sand is a perfect example of the polyphonic novelist who in the various voices of her characters echoes or recasts, confronts or parodies, in a word responds to earlier voices from her personal sphere or from fiction. Far from denying the impact of Nodier, Senancour, Balzac, and others on Sand's texts, then, I would emphasize the profoundly dialogical foundation of *Lélia*. Formally, as we saw, the novel is constructed as a series of (often philosophical) dialogues, with many of its thematic concerns directly engaging in dialogue with other texts. Sand's feminizing of Obermann's splenetic character is a good example of this kind of creative response, one that undoes any critical assertion that she did not understand Senancour's novel.

What shocks Reboul in these pages, I suspect, and what provoked his acrid commentary, is the audacity that permeates this chapter, the audacity of a female character (not to mention novelist) in the role of philosopher, while the male is reduced to a mere sounding board. But again, Sand's literary device of sexual inversion does not mean that she had misread the texts of her precursors. On the contrary, the device plays a deliberate and crucial role in this revolutionary novel. Reboul is far less nervous when Lélia ceases to philosophize and is content to be a poet. There are far fewer critical comments in the chapter entitled "Solitude."

At the center of this important chapter stands a passage which expresses, in lyrical terms, the breakdown of the individual's capacity to put knowledge into action. Using the controlling metaphor of the dream journey, a device at once poetic and liberating for the author's imagination, Sand has her heroine visualize an ideal world so perfect and in such exquisite detail that the real world can seem only a paltry imitation. The dream takes on vivid, lifelike color, while the real world appears dull and grey. Lélia begins by taking off on the wings of imagination:

> "que d'univers j'ai parcouru dans ces voyages de l'âme! J'ai traversé les steppes blanchies des régions glacées. J'ai jeté mon rapide regard sur les savanes parfumées où la lune se lève si belle et si blanche. J'ai effleuré sur les ailes du sommeil ces vastes mers dont l'immensité épouvante la pensée. . . . J'ai, dans l'espace d'une heure, vu le soleil se lever aux rivages de la Grèce et se coucher derrière les montagnes bleues du Nouveau-Monde. . . . J'ai contemplé de près la face rouge des astres errants dans les solitudes de l'air et dans les plaines du ciel. . . . Quels trésors d'imagination, quelles merveilleuses richesses de la nature n'ai-je pas épuisés dans ces vaines hallucinations du sommeil?" (129–130)

> ("how I have traveled the universes in these journeys of my soul! I have crossed the white steppes of the frozen tundras. I have cast a rapid glance over the fragrant savannahs where the moon rises, so beautiful and so white. On the wings of sleep, I have skimmed those vast seas, their sheer immensity overwhelming

the mind. . . . In the space of one hour, I have seen the sun rise over the shores of Greece, and set behind the blue mountains of the New World. . . . I have contemplated up close the red faces of the stars wandering through the solitudes of the air and on the plains of the sky. . . . What treasures of the imagination, what marvelous riches of nature have I not exhausted in these futile hallucinations of sleep?")

Sand here verifies Senancour's axiom that "Man's real life comes from within, the one he receives from the external world is only accidental and subordinate," all the while inscribing it in the feminine.[41] Lélia's voyages of the mind make any excursions into the real world superfluous:

"que la nature m'a semblé pauvre, le ciel terne et la mer étroite, au prix des terres, des cieux et des mers que j'ai franchis dans mon vol immatériel! Que reste-t-il à la vie réelle de beautés pour nous charmer, à l'âme humaine de puissances pour jouir et admirer, quand l'imagination a tout usé d'avance par un abus de sa force?"   (130)

("how impoverished nature seemed to me, how dull the sky and how narrow the sea, compared to the lands, the heavens, and the seas I have crossed in my immaterial flight! What beauty remains in real life to enchant us, what powers in the human soul to enjoy and to admire, when the imagination has already drained everything through an abuse of its strength?")

Imagination is both Lélia's power and her curse. Certainly, it corresponds to Baudelaire's definition as "la reine des facultés." But, by making life in the world unbearable, Lélia's hypertrophied imagination can be likened to an unhealthy organ that creates existential impotence, an increasing paralysis of the body and of the will, and the temptation to delve more and more exclusively, as a refuge, into the recesses of the nocturnal mind. These two chapters, then, at the novel's ideological center, can be defined as a great moment in Sand's *sensibilité noire*. *Lélia* expresses the somber, rebellious side of Sand—a sensibility that can be found again in her two other chefs-d'oeuvre, *Spiridion* and *Consuelo*.

The Novel's "Failure"

Sand's search for a new narrative voice that would incorporate both the male and the female, that would be at once more democratic and androgynous, was not satisfactorily resolved in the first version of *Lélia*. As such, it was a "failed" text for the author herself. Paradoxically, *Lélia* is both a masterpiece from our modern perspective and one of the most remarkable "failures" of nineteenth-century French fiction. A careful examination of the two versions of *Lélia*—the first redaction of 1833, analyzed in this chapter, and the 1839 version, a much altered text examined in the next—reveals to what extent Sand, in the rewriting of her novel, chose to depend more heavily on the traditional third-person narrative point of view. Trenmor's confession, for example, which is told in the first person in the 1833 version, is transposed into a third-person narration in the 1839 text.

The ending of the 1833 version is significantly symbolic in this context. Lélia is strangled by the insane monk, Magnus; Sténio drowns himself, while the other characters survive. Thus both the male voice of poetry and the female voice of the quest for a new world view are silenced. This last scene of double death is not so much an expression of the Romantic topos of suicide or an exploitation of the Gothic theme of man's sadistic violence against woman. Rather it represents a transposed avowal on the part of the author of her incapacity to invent a totally new, viable, narrative structure that would allow for the modern novel's double liberation from narrative totalitarianism and narrative phallocracy.

For all its innovative and experimental writing, then, *Lélia* did not open permanent, new narrative paths for Sand to follow in subsequent works. Immediately after writing this novel, she returned to the tried and true narrative structure used in *Indiana* and *Valentine*; we find it in *Le Secrétaire intime* (1833), *André* (1834), and *Mauprat* (1837), for example. She would never be quite so innovative again with respect to the fictional narrative structure. But as the next chapter will show, Sand's mystical novel, *Spiridion*, written several years later, was just as experimental, but with a different problematic and different solutions, while the second redaction of *Lélia* probed some of the same metaphysical questions as *Spiridion* in their feminine incarnation.

6

Two Metaphysical Novels: *Spiridion* and *Lélia* of 1839

La magie des idées qui fermentaient alors en France.

MAUPRAT

(The magic of ideas that were fermenting in France at the time.)

Histoire du rêveur, *Indiana*, *Valentine*, and *Lélia* were all set in a contemporary framework. Whether exploring the artist's quest, the mal du siècle in its feminine and peasant incarnations, or probing the social, intellectual, and spiritual dilemmas of the age, these texts of the early thirties portrayed a fictional world in the present. As the next three chapters will show, George Sand's efforts for the following decade would focus on expanding the time frame of her literary universe. She would first deploy her backward glance into the eighteenth century in three novels, *Spiridion*, *Consuelo*, and its sequel, *La Comtesse de Rudolstadt*. In the forties, novels such as *Le Compagnon du tour de France*, *Le Meunier d'Angibault*, and *Le Péché de Monsieur Antoine* would delineate the utopian future. Absorbed by her attempt to "rêver l'utopie," to cite Victor Hugo's expression, Sand would declare, in a letter dated April 1845 to Jules Michelet, "Je suis utopiste" (*Corr.*, 6:836).

At the same time she was composing *Spiridion*, Sand was also obstinately rewriting *Lélia*. The two novels, in book form, were published within months of each other.[1] The new *Lélia* was less concerned with depicting the mal du siècle in the feminine, although paradoxically some of its pronouncements were more forcefully "feminist" than the first version, and more intent on probing even further the philosophical and religious questions the heroine had begun to address in the 1833 version. Most important, by transforming Lélia into the abbess of the Camaldules, Sand made the 1839 version of *Lélia* a twin novel of *Spiridion*. Later in this chapter I shall examine the two novels intertextually.[2]

"Un Logogriphe immense": Sand's Vision of Revolution

Spiridion, which Béatrice Didier calls a kind of nineteenth-century *Name of the Rose*, is Sand's first serious novel to deal with history. Interestingly, her utopian vision is already manifest in this novel and helps to shape her understanding of the specific historical period she is studying, the French Revolution. While revolution is restricted to a prophetic role in *La Comtesse de Rudolstadt*, since the fictional thread is cut off in the year 1774, history bursts upon the scene in *Spiridion* (the year is around 1796) only to bring the novel to its dramatic conclusion. The vaguely delineated geographic setting of *Spiridion* is somewhere on the Italian coast—and clearly not in France. Nevertheless, this novel offers the most insight into the author's utopian and messianic vision of the French Revolution and revolution in general.

For Sand, as for many of her contemporaries, the Revolution did not start unexpectedly in 1789, but was the inevitable outcome of the extraordinary fermentation of ideas that preceded it. "What a strange century," she remarks in the "Notice" of *Consuelo*, "it starts in song, evolves in bizarre conspiracies and ends . . . in fantastic revolutions" (*Consuelo*, 1:39). *Spiridion* and *La Comtesse de Rudolstadt* thus concentrate on the fertile period before 1789. A remarkably coherent network of reflections, images, and tropes emerges from these two novels regarding the link between revolutionary France and the Romantic age. The two periods are intimately connected in the Romantic imagination, as exemplified by Hugo's remark:

> The nineteenth century . . . is the son of an idea . . . the nineteenth century has a majestic mother . . . the French Revolution. . . . The Revolution forged the bugle, the nineteenth century is sounding it. . . . The thinkers of the present era, the poets, writers, historians, orators, philosophers, every single one of them derives from the French Revolution.[3]

To study this period was then to examine the roots of Romanticism. Sand sensed in the "siècle des lumières" a heterogeneous era, a double century: an era in which subterranean intellectual currents counterbalanced the Apollonian rationalism of the philosophes and the lighthearted *Marivaudage* of the amoral aristocracy. She understood that, in the words of the critic René Jasinski, the "siècle des lumières" had also been a "siècle des illuminés."[4] *La Comtesse de Rudolstadt*, with its examination of secret societies as exemplified by the Sect of the Invisibles, can be envisaged as a voyage through the Revolution's various prophetic undergrounds. Europe, says one of the novel's characters, "est remplie de sociétés secrètes, laboratoires souterrains où se prépare une grande révolution, dont le cratère sera l'Allemagne ou la France" (*Consuelo*, 3:312; "Europe . . . is filled with secret societies, underground laboratories where a great revolution is being prepared, the crater of which will be Germany or France").

Sand's eighteenth century is a two-layered century, full of contrasts, characterized by a severe *décalage* between its glittery surface and its concealed depths. The eighteenth century she calls "un log-ogriphe immense," a verbal enigma that needs to be deciphered through the exploration of its binary code. It is a "brilliant nebula," characterized by enlightenment and illuminism, informed by a double source of knowledge—philosophy and mysticism. As she puts together a list that might be called her "Who's who in the eighteenth century," Sand pairs up incongruous figures. The *lumières* as embodied by Voltaire are contrasted to the *ténèbres* as represented by Swedenborg, Kant's rationalism is opposed to Mesmer's mysticism:

> [Ce dix-huitième siècle où s'épanouissent] Voltaire et Swedenborg, Kant et Mesmer, Jean-Jacques Rousseau et le cardinal Dubois . . . Frédéric II et Robespierre, Louis XIV et Philippe-Egalité, Marie-Antoinette et Charlotte Corday . . . Babeuf et Napoléon . . . laboratoire effrayant, où tant de formes hétérogènes ont été jetées dans le creuset, qu'elles ont vomi, dans leur monstrueuse ébullition, un torrent de fumée où nous marchons encore enveloppés de ténèbres et d'images confuses.   (*Consuelo*, 3:401)

> ([This eighteenth century in which flourish] Voltaire and Swedenborg, Kant and Mesmer, Jean-Jacques Rousseau and Cardinal Dubois [prime minister under Louis XV] . . . Frederick the Second and Robespierre, Louis XIV [who died in 1715!] and Philippe-Egalité, Marie-Antoinette and Charlotte Corday . . . Babeuf and Napoleon . . . a terrifying laboratory where so many heterogenous forms were thrown into the pot that they spewed forth, in their monstrous boiling, a torrent of smoke through which we still walk, surrounded by darkness and murky images.)

Since Sand redefines this enigmatic century as simultaneously an "âge des lumières" and an "âge des ténèbres," she sees in its apotheosis, the French Revolution, the intellectual mark of not only the *philosophes des lumières* but the secret societies and mystical thinkers. It is they who were blessed with a prophetic perspicacity which the rationalists lacked: "Cette mystérieuse révolution . . . que les conspirateurs mystiques du siècle dernier avait vaguement prédite 50 ans d'avance. . . . Voltaire et les calmes cerveaux philosophes de son temps . . . n'en prévoyaient [pas] les brusques orages" (*Consuelo*, 3:402; "This mysterious revolution . . . that the mystical conspirators of the past century had vaguely predicted 50 years ahead of time. . . . Neither Voltaire nor the calm philosophical minds of his time had predicted the storms brewing.") The genesis of revolution is ascribable to the "noble chimera" of that noble century's double discourse.

In opposition to the tendencies of the rationalist philosophes to secularize political theory, Sand's vision of history constitutes a re-

sacralization of the political. By insisting on the primordial role of secret societies which made up a "siècle des ténèbres" (counterbalancing
the "siècle des lumières"), she interpreted revolution as profoundly religious in nature. Revolution apprehended as a new theology is a key
concept that runs throughout Sand's writings, where the events of
1789 can be seen as the erecting of a new religious order. The heroine of
Nanon, a much later novel which also deals with the French Revolution,
for example, exclaims: "l'Eglise a péri pour avoir été cruelle. Si les jaco-
bins succombent, pensez au massacre des prisons, et alors vous direz
comme moi: On ne bâtit pas *une nouvelle Eglise* avec ce qui a fait écrouler
l'ancienne." ("The Church perished because of its cruelty. If the Jaco-
bins fall, think of the prison massacres, and then you will say, as I do:
You cannot build a new Church with what made the old one crumble.")[5] Sand is referring here to the Church's propensity for violence
and intolerance. On the one hand, the Inquisition prefigures the Terror. But on the other, if the Church was to blame indirectly for many of
the excesses of 1793, it could also be credited with helping to determine
the moral dimension of the revolutionary agenda. Sand's philosophical tale exemplifies the remark made by the historian Louis Blanc: "It is
not force that governs the world, in spite of appearances. It is
thought."[6] And thought was what flourished inside the monasteries in
the late eighteenth century. As she writes: "Toute lumière, tout pro-
grès, toute grandeur sont sortis du cloître" (*Spiridion*, 26; "All enlightenment, all progress, all grandeur have issued from the cloister").
Since the cloister was the privileged space for meditation, Sand explored the ideational sphere of a monastic order where intimations of
revolution could be articulated. That exploration resulted in *Spiridion*.

Confession of a Child of the (Eighteenth) Century

Since Sand was convinced of the primordial power of ideas in the creation of political events, it is fitting that she should have composed a
novel in which the entire fictional matter was ideational, to the exclu-
sion of any real plot. *Spiridion*, in fact, may be her most arid novel; in an
understated comment, she herself defined it as a "roman peu récréatif"
(HV, 2:160). A multifarious text, incorporating elements of autobiography, it is part philosophical treatise (the theories of the nineteenth-
century utopian philosopher Pierre Leroux play an important role),
part Gothic tale (certain fantastic decors such as a descent into the catacombs are straight out of Horace Walpole's *Castle of Otranto* or Ann
Radcliffe's *Mysteries of Udolpho*), and part novel of initiation. Set in a
monastery, the novel is entirely made up of monologues and dialogues
between monks. The fictional structure is of one piece, with no chapters or parts to halt the growing rhetorical power of the text. Nothing
truly happens—there are no events, no adventures, no love interests.

Throughout, the author appeals to her reader's most erudite faculties. With all its stunning audacity, the novel emphasizes that its form has been made austere and opaque deliberately. As far removed from a "romance" as is possible, since *Spiridion* contains no female characters[7] and can offer no love intrigue; totally unlike a pastoral, since it is pre-occupied exclusively with moral and philosophical argument rather than with lyrical nature descriptions; unsentimental in the extreme; as abstract and introspective as a novel could ever dare to be, *Spiridion* exemplifies Sand's sensibilité noire and her powerful "claustral" imagination.

The cast of main characters is limited to two monks—a young novice with the obviously resonant name of Angel and a somber old monk called Alexis, who is on his deathbed. Surrounding them are the shadowy figures of other monks and the mysterious apparitions of the dead monk and founder of the convent, Spiridion himself. Taking as her cue Pierre Leroux's utopian call for the necessity of a "new syn-thesis of all human knowledge,"[8] Sand sets out to put this need for philosophical syncretism into fiction, so that what fills the universe of *Spiridion* is a spoken confession delivered by Alexis to his chosen "spir-itual heir." As Jean Pommier reminds us, the fleshless nature of the novel is accentuated by the words the monk pronounces when he de-fines his paternity as the conceiving of a child of the mind rather than a child of one's own flesh and blood:[9] "Je ne mourrai donc pas sans avoir vécu car le but de la vie est de transmettre la vie. . . . J'ai un fils, un enfant plus précieux qu'un enfant de mes entrailles; j'ai un fils de mon intelligence" (*Spiridion*, 246; "I will not die without having lived, for the goal of life is to transmit life . . . I have a son, a child more precious than a child of my flesh and blood; I have a son of my intelligence"). What Bakhtin has called "the motif of the speaking person" in the novel,[10] a motif most often identified with Dostoevskian discourse, is already worked out extensively in *Spiridion* as one of its main rhetorical devices. Its dialogic structure perhaps explains why some have seen in it a prefigurative text for Dostoevsky's *Brothers Karamazov*.[11]

This cerebral text interprets revolution from the standpoint of utopian socialist thought of the 1830s. Sand creates a kind of master weave of many of its main threads: the perfectibility of humankind, the idea of continuous progress, the insistence on a eudemonistic vision for the future, belief in a new religion of Humanity. But the novel is not just a passive vehicle for the promotion of these concepts. It engages them in a dialogic framework, most notably, as they are expressed to Angel by the old monk. Although in the fictional chronology, the views of Alexis are those of a man of the 1790s, the doctrines he pro-motes are those of the 1830s, bearing the stamp of Pierre Leroux. Rather than a "spiritual thriller,"[12] as it has been called, the novel exemplifies the active, questioning relationship between source and new creation that Leroux, in an astonishing prefiguration of Bakhtin, called "the law of succession in the chain of all the great monuments of language."[13] *Spiridion* is not exactly a philosophical treatise, but it comes very close, verifying with particular felicity the workings of this law of succession and continuity and highlighting many of Leroux's concepts: solidarity, the march of Humanity toward a better future, spiritual heredity, continuity in the nonmaterial sphere. These utopian ideas will continue to run through Sand's writings in the 1840s, as an article she wrote in 1841 on the "utopianism" of Lamartine attests: "The awareness of life, of the future, of perfectibility, of equality, is present today in all noble hearts, whether they be the hearts of famous poets or of proletarian rhymers, and the word of truth on all eloquent lips."[14] The two concepts of perfectibility and egalitarianism underscored in Sand's text are the key issues in Leroux's utopian ideology.

In the long central section of *Spiridion*, which might be subtitled "Confession of a Child of the (Eighteenth) Century," Alexis attempts to formulate a "new credo," built around the notion of conversion, evolving from a strict and unexamined form of Catholicism to Protestantism to philosophical atheism, and finally to a tolerant and fluid Christianity. Alexis denounces any rigid interpretation of religious dogma; he questions the need for a hierarchical church; he advocates the individual's right to search for truth and the imperative need for freedom of choice. Sand will state these articles of faith again in *Mademoiselle la Quintinie* (1863), when she proclaims the novelist's privilege to include religious discussions in his or her works, drawing up a kind of "Declaration of the Rights of the Religious Man and Citizen."[15] In an attempt to restore many of Christianity's most laudable principles to their primitive and ideal form, Alexis insists on the literal responsibility of each for all. This belief will cost him his life. But death is defined as a new life, the life of the spirit being envisaged as all-encompassing. Toward the end of his confession, Alexis articulates some of the main tenets of his new theology:

> "Je crois à un engendrement perpétuel des âmes, qui n'obéit pas aux lois de la matière, aux liens du sang, mais à des lois mystérieuses, à des liens invisibles. . . . Il est pour nous deux immortalités, toutes deux matérielles et immatérielles: l'une, qui est de ce monde et qui transmet nos idées et nos sentiments à l'humanité par nos oeuvres et nos travaux; l'autre, qui s'enregistre dans un monde meilleur par nos mérites et nos souffrances, et qui conserve une puissance providentielle sur les hommes et les choses de ce monde." (*Spiridion*, 220–221)

> ("I believe in a perpetual engendering of souls which does not obey the laws of matter or the ties of blood, but obeys mysterious

laws and invisible ties. . . . For us there are two immortalities, both
are material and immaterial; one is of this world and transmits our
ideas and feelings to humanity through our works and deeds; the
other is registered in a better world through our merit and our sufferings and preserves a providential power over men and things of
this world.")

As "mythologue de la démocratie sociale,"[16] Sand used Leroux's
metaphor of the human chain, the notion that each individual and each
generation are but links in the chain of Humanity.[17] In a letter dated
August 1842 to Marie-Sophie Leroyer de Chantepie, she formulated
her own credo, reiterating many of the beliefs expounded by the hero
of *Spiridion*: "Je crois à la vie éternelle, à l'humanité éternelle, au pro-
grès éternel . . . j'ai embrassé à cet égard les croyances de Pierre
Leroux" (*Corr.*, 5:757; "I believe in eternal life, in eternal humanity, in
eternal progress . . . in this respect I have embraced the beliefs of
Pierre Leroux"). Sand's novel, however, in dialogue with those philosophical beliefs, is more readable today than the utopian socialist's
often obscure prose.

The Denial of Agency

The temptation in past critical practice has been to denounce Sand for
appropriating these concepts of Leroux's, and sometimes even to ac-
cuse her of obtaining his direct collaboration in her fictional projects.
In fact, for years an unfounded rumor circulated that parts of *Spiridion*
came from the pen of Leroux himself. The bibliographer Spoelberch de
Lovenjoul discovered that parts of the manuscript of *Spiridion* were of a
different hand than Sand's own. He immediately jumped to what for
him was the most obvious conclusion—Leroux had quite evidently
composed portions of *Spiridion*. The Leroux scholar Félix Thomas cites
a letter he received from Lovenjoul in which he asserts that "part of the
manuscript of *Spiridion* is in the hand of Pierre Leroux and *composed* by
him."[18] David Owen Evans subscribes to this thesis uncritically in his
otherwise solid book on Leroux and Romanticism, *Le Socialisme romantique*, published in 1948. He wrongly concludes that *Spiridion, Consuelo,*
and *La Comtesse de Rudolstadt* "were written in collaboration with
[Leroux]."[19]

The dean of Sand studies, Georges Lubin, reexamined all the details of this false ascription and set the matter straight. With his usual
perspicacity, he studied the two foreign handwritings in the manuscript of *Spiridion* and identified the first as belonging to Maurice Sand
and the second to Maurice's preceptor, Mallefille.[20] A letter dated 28
January 1838, in which Sand complains of a rheumatism in her arm,
explains why Maurice Sand and his preceptor had taken *Spiridion* in

dictation and testifies to her innocence.[21] A second letter to Gustave Planche exonerates her further of any blame: "My arm is almost paralyzed for hours at a time and I am forced to dictate most of my letters" (*Corr.*, 3:343). Thus, it has been proven beyond doubt that Leroux did not write one single word of the novel.

The remarks of feminist critic Joanna Russ provide an apt commentary in this context. When the author is female, notes Russ, there often is a strong tendency to denigrate her production as much as possible, either by claiming that the author in question did not write it or by asserting that she did not understand what she was writing. As Russ sees it, in its constant effort to put down women's writing, the male literary establishment has, among other strategies, invented "the denial of agency." To claim that Leroux wrote part of *Spiridion* exemplifies the phallocratic thesis that likes to claim: "She [fill in the name of any woman writer] wrote it, but she had help." A different line of attack has been used by numerous critics in the (not so distant) past to dismiss Sand's seriousness as a witness to her time, who insist that she repeated what she had read or heard without really understanding it. Ironically, the male critics tend to want it both ways. With Sand successfully exonerated from the accusation that she had other people write her books, it remains difficult to find a modern critic to take *Spiridion* seriously once it is established that no male hand contributed to its composition.

The way to deal with a woman genius or a masterpiece born of a female pen is still a stumbling block for many male critics. Even the often perspicacious critic, Mario Praz, cannot really accept that a woman could have written a work of genius. Here is his comment on Mary Shelley's *Frankenstein*, a typical manifestation of the anxiety he felt at the idea that an "authoress" could have produced a great novel: "All Mrs. Shelley did was to provide a passive reflection of some of the wild fantasies which were living in the air around her."[22] Such views suggest that, as long as female genius can be ascribed to a kind of Pythic receptivity, the world of art and philosophy remains hermetically and safely sealed against infiltration by nonmale influences. It remains restricted to the male principle. All women writers are literally written off as anomalies, plagiarists, or receptive Sybils who are mere receptacles or filters for the male Logos. In this view, the woman writer does not speak her own language. The god's word is spoken through her. She is but the body, the voice (or, in the case of writing, the hand) that gives shape to the Logos.

The concept of the purely passive sybil who enters into ecstasy and repeats mindlessly the words which are dictated to her by a higher (read "male") authority can be seen as the literary equivalent of the theory of the virgin birth. Anthropologists have long remarked on a related belief among so-called primitive societies—the naive and

phallocentric idea that the woman does not contribute in any significant way to the conception of the child. It was believed that, by depos-
iting his sperm into the inert receptacle of the woman's womb, like God
in the case of the virgin birth, the man had provided the totality of the
substance necessary for conception. Since many societies believed
(and some, to this day, continue to believe) that the sperm contained
the total child in miniature, the woman's sole contribution was the vessel of her womb.[23]

In both instances, the literary as well as the biological, the dominant patriarchal culture expresses the need to deny woman any access
to creation, whether it be the creativity of the feminine mind or the
creative possibilities of the female body. In this vision the female potential is rendered dependent upon and subordinate to the male. The
woman's mind, like her uterus, is likened to an empty space whose
only purpose is to be filled with any discourse the dominant literary
establishment chooses.

A Christic Schema

Let us not go from one extreme, however, saying that Leroux wrote
parts of *Spiridion*, to the other, affirming that Leroux had nothing to do
with the novel's composition whatsoever. This is certainly a dialogic
text. As an astute critic remarks: "The intellectual atmosphere of an era
constitutes the point of departure for [Sand]."[24] Once again, *Spiridion*
offers evidence that she was the consummate embodiment of the polyphonic novelist. To highlight the presence of Leroux and other utopian
thinkers in *Spiridion*, let me provide one example. At the end of the
novel, Alexis is attacked in a church and brutally slain by the French
revolutionaries who have invaded Italy. These are the monk's final
words:

> "nous ne sommes que des images qu'on brise, parce qu'elles ne
> représentent plus les idées qui faisaient leur force et leur sainteté.
> Ceci est l'oeuvre de la Providence, et la mission de nos bourreaux
> est sacrée, bien qu'ils ne la comprennent pas encore! Cependant,
> ils l'ont dit, tu l'as entendu: c'est au nom du *sans-culotte Jésus* qu'ils
> profanent le sanctuaire de l'église. Ceci est le commencement du
> règne de l'Evangile éternel prophétisé par nos pères." (*Spiridion*,
> 270)

> ("we are only images that are being shattered because they no
> longer represent the ideas that made their strength and their holi-
> ness. This is the work of Providence, and the mission of our execu-
> tioners is sacred, although they themselves do not understand it
> yet. Nevertheless, they said these words and you heard them: it is

in the name of the *sans-culotte Jesus* that they are desecrating the sanctuary of the church. Now is the beginning of the reign of the eternal Gospel prophesied by our fathers.")

This speech while alluding to the words from the Gospel—"Forgive them, Father, for they know not what they do"—articulates a radical reinterpretation of the traditional doctrine of forgiveness for those who do not know what they are doing. For the slayers now represent not the forces of reaction destined to perish but the avant-garde whose actions are necessary to realize the fulfillment of the revolutionary new order. The recasting of the words of Jesus, then, emphasizes the religious mission of the Revolution. Christ is identified as the incarnation of the godhead apprehended as a revolutionary force.

This episode is an instance of the theme of the "sans-culotte Jesus-Christ" which Frank Bowman, in his *Le Christ romantique*, has studied brilliantly and exhaustively. It also represents a working out of Sand's deep-rooted conviction of the profoundly dissident nature of the figure of Jesus. As she expressed it elsewhere: "Si Jesus reparaissait parmi nous, il serait empoigné par la garde nationale comme factieux et anarchiste" ("If Jesus reappeared in our midst, he would be arrested by the national guard as seditious and an anarchist").[25] But, above all, this usage of a Christian terminology to describe historical events, with the Revolution as a privileged moment, appears as a sort of mania among the French Romantics and utopian socialists of the 1830s and 1840s. The philosophers—Leroux, Fourier,[26] Enfantin,[27] and others— were inclined to collapse Christianity and the new age of Harmony into a continuous religious movement, a tendency that runs throughout *Spiridion*, where Leroux's formula of a New Religion following on the heels of the three ages of Christianity is elaborated.[28] As the utopian Alphonse Esquiros commented, "Several modern writers regard democracy as the necessary development of Christian ideas; for them the French Revolution is issued from the Gospel . . . [in fact] it is the Gospel itself embodied in an event."[29] As for the Romantic novelists and poets—Sand, Balzac,[30] Hugo, Lamartine[31]—they found in literature a medium through which they could elaborate abstract constructs based on Christian themes, which would allow them to come to grips with a postrevolutionary society.[32]

The critic Jean-Claude Fizaine notes that the distinctive feature of Romanticism might be defined as "its capacity to think through images even History, even the Revolution."[33] In their attempt to express the events of 1789 figuratively, the Romantics used religious images to an astonishing degree. The number of texts in the literature of the time which exploit religious concepts to interpret revolution is overwhelming. Early in the century the mystical philosopher Saint-Martin had remarked that the French Revolution was a religious war: "In actual fact there are in the world only two divine wars, or if you prefer, two wars of religion . . . the war of the Hebrews . . . and our present Revolution.[34] Michelet, in turn, saw the revolution of 1789 as an attempt to create a new religion: "the ill-named Revolution, was less a destruction than a creation, the foundation of a new religion, the religion of justice, as opposed to the religion of grace or of arbitrariness, which was the religion of the Middle Ages."[35] Convinced that he was "accomplishing a divine mission," Saint-Simon pronounced these *ultima verba*, in which he claimed that, on the heels of the French Revolution, his was a religious task:

> The last part of my work, new Christianity, will not be immediately understood. It was thought that all religious systems would have to disappear because we had succeeded in proving the obsolescence of the Catholic system. We were wrong: religion cannot disappear from the face of the earth, it can only be transformed. . . . We have come to proclaim that humanity has a religious future, that the religion of the future will be greater, more powerful than the religion of the past, that it will be . . . a synthesis of all the conceptions of humanity.[36]

For Sand, as well as for other thinkers of the time, a religious phraseology continued to describe the phenomenon of revolution up until the events of 1848, with the figure of Christ providing a divine incarnation of the revolutionary. In her article, "La Religion de la France" (part of her memoirs about the period of 1848), she wrote: "Jesus was the first and immortal apostle of equality. Jesus, child of the people, martyr of truth, a victim devoted to the cause of the disempowered, of the poor and the enslaved."[37] The biographer of Esquiros, J. Van der Linden, remarked that the Revolution of 1848 was "taking on the aspect of a religious event," thus announcing "the new reign of Christ, his social reign."[38]

Starting with Saint-Simon's *Le Nouveau Christianisme*, many utopian works appeared in those years which described the new society in Christian terms:[39] Leroux's "De la philosophie et du christianisme" (1832), Lamennais's *Paroles d'un croyant* (1834), Strauss's *La Vie de Jésus* (translated into French by Littré in 1838, a year before *Spiridion*), Eliphas Lévi's *La Bible de la liberté* (1840), Esquiros's *L'Evangile du peuple* (1840), Cabet's *Le Vrai Christianisme suivant Jésus-Christ* (1846), and Leroux's *Du christianisme et de son origine démocratique* (1848). Such evidence confirms the constant "Christianization" of history and social thought in the first half of the nineteenth century, where a reference to Christ was often the marker of utopianism.[40] The Gospel had been reinterpreted as a utopian text; and revolution as a new form of Christianity. Politics and theology merged. As Sand herself said in 1848 in her hotly debated "Lettre aux riches": "communism is the true form of Christianity," the term communism denoting a pre-Marxist form of thought, what Leroux more accurately called "communionism."[41]

References to Christ as revolutionary figure abound in Sand's metaphysical novel. Spiridion, the founder of the order, is portrayed as a Romantic dreamer, whose religious meditations are compared to the trials of Christ. Like Jesus, he sweats blood and tears on the mountain at the sight of his coming torment.[42] In later chapters Christ, "the friend of humanity, the prophet of the ideal" (*Spiridion*, 244), is the central point of reference for Alexis when he experiences a moment of epiphanic intensity while looking out on the blue expanse of the Mediterranean: "je me représentai cet homme divin, grand comme les montagnes, resplendissant comme le soleil. Allégorie de la métaphysique, ou rêve d'une confiance exaltée . . . tu es plus grand et plus poétique que toutes nos certitudes mesurées au compas et tous nos raisonnements alignés au cordeau!" (194; "I imagined this divine man as great as the mountains, as radiant as the sun. Allegory of metaphysics, or dream of exalted faith . . . You are greater and more poetic than all our certitudes measured out with the compass and all our rationalizations lined up with a plumb rule!"). As Jean Gaulmier remarked, *Spiridion* was a text which, like Edgar Quinet's *Le Génie des religions*, Victor Cousin's eclecticism, Michelet's historical works, and Hugo's *Contemplations*, tended to see in Jesus a divine human being, rather than the son of God.[43]

Another biblical formula crucial to the ideological structure of *Spiridion* is the image of "not by bread alone." Sand's mouthpiece, Alexis, insists that a person's fundamental nature is neither materialistic nor rational. The monk stands in favor of the French Revolution's goals, but he affirms that those goals are primarily spiritual:

> "Ce travail gigantesque de la révolution française, ce n'était pas, ce ne pouvait pas être seulement une question de pain et d'abri pour les pauvres; c'était beaucoup plus haut . . . que visait et qu'a porté, en effet, cette révolution. Elle devait, non seulement donner au peuple un bien-être légitime, elle devait, elle doit . . . achever de donner la liberté de conscience au genre humain tout entier. . . . Cette âme qui me tourmente, *cette soif de l'infini* qui me dévore, seront-elles satisfaites et apaisées, parce que mon corps sera à l'abri du besoin?"   (Emphasis added; 221–222)

> ("This gigantic task of the French Revolution was not, could not be, only a question of bread and shelter for the poor; it was something much loftier . . . that this Revolution, in fact, aspired to and attained. Not only did it have to give to the people a legitimate well-being, it had to, it still must . . . fully accomplish the task of giving

freedom of conscience to the entire human race. . . . This soul that torments me, *this thirst for the infinite* which devours me, will they be satisfied and appeased because my body is safe from want?")

Some thirty years after the publication of *Spiridion*, it was precisely Sand's position of nonmaterialism that the Russian novelist Dostoevsky would single out for praise. In his 1876 necrological article, he stated that the form of Christian socialism Sand had articulated for France in the late thirties and forties made her into "one of the most perfect confessors of Christ. . . . She based her socialism, her convictions, hopes, and ideals on the moral feeling of human beings, on the spiritual thirst of humankind, on its striving toward perfection and purity." His reading of *Spiridion* prompted him to remark: "there was no thinker or writer in the France of her time who understood with such force that *man shall not live by bread alone*."[44] Indeed the main character of *Spiridion* had spoken of the French Revolution very much in those terms:

> "Et quand ce droit [promis par la révolution] sera conquis entière-ment par les générations futures, quand tous les devoirs des hommes entre eux seront établis par l'intérêt mutuel, sera-ce donc assez pour le bonheur de l'homme? . . . Quelque paisible, quelque douce que vous supposiez la vie de ce monde, suffira-t-elle aux désirs de l'homme, et la terre sera-t-elle assez vaste pour sa pensée?"   (222)

> ("And when this right [promised by the Revolution] is entirely conquered by future generations, when all the duties of men among themselves are established through a system of mutual interest, will this suffice for human happiness? . . . No matter how peaceful, how sweet one supposes life on earth to be, will it suffice for the desires of humankind, and will the world be vast enough to encompass human thought?")

One of Sand's goals, in this novel especially, was to render some of Leroux's ideas more palatable, to "faire avaler l'idée," as she writes.[45] *Spiridion* is not only one of the best examples of Sand's theory of the invisible novel after *Lélia*, it is also an important document in pre-Marxist social philosophy.

George Sand had created in her childhood a kind of socialist utopian androgynous deity, Corambé. In *Histoire de ma vie* she drew attention to her fundamental religious temperament:

> Mystique? soit! . . . j'appartenais apparemment à ce type-là. . . .
> Il me fallait trouver, non pas *en dehors*, mais *au-dessus* des concep-tions passagères de l'humanité, *au-dessus* de moi-même, un idé-

al . . . un type de perfection immuable à embrasser, à contempler,
à consulter et à implorer sans cesse.   (emphasis added; 2:96)

(A mystic? so be it! . . . apparently I belonged to that [intellectual]
type. . . . I needed to find, not so much *outside* as *above* the tran-
sitory conceptions of humanity, *above* my own being, an ideal
. . . a type of unchanging perfection that I could constantly embrace, contemplate, consult, and implore.)

In *Spiridion*, then, Sand constructed such an ideal in the form of a utopian socialist superstructure which gave perennial meaning to tran-
sitory historical events. Unlike the eighteenth-century philosophes
who had examined sacred texts with the intention of desacralizing
them, Sand along with the nineteenth-century utopian socialists and
Romantics was intent on resacralizing the secular past through the
deliberate usage of a Christian vocabulary. On the frontispiece of
Diderot's *Encyclopédie*, a female allegorical figure of Philosophia is depicted holding Theology on a leash. The utopians did not remuzzle
philosophy and hand the reins over once again to theology. But they
insisted on an equality or identification of the two. Leroux's phrase
"philosophy is a religion" underlines this position.[46]
     Marx's famous remark—"Religion is the opium of the people"—
could be reinterpreted as an indirect attack against the utopian socialists. Since the German philosopher had read the utopians carefully,
his epigram could be taken to mean that for him a religious terminology and a sacralized superstructure were the opium of the intellectuals, idealist philosophers, and Romantic novelists alike. If God had
indeed been reinvented in the postrevolutionary years, thus confirm-
ing Voltaire's remark "Si Dieu n'existait pas, il faudrait l'inventer," with
Marx God died a second death. Of course, religion, for Sand and her
Utopian contemporaries, had not been a drug or a poison. On the contrary, it had been a powerful antidote to a desacralized universe. And
Sand's religious epic, *Spiridion*, had been yet one more variant of
Engels's paradox regarding France as a Voltairian nation permeated
with mysticism.[47]

From *Spiridion* to *Lélia* II

Sand continued to work on the second version of *Lélia* throughout the
Spiridion gestation period. As early as November 1836, writing from
Paris, she had asked her old friend Alexis Duteil to send her the copy of
Lélia she had left in Nohant, "à demi déchiré, *corrigé et barbouillé de ma
main* . . . échareugné" ("half-torn, filled with corrections and covered
with my scribbles . . . completely marked up").[48] The letter confirms
that Sand had been extensively revising her original text for some time.

Indeed that same year, two "unpublished" chapters of the new *Lélia* came out in *La Revue des deux mondes*: "Les Morts" and "Contemplation."[49] Thereafter *Lélia* was "in transition" for almost three years, until September 1839 when the revised edition was finally published in book form.

We have had to wait almost one hundred and fifty years for a critical edition of that 1839 text. Only recently the Editions de L'Aurore published this version with an introduction by Béatrice Didier and a fine scholarly apparatus, consisting of annotations, chronology, bibliography, and valuable appendices. This annotated edition (referred to here as *Lélia* II, to differentiate it from the 1960 Garnier edition that concentrates on the 1833 version) provides the complete, revised text. As such, it stands in sharp contrast to the fragmented version of 1839 supplied by Pierre Reboul at the back of his edition. Didier's edition of *Lélia* strikes us as a new novel.

This second *Lélia* is even more religiously and philosophically oriented than the first. From a Romantic enfant du siècle lyrically giving vent to her nihilistic outbursts, Lélia has been transformed into a heretical thinker, a fact that Sand emphasized when she remarked in June 1836: "je ne conclus pas *Lélia* dans le sens catholique. . . . Lélia est à la fin du livre chassée de son couvent par les prêtres, pour avoir été trop charitable et trop évangélique, par conséquent *hérétique*" (*Corr.*, 3:449; "I do not conclude *Lélia* in a Catholic fashion. . . . At the end of the book Lélia is driven from her convent by the priests for having been too charitable and evangelical, therefore *heretical*"). Sainte-Beuve's remark concerning the "dithyrambic, grandiose and symbolic" tone of the first version of *Lélia*, in which he discerned moments of apocalyptic intensity, is even more relevant to the 1839 text.[50] Sand's portrayal of the new Lélia as a nun shows the way in which the two novels share the same religious sphere.

The trope of frigidity, pervasive in the 1833 *Lélia*, now extends itself to the religious sphere. A description of Lélia's cell reinforces the abstract connotations of whiteness, of cold and marble, images associated with the character from the first. "Cette cellule était simple et recherchée à la fois. Elle était toute revêtue . . . d'un stuc blanc comme l'albâtre. Un grand Christ d'ivoire . . . se détachait sur un fond de velours violet" ("This cell was simple and sophisticated at the same time. The walls were completely covered . . . with stucco as white as alabaster. A large ivory Christ . . . stood out against a purple velvet background"). When Sténio, who plays the part of voyeur in this scene,[51] finally distinguishes Lélia from her surroundings, he is disappointed not to see a woman of flesh and blood. His erotic expectation is undermined when he gazes only at a phantom: "il ne sut si c'était elle ou une statue d'albâtre toute semblable à elle, ou le spectre qu'il avait cru voir dans des jours de délire et d'épuisement" ("he did not know if it was her or a perfect alabaster statue of her likeness, or a ghost he recalled having seen during the days of his delirium or exhaustion"). Lélia has reached such a degree of immateriality that she has almost completely transcended the material world. She has become a statue, a ghost, a snow queen, a prefiguration of death:

> Elle était assise sur sa couche, cercueil d'ébène gisant à terre. Ses pieds nus reposaient sur le pavé et se confondaient avec la blancheur du marbre. Elle était toute enveloppée de ses voiles blancs . . . l'éclat de ce vêtement sans tache et sans pli avait quelque chose de fantastique qui donnait l'idée d'une existence immatérielle. . . . Sténio ne sut si elle dormait ou si elle méditait, tant elle demeura immobile. . . . Ses mains de neige posées l'une sur l'autre n'indiquaient ni la souffrance, ni la prière, ni l'abattement. On eût dit d'une statue allégorique représentant le calme. (2:130)

> (She was seated on her couch: an ebony coffin lying on the ground. Her bare feet rested on the stones and blended into the white of the marble. She was completely enshrouded in her white veils . . . the sheen of this dress, spotless and unwrinkled, had an eeriness that suggested an immaterial existence. . . . Sténio could not tell if she was sleeping or meditating, so still was she. Her snow white hands motionless one on top of the other indicated neither suffering, nor prayer, nor despondency. One might have taken her for an allegorical statue representing tranquillity.)

This reworking of the theme of frigidity, in which its abstract and non-sexual meaning is further accentuated, corresponds more closely to Sand's original intentions. Six years earlier, she had been shocked when the critics responded to the original *Lélia* with accusations of obscenity and immorality. The new version seems to prove Francine Mallet right when she argues that to examine *Lélia* "through the grid of the search for the absolute" corresponds more accurately to the author's original figuration of the main character and that the interpretation of sexual frigidity as a key to the novel should be downplayed.[52]

In *Spiridion* Sand used many of the same devices exploited in *Lélia*. One such device, in which the figural and the architectural echo one another, is at work in the scene where Alexis is wandering outside the convent. As he comes upon a decrepit tower, he immediately compares himself to the structure: "C'était un endroit sauvage, et la mer le remplissait d'harmonies lugubres. Une vieille tour ruinée . . . semblait prête à crouler sur ma tête. Rongées par l'air salin, ses pierres avaient pris le grain et la couleur des rochers voisins . . . Je me comparai à cette ruine abandonnée que les orages emportaient pierre à pierre" (*Spiridion*, 212; "It was a wild place, and the sea filled it with gloomy harmonies. An old ruined tower . . . seemed about to crumble down on my head. Worn down by the salt air, its stones had acquired the grain and the color of the surrounding rocks . . . I compared myself to this abandoned ruin which the storms were taking apart rock by rock"). In the descriptions of Lélia's cell and Alexis's tower, an identification is made between the characters' mental states and the architectural world surrounding them. From our modern perspective, obvious sexual—or at least physiological—identifications could be made between Lélia's femininity and her cell, and Alexis's masculinity and his tower. But in spite of the possible sexual resonance of the two settings, what is exploited here is a crucial Romantic form of poetic correspondance, in which landscape designates the characters' frame of mind ("un paysage est un état d'âme") rather than their sexuality. The two scenes emphasize the imminent departure of Alexis and Lélia from the world of the senses. They live on the edge of the ideal realm that will claim them both at the end.

Many parallels between the new *Lélia* and *Spiridion* are striking. *Spiridion* was the "complement" of *Lélia*, remarked Gustave Planche, since both novels sought "to revive the flames of Christian spiritualism."[53] Reflecting on the deaths in the two novels, Planche concluded that Lélia died "because the old religion is losing ground every day," since "Catholic spiritualism . . . is powerless to cure the moral wretchedness of our century." The same idea structures the ideological framework of *Spiridion*. When Alexis makes it clear that the monks have outlived their usefulness on the eve of a new age, he renounces the old Catholicism in favor of a new Christianity: "Le règne de l'Evangile éternel arrive, et vous [les moines] n'êtes plus ses disciples . . . la bannière du vrai Christ est dépliée, et son ombre vous enveloppe déjà" (*Spiridion*, 264–265; "The reign of the eternal Gospel is upon us, and you [the monks] are no longer its disciples . . . the banner of the true Christ is unfurled and its shadow is already enveloping you"). Similarly, the new Lélia yearns to articulate a new religion.

Lélia and Alexis have the same eschatological visions; they speak the same language. Lélia is "prey to a nameless delirium, to an unbounded despair" (*Lélia* II, 2:158); Alexis is "prey to every weariness and every worry of a soul groping for his way" (*Spiridion*, 230). They use many of the same metaphors. The image of the "shoreless sea," which expresses their sense of metaphysical disarray and the temptation of the infinite realm, is a dominant metaphor. Lélia is talking about the modern prophets: "En vain quelques groupes épars de sectaires impuissants essaient de rallumer une étincelle de vertu. Derniers débris de la puissance morale de l'homme, ils surnageront un instant sur l'abîme, et s'en iront rejoindre les autres débris au fond de cette *mer sans rivage* où le monde doit rentrer" (emphasis added; 1:135; "Several scattered groups of powerless sectarians are trying in vain to reignite the spark of virtue. As the last fragments of man's moral power, they will momentarily float above the abyss and then sink to join the other debris at the bottom of this *shoreless sea* to which the world must return"). Alexis, in the most lyrical passage of the book, cries out: "O ma religion! ô mon espérance! vous m'avez porté comme une barque incertaine et fragile sur des *mers sans rivages*, au milieu des brumes décevantes, vagues illusions, informes images d'une patrie inconnue" (emphasis added; 192; "O my religion! O my hope, you have borne me like an unsteady boat on *shoreless seas*, amid deceptive mists, vague illusions, shapeless images of an unknown homeland").

Both characters have devoted their lives to a quest for the ideal and have not found it. Lélia, in her last dithyrambic outburst, proclaims her failure through the conflation of pagan and Christian figures:

> "O vérité, vérité! pour te trouver je suis descendue dans des abîmes dont la seule vue donnait le vertige de la peur aux hommes les plus braves. J'ai suivi Dante et Virgile dans les sept cercles du rêve magique. J'ai suivi Curtius dans le gouffre . . . j'ai suivi Régulus dans son hideux supplice . . . j'ai suivi Madeleine au pied de la croix, et mon front a été inondé du sang du Christ et des larmes de Marie. J'ai tout cherché, tout souffert, tout cru, tout accepté . . . vérité! tu ne t'es pas révélée, depuis dix mille ans je te cherche et *je ne t'ai pas trouvée.*"   (emphasis added; *Lélia* II, 2, 158–159)

> ("O truth, truth! to find you I have descended into abysses, the merest sight of which inspired the dizziness of fear in the bravest of men. I have followed Dante and Virgil into the seven circles of the magic dream. I have followed Curtius into the bottomless pit . . . I have followed Regulus in his hideous ordeal . . . I have followed Mary Magdelene to the foot of the cross and my brow was bathed with the blood of Christ and the tears of Mary. I have sought after everything, suffered everything, believed everything, accepted everything . . . truth! You have not revealed yourself, I have sought you for ten thousand years and yet *I have not found you.*")

Alexis expresses the same anguish: "Il y a en moi une ambition de l'infini qui va jusqu'au délire. . . . J'ai cherché l'idéal partout avec l'ardeur d'un cerf qui cherche la fontaine dans un jour brûlant; j'ai été consumé de la soif de l'idéal et *je ne l'ai pas trouvé*" (emphasis added; 230, 234; "There is a desire in me for the infinite which reaches delirium. . . . I have sought the ideal everywhere with the ardor of a deer seeking a spring on a scorching day; I have been consumed by my thirst for the ideal and yet *I have not found it*"). The quest embarked upon in pain and resulting in despair links both passages and both characters.

Finally, like Lélia who is incapable of "resigning herself to *la vie positive*" (Sand's contemptuous term for the banality of quotidian existence), Alexis also has "forgotten to live." Having given herself over exclusively to the life of the mind and of the imagination, Lélia is "burned out" before her time: "Quand vint l'âge de vivre, il fut trop tard: j'avais vécu" ("When it came time to live, it was too late: I had already lived").[54] Alexis makes the same remark: "Le portier me demanda si j'avais oublié quelque chose. Oui, lui répondis-je avec égarement, j'ai oublié de vivre" (217; "The porter asked me if I had forgotten something. Yes, I answered distractedly, I have forgotten to live"). Both characters, in their frantic search for the "jouissances de l'âme," have denied the pleasures of the senses and permanently relinquished their corporeal existence.

The story of Alexis had evidently been in gestation for years, since the plot of *Spiridion* in miniature can be discerned in the earliest version of *Lélia* published in 1833. The episode in question (which was retained in the revised version of 1839), recounted by Lélia during her confession to her sister Pulchérie, describes the heroine's retreat to an abandoned monastery. As she discovers a hidden vault and descends into the catacombs, the reader in turn recognizes the embryonic presence of *Spiridion*: "en errant un jour parmi les décombres, j'avais découvert l'entrée d'un caveau qui, grâce aux éboulements dont elle était masquée, avait échappé aux outrages d'un temps de délire et de destruction" (*Lélia*, 189; *Lélia II*, 1:182; "wandering through the rubble one day, I discovered the entrance to a vault which, due to concealing landslides, had escaped the desecration of a time of frenzy and destruction"). In the course of her descent she finds the perfectly conserved figure of a dead monk, who is kneeling in a meditative pose. Pondering on the possible reasons for the figure's presence among these ruins, Lélia links it to the aftermath of 1789:

> C'était donc l'orage révolutionnaire qui avait surpris ce martyr dans sa retraite. Il était descendu là peut-être, en entendant les cris féroces du peuple, pour échapper à ses profanations, ou pour recevoir le dernier coup sur les marches de l'autel. . . . Il avait rendu son âme à Dieu, prosterné devant le Christ et *priant pour ses bourreaux*. (emphasis added; *Lélia*, 190; *Lélia II*, 1:183)

> (It was therefore the revolutionary storm that had surprised this martyr in his retreat. He had sought refuge there perhaps upon hearing the ferocious cries of the people, to escape from their desecrations, or to receive the last blow on the altar steps. . . . He had committed his soul to God, prostrated before Christ and *praying for his executioners*.)

In this passage, which exactly prefigures the entire ending of *Spiridion*, Lélia is overwhelmed by emotion as she ponders on the profound message of expiation. The monk is a martyr to the future, a Christ-like figure. Lélia's words suggest the conflation of the two stories—her own and that of Alexis:

> "Quelle plus grande pensée, quel plus profond emblème que ce Dieu martyr, baigné de sang et de larmes, étendant ses bras vers le ciel! O image de la souffrance, élevée sur une croix et montant comme une prière . . . de la terre aux cieux! Offrande expiatoire de la douleur qui se dresse toute sanglante et toute nue vers le trône du Seigneur! Espoir radieux, croix symbolique . . . Bandeau d'épines . . . sanctuaire de l'intelligence, diadème fatal . . . Je vous ai souvent invoqués, je me suis souvent prosternée devant vous! Mon âme s'est offerte souvent sur cette croix, elle a saigné sous ces épines; elle a souvent adoré, sous le nom de *Christ*, la souffrance humaine relevée par l'espoir divin." (*Lélia*, 191; *Lélia II*, 1:183–184)

> ("What grander thought, what more profound emblem than this martyr God; bathed in blood and tears, stretching his arms heavenward! O, image of suffering, raised up on a cross and ascending like a prayer . . . from earth to heaven! Expiatory offering of pain that rises bloody and naked toward the Lord's throne! Radiant hope, symbolic cross . . . crown of thorns . . . sanctuary of intelligence, fatal diadem . . . I have often invoked you, I have often knelt before you! My soul has often offered itself on this cross, it has bled under these thorns; it has often adored, in the name of *Christ*, human suffering uplifted by divine hope.")

The formula "human suffering uplifted by divine hope" encapsulates the essence of *Spiridion* and its hero. Like the monk Lélia discovers, Alexis is portrayed prostrated before the altar and he dies praying for his executioners. Lélia and Alexis are not so much twin spirits as kindred minds separated in time by more than a generation. We must suppose that, in the novelistic chronology of *Spiridion*, Alexis was attacked and slain by French soldiers during the first Italian campaign, sometime in the mid-1790s. Some four (fictional) decades later, in 1833, Lélia found the remains of an unknown monk. Lélia's discovery unearths for the reader a literal underground passageway between the two texts. While the crumbling monk cannot be said to be an exact replica of Alexis, he nonetheless represents a *mise-en-abyme* of the main character of *Spiridion*. The figuration of Alexis expresses a "retour aux sources" for the character of Lélia. Alexis is the embodiment of Sand's search for the intellectual and metaphysical roots of her heroine. Alexis, then, is not a brother but a chosen ancestor, a past master of whom Lélia can consider herself the privileged pupil. Lélia's sufferings take over where Alexis's martyrdom left off.

Alexis and Lélia on the Edge

Two chapters added to the 1839 edition of *Lélia* portray the heroine wandering on a rocky ledge. The pages have much in common with a scene of *Spiridion* which depicts its hero in a comparable landscape. The first chapter especially, entitled "Lélia au rocher," depicts a setting common to both texts—a cliff, a rocky crag hovering over the tumultuous ocean, on an unspecified portion of the Italian coast. Here is a veritable palimpsest. Underlying both passages two preromantic heroes, the melancholic René perched on his rock and Corinne on the Cape Misène can be discerned. And beneath them lurks Sand's recurrent Empedocles complex which expresses itself as the desire for vertigo. Alexis and Lélia express a similar longing for excess and cataclysm. The valorization of contemplative solitude which cohabits uneasily with a profound sense of alienation from the communities in which they live, and their verbalization of metaphysical anguish tighten the bonds between the two heretics and emphasize their similar psychic makeup. Sand highlights in both the same religious raison d'être, a solitary aloofness, a strongly intellectualized religiosity, a heretical world view, a desire to grapple with the large question of humanity's place in the hierarchy of creation, an eagerness to match God's wit, a disposition to express rebellion at any preestablished hierarchical order, a willingness to denounce the gap between mind and matter, a capacity for intellectual improvisation in which the mind becomes its own object of inquiry. Alexis is on his way to the old hermit's abode, where he will help care for the plague victims. He is dazzled by the vertiginous panorama that spreads out before him:

> Quand j'eus gravi la montagne, je fus ravi de l'aspect de la mer. Vue ainsi en plongeant de haut sur ses abîmes, elle semblait une immense plaine d'azur fortement inclinée vers les rocs énormes qui la surplombaient; et ses flots réguliers, dont le mouvement n'était plus sensible, présentaient l'apparence de sillons égaux tracés par la charrue. Cette masse bleue, qui se dressait comme une colline et qui semblait compacte et solide comme le saphir, me saisit d'un tel vertige d'enthousiasme, que je me retins aux oliviers de la montagne pour ne pas me précipiter dans l'espace. Il me semblait qu'en face de ce magnifique élément le corps devait prendre les forces de l'esprit et parcourir l'immensité dans un vol sublime. Je pensai alors à Jésus marchant sur les flots.   (*Spiridion*, 194)

> (When I had scaled the mountain, I was overcome by the view of the sea. From far above its depths, it appeared an immense azure plain sharply tilted toward the enormous overhanging rocks; and its regular waves, whose motion was no longer noticeable, suggested evenly plowed furrows. This blue mass, which rose up like

a hill and seemed as dense and solid as a sapphire, gripped me with such a dizzing enthusiasm that I clung to the mountain olive trees to avoid throwing myself into space. It seemed to me that facing this magnificient element the body must assume the mind's forces and cross the vastness in a sublime flight. I was reminded in that moment of Jesus walking on the water.)

By contrast, Lélia's promontory is depicted in a nocturnal mode. The Evangelical image of Jesus walking on the water alluded to by Alexis is here transmuted into the somber parable of Christ on the mount. Lélia wrestles with the dark angel, resisting the temptation of the reign of the material; she struggles against her feelings of jealousy for Sténio, jeering the "priestesses of matter" he has preferred to her. Her trial lasts through the night, after which she declares "ma lutte est finie" and climbs calmly down from her rock.

The ending of the 1839 version of *Lélia*, which was completely reconceptualized, presents a sequel to this scene. In an entirely new chapter, entitled "Délire," Lélia delivers her last oral improvisation. She has been exiled to an abandoned charterhouse in the north. Trenmor finds her wandering aimlessly in the mountain, oblivious to the night storm, the lashing rain, and the slippery rocks. Sensing that her strength is failing, the abbess embarks on a final lamentation:

> "Il est des heures dans la nuit où je me sens accablée d'une épouvantable douleur. . . . La nature toute entière pèse sur moi, et je me traîne brisée, fléchissant sous le fardeau de la vie comme un nain qui serait forcé de porter un géant . . . alors l'élan poétique et tendre tourne en moi à l'effroi et au reproche." (*Lélia* II, 2:157)

> ("There are hours during the night when I feel oppressed by an unbearable pain. . . . All of nature weighs down on me, and I drag myself, broken and bent down under the burden of life, like a dwarf forced to carry a giant . . . it is then that the poetic and tender fervor turns to dread and reproach in me.")

By situating herself deliberately in a long line of rebellious sibyls, the Romantic heroine becomes the most recent embodiment of the doomed feminine search for the appropriation of the Word:[55]

> "Depuis dix mille ans j'ai crié dans l'infini: Vérité, vérité! Depuis mille ans, l'infini me répond: Désir, désir! O Sibylle désolée, ô muette pythie, brise donc ta tête aux rochers de ton antre, et mêle ton sang fumant de rage à l'écume de la mer; car tu crois avoir possédé le Verbe tout-puissant et depuis dix mille ans tu le cherches en vain." (*Lélia* II, 2:159)

("For ten thousand years I have cried out into the infinite: Truth, truth! For a thousand years, the infinite has answered me: Desire, desire! O grieved Sibyl, o mute Pythia, why don't you smash your head against the rocks of your cave, and mingle your blood smoldering with rage with the seafoam; for you think you once possessed the all-powerful Word and for ten thousand years you have sought it in vain.")

As Lélia's delirious speech comes to a close, she cries "comme si elle allait se précipiter" ("as if she were about to throw herself down"). Held back by her friend, she collapses: "Elle retombait sur le rocher: elle avait cessé de vivre" ("she fell back against the rock: she had ceased to live"). Lélia's death is a form of "invisible suicide," in which the heroine kills herself through an act of will alone. This "natural" death replaces Lélia's death by strangling in the first version, thereby allowing her to spill out her definitive credo before her final collapse. Having steered away from the inspiration of the frenetic school evident in the earlier version, Sand now capitalizes on the closing scene to proclaim Lélia's poetic intensity, the seriousness of her claims, and the strength of her intellect.

Whereas both texts are concerned with the future and announce the coming of a new religion, *Lélia* II ends in doom while *Spiridion* closes with an affirmation of the imminence of a new Humanity. Alexis says, "ma vie a été un long combat entre la foi et le désespoir; elle va s'achever dans la tristesse et la résignation. . . . Mais mon âme est pleine d'espérance en l'avenir éternel" (217; "my life has been a long struggle between faith and despair; it is going to end in sadness and resignation. . . . But my soul is full of hope in the eternal future"). In the 1839 text of *Lélia*, it is true, Trenmor had announced that "une philosophie nouvelle, une foi plus pure et plus éclairée va se lever à l'horizon. Nous n'en saluons que l'aube incertaine et pâle" (2:156; "a new philosophy, a purer and more enlightened faith will appear on the horizon. We shall greet only its pale and uncertain dawn"). But Lélia is sceptical to the bitter end. At her death scene, her greatest torture lies in her continuing incapacity for any positive visionary thinking: "l'idée de voir l'ancien monde finir sans faire surgir un monde nouveau lui était amère et insupportable" (2:156; "the idea of watching the old world end without bringing forth a new one was bitter and unbearable to her"). Alexis, on the contrary, knows at his death that the new age is on the verge of being born: "Je voyais les sociétés prêtes à se dissoudre, les trônes trembler comme des roseaux que la vague va couvrir, les peuples se réveiller d'un long sommeil et menacer tout ce qui les avait enchaînés." (*Spiridion*, 200; "I saw societies ready to dissolve, thrones trembling like reeds before an oncoming wave, people waking from a long sleep and threatening everything that had enslaved them"). This crucial difference between the two texts, in spite of many parallels, explains why *Spiridion*, although its publication precedes that of *Lélia* II by a few months, is ideologically more in tune with the utopian novels of the forties. The new *Lélia*, in spite of all of its reconceptualizing, remains more solidly attached to the somber text of 1833 than to the new ideas Sand would spend the next decade in promulgating. Still, *Lélia* II and *Spiridion*, with their similar religious tropes, with their use of a hagiographic chronotope, with their comparable psychology of the infinite and Gothic atmosphere, point up two salient moments of Sand's black period.

The Transmission of the Book

Both versions of *Lélia* continued to occupy a unique place in Sand's intellectual development. More than twenty years after the 1833 text, she remarked, in her preface to the Hetzel edition, that after having read *Lélia* readers who subsequently read the story of her intellectual life in *Histoire de ma vie* would no longer be surprised that "doubt had been for [her] such a serious issue and such a terrible crisis" ("Préface de 1854," *Lélia*, 357–358). Sand's suggestion here of parallels between her own life and her heroine's is nonproblematic in the traditional critical perspective that routinely collapses author and hero. But note that the parallels are not those physical traits some critics prefer to insist upon, such as sexual frigidity or an overabundance of body hair (see *Lélia*, 185, 157, notes). Rather they are parallels rooted in the mental and spiritual life of the author. Much more troubling to some critics, on the other hand, is Sand's declaration in her memoirs that encourages the reader to view Father Alexis as another autobiographical projection alongside Lélia. A most revealing intertext for *Spiridion* is provided by *Histoire de ma vie* (1854–1855), in which the author reiterates her overwhelming concern for religious questions, a preoccupation that began in childhood:

> Ce qui m'absorbait à Nohant comme au couvent, c'était la recherche ardente ou mélancolique, mais assidue, des rapports qui peuvent, qui doivent exister entre l'âme individuelle et cette âme universelle que nous appelons Dieu.   (HV, 2:95)

> (What absorbed me at Nohant, as in the convent, was the always assiduous investigation, whether it was ardent or nostalgic, of the rapport that could, that must exist between the individual soul and this universal soul that we call God.)

It is not surprising, then, that some of these issues that had occupied her for years emerged in fictional form in *Spiridion*. But of special interest is a revealing episode recounted in great detail and with astounding precision at the end of Part 3 of the memoirs. The *Tolle, lege* incident at the Couvent des Anglaises had a direct thematic impact on *Spiridion*, being an event in Sand's life which took on mythical dimensions and subsequently provided the novelist with a series of literary tropes for writing about spiritual life.

The narrator is looking back on the turbulent Aurore Dupin and tracing her psychic itinerary as she comes into contact with the mystical realm. Sand describes at great length the chapel in which the pensionnaires regularly attended the religious services. Her narrative is effected through a series of visual observations—a standard device for Sand by now—as it concentrates on two sacred paintings. The first description emphasizes the play of light and dark on a painting by Titian as a metaphor to express divine revelation and human blindness:

> Placé trop loin des regards et dans un coin privé de lumière . . . on ne distinguait que des masses d'une couleur chaude sur un fond obscur. . . . Il y avait un seul moment dans la journée où j'en saisissais à peu près les détails, c'était en hiver, lorsque le soleil sur son déclin jetait un rayon sur la draperie rouge de l'ange et sur le bras . . . du Christ. Le miroitement du vitrage rendait éblouissant ce moment fugitif, et à ce moment-là j'éprouvais toujours une émotion indéfinissable.   (HV, 1:947–948)

> (Situated at a great remove from the viewer and in a corner deprived of light . . . one could make out only shapes of warm color on a dark ground. . . . There was only one moment during the day when I could perceive more or less clearly the details; that was winter, when the sun as it set cast a ray of light on the angel's red drapery and on the arm . . . of Christ. The shimmering reflection of the stained glass made this fleeting moment dazzling, and at that moment I always experienced an indescribable emotion.)

The description in chiaroscuro uses an artistic vocabulary to talk about theological questions. Light and dark articulate in a painterly way the child's capacity to see the divine truth or the inability to perceive the invisible. The holy portrait of Jesus on the Mount of Olives encapsulates a prefiguration of a revelation to come. The rays of the setting sun falling onto the picture are especially meaningful in terms of the way the image is used again in *Spiridion*. The illuminated portrait, then, provided Sand with a key symbol with which to express the manifestation of the divine. Light was made synonymous with illumination.

The same theme of light falling on a painting is recaptured in *Spiridion*. Angel is in the "salle du chapitre" where he admires the elegant moldings and the portraits:

On était aux derniers beaux jours de l'automne. Le soleil, entrant par les hautes croisées, projetait de grands rayons d'or pâle sur les traits austères de ces morts respectables, et donnait un reste d'éclat aux dorures massives des cadres noircis par le temps. Un silence profond régnait dans les cours et dans les jardins.   (*Spiridion*, 45)

(It was during the last fine days of autumn. The sun, streaming in through the upper transepts, cast long pale golden rays onto the austere features of those respectable dead and lent a residual gleam to the massive gilded frames now blackened with age. A profound silence reigned in the courtyards and the gardens.)

Again the same chiaroscuro atmosphere saturates this scene, which also stands as a prelude to a full-scale religious epiphany.

But the painting in *Histoire de ma vie* was only a preliminary step leading to Aurore's revelation, as the text moves from one description to another, this time focusing on a portrait of Saint Augustine "avec le rayon miraculeux sur lequel était écrit le fameux *Tolle, lege,* ces mysté-rieuses paroles" (HV, 1:948; "with the miraculous ray on which was written the famous *Tolle, lege,* those mysterious words"). This second instance of divine revelation is even more crucial. The metaphor of the sunray makes itself more precise, identified as miraculous and as bear-ing mysterious words. The narrative then leads Aurore out of the chapel, to digest what she has just witnessed. That evening, wander-ing about in the convent and looking for something to do, she decides to go back into the church. The "miracle" about to take place, what she calls her version of the *Tolle, lege,* whether imagined or real, is her ex-planation for her instantaneous transformation from a prank-loving fifteen-year-old devil into a mystically inclined adolescent. As she steps into the dark church, emphasis is placed once again on the light, emanating from a silvery lamp. But now the sense of sight, expanded by the senses of smell and hearing, creates a moment of sensory completeness:

l'église . . . n'était éclairée que par la petite lampe d'argent du sanctuaire, dont la flamme blanche se répétait dans les marbres polis du pavé, comme une étoile dans une eau immobile. . . . Les parfums du chèvre-feuille et du jasmin couraient sur les ailes d'une fraîche brise. Une étoile perdue dans l'immensité était comme en-cadrée par le vitrage. . . . Les oiseaux chantaient; c'était un calme, un charme, un recueillement, un mystère, dont je n'avais jamais eu l'idée.   (HV, 1:952–953)

(The church . . . was illuminated only by the little silver lamp in the sanctuary whose white flame was reflected on the polished

marble floor like a star in still water. . . . The scent of honeysuckle
and jasmin wafted through on the wings of a fresh breeze. A star
lost in the vastness appeared as if framed in the stained glass. . . .
Birds were singing; it was a moment of stillness, of enchantment,
of serenity, of mystery such as I had never imagined.)

Synesthesia and rapture, ecstasy of the senses and of the soul, beatitude in the midst of chaos and rebellion. Sand describes a scene of imminent mutation, a character on the verge of transformation. Aurore
falls into a somnanbulesque reverie. Time passes. The church is about
to be closed for the night:

> Je ne sais ce qui se passait en moi. Je respirais une atmosphère
> d'une suavité indicible. Tout à coup je ne sais quel ébranlement
> se produisit dans mon être, un vertige passe devant mes yeux
> comme une lueur blanche dont je me sens enveloppée. Je crois
> entendre une voix murmurer à mon oreille: *Tolle, lege.* Je me re-
> tourne . . . J'étais seule.   (HV, 1:953–954)

> (I do not know what was happening within me. I was breathing
> an atmosphere of indescribable sweetness. Suddenly some un-
> known disturbance occurred within my being, a sensation of dizzi-
> ness passes before my eyes like a white glow that seems to envelop
> me. I think I hear a voice murmur in my ear: *Tolle, lege.* I turn
> around . . . I was alone.)

The text emphasizes the role of the book as sacred object in the discovery of the Holy Word. "Take this book and read it," is the Augustinian
message that creates an "ébranlement" in Aurore's psychic life. The
passing on of the book can be identified as a crucial event in her mental
development. This theme of *translatio* will here-to-fore be highlighted
in Sand's oeuvre as a crucial element in the individual's sense of
community:

> ma pensée embrassait . . . pleinement cet idéal . . . de sain-
> teté . . . avec lequel je ne m'étais jamais trouvée en communica-
> tion directe; je sentis enfin cette communication s'établir
> soudainement. . . . Je voyais un chemin vaste, immense, sans
> bornes, s'ouvrir devant moi . . . mes larmes coulaient comme une
> pluie d'orage, mes sanglots brisaient ma poitrine, j'étais tombée
> derrière mon banc.   (HV, 1:954)

> (my thoughts fully embraced this ideal . . . of holiness . . . with
> which I had never been in direct contact; I finally felt this contact
> suddenly established. . . . I saw a vast, immense, limitless path
> open up before me . . . my tears gushed forth like a cloudburst,
> sobs wracked my chest, I had fallen behind my pew.)

The *Tolle, lege* episode can be interpreted as a prefiguration of Sand's future vocation as a writer. We remember that, throughout her memoirs, she tends to collapse the concepts of "religion" and "novel" into one signifying whole. The image of the "limitless path" opening up before her can be seen as a metaphor for her own future itinerary as a novelist writing for her life. Furthermore, the emphasis on her conversion as establishing a "contact" with the Other indicates the extent to which she saw the book, whether sacred or fictional, as a powerful object meant to be handed down from one generation to the next. The idea that books form a chain transmitting humanity's accumulated wisdom is one of the underlying motifs in *Spiridion*.

It is significant that Sand uses Saint Augustine in *Histoire de ma vie* as her model, since his *Confessions* are built upon a similar construct of psychic reversal. Augustine's *Tolle, lege*, the moment that spells reversal and takes place almost exactly at midpoint in the book, is heard "all at once." The profound change occurs in a fraction of time: "*in an instant . . .* it was as though the light of confidence flooded into my heart and all the darkness was dispelled."[56] For Saint Augustine, as for George Sand, "vocation," whether religious or literary, is expressed as a nonlinear progression, in terms of unexpected psychological mutations. This structure of discontinuity and reversal of behavior is a typical device throughout Sand's memoirs.

In *Spiridion* a portrait of the founder of the religious community also carries a verbal message. *Hic est veritas*, Spiridion's favorite motto which is used as the epigraph for his final testament, is written on the cover of the book he carries. Fictional and autobiographical text alike issue from the same set of devices—the double portrait, the tropes of illumination and enlightenment, manifestation of a saintly presence, and especially the existence of a divine word.

An episode later in *Spiridion* follows perhaps even more closely the model set up in *Histoire de ma vie*, as it involves the same cluster of themes, a hushed atmosphere, a portrait, a strange apparition or vision. Now Alexis is telling his story. Like Aurore he is "perfectly alone in the church" where "a profound silence" reigns. The emphasis shifts onto various light motifs: the "golden strips of the tabernacle," the "celestial light," the "colored stained-glass windows ablaze with sunlight," the "dull white flame of the lamp" burning before the altar. The stained-glass windows and the church lamp are recurrences of Aurore's *Tolle, lege*. There follows a "moment of beatitude" for Alexis that replicates the "state of indescribable beatitude" (1:955) Aurore described in *Histoire de ma vie*: "Ce fut dans cet instant de béatitude intellectuelle et physique . . . que j'entendis la porte . . . s'ouvrir doucement, et des pas . . . retentirent dans le silence du lieu saint avec une indicible harmonie. . . . L'esprit s'était manifesté à un seul de mes sens . . . tout rentra dans le silence" (*Spiridion*, 110–111; "It was in that moment of intellectual and physical bliss . . . that I heard the door . . . open gently, and steps echo in the silence of that holy place with an indescribable harmony. . . . The revelation had made itself manifest to only one of my senses . . . everything was again plunged into silence"). True to the Augustinian model of abrupt discontinuity and reversal, the time structure is epiphanic. The saintly presence here is discerned not through the whispering of words, but rather the echoing of steps. As in the memoirs, everything returns to normal almost instantaneously, the aftermath marked only by the overwhelming silence. The two texts have explored the same state of mind using the same images.

The main theme of *Spiridion*, which is highlighted by the *Tolle, lege* episode in *Histoire de ma vie*, is the transmission of the sacred Logos, depicted either as an oral message or through the medium of the Holy Book. *Spiridion* explores the double power of written and spoken words. Conversations, speeches, mysterious words spoken by a disembodied voice, oral confessions, phantoms pronouncing prophetic words, and doctrines passed on from father to spiritual son structure much of the text. The end of the novel, however, over which Sand labored and of which two very different versions exist, emphasizes the power of the written word. In the wake of Alexis's "livre blanc" with its invisible writing, Spiridion's testament is exhumed from his tomb. It consists of three manuscripts: the Gospel according to Saint John, considered by Spiridion to be the most divine; Jean de Parme's "Introduction to the Eternal Gospel," denounced as heretical and burnt by the church in 1260; and Spiridion's own final commentary. The monk praises Jean de Parme's division of Christianity into three reigns: the reign of the Father (the period of Mosaic law) which has ended; the reign of the Son which is about to end; and the reign of the Holy Ghost, a doctrine of liberty, equality, and fraternity, which is about to begin. Spiridion announces "a new revelation," "a new religion," "a new humanity," "a new society," using a series of feminine personifications:

"Cette religion, fille de l'Evangile, ne reniera point sa mère, mais elle continuera son oeuvre; et ce que sa mère n'a pas compris, elle l'expliquera; ce que sa mère n'a pas osé, elle l'osera; ce que sa mère n'aura fait qu'entreprendre, elle l'achevera." (*Spiridion*, 259)

("This religion, daughter of the Gospel, will not repudiate its mother, but will continue her work; what its mother did not understand, it will explain; what its mother did not dare to do, it will dare; what its mother only started, it will fully accomplish.")

As Alexis interprets Spiridion's testament to Angel, he likens his disciple to an initiate whose brain is now "like a book that carries life within it" (*Spiridion*, 260).

Aurore's mind, divinely infected by the instruction to "Take the book and read" and Alexis, whose brain is likened to a book, both express a fundamental Sand myth: the transmission of Humanity's ultimate and often hidden goals in its itinerary toward the future, from hand to hand, from mouth to mouth, and from book to reader. *Spiridion*, then, marks a crucial moment in the evolution of Sand's thought. After such novels of rebellion as *Indiana*, *Valentine* and *Lélia*, she embarked on the search for the great myths of humanity which would form a double furrow in her works. In the utopian novels of the 1840s she would explore the myths of social rejuvenation. In *Consuelo* and *La Comtesse de Rudolstadt* she would give a voice to the classical myths as they were reformulated by the Romantic collective unconscious.

7

From *Desolatio* to *Consolatio:* The Utopian Convalescence of an Enfant du siècle

Notre âme est un trois-mâts cherchant son Icarie.

BAUDELAIRE

(Our soul is a three-masted ship seeking its Icaria.)

Romantic Poison, Utopian Antidote

"The woman-genius, known under the name of George Sand, is indisputably the foremost poetic glory of the contemporary world," wrote the Russian critic Belinsky in 1842.[1] During her lifetime, such words of praise were not unusual among the Russian intelligentsia who responded to Sand with unparalleled intensity. In his *History of Social Thought*, Maxime Leroy insisted on the extraordinary impact of Sand's novels abroad in the mid-nineteenth century and their importance for the propagation of certain social ideas in the cultural air at the time: "Through her, socialist ideas were diffused to a very large public; she conferred to them, bathing in a magnificent halo, an unheard of prestige; it is hard for us today to imagine this diffusion."[2] In Russia especially, where most foreign books in economics, philosophy, social thought, and history had been banned since the aborted Decembrist uprising of 1825, novels became the great medium through which ideas from the West could travel. Sand's position, from the late 1830s on, was privileged in this respect with her fictions increasingly recognized as vehicles for many of the so-called new ideas.

Among the early novels, *Spiridion* without doubt was Sand's most influential in Saint Petersburg and Moscow. After it, Russian critics most often singled out her utopian novels of the 1840s. Belinsky, for example, devoted a lengthy and laudatory book review to *Le Meunier d'Angibault*, a novel that by contrast had made little impression in France. Bakunin called her a modern Joan of Arc and commented that she was the "star of salvation and the prophet of a glorious future."[3] Turgenev referred to her as "one of our saints." In *Diary of a Writer*, Dostoevsky described "with fervor the great admiration he and other Russian *dreamers* of the forties had experienced in reading the novels of

G. Sand, novels that expressed a burning faith in humankind [and] a belief in the greatness of humanity's moral possibilities."[4] Still today, the Sand titles Soviet specialists single out are different from those usually considered her greatest works in the West.[5] Sand's "extraordinary decade" is considered by the Russians to be the period of her utopian novels. The scholar N. Treskunov, while discussing some of the novels that constitute Sand's most popular works in the West, such as *Indiana*, *Valentine*, *Lélia*, *Consuelo*, and the pastoral novels, also provides chapters dealing with her utopian and socialist texts: *Le Compagnon du tour de France*, *Horace*, *Le Meunier d'Angibault*, and *Le Péché de Monsieur Antoine*.[6]

The Russian discourse about Sand, therefore, brings us to the following paradox. There seem to be two Sands: one steeped in mal du siècle, the other intent on *guérison du siècle*. One nihilist, the other socialist; one denouncing existing social structures, the other announcing the advent of a new social order. On the one hand, a myth of rebellion and punishment is embodied in Lélia seen as a figure of revolt; on the other, a myth of a New Jerusalem finds its expression in the utopian socialist dreamers who make up Sand's fictional cast of characters in the forties. The world is decomposing in *Lélia*, and being recomposed in *Le Péché de Monsieur Antoine*. Is it then possible to reconcile two seemingly antithetical fictional tendencies in Sand's works, to find the thread leading from one series of novels to the other, from such early works of sensibilité noire as *Lélia* and *Spiridion* to the utopian novels so clearly reflecting another ideological framework? In these later texts, a different kind of narrative structure is articulated, a new set of characters enters Sand's fictional repertoire, and familiar themes or devices, such as the dream or the use of religious terminology, are exploited to underscore a new message. When Sand coined two antithetical terms, desolation making and consolation making, to differentiate Flaubert's style of literary discourse from her own, she unwittingly provided useful labels with which to describe her own duality as a novelist. In fact, the 1840s mark Sand's moving away from her own novels of desolation and adopting a fiction of consolation. The concept of *consolatio*, of course, is encapsulated in the title of her great sage, *Consuelo*.

The ideological itinerary Sand followed from those novels that revel in the mal du siècle to those that aim to articulate the possibility for a *santé du siècle* can be traced in her autobiography and correspondence. Examining her beginnings as an artist, Sand diagnosed her ailment as having both temperamental and sociocultural origins. As a young woman her natural tendency to live within herself had encouraged a Romantic form of egotism which developed into melancholia: "I lived too much in myself, by myself, and for myself," she writes in *Histoire de ma vie* (2:302). When she began timidly to peek out of her shell at the various political, historical, social, and cultural spheres in the early 1830s, what she saw only exacerbated her nascent symptoms:

> Quand mon horizon se fut élargi, quand m'apparurent . . . tous les vices du grand milieu social, quand mes réflexions n'eurent plus pour objet ma propre destinée, mais celle du monde où je n'étais qu'un atome, ma désespérance personnelle s'étendit à tous les êtres, et la loi de la fatalité se dressa devant moi si terrible que ma raison en fut ébranlée.   (HV, 2:195)

> (When my horizons were broadened, when all the vices of the larger social sphere . . . appeared clearly before me, when my thoughts no longer had as their subject my own destiny, but rather that of the world where I was only an atom, my personal hopelessness extended to all beings, and the law of fatality rose up so terrible before me that my reason was shaken by it.)

With selective perception, she drew up a catalogue of catastrophes. It seemed to her that all domains—politics, medicine, philosophy, the arts—were marked by dashed hopes and rampant pathology. Her description of the mood in the early 1830s conjures up a gloomy picture of a sick society, suffering an epidemic of spiritual afflictions:

> La République rêvée en juillet aboutissait aux massacres de Varsovie et à l'holocauste du cloître Saint-Merry. Le choléra venait de décimer le monde. Le saint-simonisme . . . était frappé de persécution et avortait. . . . L'art aussi avait souillé, par des aberrations déplorables, le berceau de sa réforme romantique. Le temps était à l'épouvante et à l'ironie, à la consternation et à l'impudence . . . personne ne croyant plus à rien, les uns par découragement, les autres par athéisme.   (HV, 2:195–196)

> (The Republic dreamed of in July had ended in the Warsaw massacres and the holocaust of the Saint-Merry cloister. Cholera had just decimated the world. Saint-Simonianism . . . was struck by persecution and was dying prematurely. . . . Art also, by deplorable aberrations, had sullied the cradle of its romantic reform. It was a time of dread and irony, consternation and impudence . . . no one believed in anything anymore, some because of discouragement, others because of atheism.)

In this atmosphere of disillusionment and moral apathy, Sand set out to write *Lélia*, "sous le coup de cet abattement profond . . . éprouvant une sorte de soulagement triste à céder à l'imprévu de ma rêverie" (HV, 2:196; "under the influence of this deep dejection . . . experiencing a kind of forlorn relief in giving myself up to the unexpected in my musings"). *Lélia* then is identified as the highpoint of her scepticism, doubt, and despair.

The period of *Lélia*, *Lettres d'un voyageur*, *Jacques*, and *Spiridion* was stamped with a pessimism and a melancholia that the author transfused directly into the bloodstreams of her characters. Lélia, the "voyageur," Jacques, and Alexis are all, in one way or another, afflicted by the mal du siècle, poisoned by the venom of nihilism, tempted by suicide, cursing the materialistic age in which they live, and repudiating the possibility of improvement. By the time of *Consuelo*, however, Sand's world view had been turned on its head. Hopelessness had given way to optimism, tragic denouements were replaced by happy endings, no longer was suicide a viable option. Characters began to make affirmations of faith which replaced assertions of doubt and atheism. Clearly, a major change had taken place.

For some contemporary critics, Sand's progression from black Romanticism to rosy utopian socialism was indicative of the natural development of literary history. Sainte-Beuve, in an article entitled "Hope and Desires of the Literary and Poetic Movement after the Revolution of 1830," claimed that the mission of art in his day was "to constantly reflect and radiate in a thousand colors the feeling of progressive humanity."[7] For Hugo, Romanticism and socialism were "the same phenomenon."[8] To concentrate intensely, as George Sand had done, on diagnosing the ailments of the age naturally led to the desire, just as intense, to find remedies for these ills. The second half of the thirties, when she was writing *Spiridion* and rewriting *Lélia*, marks the turning point of this shift.

From 1836 to 1839, even as her fictions tended to depict a predominantly nihilistic universe, her correspondence expressed a world view in flux. For Georges Lubin, the shift in Sand's frame of mind begins to appear in the correspondence from approximately 1837 on.[9] While a letter to Michel de Bourges, dated January 1837, still employs the phraseology of Lélia, expressing at once the "malheur de vivre" and the adherence to desperation which marks Sand's great nihilistic heroine, an undercurrent of measured hope can be sensed.[10] An earlier letter to Marie d'Agoult, in which Sand not only draws up the framework for a life in search of the ideal but also suggests that the ideal has been found, hints that her priorities, both in and out of literature, are in transition:

> pleurer avec la misère du pauvre . . . vivre de presque rien, donner presque tout, afin de rétablir l'égalité primitive . . . voilà la religion que je proclamerai dans mon petit coin et que j'aspire à prêcher à mes douze apôtres sous le tilleul de mon jardin.   (10 July 1836; *Corr.*, 3:474–475)

(to cry with the poverty of the pauper . . . to make do with almost
nothing, to give away almost everything, in order to reestablish
primeval equality . . . this is the religion that I will proclaim in my
little corner and that I intend to preach to my twelve apostles under
the linden tree in my garden.)

She amplified the metaphor of illness and recovery to designate literary inspiration: "je refais *Lélia*. . . . Le poison qui m'a rendue malade
est maintenant un remède qui me guérit. . . . Ce livre m'avait pré-
cipitée dans le scepticisme; maintenant, il m'en retire; car vous savez
que *la maladie fait le livre, et de même pour la guérison*" (emphasis added;
10 July 1836; *Corr.*, 3:474; "I am reworking *Lélia*. . . . The poison that
made me ill is now a healing remedy. . . . This book originally threw
me into skepticism; now, it is pulling me out of it; for you know that
illness makes the book, and so does the cure"). December of the same year
finds Sand measuring the emotional gap between the first and second
versions of *Lélia*: "I want to complete . . . [*Lélia*] in which earlier I
placed all the bitterness of my suffering and into which I now intend to
insert the ray of hope which has appeared to me" (*Corr.*, 3:595). The
1839 text, although still steeped in pessimism, was a first step toward
philosophical convalescence.

Still, can one actually speak of a conversion, as Georges Lubin
and Julie Sabiani do?[11] Such a conversion would divide Sand's intellectual and literary life into an early period (the 1830s), primarily concerned with exploring the philosophy of doubt, and a second period
(the 1840s on) marked by the contrary attitude of hope. The essential
role played by Leroux in this philosophical transformation cannot be
overemphasized. The utopian thinker who, according to Balzac, had
"shaken up his century,"[12] was for Sand a being whom she venerated
"as a new Plato, as a new Christ" (letter to C. Marliani, 8 Mar. 1839;
Corr., 4:590). One can readily understand the appeal that Leroux's
thought had for her, since many of her earliest intellectual tendencies,
which could be grouped under the rubric of mystical Romanticism,
found their echo in Leroux's antimaterialistic doctrine.[13] Sand's "shock
of recognition" can already be felt in *Spiridion*. Furthermore, the poetic
intensity of Leroux's prose made him the most Romantic of all the utopian socialists.[14] His understanding of poetic ecstasy as a variant of
mysticism coincided with Sand's own view of poetic inspiration.[15]
Leroux did provide the novelist with something *new*, however: a program, a plan, a set of measures to bring about social change. After the
diagnosis, a prognosis; after the denunciation of the present, an an-
nunciation of the future. That is why many of Leroux's more progressive teachings were incorporated into Sand's utopian novels. Key
concepts such as solidarity (a utopian cognate for Christian charity),
Humanity (the common denominator linking past, present, and fu-

ture), and perfectibility made their entry forcefully into Sand's novels of the forties. Her discovery of Leroux's philosophy had in part been prompted by Sainte-Beuve.[16] "I plunged myself in [Leroux's philosophy] and I was *transformed* by it," she writes Charles Poncy, a proletarian poet from Toulon. "I found in it calm, strength, faith, hope, and the patient and persevering love of humanity" (emphasis added; 26 Feb. 1843; *Corr.*, 6:68). This articulation of a *vita nuova* was more the reemergence of a tendency that had been part of the author's "semimystical and semiartistic" temperament in childhood. She had always led a double existence, she explains in *Histoire de ma vie*, at once prone to attacks of doubt which provoked spleen—"an old chronic ailment," as she calls it, which she had contracted and fought against since her earliest years (HV, 2:300)—and attracted to finding solutions of hope. She likened the attacks to "veils falling like a tempest" on her imagination (HV, 2:302) which would plague her until death: "I will die in this thick cloud which surrounds and oppresses me" (HV, 2:303). These moments of gloom were broken up by privileged periods of serenity, marked by a distancing from the egotistical self, "a sincere detachment from my personality before God" (HV, 2:304).

Although she would transcend it, Sand would never disavow the 1830s as a crucial period in her intellectual development. To Flaubert, who likened writing to a sacred agony, she acknowledged that all writing need not issue from optimism. Although by the 1860s, she herself had given up inspiration borne of desperation, she recognized its potential in sustaining the artist's fervor. Despair, anger, or even anguish of the soul could serve as literary inspiration. If anything, they were preferable, in Sand's view, to literature nourished by the gross materialism prevailing then in her society. To readers who criticized the mal du siècle and its victims, she retorted in 1866: "Peut-être notre maladie valait-elle mieux que la réaction qui l'a suivie; que cette soif d'argent, de plaisirs sans idéal et d'ambitions sans frein, qui ne me paraît pas caractériser bien noblement la *santé du siècle*" ("Perhaps our illness was worth more than the subsequent reaction to it; more than this thirst for money, for pleasure without ideals, and for unrestrained ambitions, which to me do not very nobly portray the *health of the century*").[17]

Sand had already made this point in her autobiography: "je me persuade encore que l'effet de ces sortes de livres [tels que *Lélia*] est plutôt bon que mauvais . . . dans un siècle matérialiste, ces ouvrages-là valent mieux que les *Contes drôlatiques*, bien qu'ils amusent beaucoup moins la masse des lecteurs" (HV, 2:202; "I still tell myself that the effect of these kinds of books [such as *Lélia*] is more good than bad . . . in a materialist age, such works are worth more than the *Contes drôlatiques*, even if they are much less entertaining to the general reading public"). But while a hopeless search for the absolute was preferable to the crass materialism that characterized her age, it was not until Sand was able, with the help of Leroux and other utopian thinkers, to fashion for herself an idealist philosophy, which at once transcended the self and promised collective hope, that her "conversion" truly took place. The crucial step was the permanent rejection of the Romantic "moi admirable" in favor of a "moi humanitaire," which merged with the larger human collective. From the 1840s on, living outside the self would be a leitmotif in Sand's writings: "Nous n'arrivons à nous comprendre et à nous sentir vraiment nous-mêmes qu'en nous oubliant, pour ainsi dire, et en nous perdant dans la grande conscience de l'humanité" (HV, 2:199; "We succeed in understanding ourselves and feeling truly like ourselves only by forgetting ourselves, so to speak, and by losing ourselves in the collective consciousness of humanity"). Her correspondence with Flaubert in the 1860s and 1870s would make frequent references to "l'horreur du *moi*"[18] and to the desire to live "outside the self."[19]

The critic Daniel Halévy traced Sand's search for reconciliation as early as *Lettres d'un voyageur*, where, he argued, the writer hesitated "between a life of despair and humanitarian enthusiasm."[20] Sand's ideological itinerary from *desolatio* to *consolatio* is exemplified in her return from the austere desert of meditation and her voluntary reintegration into society. Years after her "conversion," she would address a credo to her friend Desplanches, which affirmed her will to believe and betrayed its utopian inspiration in the simultaneous allusion to the Christian virtues alongside the great trinity of revolutionary principles:

> Croyons au progrès; croyons en Dieu dès à présent. . . . La foi est . . . un état de grandeur intellectuelle qu'il faut garder en soi comme un trésor. . . . Croyons quand même . . . et disons: *Je crois*! ce n'est pas dire: "J'affirme"; disons: *J'espère*! ce n'est pas dire: "Je sais." Unissons-nous dans cette notion, dans ce voeu, dans ce rêve. . . . Nous sentons qu'il est nécessaire que, pour avoir la charité, il faut avoir l'espérance et la foi, de même que, pour avoir la liberté et l'égalité, il faut avoir la fraternité.   (25 May 1866; *Corr.*, 19:897–898)

> (Let us believe in progress; let us believe in God from this very moment. . . . Faith is a state of intellectual grandeur that we must preserve within us like a treasure. . . . Let us believe all the same . . . and say: *I believe*! which is not to say: "I affirm"; let us say *I hope*! which is not to say: "I know." Let us unite in this idea, in this desire, in this dream. . . . We feel it is necessary that, in order to have charity, we have hope and faith, just as to have liberty and equality, we must have fraternity.)

Sand was recasting in epistolary form what the first of her utopian heroes, Pierre Huguenin, had declared two decades earlier in *Le Compagnon du tour de France*:

> La résignation pour soi-même est une vertu qu'il faut avoir. . . .
> Mais se résigner au malheur d'autrui, mais supporter le joug qui
> pèse sur des têtes innocentes, mais regarder tranquillement le
> train du monde sans essayer de découvrir une autre vérité,
> un   autre   ordre,   une   autre   morale!   oh!   c'est   impossi
> ble.   (*Compagnon*, 303)

> (Resignation in and of itself is a virtue one must have. . . . But to
> resign oneself to the unhappiness of others, to tolerate the yoke
> weighing down on innocent heads, to calmly watch the course of
> events without trying to discover another truth, another order, an
> other moral system! oh! that is impossible.)

This denunciation of philosophical passivity supports a position that
diametrically counteracts the outbursts of despair uttered by Sand's
Romantic characters. Exploiting the same metaphor of disease with
which Lélia had designated the social body, the *compagnon* makes quite
a different diagnosis which insists more on the cure than on the
affliction:

> Est-ce donc chercher le remède que de détourner les yeux avec hor
> reur et de se boucher le nez, en distant qu'il n'y a que corruption et
> infection dans l'infirmerie? Que penseriez-vous d'un carabin qui
> ne pourrait voir sans s'évanouir de dégoût un membre gan
> grené? . . . osez . . . descendre dans les léproseries de l'huma
> nité morale . . . *ne perdez pas le temps à dire que cela est horrible à voir;
> songez à y porter remède.*[21]

> (Is it really seeking a remedy merely to avert one's eyes with horror
> and hold one's nose, while saying that there is only corruption and
> infection in the sick ward? What would you think of a medical stu
> dent who could not set eyes on a gangrened limb without fainting
> in disgust? . . . dare . . . to descend into the leper colonies of
> moral humanity . . . *do not waste time saying that this is horrible to
> look at; think of finding a remedy.*)

Whereas the characters with Lélia's proclivities dwelt on the horror
of a given situation without attempting to prescribe any remedies,
the utopian Huguenin insists on finding cures. Sand's utopian novels
have as an ideological base the valorization of the search for happiness in the great progressive march toward a better future. The lyrical

lamentations of a Lélia or an Alexis are replaced by the social philosopher's therapeutic vision. The Stendhalian "goût du malheur" expressed in Sand's Romantic novels now gives way to what Rimbaud called the "magic study of happiness."[22]

After the Romantic poison of the 1830s comes the utopian antidote of the 1840s: *Le Compagnon du tour de France* (1840), *Horace* (1842), *Consuelo* and *La Comtesse de Rudolstadt* (1842–1844), *Jeanne* (1844), *Le Meunier d'Angibault*,[23] *Le Péché de Monsieur Antoine* (1845), *La Mare au diable* (1846). To these titles could be added two novels of the sixties, *Mademoiselle la Qunitinie* (1863) and *Monsieur Sylvestre* (1866). All are underscored by a similar discourse of consolation; the narrative framework, for the most part, ensures a happy resolution; characters are imbued, to various degrees, with Utopian ideas; and the narrator is convinced of a specific philosophic point of view based on generosity of vision and idealism. Sand composed *Lélia* during a time when she could not find "in the Republican and socialist ideas . . . a light strong enough to combat the shadows that Mammon was brazenly spreading across the world" (HV, 2:196); by contrast the decade following the composition of *Spiridion* represents a very different turn of mind when the author wants "to see the right prevail."[24] The 1840s, which culminated in the Revolution of 1848 (in which Sand actively participated) represent Sand's utopian decade. And the fictional universe which issued from Sand's utopian imagination called for a new set of narrative principles.

Articulating the Future

While Sand increasingly called for the right of novelists to weave into the fabric of their fictional texts consideration of abstract concepts as expounded by the proponents of various utopian ideologies, she was well aware that she could not do so using the same rhetorical devices as the social thinkers. "A novel is not a treatise," she wrote to Jean Dessoliaire in November 1848. But because she was always able to grasp fully the potential of the fictional form, she was able to work on the boundaries of novelistic structures, writing on the seam, so to speak, of fiction and nonfiction. In *Lélia* she had aimed at writing an invisible novel, in *Spiridion* a completely plotless fiction. In her utopian works, the challenge was to fictionalize the abstract sphere of contemporary social thought; to find literary devices enabling the undidactic inclusion of ideological topics into the marrow of her fiction. As she noted in the same letter to Dessoliaire:

> J'ai essayé de soulever des problèmes sérieux dans des écrits dont
> la forme . . . permet à l'imagination de se lancer dans une re-
> cherche de l'idéal absolu. . . . Les romans parlent au coeur et à

l'imagination. . . . Laissons l'imagination de chacun apprécier selon son goût et sa partie les ouvrages d'imagination. Pourvu que
ces ouvrages soient animés d'un esprit de générosité et qu'ils ten-
dent à l'amour du bien, ils ne peuvent faire de mal et même ils
peuvent faire un peu de bien.   (*Corr.*, 8:685)

(I have tried to raise serious questions in works whose
form . . . might incite the imagination to search for the absolute
ideal. . . . Novels speak to the heart and to the imagination. . . .
Let each one's imagination appreciate works of imagination according to his or her taste. . . . Provided that these works are endowed with a spirit of generosity and that they lend themselves to
the love of the good, they can do no harm and can even be of some
small benefit.)

Sand, then, faced the challenge of appealing to the imagination of her
readers rather than to their rational faculties when presenting certain
philosophical concepts of the utopian socialist thinkers she wished to
promote. Therefore, all her utopian texts betray a tension between the
artist's desire for a free dialogue with the reader and the writer's interest in promoting the "right" solution.

The favorite daydream of the utopian thinker, says W. H. Auden,
is of a New Jerusalem, a future world in which the contradictions of the
present world have been resolved.[25] Sand illustrates Auden's remark
because she projected her novels into the future so as to give free reign
to her utopian imagination. Renan's comment—"Make no mistake.
Man is guided only by the idea of the future"[26]—incapsulates a fundamental tenet of Sand's utopian strategy: to direct her vision toward an
invisible but auspicious future. The novel of the forties added a new
dimension to Sand's fictional time structure. Her "études de moeurs"
in novels such as *Indiana* and *Valentine* had examined the pulse of the
present; her historical novels had probed the mysteries of the past, the
eighteenth century in *Spiridion* and *Mauprat*, the sixteenth century in
L'Uscoque; her utopian fictions would increasingly depict the future.
Saint-Simon's belief in the perfectibility of the human race was expressed in his claim: "The Golden Age, which tradition has up to now
placed in the past, is before us."[27] The philosopher's famous line found
its concretization in Sand's fiction. "It is from Sand [along with other
Utopian socialists] that a ray of light shone," remarked the Russian
writer Saltykov-Shchedrin in his memoirs, insisting on this forward-
looking gaze now apparent in her novels, "which made us understand
that the Golden Age was not in the past but truly in the future."[28] If the
utopian imagination can be defined above all as the capacity to look
into the future, we are tempted to speculate on the powerfully anti-
nostalgic vision of Sand's novelistic eye. For while her pastoral mode

might be seen to depict a kind of backward glance on social structures that predate the nineteenth century, many more of her novels encapsulated a vision of the future, with the present often articulated as a harbinger of a new order, poised on the threshold of a utopian society. She exploited primarily three strategies to fictionalize the future in her utopian novels: the description of dreams, the employment of two spatial metaphors (the road and the garden), and the use of a recurrent character who announced the new social order.

"Promontorium Somni"

"To dream a dream is good, to dream utopia is better," remarked Hugo.[29] Dreaming utopia is the visionary occupation of Sand's utopian characters—the heroine of *Consuelo*, Marcelle de Blanchemont in *Le Meunier d'Angibault*, Pierre Huguenin in *Le Compagnon du tour de France*, M. de Boisguilbault in *Le Péché de Monsieur Antoine*, the old hermit in *Monsieur Sylvestre*, and M. Lemontier in *Mademoiselle la Quintinie*. In order to describe the elusive vision, the protagonist is removed from his or her isolation, and integrated into a community, so that the utopian future is almost entirely envisaged from a communal point of view. The Sandian hero verifies Leroux's vision of the existence of a unit larger than the individual, the unit Humanity: "the individual is a real being in whom there lives, in a virtual state, the ideal being called humanity." Leroux's *communionism* stressed the binary poles of religiosity and fraternity which Sand attempted to incorporate in her fictions.[30]

An archetypal example of the utopian dream appears in *Le Compagnon du tour de France* where the hero, Pierre Huguenin, defined as "l'homme . . . de la société future," looks into a crystal ball through the transforming lens of socialist theory (*Compagnon*, 439). By giving oneiric form to the desire for an improved world, Sand poeticizes the search for a new realm of existence, in which a new social structure can be erected. Pierre is typical of a group of privileged Sandian utopian dreamers whose rich mental faculties explore the future. His vision stems from a noble refusal to resign himself to the misfortune of others; it reflects his overwhelming need for hope and his yearning for the elaboration of a plan of action out of which a new moral order can emerge. At the same time, the author's "courage de rêver tout haut" (*Corr.*, 7:187) is conveyed:

> Il fit un rêve étrange. Il lui sembla qu'il était couché, non sur des copeaux, mais sur des fleurs. Et ces fleurs croissaient, s'entr'ouvraient . . . et montaient en s'épanouissant vers le ciel. Bientôt, ce furent des arbres gigantesques qui embaumaient les airs et, s'échelonnant en abîme de verdure, atteignaient les splendeurs de l'em-

pyrée. L'esprit du dormeur, porté par les fleurs, montait . . . vers le ciel, et s'élevait, heureux et puissant. . . . Enfin il parvint à une hauteur d'où il découvrit toute la face d'une terre nouvelle. (*Compagnon*, 289)

(He had a strange dream. It seemed to him he was lying down, not on wood shavings, but on flowers. And these flowers were growing, half opening . . . and blooming as they rose up toward the sky. Soon, they were huge trees that perfumed the air and, stretching out in an endless green expanse, reached the heights of the empyrean. The sleeper's mind borne up by the flowers, rose . . . toward heaven, and was elevated, happy and powerful. . . . Finally he reached a height from which he could see entire the countenance of a new world.)

Pierre's dream encapsulates many elements of utopian prophecy making. The future is anticipated as being predominantly agrarian. The lavish nature description has a lyrical effect on the reader. Appeal is made to the aesthetic faculties rather than to rational understanding. When the human hand is in evidence, the architectural and artistic is privileged over the scientific or technological. The utopian model is far from the futuristic world of science fiction:

Des constructions d'une architecture élégante, des monuments admirables . . . s'élevaient de tous les points de ce jardin universel, et des êtres qui semblaient plus beaux et plus purs que la race humaine, tous occupés et tous joyeux, l'animaient de leurs travaux et de leurs concerts. Pierre parcourut tout ce monde inconnu avec autant de rapidité qu'un oiseau peut le faire; et partout où son esprit se posait, il voyait la fécondité, le bonheur et la paix fleurir sous des formes nouvelles. (*Compagnon*, 288–289)

(Rising up everywhere in this universal garden were elegantly designed buildings and wonderful monuments . . . and beings who seemed more beautiful and pure than any mortals, all busy and full of joy, animated the scene with their works and their concerts. Pierre flew across this unknown world with the speed of a bird, and everywhere his spirit rested, he saw abundance, happiness, and peace flowering in new guises.)

The dream emblematizes what Hugo called "Promontorium Somni," the privileged promontory that the oneiric state provides. The dreamer's flight in Sand's text highlights the remarkable advantage the panoramic overview gives to the viewer. In *Lélia* and *Spiridion*, on the other hand, the metaphor of the promontory was used to underscore the despairing present rather than the utopian future. Both Lélia and Alexis were portrayed on their "rocky heights" reaching paroxysms of vertigo and experiencing suicidal urges. The cerebral superiority of Lélia and Alexis which spelled despair and defeat is counteracted here with the panorama offering a beneficient view that makes total understanding possible. In *Le Compagnon du tour de France*, to fly is to know and to reconcile contradictions, while in *Lélia*, to know is to despair and to measure the gap between possibility and actuality. Thus this dream text felicitously reworks in the utopian mode two of Sand's epiphanic tropes, the travels of the soul ("les voyages de l'âme") and the flying being ("l'être volant").

In Sand's preutopian novels, the capacity to climb to great heights (Lélia's rock, Alexis's ledge) or to plumb great depths (the *rêveur* falling into the volcano, the *voyageur*'s "abîmes du désespoir," LV, 162) expressed a spatial metaphor for the characters' superior mental faculties. Their visionary reflections, however, consistently resulted in despair and disillusionment; their superior minds were a curse leading only to suffering. In her utopian period, however, Sand's spatial cosmology took on a different meaning. The capacity to see at a great height became the spatial equivalent of being able to look into the future. And that future society has spontaneously evolved into a terrestrial promised land. This paradise is but the old world now unrecognizable, peopled by new beings who have been "transformed and idealized."

> un être qui voltigeait près de lui depuis longtemps . . . lui dit: Vous voici enfin dans le ciel que vous avez tant désiré de posséder . . . les temps sont accomplis. . . . Alors Pierre, ouvrant les yeux, reconnut le lieu où il était et l'être qui parlait. C'était le parc de Villepreux, et c'était Yseult; mais ce parc touchait aux confins du ciel et de la terre . . . il reconnut enfin tous ceux qu'il aimait et tous ceux qu'il connaissait. . . . Yseult lui dit: Ne vois-tu pas que nous sommes tous frères, tous riches et tous égaux? La terre est redevenue ciel, parce que nous avons arraché toutes les épines des fossés et toutes les bornes des enclos; nous sommes redevenus anges, parce que nos avons effacé toutes les distinctions et abjuré tous les ressentiments.   (*Compagnon*, 289)

> (a being who had been fluttering near him for a long time . . . said to him: Here you are finally in the heaven that you have so wished to possess . . . the times have been fulfilled. . . Then Pierre, opening his eyes, recognized the place where he was and the being who was speaking. It was the park of Villepreux, and it was Yseult, but this park extended to the limits of heaven and earth . . . finally, he recognized everyone he loved, everyone he knew. . . . Yseult said to him: Do you not see that we are all brothers, all rich and all equal? Earth is become heaven again, because we have pulled up

all the thornbushes from the ditches and all the hedges from the
pastures; we have become angels again, because we have erased
all distinctions and forsworn all resentment.)

Sand's utopian dream, while employing a celestial terminology—
flight, angel, sky, paradise—is nevertheless intent upon depicting the
world in which we live, not an afterlife beyond the grave in which the
bipartite system of heaven and hell allots reward and punishment to
each individual on the basis of earthly merit or lack of it. As Yseult reminds the hero: "The earth has become the sky once again," that is to
say, the world as we know it has been cured of its Romantic affliction
and transformed by a certain number of utopian values. The transformed, angelized Yseult does not ascribe the change to any specific
discovery—technological, scientific, or otherwise—but to a mysterious, inexplicable psychological mutation, which is the result of a
triple profession of faith, based on love, belief, and toil: "Aime, crois,
travaille, et tu seras ange dans ce monde des anges" ("Love, believe,
work, and you will be an angel in this world of angels," *Compagnon*,
289). Here is an echo of Leroux's conviction that progress is inevitable,
effected through the birth of ideas that are then realized and become
incarnate.[31] The passage from the realm of ideas to that of matter is
comparable to the Logos made flesh in the Old Testament. Christian
idealism underlies the framework of utopian thinking.

The dream in *Le Compagnon du tour de France* also illustrates another utopian "law" according to which the predominant human value
is sociability. Since, according to the Saint-Simonian doctrine,
humanity is "a collective being in development,"[32] the representation
of the future depicts the individual as part of a human community.
Huguenin's vision animates the remark Sand made to Giuseppe
Mazzini in 1849—"Triste vie que celle qui n'est pas une émanation de
la vie collective" (4 Aug. 1849; *Corr.*, 9:243; "It is a sad life that is not an
emanation of the communal life")—and is a radical departure from the
solitary broodings of a Lélia or an Alexis. The dream lives of Sand's
afflicted characters reveal the individual "isolated from the universe,"
(*Lélia*, 130) in conflict with the group. Lélia's oneiric explorations
develop into a series of grotesque visions, and only serve to further
alienate her from the human community. In *Spiridion*, Alexis's apocalyptic point of view is embedded in a hideous eschatological night-
mare that emphasizes disunity and dissension. His bloody vision of
dismembered and suffering bodies is to be deciphered as the expression of his own inner malaise. After a terrifying scene in which Alexis dreams that his heart is ripped out and that he is buried alive,
Spiridion interprets this vision as the image of the former's fear of the
unknown. As "martyr of the new truth" (*Spiridion*, 172), the monk is
also the sole bearer of revelation. By contrast, Huguenin who sees the

Villepreux estate transfigured and idealized, dreams of a future society in which everyone has been enlightened. Martyrs are no longer necessary. Everyone is on the same rung of the utopian ladder. Huguenin's dream proposes an ideal of fraternity as a centripetal force that binds all humankind. The locale in which the story unfolds promises a future of equality between the sexes and between the classes.

The fantastic panorama depicting an idealized state of being structures all Sand's utopian novels, celebrating the forward march of humanity, glorifying thinking in the future. Marcelle de Blanchemont in *Le Meunier d'Angibault*, the young artisan Michel of *Le Piccinino*, and M. Sylvestre dream feminine and masculine versions of the utopian ideal. The imagination had always been Sand's favorite sphere for the search for the ideal, and the utopian vision is the culmination of that search, suggesting that the Ideal has been found.

Sand, of course, offers no concrete theories in these texts which spell out precisely the way the transition from the old world to the new will be effected. She is interested not so much in putting Leroux's ideas into actual practice as in stretching the boundaries of fictional possibilities. The idealized image of the future she offers leaves us at once gasping and dazzled by her leaps of imagination. M. Sylvestre, who "dreams quite a bit and whose dreams are generally pleasant,"[33] predicts a radical break in the way humans think which will bring about the change. Discussing the felicity that humans will one day discover in themselves and in others, he simply comments: "l'homme . . . s'apercevra que cette terre tant excommuniée par les mystiques, cette vallée de larmes, ce champ de bataille, est une délicieuse oasis parmi les innombrables oasis de l'immensité" (253; "man . . . will see that this earth so often cursed by the mystics, this vale of tears, this battlefield, is a lush oasis among the innumerable oases of vastness"). Not through mechanical progress will change take place but through a nonprogrammable psychological mutation. Sand's prose stressed the power of the Idea to bring about change and the promise of a new human essence. She insisted repeatedly that change would come about not through coercion but through faith, not through an intervention of the state, but through the individual's free choice. *Libre-arbitre* is surely one of her key words.

Sand's Way

If the dream is Sand's temporal medium for expressing utopia, the garden and the road are her spatial metaphors to designate the future. The garden, of course, is immediately reminiscent of the perfect community of Clarens in *La Nouvelle Héloïse*, and the road has been associated with liberated space ever since Sand's own *Valentine*. At the same time, the use of spatial metaphors to express a utopian ideal is a standard device in the writings of the utopian socialists in the thirties and forties. Architectural and botanical images are constantly created to talk about theoretical social problems. The New Society is described as an ideal landscape, or a glorious edifice, or a garden: Cabet's Icaria, Fourier's phalanstery, Leroux's paradise regained as socialist views expressed through architectonic or botanical images. Sand's insistence on the future transformation of the material world into an earthly garden of paradise through immaterial forces is reminiscent of Leroux, in whose writings we find this 1846 reflection: "Make haste to leave behind the present world and you will sooner find the future world, which will be this same world transformed and made more beautiful."[34] And elsewhere: "You have taken from me the paradise in the sky, I want it here on earth."[35] The perfect society of the future is portrayed as Edenic, based on a primitive pastoral model, in which the natural world is preferred, where the earth's fertility becomes the trope of abundance and equanimity.

The ending of *Le Péché de Monsieur Antoine* expands on the idea of a utopian horticultural space. The "garden of the commune" is the centerpiece of M. de Boisguilbault's image of the future thanks to which his mal du siècle is transmuted into a vision of the remède du siècle. The old man imagines that a few centuries hence he will return to his estate:

> mon ombre . . . y verra des hommes libres, heureux, égaux, unis, c'est à dire justes et sages. Ces ombrages où j'ai promené tant d'ennuis et de douleurs, où j'ai fui avec épouvante la présence des hommes d'aujourd'hui, abriteront alors, *ainsi que les voûtes d'un temple sublime*, une nombreuse famille prosternée pour prier et bénir l'auteur de la nature. . . . Ceci sera le *jardin de la commune*, c'est à dire aussi son gynécée, sa salle de fête et de banquet, son théâtre et son église.[36]

> (There my spirit . . . will see men who are free, happy, equal, united, that is to say, just and wise. This shadow world where I have walked with so many cares and sorrows, where, horrified, I have taken refuge from the presence of contemporary men, will then shelter, *like the vaults of a sublime temple*, a large family bowed in prayer, blessing the author of nature. . . . This will be the *communal garden*, which is also to say, its gynaeceum, its auditorium, its banquet hall, its theater, and its church.)

In this sublime setting, a natural temple, created by the interweaving of the tree branches, will metaphorically express the poetic religiosity of the future society. The utopian edifice is integrated into the landscape. The garden allows the spirit to soar and roam at will in contrast to the stone and cement that confine the human mind:

ne me parlez pas des *étroits espaces* où la pierre et le ciment parquent les hommes et la pensée; ne me parlez pas de vos riches colonnades et de vos parvis superbes, en comparaison de cette architecture naturelle dont le Créateur suprême fait les frais! . . . N'ôtez pas au vieux planteur son illusion. . . . Il en est encore à cet adage que Dieu est dans tout et que *la nature est son temple.*   (emphasis added; *Monsieur Antoine,* 374)

(Do not speak to me of *narrow places* where stone and cement confine men and thought; do not speak to me of your rich colonnades and your splendid church squares, in comparison to this natural architecture whose cost the supreme Creator assumes! . . . Do not take away from the old planter his illusions. . . . He still lives by the old saying that God dwells in everything and that *nature is His temple.*)

This lyrical statement, which closes the novel, immediately conjures up Baudelaire's "Correspondances." Even more readily, it recalls the words spoken by Sand's first poetic hero, Ralph— "Pour nous *l'univers est le temple* où nous adorons Dieu" (emphasis added; *Indiana,* 307), as well as the words of the "voyageur" in the sixth letter: "La nature sera un temple" (LV, 183).

Two remarks can be made at this point. The first is that the Romantic writers, to judge from their literary texts, are indifferent to the man-made edifices of the physical world. From Rousseau on, natural landscapes, in their tamed and wild variations, are preferred to built environments. The wilderness of "le désert," whether exotic or familiar, and the cultivated garden structure the spatial dimension of a work. Where architectural motifs enter the Romantic fictional universe, they tend to be ruins. Lélia's retreat to an abandoned monastery in the Italian countryside is an extended example of this rich motif. Thus it comes as no surprise that in her utopian writings, Sand should have been unwilling to erect an edifice, and that she preferred a pastoral setting for her future society. The image of the garden is fitting here since it symbolizes the harmonious interaction of the natural world under the guiding hand of human intervention. This predilection, which further affirms Sand's affinity to Leroux since the garden is his prefered metaphor for the utopian future, also prefigures images of the "fertile furrow" in *La Mare au diable* and recalls Aurore's childhood dream of the "garden of the world." Furthermore, the gardens of Patience in *Mauprat* and that of the canon in *Consuelo* exemplify the theme of cultivation as a compelling image of culture.

Second, in contrast to the Romantic novelists and thinkers, several utopian socialists such as Cabet and Fourier were intent on building. Cabet's detailed descriptions of the architectural marvels in Icaria and

Fourier's meticulous drawings and verbal descriptions of the phalanstery are noteworthy in this respect. The garden in the utopian system of images, then, is a motif that separates the determinist philosophers, such as Fourier and Cabet, from the nonmaterialist thinkers, such as Sand and Leroux. In Sand's cosmology this image spelled open-endedness and liberty of thought and emphasized the imagination's propensity to wander at will.

Significantly, the only architectural structure that Sand conjures up in reference to her utopian society can be found in *Le Meunier d'Angibault*, where the image of the ark is used to denote the temporary shelter from an evil society in the expectation that a new social order is in the making. The heroine, Marcelle de Blanchemont, explains:

> On parle d'une religion de fraternité et de communauté, où tous les hommes seraient heureux en s'aimant, et deviendraient riches en se dépouillant. . . . On dit encore que cette religion est prête à descendre dans le coeur des hommes . . . du choc immense, épouvantable, de tous les intérêts égoïstes, doivent naître la nécessité de tout changer, la lassitude du mal, le besoin du vrai et l'amour du bien. . . . Mais . . . j'ignore quels jours Dieu a fixés pour l'accomplissement de ses desseins . . . et, réfugiée dans l'arche comme l'oiseau durant le déluge, j'attends, je prie, je souffre et j'espère.[37]

> (Some talk of a religion of brotherhood and solidarity, where everyone would be happy loving one another, where all would become rich by casting aside their wealth. . . . They also say that this religion is ready to descend into the hearts of humans . . . the enormous, frightening collision of all selfish interests must give birth to the necessity of changing everything, the exhaustion of evil, the need for truth, and the love of the good. . . . But . . . I do not know which days God has appointed to bring about his plans . . . and so, having taken refuge in the ark, like the bird during the Flood, I wait, pray, suffer, and hope.)

The ark, denoting a temporary abode out of which "the new church" can emerge, conjures up a utopia in the making, rather than the static and rigid image of a utopian palace. Likening herself to "the first Christians of the desert" (297), Marcelle bemoans that "the church of the poor has not been erected" (299). Like Consuelo, she announces the reign of a future church of humanity. Sand's evangelical phraseology remains at the service of a profoundly fluid vision, where waiting rather than programmatic implementation is advocated.

The other spatial metaphor Sand exploits is the road, once again an image highlighting freedom of movement. While buildings in Sand's utopian architecture are the equivalent of emprisonment and despair, the road is the spatial equivalent of hope. The fourth letter of the "Lettres à Marcie" is especially eloquent on this point: "Si nous ne pouvons marcher, traînons-nous. Tant qu'il y aura de l'espace devant nous, il y aura aussi de l'espérance" ("If we cannot walk, let us crawl. As long as there is space before us, there is also hope").[38] In *Consuelo*, the heroine, cloistered in the sinister Château des Géants, wistfully marks the difference between enclosure and liberation: "Qu'y a-t-il de plus beau qu'un chemin . . . le libre chemin qui s'enfuit et se cache à demi dans les bois m'invite et m'appelle à suivre ses détours et à pénétrer ses mystères. Et puis ce chemin, *c'est le passage de l'humanité*, c'est la route de l'univers . . . le chemin est une terre de liberté" ("What is more beautiful than a path . . . the open path that runs ahead and half-disappears in the woods, beckons me to follow its turns and penetrate its mysteries. This path is also *the passage of humanity*, it is the highway of the universe . . . the path is a land of freedom"). By extension, the road is the spatial expression of equality, of communal ownership: "A droite, à gauche, les champs, les bois appartiennent à des maîtres; le chemin appartient à celui qui ne possède pas autre chose. . . . Le plus grossier mendiant a pour lui un amour invincible. Qu'on lui bâtisse des hôpitaux aussi riches que des palais, ce sont toujours des prisons" (emphasis added; *Consuelo*, 1:394; "To the right, to the left, the fields, the woods have owners; the path belongs to the one who owns nothing else. . . . The coarsest beggar has for it an invincible love. One could build him hospices as rich as palaces, they would still be but jails to him"). The road is the metaphor which closes the novel, as the reader encounters the little group of Consuelo, Albert, and their children wandering down "le chemin *sans maître* de la forêt" (3:467; "the forest road that has *no master*"). The road as a metaphor for life is a traditional one, of course, which the narrator of *Consuelo* expresses in the last paragraph of the novel: "la vie est un voyage qui a la vie pour but" ("life is a voyage which has life as a goal"). But Sand's way does not designate any random life, any haphazard itinerary. The "voyage without rest" sends her heroes on their way to encounter "action without a faltering of heart." And the book's final words make clear that "the road to progress"[39] leads inexorably "to triumph or to martydom" (3:467).

The Old Hermit

Several of Sand's characters figure in at least two separate novels, thus prompting the supposition that she was exploring the potential of the Balzacian "retour des personnages" in a limited way.[40] However, there is one striking instance of a recurrent character in her oeuvre. No Rastignac or Vautrin, this character is male, often elderly, simultaneously wise and aloof, described as a hermit, a saint, a philosopher, a sage. Often, he articulates a utopian ideal. Although his name and identity vary from novel to novel, he nevertheless remains a stable type. He is the anonymous "traveler" in *Lettres d'un voyageur* and *Nouvelles Lettres d'un voyageur*, the marquis de Carabas in *Rose et Blanche*, Trenmor in *Lélia*, Patience in *Mauprat*, M. de Boisguilbault in *Le Péché de Monsieur Antoine*, and M. Sylvestre in the novel by that name. The underlying link among all these characters is finally revealed in an essay from *Nouvelles Lettres d'un voyageur*, entitled "A propos de botanique," a late text written in 1868. Reflecting on the possible discontinuities in her life, Sand contrasts the "ancien moi" with the person she has become. As she compares the past to the present, her literary musings instinctively take her back to a text written by her some thirty-four years earlier, *Lettres d'un voyageur*, which lies in palimpsest underneath the present project. She cites verbatim a passage from the fourth letter which refers to a recurrent character in her prose, an old man:

> "vous verrez, mes amis, *quels profonds philosophes, quels antiques sto-ïciens, quels ermites à barbe blanche se promèneront à travers mes romans.* Quelles pesantes dissertations, quels magnifiques plaidoyers, quelles superbes condamnations découleront de ma plume!"[41]

> ("you will see, my friends, *what deep-thinking philosophers, what antiquated stoics, what white-bearded hermits will wander through my novels.* What weighty discourses, what splendid speeches for the defense, what superb condamnations will flow from my pen!")

Having cited this earlier text, she then proceeds to make a double confession. First, she admits that indeed an old man has been wandering throughout her oeuvre for several decades. Second, she reveals his identity: "Aujourd'hui, en 1868, il y a bien un vieux [sic] ermite qui se promène à travers mes romans; mais il n'a pas de barbe, il n'est pas stoïcien, et certes il n'est pas un philosophe bien profond, car *c'est moi*" ("Today, in 1868, there is indeed an old hermit who wanders through my novels; but he is beardless, he is not a stoic, and he is certainly not a very deep-thinking philosopher, for *the hermit is I*").[42] I propose that the old hermit is Sand's most visible recurrent character. He is crucial for two reasons. First, he links many apparently disparate protagonists in the cast of characters, thereby making clear the underlying unity of Sand's oeuvre as a whole. Second and more important, the old philosopher is the boldest embodiment of her own fictional androgynous persona. Sand's seemingly enigmatic identification with a series of male characters—Amédée, Ralph, Bénédict, and Alexis—now takes on heightened meaning. It allows the reader to posit the existence of a fundamental, double-gendered fictional vision in both the Romantic and the Utopian novels.

At the same time, this series of male sages must not be confused with a one-dimensional autobiographical transference. In fact, Sand herself encouraged us not to do so. In *Histoire de ma vie*, recalling the mood in which she had composed *Lettres d'un voyageur*, she accentuated the deliberate gap that existed between the controlling voice of the narrator and the autopsychological projection:

> je créai . . . un moi fantastique très vieux, très expérimenté et partant très désespéré. Ce troisième état de mon *moi* supposé, le désespoir, était le seul vrai, et je pouvais, en me laissant aller à mes idées noires, me placer dans la situation du vieil oncle, du vieux voyageur que je faisais parler. . .   (HV, 2:299)

> (I created a fantastical self, quite old, very experienced, and therefore quite desperate from the start. This third state of my supposed *self*, despair, was the only true one, and I could, by giving free reign to my dark moods, put myself in the place of the old uncle, the old traveler through whom I spoke. . .)

Furthermore, she insisted that *Lettres d'un voyageur* was a piece in which she was not the real character ("le personnage réel") but the thinking and analyzing character ("Le personnage pensant et analysant"). The distinction dismisses any identification at the autobiographical level and highlights the importance of the *intellectual self* in her autopsychological characters.

A variant of the old hermit appears in Sand's very first work, *Rose et Blanche*. Although the novel was initially a joint venture (see Introduction), we can be reasonably sure that the Marquis de Carabas was Sand's creation because the character was retained in the much-amended second version which, as she tells us, was almost entirely of her composition.[43] Even in *Lélia*, where she is very closely linked to the heroine, Sand herself explains that Trenmor represents the wisdom of her old age. When, at the end of *Lélia*, he picks up his stick and gets back on the road, this gesture not only symbolizes the act of the writer's picking up the pen in readiness for the next novel, but also identifies him as another incarnation of Sand's recurrent character. In *Le Péché de Monsieur Antoine* M. de Boisguilbault's evolution echoes Sand's own ideological trajectory from melancholia to eudemonism. Regarding the old philosopher of *Monsieur Sylvestre*, she writes at the end of her life: "J'ai la foi du vieux Sylvestre" (*Corr.*, 19:292).

The old hermit is also Sand's privileged bearer of ideas. A letter to Anténor Joly, journalist at *L'Epoque*, insists on the importance of *ideas* as fictional material in addition to *facts*: "il faut . . . que chaque personnage d'un livre soit le représentant *d'une des idées qui circulent dans l'air* qu'il respire, qui dominent ou s'insinuent, qui montent ou tombent, qui naissent, qui règnent ou qui finissent" (emphasis added; 13 Aug. 1845; *Corr.*, 7:51–57; "each character in a book . . . must represent *one or another of the ideas circulating in the air* that he or she breathes, ideas that impose themselves or slip in, that rise or fall, that are born, that reign or die out"). The character as bearer of one of those ideas flying about in the air is an uncannily Dostoevskian notion.[44] It accentuates the central position of the philosophical dimension in Sand's works, and marks with particular intensity her utopian imagination. The marquis de Carabas has learned how to live and is ready to share his program; Trenmor has weathered successfully the double trial of addiction to gambling and forced labor; M. de Boisguilbault has traveled through the desolate plains of spleen and has found his way out; M. Sylvestre has learned how to live on almost nothing and to concentrate his attentions on the future happiness of humankind. The "voyageur" has gone on to find the road out of the land of despair: "j'ai cherché un chemin, je l'ai trouvé, perdu, retrouvé, et je peux le perdre encore" ("I looked for a path, I found it, lost it, found it again, and I can lose it yet again").[45] In 1868 she was only reiterating what she had expressed gropingly about the independent life of ideas in *Lettres d'un voyageur*: "Nous périrons . . . mais les idées ne meurent pas, et celle que nous avons jetée dans le monde nous survivra" (232–233; "We will perish, but ideas do not die and the one that we have sowed in the world will outlive us"). Years later, when she was writing *Monsieur Sylvestre*, she repeated: "Je n'ai que la passion de l'idée" ("I have only the passion of ideas").

The utopian decade of the 1840s is then a transitional period showing Sand at the crossroads in her literary voyage. *Spiridion* had ended with the unearthing of a new gospel, an unknown Book of Revelations. But it served little practical purpose within the fictional framework of the novel. It had been written, transmitted, lost, then finally found. Nothing further had been done with it. In the utopian mode that will culminate with *Consuelo*, however, the Sacred Book is transformed into a praxis. The fluid practice of evangelization replaces the static evangelical text. The reader is transported from the rigid and closed world of the monks to the open and dynamic world of the wandering Bohemians. *Consuelo*, then, can be seen as the most perfect expression of Sand's utopian imagination. By reworking several Greek myths and exploring further the nineteenth-century social myths, this novel would achieve a remarkable literary synthesis.

Consuelo and *La Comtesse de Rudolstadt:* From Gothic Novel to Novel of Initiation

As Jean Cassou reminds us in his article on *Consuelo* and its sequel, *La Comtesse de Rudolstadt*, the early nineteenth century was a fertile period in the development of the novel, an era that gave birth to a number of new fictional genres.[1] *Consuelo*, Cassou points out, is particularly rich in novelistic innovation, incorporating elements drawn from at least four types: the *roman-feuilleton*, the musical novel, the Gothic novel, and the novel of initiation.[2]

Originally, of course, *Consuelo* did appear as a series of feuilletons, from 1 February 1842 to 10 February 1844 in the *Revue indé-pendante* (a journal founded by Pierre Leroux in 1842 in conjunction with Louis Viardot and George Sand herself). Nor can we deny the central presence of music in *Consuelo*, the novel being, among other things, an exploration of eighteenth-century musical circles in Venice, Vienna, and Berlin, with at least two real musicians of the age, Nicola Porpora and Joseph Haydn, playing major fictional roles.[3] But neither serialized novel nor musical novel designates a formal genre. Neither conjures up the combination of an established set of thematic elements, together with a predictable cast of characters, certain formal exigencies, and a traceable tradition, the way established genres such as Gothic novel ("roman noir") and novel of initiation do.[4]

Sand's triple-decker novel participates mainly in these two traditions. In its use of the established narrative of terror, inherited from the eighteenth-century Gothic writers, and by the choice of both a temporal and physical setting *Consuelo* belongs to the tradition of the Gothic novel. But with its attention to the initiation topos and its innovative concern for the coining of a modern psychological language, it constitutes one of the most remarkable novels of initiation of the Romantic age. In addition to this double focus, furthermore, Sand's own feminizing of the canon led her to construct in *Consuelo* a feminine version of the metaphysical sublime.

The Gothic Voice

A privileged theme of Gothic fiction is the fortified castle, in which the underground spaces—dungeons, labyrinths, subterranean prisons, secret passageways, crypts, and catacombs—are equated with terror. When such a castle is introduced in *Consuelo*, Sand immediately establishes the link between her Château des Géants and the archetypal edifice of terror, Udolpho, thereby placing herself in the tradition of the most celebrated female writer of Gothic novels, Ann Radcliffe. She also specifically addresses her reader in the feminine, thus creating an unusual literary triad in which writer, reader, and foremother are all women:

> Si l'ingénieuse et féconde Anne Radcliffe se fût trouvée à la place du candide et maladroit narrateur de cette très véridique histoire, elle n'eût pas laissé échapper une si bonne occasion de vous promener, madame la lectrice, à travers les corridors, les trappes, les escaliers en spirale, les ténèbres et les souterrains pendant une demi-douzaine de beaux et attachants volumes, pour vous révéler, seulement au septième, tous les arcanes de son oeuvre savante. (*Consuelo*, 1:265)

> (If the resourceful and prolific Ann Radcliffe had found herself in the place of the candid and awkward narrator of this very real story, she would not have let such a good opportunity go by to take you, madame reader, through corridors, trapdoors, spiral staircases, shadows, and underground passageways during half a dozen volumes, in order to reveal to you only in the seventh, all the mysteries of her learned work.)

Despite Sand's gently ironic tone in referring to Radcliffe's use of spaces of terror, Gothic edifices occupy large portions of her text: the Château des Géants is the setting for more than one-third of *Consuelo*,[5] while the events in the Spandau fortress make up approximately one-fifth of *La Comtesse de Rudolstadt*.

Udolpho, with its huge portcullis, back staircases, winding passages, wide chambers, vaulted galleries, underground chapel, and slender watchtowers, is an exquisite mechanical contraption. A fitting embodiment of Edmund Burke's notion of the sublimity found in a terrible object, it lies in wait for its next victim. Yet, for all of its ominous appearance, Udolpho is a static place. Immutable, silent, forbidding, its mysteries locked up inside it, Udolpho has a menacing grandeur more illusory than actual. When all the mysteries have been elucidated, Udolpho is reduced to nothing more than a white (or should I say black?) elephant.

Inversion of the natural order in Radcliffe's castle, both temporal and spatial, suggests another level of meaning, however. Time and space appear to be strangely warped. Plot time is invariably marked as nocturnal, midnight being the favored hour for the heroine to set out on her wanderings and explorations. The reversed time structure is accompanied by a strangely altered allocation of space. The corridors, passageways, and staircases take up more room than the various chambers, apartments, and reception halls. It is as though the architect, a modern Daedalus, had concentrated his efforts on building a labyrinth inside the castle, and in his single-mindedness, had forgotten to include sufficient living space.

Udolpho provides what Peter Brooks has called an epistemological model of the depths, an architectural approximation of the Freudian structure of the mind.[6] The walks Radcliffe's Emily takes inside the castle are "voyages of the mind." The bedroom doors, which can be locked or unlocked only from the outside and by forces beyond the heroine's control, suggest that she is prey to the intrusion of her unconscious fears and desires. Her alarm at becoming lost "in the intricacies of the castle"[7] is an expression of her reluctance to make frightening discoveries about her own psyche. Emily's dream life, constituting what Nerval called "une seconde vie," fills up the major portion of the narrative time spent in Udolpho.

Maurice Lévy, in his authoritative *Le Roman "gothique" anglais*, has provided a Bachelardian reading of those "Gothic heroines who at [midnight] come out of the melancholic torpor that weighs them down during the day so as to walk unflaggingly up and down corridors without end and go down interminable staircases."[8] If going up and down the stairs of a house is a metaphor for changing from one level of consciousness to another, Emily's descent into the catacombs of Udolpho can be read as a plunge into the deeper parts of her consciousness. In an archetypical dreamlike sequence, she descends into an underground chapel, going down into the vaults, and through an adjoining passage to a pair of iron gates that lead to a flight of steps. As Lévy reminds us: "to descend into the subterranean parts of the castle is to descend into ourselves, down into the deepest part of our inner life. It means leaving the level of rational consciousness to become engulfed in the most archaic levels of being" (630). As Emily starts climbing back, her perceptions of the castle confirm this vision of the archaic self: "As [she] passed up . . . [she] discovered more fully the desolation of the place—the rough stone walls, the spiral stairs, *black with age*, and a suit of *antient* armour, with an iron visor, that hung upon the walls, and appeared a trophy of some *former* victory" (emphasis added; *Udolpho*, 346).

Emily's escalating sense of dread and her growing claustrophobia as she explores this fantastic architectural structure is symptomatic of her own dangerous inner journey. Bachelard explains the relationship between the dreamer's perception of his or her environment and his or her private emotional gyroscope: "It is not because the passage is narrow that the dreamer feels compressed . . . [it is because] the dreamer is experiencing anguish that she or he sees the passage becoming narrower."[9] In a room off one of the landings Emily comes across some instruments of torture—an iron chair, iron bars and rings to confine the hands and feet: "it occurred to her . . . that she herself might be the next [victim]! An acute pain seized her head, she was scarcely able to hold the lamp, and, looking round for support, was seating herself, unconsciously, in the iron chair itself" (*Udolpho*, 348). Emily's unconscious willingness to offer herself as the next victim by sitting in the iron chair confirms what William Patrick Day has found to be at the crux of Gothic ideology, the fixed presence of a victim and a torturer. In this relationship based on violence, the Gothic character is "defined through conflict, as giver or receiver of pain in an sadomasochistic dynamic."[10] It is the feminine characters who are invariably the victims of men's brutality in Gothic fiction. Radcliffe's novel epitomizes the message that good behavior in women is "equated with victimization and obedience to authority."[11] But the worst is still to come for Emily as she discovers a bloody and hideously disfigured corpse. Having reached the epitome of what Julia Kristeva calls "abjection," that state in which "the boundaries between the inner and the outer, the Self and the Other" are perturbed, Emily faints and is taken back to her room.[12]

Thus is completed a circular itinerary: from the bedroom, down into a cave (the locus of *l'être obscur*) and a chamber of horrors, and back. This structure is typical of Gothic narrative, since the phenomena of "transformation and metamorphosis," to quote Day, "lead only back to the place from which one started."[13] The image of circularity makes clear that, on the psychological level, increased self-awareness or self-discovery is next to impossible. A psychic impermeability to potentially traumatic or revelatory events persists throughout Emily's confinement within Udolpho. In spite of repeated assaults on her sensibility, her character is not permanently altered in any way. She withstands events, but does not incorporate them into her own mental life. When she escapes from prison, the Gothic heroine is identical to the person she was before claustration. Emily leaves, taking only "a small package" (*Udolpho*, 399), an indication of how little psychic growth has taken place.[14] Incarceration leaves no permanent scars. Once she is beyond the reaches of Udolpho, it ceases to play any active role in her imagination. The memory of it simply fades like "a distempered dream."[15]

Sand's reading of Gothic novelists (Radcliffe foremost among them) provided her with techniques for building narratives of suspense. She learned to place an emphasis on mood building, to create an aura of mystery, and to make use of a claptrap of Gothic stage sets and props (to use Lowry Nelson's formula). Many Gothic details—such as mysterious voices, uncanny statues, magic portraits, masked messengers, blood stains, corpses—appear in *Consuelo* and combine with the dominant edifice of the menacing castle, with its enticing and terrifying underground galleries, to make this the most Gothic of Sand's novels.[16] But, as we shall see, these Gothic motifs are at the service of a different ideology in *Consuelo*; they serve a different set of narrative priorities.

The Initiation Topos

In the first volume Sand describes her heroine's descent into the castle's underground by means of a well that has been temporarily emptied of water. A structure of terror, worthy of Radcliffe, unfolds as the character, who has taken the wrong passageway, finds herself walking inexorably down a gallery as the water comes rushing behind her. In true Gothic fashion, escape, here in the form of a foothold leading to a higher landing, is provided only at the very last moment. As Consuelo continues her wandering through a vast cave, she encounters further dangers, notably the threat of being buried alive—a favorite device of terror in Gothic fiction and a recurrent motif throughout the text. Here also, the symbolic weight of these motifs—torrential water, being buried alive—is significant in psychological terms.

But as the heroine proceeds through this labyrinth of fear toward the subterranean retreat of Albert de Rudolstadt, the hero, the narrative tone changes. The Gothic voice of terror recedes. A different language of solace now dominates. The landscape of terror gives way to one of serenity and harmony:

> un sentier de sable frais et fin remontait le cours de cette eau limpide et transparente. . . . Ce sentier était relevé en talus dans des terres fraîches et fertiles; car de belles plantes aquatiques . . . dans ce lieu abrité . . . bordaient le torrent d'une marge verdoyante. . . . C'était comme une serre chaude naturelle. (1:322)

> (a path of cool, fine sand ran upstream alongside the limpid and transparent water. . . . This path ran along the top of a raised embankment of fresh and fertile earth; for beautiful aquatic plants . . . in this sheltered place . . . edged the torrent forming a verdant border. . . . It was like a natural, warm greenhouse.)

Inner and outer landscape correspond. The beneficial effect of this site on Consuelo's mood is almost instantaneous: "Consuelo commençait à ressentir l'influence bienfaisante qu'un aspect moins sinistre et déjà poétique des objets extérieurs produisait sur son imagination bouleversée par de cruelles terreurs. . . . Elle se sentait renaître" (1:322; "Consuelo began to feel the beneficial influence exerted on her by the less sinister and already poetic aspect of exterior objects. Her imagination had been prey to cruel terrors. . . . Now she felt herself being reborn"). On the verge of a "minor initiation," Consuelo reflects on her preinitiatory state of mind: "une âme fervente, une résolution pleine de charité, un coeur tranquille, une conscience pure, un désinteressement à toute épreuve" (1:323; "a fervent soul, a resolution full of charity, a peaceful heart, a pure conscience, an unfailing selflessness").

In Albert's "melancholy sanctuary," whose access is reached symbolically by opening three doors, the two protagonists engage in a bizarre dialogue, halfway between madness and revelation. As in *The Mysteries of Udolpho*, the scene ends with the heroine fainting. But unlike Emily, Consuelo succumbs not to horror but to exhaustion and relief. Whereas Udolpho ultimately led its heroine to objects symbolizing pain, death, and decay, the Château des Géants takes "la Porporina" (Consuelo's nickname) to an innermost sanctum of rebirth, forgiveness, and absolution. Although in Radcliffe's and Sand's texts the two itineraries are remarkably similar, Consuelo's quest for Albert has quite a different meaning from Emily's search for her aunt. When Emily finally locates Madame Montoni on her deathbed, the scene only confirms her worst fears. In Sand's novel, however, Consuelo's discovery of Albert resembles a successful quest. The heroine's suffering is given a purpose. The Romantic search ends in initiation and growth while the Gothic finishes in hopelessness and gloom.

The crucial difference, however, lies in the contrasting consequences of stasis versus change in each heroine after her trial by terror. In *The Mysteries of Udolpho*, as Ellen Moers notes, Emily retains her respectability in the worst situations: "her sensibility and her decorum never falter; and however rapid or perilous her journeys, the *lares* and *penates* of proper English girlhood travel with her."[17] Yet there is a moment in the novel when this principle of proper behavior is put to the test. After a hurried flight from Udolpho Emily finds herself without the necessary hat. On the very next day Radcliffe has her heroine acquire "a little straw hat, such as was worn by the peasant girls of Tuscany" (*Udolpho*, 455) and the awkward situation is thus remedied. The detail would be merely amusing if it did not highlight a major component of the Radcliffe heroine. Through attention to the proprieties she keeps her sense of identity intact. Respectability points to the only form of power available to the feminine archetype in the Gothic world,[18] a power that ensures her firm grip on reality. This stability of character allows her to undergo unspeakable ordeals looking none the worse for wear (give or take the loss of a hat). From our modern perspective, the Gothic heroine may well seem an unexciting character because of her static psychology. But ultimately she displays that steadfast endurance and sheer pluck in the face of danger that are the counterbalancing virtues of such characterization. (We see this model most often in male heroes of the picaresque tradition.) Her hanging on to her hat, then, is more a mark of courage, what Moers calls her "heroinism," than mere passive acceptance of the etiquette of her time.

How different is the aftermath of Consuelo's trial. Back in her room she collapses in bed with a fever and spends several weeks harboring an illness of the soul, "un cas extraordinaire d'affection morale" (1:357; "an extraordinary case of moral illness). Displaying many of the symptoms of hysteria—clenched teeth, livid mouth, alternating moments of fever and pallor (the canoness sees her changing color from "une rougeur dévorante," "a devouring blush," to "une pâleur bleuâtre," "a bluish pallor," 1:360)—she is literally possessed by the need to absorb and to make sense of the events witnessed in the grotto's mythic decor:

> Consuelo, en proie à un délire épouvantable, se débattait dans les bras des deux plus vigoureuses servantes de la maison. . . . Tourmentée, ainsi qu'il arrive dans certains cas de fièvre cérébrale, par des terreurs inouïes, la malheureuse enfant voulait fuir les visions dont elle était assaillie; elle croyait voir, dans les personnes qui s'efforçaient de la retenir . . . des monstres acharnés à sa perte. (1:363)

> (Consuelo, a victim of the most alarming delirium, struggled against the grip of the two strongest servants of the house. . . . Tormented, as it happens in certain instances of cerebral fever, by extraordinary terrors, the unhappy child wanted to flee from the visions assailing her; she believed that the people struggling to hold her back . . . were monsters furiously trying to kill her.)

The illusory monsters that Consuelo's feverish state creates are metaphors for her psychic growth. Whereas in *Udolpho* the monsters belong to the castle and thus cease to haunt Emily the minute she steps off the property, Consuelo's visions of the depths of the Château des Géants continue to torment her until she is able to give them meaning. Significantly, her illness oscillates between gestures of madness and of religious ecstasy, thus running almost exactly parallel to Albert's own erratic behavior. As a madwoman, she looks like "un spectre échappé de la tombe" (1:364; "a ghost escaped from the tomb"); as a saint she resembles a feverish mystic in the throes of a passionate communion with God. The opposition of pallor and fever, of spectrality and ecstasy, to describe the process of psychic "digestion" clearly demonstrates Sand's emphasis on the psychological change brought about by experience in her heroine. Consuelo is not only becoming more like Albert, her guide and initiator, she is also developing into a more complex character. In the final stage of growth Consuelo falls into a state of "limp tranquillity" ("molle quiétude," 1:370–371) such as normally follows a "great crisis" (1:373). At the end of her trial by illness, she is reborn and ready to embark upon a new life. Such a narrative differs fundamentally from the Gothic. To be sure, the Romantic predilection for freneticism, an offshoot of Gothic sensibility, can be detected in these pages. Consuelo turning blue makes her a sister of the frenetic Lélia in the throes of a cholera fit. But it is also a marker of the initiation narrative. The initiate must travel through nightmarish geographic and mental landscapes before she can be reborn. The subsequent illness and fever only verify that change has taken place.

The quest for a major initiation, in the Château du Graal (the castle's name needs no comment), sends Consuelo down into the catacombs a second time. Here again terror is at the service of initiation. The grand master informs her:

> "tu vas être soumise par nous à quelques souffrances morales. . . . Ce n'est pas dans le calme du repos, ni dans les plaisirs de ce monde, c'est dans la douleur et les larmes que la foi grandit et s'exalte. Te sens-tu le courage d'affronter de pénibles émotions et peut-être de violentes terreurs?" (3:379)

> ("You will be subjected to several moral torments. . . . It is not in the tranquillity of rest, nor in the pleasures of this world, but in suffering and in tears that faith grows and is exalted. Do you feel courageous enough to confront these painful emotions and maybe violent terrors?")

Alone, with only a silver lamp to guide her, forbidden from looking back, Consuelo proceeds to this last trial in several stages. Sand uses the word "stations," to indicate that, in Christ-like fashion, this is Consuelo's passion, with the various stops making up a catalogue of the "misfortunes and crimes of humanity." The culmination is a chamber of horrors, filled with numerous instruments of torture, similar to the one Emily had discovered in Udolpho. Consuelo's eye focuses on a particularly hideous contraption:

> elle contemplait une sorte de cloche de bronze qui avait une tête monstrueuse et un casque rond posés sur un gros corps informe. . . . Consuelo . . . comprit . . . qu'on mettait le patient accroupi sous cette cloche. Le poids en était si terrible, qu'il ne pouvait, par aucun effort humain, la soulever. (3:388)

> (she was contemplating a kind of bronze bell which had a mon-
> strous head and a round helmet placed on top of a large, shapeless
> body. . . . Consuelo . . . understood . . . that the victim was
> placed under this bell. The weight was so terrible that he or she
> could not, despite the greatest of human efforts, lift it.)

Through the contemplation of this hideous bell, a powerful metaphor
for extreme claustration of the body and spirit, Consuelo literally
reaches out of herself, in a moment of identification with the victim.
Much like Emily had sat in the iron chair, so Consuelo imagines herself
under the bell. The result is, once again, abjection, as Consuelo ceases
to exist as a separate being: "Consuelo ne vit plus rien et cessa de souffrir . . . son âme et son corps n'existaient plus que dans le corps et
l'âme de l'humanité violentée et mutilée, elle tomba droite et raide sur
le pavé" (3:389; "Consuelo saw nothing more and suffered no longer.
. . . Her soul and body existed only in the body and soul of violated
and mutilated humanity, she fell straight and stiff on the ground"). In
spite of its evident Gothic tonality, the scene transcends its initial
model. Emily was transfixed with horror when she surmised that the
tools of torture might be meant for her. Consuelo, on the contrary,
experiences abjection because she identifies with all those outside of
herself who have suffered at the torturer's hands. As Lucienne Frappier-Mazur remarks: "having merged her existence with that of violated and mutilated humanity, a sublime Consuelo . . . is reborn
. . . [who] rejects any thought of happiness on earth."[19] Indeed, Consuelo's initial reaction is to insist on living with the constant reminder
of the horrors she has witnessed:

> "Que me parlez-vous de liberté . . . d'amour et de bonheur? . . .
> Ne venez-vous pas de me faire traverser des épreuves qui doivent
> laisser sur un front une éternelle pâleur. . . . Quel être insensible
> et lâche me croyez-vous, si vous me jugez encore capable de rêver
> et de chercher des satisfactions personnelles après ce que j'ai
> vu. . ."   (3:396)

> ("Why do you speak to me of freedom . . . of love and hap-
> piness? . . . Haven't you just made me undergo trials that are sup-
> posed to leave an eternal pallor on my forehead. . . . What kind of
> insensitive and cowardly being do you think I am, if you judge me
> capable of dreaming and seeking personal satisfaction after what I
> have seen. . .")

Here again the narrative stresses the changes in the heroine's psychological makeup. Whereas Emily withstands experience, Consuelo un-
derstands it and, in a moment of Romantic fervor, transcends it.
    We are now in a position to formulate the crucial difference

between a Gothic narrative and a novel of initiation based on Gothic discourse. The former "refuses to offer a transcendent vision and em- powering mythology, a new cosmogony and an ethical imperative," while the latter makes it imperative.[20] The closed circuit of the Gothic novel is broken in the text of *Consuelo*, where each episode of horror has a particular purpose, leading the heroine and the reader along with her to new heights of reflection. The opposition between stasis as dom- inating element in the Gothic novel and movement as primary force in the initiation novel is further articulated by the road motif in the two novels. In *The Mysteries of Udolpho* the road has a double resonance. In the early part of the novel it is considered by Emily as a pleasurable place as she and her father journey from their family estate in Gascony toward better climates in Provence. In the latter portion of the book, however, the road is a means of getting away from Udolpho and back home (with quite a few detours, it is true). By its circularity, the road motif very much resembles Emily's excursions into the depths of the Gothic castle. The novel which had begun at the chateau at La Vallée also ends there, with nothing changed in the surrounding landscapes or in the interiors: "the . . . furniture of the pavilion remained exactly as usual, and Emily thought it looked as if it has not once been moved since she set out for Italy" (*Udolpho*, 585). Indeed it is the very immu- tability of the place which has its greatest appeal for the heroine. The final lines of the novel insist on the two heroes being "restored to each other" and to "the beloved landscapes of their native country" (*Udolpho*, 672), as if happiness and goodness resided specifically in this act of restoration, turning the clock back, denying time, reaching for what existed before the adventures began, in a word, finding stasis again.

By contrast, Consuelo yearns not for paradise regained but for the exhilarating freedom and uncertainty of "le grand chemin." Locked up in her gloomy fortress ("cette noire forteresse") at the Riesenburg, she muses on the significance of the road, "le symbole et l'image d'une vie active et variée" ("the symbol and the image of an active and varied life"). While the comfort of domesticity is Emily's ide- al, Consuelo prefers "le libre chemin qui . . . m'invite et m'appelle à suivre ses détours et à pénétrer ses mystères" ("the open road that . . . invites and calls me to follow its winding paths and penetrate its mysteries"). For her, the house—whether haven or palace—is al- ways a prison ("Un mur ou une palissade . . . ferme l'horizon"; "A wall or a hedge . . . closes off the horizon"), while the road is a space of freedom (1:394).

The *Mysteries of Udolpho* culminates in an apotheosis of the famil- ial ideal, represented by the symbolic hearth. By contrast, the control- ling image in *Consuelo* is the road, surprisingly identified with the maternal figure:

"[la] poésie, [le] rêve, [la] passion [du vagabond], ce sera toujours le grand chemin. O ma mère! ma mère! . . . que ne peux-tu me reprendre sur tes fortes épaules et me porter là-bas, là-bas où vole l'hirondelle vers les collines bleues, où le souvenir du passé et le regret du bonheur perdu ne peuvent suivre l'artiste aux pieds légers." (1:394)

("[the] poetry, [the] dream, [the] passion [of the wanderer] will always be the great road. O my mother! my mother! . . . I wish you could take me on your strong shoulders and carry me over there, over there where the swallows fly toward the blue hills, where the memory of the past and the yearning for lost happiness cannot follow the light stride of the artist.")

The nostalgic desire for return to the maternal body is no longer associated with the traditional desire for enclosure. Sand subverts the standard associations to equate the mother with strength and an ideal landscape of art and liberation. Significantly, Consuelo will end up, as did her mother before her, on the road.

In fact Sand's entire text can be seen as an apology for a life on the road, since it begins in the streets of Venice where Anzoleto and Consuelo, like two noble savages, lead a life of freedom, outside the confines of house, family, and bourgeois morality. Living, singing, eating, and sleeping on the street, the two children reinforce Sand's designation of open spaces as the locus of freedom: "ils chantèrent devant les chapelles . . . sans songer à l'heure avancée, et sans avoir besoin d'autre lit jusqu'au matin que la dalle blanche encore tiède des feux du jour" (1:54–55; "they sang in front of chapels . . . unaware of the late hour, and needing until morning no other bed than the white paving stones, still warm from the heat of the day.")

At the end of the novel, unlike Emily whose wealth and property are restored to her, Consuelo renounces the aristocratic surname Rudolstadt, all inheritance rights and material comfort for a life of poverty and wandering with her mad Albert and their three youngest children. As the narrator watches these characters disappear at the close of the book, the path they tread is freighted with prophetic value, promising the way to a paradise based on liberty and equality. Sand here inverts the traditional symbolic allotment of space according to gender—the open air as the exclusive domain of the male, the interiors restricted to the female. It is as if the writer had provided us with a new Ariadne's thread, leading us out of the great claustrophobic labyrinth of Udolpho for good.

Based on the examination of these two novels by Radcliffe and Sand, I would argue that in Gothic fiction and its younger cousin, the initiation novel, two very different views of psychology, each in harmony with its age, are expressed. The eighteenth century still viewed the individual as static, personality as a homogeneous integral whole. Since personality was considered fixed at adulthood, it could not be altered by experience after the formative years. Adult experience simply provided personality opportunities to manifest itself. Based on such a stable view of psychology, the Gothic novel experimented with the amount a hero or heroine could withstand before disintegrating. Horror, torture, fear, and imprisonment were exercised as tests of the personality. The individual, comparable to a manufactured object, was subjected to a sequence of "quality testing." Radcliffe's Emily, then, is a later, female version of La Mettrie's "homme machine," a tough, complex, but mechanized being who, when put to the test, to the satisfaction of both narrator and reader, does not overheat or crack.

In *Consuelo* we encounter something quite different, a psychology of metamorphosis through various stages of epistemological development which expresses a Romantic vision of human personality. The machine has been exploded and replaced with nonmechanical manifestations of psychic life. Sand's novel explores such areas of irrational behavior as madness, genius, artistic inspiration, the dream life, nightmares, visions, extreme fear, and passionate desire, in a word, the workings of the unconscious upon reflection and behavior. Sand's attempt to translate the most elusive of the soul's states of being into narrative is one of her most admirable enterprises.

If the Romantic aesthetic is primarily concerned with new definitions of psychology, Romantic discourse is an exploration of character through the use of dominant figures of speech—oxymoron, hyperbole, antithesis. In this light, Consuelo's ambivalence regarding crucial issues in her life reflects Sand's interest in constructing a generally coherent and yet strangely dissonant character: she loves and yet does not love Albert; she considers her art to be at once divine in the abstract and sullied in the theater; her voice is a manifestation of the divine and yet the cantatrice loses her capacity to sing soon after her final initiation. When Michel Foucault talks of the mutation of Order into History, at the juncture of the eighteenth and nineteenth centuries, he is also referring to this great change in representing character.[21] Movement has replaced immobility. Animated sequences have superseded fixed images.

But let us be fair to Gothic prose. In their depictions of castles, the Gothic writers developed a catalogue of architectural images which provided a language for talking about the dark side of the psyche. Gothic heroes and villains were the prototypes for the more complex characters who would inhabit the nineteenth-century novel. Lowry Nelson rightly sees an evolution in Gothic fiction away from "the rigged supernatural" and toward a recognition of "the 'subnatural,' that is, the irrational, the impulse to evil, the uncontrollable unconscious."[22]

Viewed from this perspective, Ann Radcliffe provided a model of "pre-psychology" which Sand adopted and extended in the creation of one of her most innovative and haunting novels. In the end Sand transforms the roman noir into a roman blanc. Her novel moves from colorful music to pure silence, from black terror to limpid serenity, from the dark abysses of ignorance and fear to the luminescent realm of initiation.

The Power of Bringing into Idea

La création est éternelle. Créons donc, c'est à dire, obéissons au souffle de l'Esprit.

(3:464)

(Creation is eternal. Let us therefore create, that is to say, let us obey the breath of the Spirit.)

The novel of initiation, skillfully studied by Léon Cellier, takes us into the very heart of the Romantic ethos.[23] Many of the French Romantics participated in this novelistic genre. Balzac's *La Peau de chagrin* and *Séraphita*, Hugo's *L'Homme qui rit*, Nerval's *Aurélia*, Gautier's *Spirite*, Sand's *Spiridion* are a few key examples. Although the initiation novel traces the spiritual itinerary of a character, it is not identical to the Bildungsroman, that novel of education of which Flaubert's *L'Education sentimentale* and Stendhal's *Le Rouge et le noir* are prime examples. The former takes its hero through the formative years into adulthood; the latter traces a character's symbolic death and rebirth into a higher realm. As Cellier puts it: "[The Bildungsroman] on the one hand resembles the initiation novel, since the hero or heroine follows an itinerary marked with trials, but on the other hand, at the end of his or her journey, he or she discovers wisdom, happiness, he or she matures, and becomes a man or woman. The fate of the character's soul is not at stake, the problem of his or her salvation is not in question."[24] The novel of initiation reveals the Romantics' almost obsessional fascination for the abstract, the invisible, the spiritual.

Merely to acknowledge the existence of a novel of initiation puts into question the conventional definition of the novel as almost entirely identifiable with Realism. In fact the standard equation of novel and Realism is manifestly false because incomplete and totalitarian in view of the multifarious nineteenth-century novel forms. Such a uniform vision of the nineteenth-century novel does not take into account the extraordinary experimentation that moved the novel in widely different directions. Increasingly, critics are discovering that our discourse about the nineteenth-century novel has been truncated and needs to be expanded. More and more we find that many fictional genres cannot fit into the narrow category of "Realism."[25]

As Naomi Schor has made clear in her article, "Idealism in the Novel: Recanonizing Sand," the critical discourse about the novel in the nineteenth century made use of two major terms that coexisted in fertile dialogical opposition—Realism and Idealism.[26] From Quatremère de Quincy's series of articles in *Les Archives littéraires de l'Europe* in 1805 to his *Essai sur l'Idéal* in 1837 to Taine's *De l'Idéal dans l'art* of 1867, the nineteenth century opposed the two antithetical sensibilities with contrasting categories: imitation versus transcendance, mimesis versus eidos, document versus vision, Realism versus Idealism. In this opposition of the documentary and the visionary, nineteenth-century fiction defined itself in binary terms. Thus, the category of "idealist novel," far from being an oxymoronic impossibility, is the counterbalancing prose form to Realism. From Chateaubriand's fictions depicting *le vague des passions*, through Senancour's study of existential impotence and paralysis, to Eugène Fromentin's study of nostalgia in *Dominique* (1863), the idealist novel assumed different guises. Sand's pastoral novels may be seen as experiments in idealist fiction. And when, in *La Mare au diable*, the author opposes "l'étude de la réalité positive" ("the study of actual reality") to "la recherche de la vérité idéale" ("the search for ideal reality," *La Mare*, 33), she is reformulating the great binary opposition that defined prose in her century. The pastoral novel, literature of the fantastic, "intimist" prose, the psychological novel make up the various facets of Idealism. But I would argue that Idealism's most original and fertile embodiment is the novel of initiation.

In his definition of Idealism Quatremère used the metaphor of the "concave mirror" in opposition to the "faceted glass" of Realism.[27] In another transposition of the visual metaphor, he referred to a certain kind of abstract visibility, one that appealed to the mind rather than to the senses. His arguments are curiously reminiscent of Sand's own discussion of the invisible novel in her article on *Obermann*:

> The word *ideal*, joined to the word *beautiful*, expresses therefore the beauty that art doubtlessly renders visible, but more specifically so to the soul, to the capacity for comprehension, to feeling, and to the mind's eye, rather than to the material organ; it expresses that beauty, of which no isolated model can be the exemplar, of which no individual can furnish the complete image, and

which the artist achieves only by his or her capacity to *ideate* ("la puissance d'*idéer*").[28]

If artistic rendering of the ideal can be only a fragmented and partial image of the whole, the essential faculty the writer exploits is the capacity to "perceive by means of the imagination."[29] This, in the words of Cellier, is the essential compositional exploit of the roman initiatique: "In order to write a novel of initiation, one must be a romantic, that is to say, one must believe in the realm of the imagination, believe in the supreme dignity of the soul."[30]

This kingdom of the imagination celebrates the realm of *ideating* (Quatremère's verb *idéer* is a neologism), and the *cerebrality* of the artist's fictional universe. In the novel of initiation this is translated into the search for hierophanies, those manifestations of the divine which challenge the definition of homo sapiens as a wholly materialist creature. Just as the novel of initiation proposes a new literary language to denote a psychology that insists on development and mutation, so it subverts the materialist equation of *homme* with *machine*. From this perspective, we can better understand Léon Cellier's interpretation of *Consuelo* as "a methodical investigation of the powers of the imagination."[31]

In *Histoire de ma vie* George Sand avowed her allegiance to the realm of the imagination which she defined as the "violent désir, si naturel à l'imagination poétique, de sortir du monde positif et d'entrer dans une voie inconnue" (2:266; "violent desire, so natural to the poetic imagination, to leave the positive world and enter into an unknown path"). The "voie inconnue" she embarked upon in *Consuelo* was rich in discoveries, including foremost among them her discovery of a personal mythology, a system of beliefs that incorporated heterogeneous elements of pagan mythology and of Christian dogma. More important still, through the articulation of these important myths, Sand paved the way for her own psychic recovery. She defined her place as a writer in society and articulated her vision of the artist's mission in the world. *Consuelo* was a novel of consolation both thematically and for its author.

The huge work of *Consuelo*, which took Sand over two years to write, represents a kind of Sandian summa; not so much a *summa theologica* (that is perhaps the role filled by *Spiridion*) as a *summa litteraria*, in which the author was able to rewrite and reinterpret certain traditional literary plots. By concentrating on these revisions and rewritings, we can clearly see emerge some of Sand's most fundamental mythological obsessions. In rewriting three classical myths, she formulated her vision of the Ideal, her search for religious syncretism, and her subversion of opinions accepted as axioms by her society.[32]

A Reservoir of Myths: Orphea

As Mircea Eliade reminds us in his monumental *Images and Symbols*, the nineteenth-century novel is the depository for the sacred in a de-sacralized universe:

> It would be a worthwhile enterprise to study the survival of the great myths throughout the nineteenth century. We would see how, having been humbled, diminished, and condemned constantly to changing banners, they nonetheless survived this hibernation, thanks for the most part to literature. . . . What a glorious enterprise it would be to reveal the truly spiritual role of the nineteenth-century novel which, in spite of all the scientific, realistic, social "formulas," was the great "reservoir" for degraded myths.[33]

These myths, desacralized, deteriorated, eroded,[34] seen in such master stories as the Garden of Eden, the myth of the eternal return, or the descent into hell, are evident in many nineteenth-century novels, with the novel of initiation a privileged genre among them, since it was more capable than the realist novel of a transmutation into the ideal. Cellier has shown that the journey frequently structures this type of novel, transforming the human adventure into a mythic quest:

> The archetypes of the journey of initiation, of the journey into the depth of the night, will then appear just beneath the surface of all the works which describe the journey of the soul: the search for the castle, for the sanctuary, for the Treasure, for the Secret; the Crossing or the Ascension; the March through the labyrinth or through the dark forest; the Climb up the spiral staircase, the Descent into Hell.[35]

This topos can already be detected in the early Sand (in *Lettres d'un voyageur*, especially). In *Consuelo*, via the theme of the descent into hell—transposed as a descent into a Gothic castle and a second descent into the catacombs of the Château du Graal—Sand adheres most strongly to the initiation genre and incorporates several mythical retellings.

Cellier reminds us that the initiation topos is usually structured into a text at least twice, in a minor and major key, the former often a preview of the grand-scale initiation. In *Consuelo* the minor initiation occurs when the heroine goes in search of Albert in the depths of the Schreckenstein grotto beneath the Château des Géants. The entire scene is a retelling of the Orpheus myth but with the genders reversed, a device that Sand employs quite often. In the Greek original Orpheus is poet and singer while in Sand's novel it is the heroine who is both singer and composer. Orpheus seeks to free Eurydice from Hades, just as Consuelo rescues Albert, her future husband. While both Orpheus and Consuelo undergo trials through terror and tests of courage, the outcome of each tale is different. Orpheus loses Eurydice for good when he turns back to make sure she is safely behind him. Consuelo, on the other hand, manages to bring Albert back temporarily to the land of the living. The author notes the resemblance between her novel and the Orphic myth through the theme of turning back:

> comme le héros fabuleux, Consuelo était descendue dans le Tartare pour en tirer son ami. . . . Ils recommençaient ensemble une vie nouvelle . . . n'osant guère regarder en arrière, et ne se sentant pas la force de se replonger par la pensée dans cet abîme. (*Consuelo*, 1:373)

> (Like the mythical hero, Consuelo had descended into Tartarus to save her friend. . . . They were beginning a new life together . . . hardly daring to look back, and no longer possessing the strength to plunge once again, even in thought, into that abyss.)

With Consuelo described as a "héros fabuleux," Sand displays yet once again her favorite gender inversion. In passing she also makes reference to the Dantean theme of *la vita nuova*, and alludes to the Orphic warning of not looking back.

Like Eurydice, Albert will return to the Netherworld. Prey to cataleptic fits that plunge him into deathlike trances, Albert convinces everyone, including his doctor, that he has died. Although this symbolic death is a prelude to his spiritual and affective regeneration, he never fully returns to the world of the living. He gives up his identity, his title, and all rights to his inheritance and estate. Spiritually reborn at the end of the novel, in a hierogamous scene with Consuelo, he remains partially entrapped in the underworld, transformed into a shadowy character, no longer quite of this world, believed dead by all but a few initiates. When he tries once to return home to pay his final respects to his father, the servants take him for a ghost and run off in terror. Sadly, he makes a Eurydice-like remark: "Il semble que Dieu veuille me fermer l'accès de ce monde" (3:363; "It seems that God wants to close off my access to this world"). Albert's words reinforce for the reader his alienation from reality.

In a novel of initiation a character's descent into hell ensures that he or she will undergo a metamorphosis. To paraphrase Kierkegaard, "only he who goes to hell finds Eurydice," one could say about Albert: "only he who goes to hell finds himself." Albert's second descent into Hades puts him in a state of mind, allowing "the superior forces, which slumber in a human being, to be restored."[36] These superior forces transform Albert from a sickly and bewildered young man into a poet, visionary, and musician. At the end of the novel, he himself, like Consuelo, has become an Orphic figure.

As the ending of *Consuelo* makes clear, Orpheus is not only the prototype of the poet whose destiny is to plunge beneath the mundane surface of existence, he is also the artist-prophet, a sacrificial victim to inspiration and the divine. The theme of Orpheus as savior of humanity is evident in Ballanche's initiatic poem *Orphée*, for instance, which Sand professed to "love passionately" (*Corr.*, 3:387–388), and which was, according to Cellier, a vital text for the Romantics "a great disseminator of ideas around 1830."[37] Hugo's narrative poem of 1855, *Dieu*, takes up again the theme of Orpheus as the savior of humankind in a scene where the poet meets Orpheus who has delivered Prometheus from the vulture. Thus "Orpheus has completed the work of Prometheus."[38] The poet-narrator then associates himself with the rebellious Prometheus and becomes an active participant in the everyday world, a bringer of the holy fire to all.

The redemptive aspect of the myth is relevant for the major initiation scene in which Consuelo undergoes the rites of passage prescribed by the sect of the Invisibles. Here she is no longer searching for Albert but seeking to merge with all of suffering humanity. Thus the Orpheus myth is both inverted and transcended, so that the pair Orpheus/Eurydice becomes Consuelo/Humanity. This element of the myth points to the significance of the Orphic revelation as syncretic. As Orpheus is "destined because of his gifts to aspire to a triple role: political, social, religious,"[39] so Consuelo commits herself in her final initiation to political action and religious activism. Henceforth, her life will be linked to Albert's and the two will devote themselves to the "redivinization" of humankind (the expression "l'homme redivinisé" is Sand's, LV, 200). Indeed *Consuelo* explores the possibility of Orpheus being a woman and thus posits the existence of Orphea.

Psyche's Lamp

A second myth is alluded to in this scene of *initatio major*. Consuelo receives a little silver lamp to guide her through the labyrinth of horrors, when she is warned not to look back:

> [Marcus] présenta à la néophyte une petite lampe d'argent. . . .
> "Craignez, [dit-il] de ne jamais arriver à la porte du temple, si vous avez le malheur de regarder une seule fois derrière vous en marchant . . . ne vous retournez pas. C'est . . . la prescription rigide des antiques initiations." (3:381)

([Marcus] presented the neophyte with a small silver lamp. . . .
"I'm afraid I must warn you [he explained] that you will never
reach the door of the temple, if you have the misfortune to look
back even once as you walk . . . don't turn around. It is . . . the
rigid regulation of ancient initiations.")

The silver lamp belongs to the myth of Psyche, and the warning
not to look back is yet another allusion to the Orphic myth and rites.
This culminating scene therefore incorporates two myths, though both
are reworked and adapted to fit Sand's vision. The Orpheus story is
still operating as the poet-singer Consuelo descends again into hell, ultimately to emerge triumphant and to be reunited with her lost husband. But Psyche's story is also very present as Sand alludes to the
myth several times in her narration. First of all, there is an allusion to
Psyche's curiosity regarding the identity of her lover. Consuelo is phys-
ically attracted to Liverani, a masked member of the Invisibles who has
rescued the young woman from prison. In the person of Liverani the
erotic makes its entrance into Consuelo's life for the first time. Although he pursues her with letters, declarations of love, and illicit visits, he maintains his masked identity. But one evening Consuelo
encounters him in the garden and watches, mesmerized, as he begins
to remove his mask: "Liverani porta la main à son masque, il allait l'ar-
racher et parler. Consuelo, comme la curieuse Psyché, n'avait plus le
courage de fermer les yeux" (3:303; "Liverani put his hand to his mask,
he was about to tear it off and speak. Consuelo, like the curious Psyche,
no longer had the courage to close her eyes"). In this episode, in order
to convey Consuelo's growing sexual awareness, Sand exploits the
Psychian theme of the masked lover who arouses the curiosity of the
woman he loves. In the Latin myth Psyche/the soul falls in love with
Cupid, that is, with Eros, sensual love. In the myth's finale Love and
the Soul are reunited. Apuleius is reworking the idea of the comple-
mentarity of human love, where sexual wholeness is obtained by the
merging of opposites. In accordance with the much earlier Platonic
myth as presented in *The Symposium*, the lover is an incomplete being
until he or she is reunited with his or her other half. Sand retains the
idea of human plenitude in love, but her schema is trinary rather than
binary. Consuelo is the Psychean figure in this case, but her lover is
double, since Liverani, the man she desires, represents Eros, while Albert, the man she married out of compassion, is Agape. When Consuelo finally realizes that the two are the same person, the opposition
of sexual and altruistic love is transcended. The dichotomy disappears
and Consuelo discovers that psychic integration can take place. Sand
uses Psyche's story not only as a myth about faithfulness and the willingness to undergo hardships for the sake of love, but also as a story
about the perfect, mysterious ideal of the *coincidentia oppositorum*,

which both Jung and Eliade find at the basis of many of our interpretations about the sacred realm.[40]

Psyche is sent to the underworld in her final trial to bring back to Venus a box in which Proserpina was to have put some of her own beauty. Psyche cannot resist opening the box and falls into a deep sleep as a result. She is rescued by Cupid himself. Likewise, Consuelo descends into the catacombs for her final preinitiatory trial and, witnessing the hideous bell, falls into a faint. Like Psyche, she is saved by her lover, Liverani. Both rescue scenes are followed by a triumphant hierogamy. Jupiter proposes to bestow immortality on Psyche. In a comparable gesture, Marcus presents Consuelo for membership into the Order of the Invisibles. Thus the apotheosis of both Psyche and Consuelo is underscored by a triple mark of integration—reunion with the spouse, inclusion into a privileged group of gods or initiates after a period of exile or imprisonment, and a psychic sense of inner unity— what Jung called personal integration. The heroine comes into her own; by becoming more harmonious within herself, she is free to be reunited with others. Inner wholeness is coupled with social integration. The sacred marriage in both stories at once closes the text with a traditional "happy ending" and leaves the reader with an image of the individual's harmonious relationship with the group, after much struggle and tribulation.

Why does Sand so obviously make use of these classical myths? In part, it reflects a fascination common to the Romantics. Orpheus, for example, is a figure with strong appeal, who confirms them in their glorification of the poet as prophet, as martyr, as the ultimate adventurer of the soul, and his story represents a powerful myth about the acquisition and danger of knowledge. Psyche was also a popular Romantic figure, as Victor Laprade's rewriting of her story in *Psyché* (1841) attests. In both cases it is interesting to note what René Canat has called "the use of ancient myths to express new ideas." Apuleius's story, for instance, is transmuted by Laprade into a series of Christian equivalents. Thus Psyche becomes Eve; her beautiful estate, a kind of Garden of Eden; and her exile, the equivalent of the Fall. Finally Psyche's ascension to Olympus represents the Christian soul being purified after the expiation of sins.[41] Laprade's Psyche, as well as Ballanche's Orpheus and Quinet's Prometheus, are Romanticized classical figures whose adventures unfold in what Gilbert Durand has called the nocturnal state.[42] All three are heroes plumbing the depths of humankind's psychological dissatisfaction, rebelliousness, and refusal to accept fate passively, whether in life or in death.

The Romantic rewritings of the old myths are manifestations of the century's need for religious syncretism. Canat criticizes Laprade for his overly ambitious synthesis of all religions and philosophies in *Psyché*: "Too large an eclecticism which is an amalgam of the Gospel,

Plato, Victor Cousin, Lamartine, Vigny, and the humanitarian philoso-phers."[43] The conflation of pagan and Christian elements, so evident in all the Romantic appropriations of classical myths, is epitomized by Quinet's *Prometheus*, in which the archangels Michael and Raphael visit earth and come across the crucified figure of Prometheus in the Cau-casus. They deliver him and as he ascends to heaven, a company of seraphims sings of the new age of hope: "The song of desperation has transformed itself into a hymn of pardon."[44]

Consuelo is a product of the same syncretic sensibility. Sand too created an eclectic novel, incorporating Greek and Latin mythology, Hussite lore, sectarian heresy, the philosophy of Pierre Leroux, histor-ical documents of the eighteenth century, Freemasonry texts. (Sand writes to Leroux that she has lost herself in research: "You can't imag-ine what labyrinth I have gotten myself into because of your free-masons and your secret societies"; *Corr.*, 6:179). She combines the pagan rites of initiation with those of the eighteenth-century secret so-cieties (Freemasons and others) in the scene of Consuelo's initiation. The sect of the Invisibles incorporates elements of the Egyptian myth of Hiram (3:377–378), of dogmas of the Lollard sect, of Freemason phi-losophy; their code names are of Greek origin (3:414); one of their main spiritual leaders is a woman who attacks the social inequalities of the sexes, the legal prostitution of marriage, and the enslavement of love to law. She is at once a feminist, a spokeswoman for Leroux's theories, and a reincarnation of a Greek sybil whose face reminds Consuelo si-multaneously of the expiring Niobe and the Virgin Mary "fainting at the foot of the cross" (3:322). These two images—one pagan, the other Christian—describe Albert's mother, the priestess Wanda, as exemplar of suffering motherhood. Later Albert describes Consuelo as both a poet (a pagan and Romantic ideal) and an angel (a Christian and Ro-mantic ideal) (3:365). More than any other Romantic writer, Sand be-lieved in her century's capacity to synthesize, to effect the harmonious cohabitation of philosophy and religion, to resacralize the world with-out binding it in rigid dogma. More often than not, she created images that were expansive and inclusive rather than prescriptive and exclusionary.

The character Albert is Sand's master-synthesizer, the philoso-pher who can reconnect the broken links among the various human faculties, who can propose a religious syncretism that incorporates all the fragmented pieces of past and present thought:

> Dans les choses qui nous avaient toujours semblé mortes ou con-damnées, [Albert] retrouva les éléments de la vie, et, des ténèbres de la Fable même, il fit jaillir les éclairs de la vérité. Il expliqua les mythes antiques; il établit . . . tous les liens, tous les points de contact des religions entre elles. . . . Il reconstitua à nos yeux

l'unité de la vie dans l'humanité et l'unité du dogme dans la religion; et de tous les matériaux épars dans le monde ancien et
nouveau, il forma les bases de son monde futur.   (3:461)

(In things that had always seemed dead or doomed to us, [Albert]
rediscovered the elements of life, and even from the darkness of
the Fable itself, he caused flashes of truth to fly up. He explained
the ancient myths; he established . . . all the links, all the points of
contact among the various religions. . . . He reestablished for us
the unity of life in humanity and the unity of dogma in religion;
and with all kinds of scattered materials from the ancient and modern worlds, he formed the basis of his future world.)

One finds a similar desire to unite knowledge and feeling in Sand's
mystical play, *Les Sept Cordes de la lyre* (1839), in which Mephistopheles
says to the philosopher Albertus (notice the name): "Pédant mystique,
tu me donnes plus de peines que maître Faust, ton aïeul . . . voici des
philosophes qui veulent à la fois *connaître et sentir*" ("Mystical pedant,
you give me more trouble than master Faustus, your forefather . . . here are philosophers who want simultaneously *to know
and to feel*").[45] Here and in *Consuelo* Sand clearly expresses her vision of
knowledge acquired through feeling rather than at its expense.

Likewise, the "new ideas" that emerge through a rewriting of the
old myths are connected to the nineteenth century's capacity for self-
reflection. Each age has plundered old stories and delved into them to
extract those myths best suited for itself, those that most accurately reflect the sensibility and values of the period. We in the twentieth century seem to have selected Oedipus (Freudians), Medusa (feminists),
and perhaps Antigone (*littérature engagée*), as those Greek heroes who
best describe our own obsessions. In selecting Prometheus, Orpheus,
and Psyche, the Romantics chose to emphasize the *questing* of their
contemporaries, their restlessness, and their need to seek meaning in
new kingdoms of thought. By plunging into the underworld in search
of knowledge, both the Romantic Orpheus and Psyche revealed to
what extent the dark side of the soul, the oneiric realm, was the other
side of the mirror.

The Daughter's Search for the Mother

The myth of Persephone and Demeter epitomizes the mother-
daughter relationship cast in an ideal mold. It is a story unsullied by a
Freudian sense of competitiveness between the older and the younger
woman for possession of the father. Demeter and Persephone are
united by a bond of such strength that it allows the mother to rescue
her daughter from the underworld, thereby ensuring that the two will

be reunited for two-thirds of each year. In this story the male is portrayed either as a predatory creature, as in the case of Hephaestos, the
rapist, or as a weak and indifferent parent, as in the case of Zeus, who
allows his daughter to be abducted because he does not want to confront his violent brother. The paternal figure, then, shrugs his shoulders and looks away. He gives no moral direction, provides no
patriarchal authority. In fact Demeter's search for her lost daughter is a
crucial instance of women's power over man's violence and over death.
Since it valorizes women living together as opposed to the patriarchal
breaking-up of the women's gynaeceum through marriage, it is a
powerful myth of gynocracy. Demeter and Persephone, goddesses of
fertility and of the harvest, are also, particularly for our purposes, goddesses of maternal devotion and filial love.

Such a relationship exists in Sand's novel between the sibyl Wanda and her protégée and confessee Consuelo. Wanda is an enigmatic
and eccentric character about whom there is surprisingly little discussion in the critical literature on *Consuelo*. Cellier, in his masterful commentary, merely notes that she represents the "soul of Leroux" and
that her speeches are a "summary of Leroux's ideas on the feminine
question."[46] But, although Wanda can be seen as a cypher for Leroux's
philosophical ideas, she is no less a powerful embodiment of the
Chthonian mother, her life a reenactment of Demeter's. In Wanda we
can see Sand reworking the story of Demeter's search for her lost child.

Wanda first appears to the reader as one of the seven members of
the tribunal of the Invisibles. She is dressed in a red cloak and wears a
white mask, so that both her identity and gender are concealed. Subsequently Wanda, still incognito, is assigned to the heroine as her "father
confessor." The two characters mostly discuss Consuelo's attraction to
Liverani and her sense of duty toward her husband, Albert, who, although presumed dead, possibly is alive after all. Only in the fourth
interview does Wanda reveal her true identity to Consuelo, not only as
a woman but as a mother:

> "Une mère t'a manqué, lorsque tu as prononcé, avec un en-
> thousiasme plus fanatique qu'humain, le serment d'appartenir à
> un homme que tu aimais d'une manière incomplète. Une mère
> t'est donnée aujourd'hui pour t'assister et t'éclairer dans tes
> nouvelles résolutions à l'heure du divorce ou de la sanction défini-
> tive de cet étrange hyménée. Cette mère, c'est moi, Consuelo, moi
> qui ne suis pas un homme, mais une femme." (3:321)

> ("You were lacking a mother when you pronounced, with an en-
> thusiasm more fanatic than human, a solemn oath to belong to a
> man whom you loved in an incomplete way. Today a mother is
> being restored to you, to assist you in shedding light on your new

resolutions in this hour of need. Will you decide on divorce or on the definitive sanction of this strange marriage? This mother is I, Consuelo. For I am not a man, but a woman.")

Wanda proceeds to remove her mask, her fake beard, and her false hair before the astonished Consuelo. As the woman hidden under her disguise emerges, the narrator studies her physiognomy and deciphers three dominating traits on her face: maternal goodness, intellectual power, and traces of great suffering:

> Consuelo vit une tête de femme vieillie et souffrante . . . mais d'une grande beauté de ligne incomparable, et d'une expression sublime de bonté, de tristesse, et de force. Ces trois habitudes de l'âme, si diverses, et si rarement réunies dans un même être, se peignaient dans le vaste front, dans le sourire maternel et le profond regard de l'inconnue . . . son visage annonç[ait] une grande puissance d'organisation primitive; mais les ravages de la douleur n'étaient que trop visibles.   (13:322)

> (Consuelo saw the face of an old and suffering woman . . . but one whose incomparable features displayed great beauty and a sublime expression of goodness, sadness, and strength. These three habits of the soul, so diverse, and so rarely reunited in one being, were imprinted on the stranger's large brow, on her maternal smile, and in her deep gaze. . . Her face reveal[ed] the formidable power of a primeval constitution but the ravages of pain were all but too visible.)

As Albert's natural and Consuelo's adoptive mother, Wanda is the image of the ideal maternal figure in Sand's terms. She has wept and searched for both children. In this portrait of the rebellious sybil, which insists on her intellect, strength of feeling, and asexual beauty, Sand creates a feminine version of the sublime old man. Finally we find a version of Sand's own recurrent hermit in its feminized variant. How rarely in literature do we find such positive physiognomies of old women! Wanda here is portrayed as the antithesis of all the Mme Vauquers of literature, with their wrinkled faces and hairpieces denoting the withering and corruption of their souls. The very opposite of a witch, Wanda is here portrayed as a goddesslike figure. Had Demeter appeared in a nineteenth-century novel, this is how she would have looked.

The narration of her life story is also a triple expression of faith. Wanda is a feminist who directs a diatribe against a society that has erected a legal structure enforcing marriage without love or equality between the sexes. She is an apologist for the wisdom and guidance that older women can provide humanity. Finally, she is a religious heretic whose intellectual path has led to the secret society of the Invisibles.

The climactic event of her life—being buried alive—is analyzed with clinical detachment and yet conjures up echoes of Gothic entombment scenes in the reader's mind. Wanda describes her long periods of catalepsy, how she is taken for dead and buried during one of them, how, as a result, she enters into a kind of netherworld. But even though she is technically alive, she never returns to her former position in life. Abandoning all the ties of her former life, save one, she embarks on an existence of wandering and concealed identity. At that moment, when she enters this death-in-life, her story bears a marked resemblance to Demeter's.

Wanda begins to search for her son, Albert, who has been sent away from the paternal home for an educational tour of Europe. She follows him from city to city for seven years as he pursues his formative travels. Albert, who resembles his mother temperamentally, pathologically, and intellectually ("Combien de fois il nous a semblé que nous étions le même être," Wanda says; 3:342; "How frequently it seemed to us that we were the same being"), undergoes the same trial as his mother. He also is buried in error, during a cataleptic swoon. Now it is Wanda who unearths him. Thereupon, Albert, like his mother, renounces all ties to his former life and joins in her cause. Thus, through an ironic (and scarcely realistic) twist of the plot, both mother and son die symbolic deaths, only to be resurrected into a higher and mysterious realm that maintains them in a kind of halfway world. While Demeter had pursued the abducted Persephone into Hades, here it is Albert who follows his mother into a netherworld to be reunited with her.

It might be argued that since Demeter searched for a daughter while Wanda searched for a son, the two stories are not close enough to warrant juxtaposition. We might even see here the Egyptian myth of Isis seeking for her dismembered son, Osiris. But two points need to be made. Sand's text repeatedly suggests that Albert and his mother are not so much an incestuous mother and son couple (such as we encounter in François le champi, as incest is a Sandian theme), but rather two embodiments of the same person. Their lives are parallel, they have the same character, think the same thoughts, are prey to the same illnesses, experience the same symbolic death and rebirth, undergo the same initiation. Wanda emphasizes this tightly knit symbiosis between them: "Nous avons souffert ensemble des mêmes douleurs physiques, résultant des mêmes émotions morales" (3:342; "We have both suffered from the same physical pains, resulting from the same moral emotions").

Furthermore, this novel centers on neither Wanda nor Albert, being fundamentally concerned with Consuelo. Both mother and son are shadowy background figures who intermittently come to the fore during the narration of Consuelo's trajectory through the novel's fictional universe. And, quite literally, Consuelo's search for her husband takes her to Wanda. For the heroine, then, Wanda and Albert are essentially the same person.

Béatrice Didier has remarked that Consuelo's itinerary is a pilgrimage toward the Mother. Her trip to Bohemia retraces her mother's Bohemian vagrant footsteps. Didier, in fact, sees in Albert a mother figure and she identifies him as a prime example of the peculiarly Sandian "fantasme de l'homme-mère," ("phantasm of the man-mother").[47] Since there is nothing strikingly maternal about Albert, Didier's interpretation may seem puzzling. But its pertinence and meaning emerge clearly when we realize that Albert and Wanda are, for Consuelo, very much interchangeable. Her quest and her initiation culminate in the scene where she is simultaneously given a husband and a mother, a mother-husband. In this most consoling of her novels, Sand expresses her ideal of a perfect trinity: the son, the daughter, and the mother. The final scene achieves the perfect fusion of the three classical myths employed by Sand. Orpheus-Psyche-Persephone represent Consuelo; Demeter is Wanda; Eurydice-Cupid is Albert. Singularly missing is a patriarchal figure. Consuelo has no father, no patronym, and does not live under any patriarch's law. She is called "la fille sans nom" ("the girl or daughter without a name," 3:264). Her mentor, Porpora, is less a father figure than a grandfatherly, impotent old grouch whose influence on Consuelo is limited. The one dominant parental figure is Wanda as she fulfills the dual role of father-confessor and mother.

In Sand's fictional world the mother is the powerful deity. Like a Demeter controling the seasons and the world's fertility, Wanda presides at her children's wedding ceremony. Her sermon dominates the scene, just as her world view guides the sect of the Invisibles. If Sand expressed in *Consuelo* the phantasm of "l'homme-mère," she also expressed the phantasm of "la mère-père" ("the mother-father").

Sand's recasting of the three classical myths of Orpheus, Psyche, and Demeter in one novel makes clear the connections among them. All are stories about solitude and about longing for reunion with the loved one. All three involve a descent into the underworld and a psychic transformation. All three are structured around the motifs of the labyrinth leading down to hell and the triumphant ascension in an apotheosis of integration. This quest for the Other, whether wife, husband, or child, points to Sand's obsession with the longing for the ideal via the search for the ideal person. If, for a moment, we can view Sand's desires expressed in Consuelo's quest, we can identify an emblematic Sand structure whereby the woman-artist leads a life of deliberate solitude and, through total devotion to her art, finally enters into a community of fellow travelers.

The Novel of Consolation

Consuelo, then, is a novel of healing because, unlike *Lélia* which ends in suicide and murder, or *Spiridion* in martyrdom, its final scene presents the ideal human community. The configuration of characters and denouement in *Consuelo* illustrate one of her key beliefs—a conviction Lélia in her fiction of solitude had not yet discovered, but which Sand began to articulate in the watershed text of *Spiridion* and explored further in the utopian novels: the conviction that humans are not made for isolation but must live in an harmonious group. Lélia must climb down from her rock; Consuelo must step down from the stage; Angel, Alexis's protégé, must leave his monastery. Together they must seek a solution that lies not in pure contemplation, but in praxis.

In the final portion of the book Albert becomes Sand's spokesperson. The device of the man having the final word echoes the ending of *Indiana*. The male point of view represents perhaps, not so much masculine authority as the symbiotic relationship between hero and narrator. The idea of community is woven into the very fabric of our spiritual life, insists Albert, since God is not one but three, and since the theory of the "divine tétrade" (3:456) can be found in numerous cults, Christian, Indian, Egyptian, Greek. Here again Sand's hero emphasizes the underlying interconnectedness of human thought and the large network of the human family.

This trinity is also present in each individual, thus making each person in the likeness of God: "l'homme est une trinité, comme Dieu. Et cette trinité s'appelle, dans le langage humain: sensation, sentiment, connaissance. Et l'unité de ces trois choses forme la Tétrade humaine, répond à la Tétrade divine" (3:457–458; "Man is a trinity, like God. And this trinity in our human language is called sensation, feeling, knowledge. The unity of these three things forms the human tetrad and corresponds to the divine tetrad"). We have entered, continues Albert, into a period of fragmentation in which these three faculties of human nature have become separated. As a result, each alienated faculty has produced its own false prophets. Each of the three different roads leads to an abyss. The prophets of physical sensation preach materialism; the prophets of immaterial feeling, mysticism; and the prophets of knowledge, atheism. Albert denounces this schism in favor of a restored unity: "Il n'y a qu'une route certaine vers la vérité: c'est celle qui répond à la nature humaine complète, à la nature humaine développée sous tous les aspects" (3:458; "There is only one certain road toward the truth: the road that corresponds to complete human nature, to human nature that has developed fully").

This "complete human nature" is symbolically expressed in the final scene of the sacred marriage between Albert and Consuelo, with Wanda presiding. The three characters, before they are bonded into a family, stand at the ceremony as the embodiment of the ideal human trinity. In each character, one of the three faculties is dominant, with Wanda representing feeling, Albert knowledge, and Consuelo sensation. The initiation consists in the synthesis of these three features and the union of the mother-husband with the virgin. The three characters are interconnected in a kind of triangular scheme, each sharing a common point with the other. Albert and Consuelo are husband and wife, fellow wanderers and initiates; Consuelo and Wanda are daughter and mother, doubles, who have integrated their sexual, artistic, and intellectual lives; Wanda and Albert are mother and son, both travelers along the same via dolorosa, who reach fulfillment when Consuelo enters their lives. All three form a harmonious crucible out of which the new society can emerge.

In his preface to H. J. Hunt's *The Epic in Nineteenth-Century France*, the scholar Gustave Rudler reflects on the prodigious capacity of the Romantic writers for myth making:

> [They] incorporated their own original messages into myths, some of which they sometimes invented, but most of which they borrowed, and then reinterpreted, probed further, sometimes damaged or defaced by loading them down with superfluous embellishments. The Romantic imagination gave itself carte blanche in every domain. The great initiators, great criminals, great victims of religions and mythologies became the natural prey for seekers of symbols: Prometheus, Orpheus, Psyche, Euphorion, Adam, Cain, Satan, Ahasverus, and Lilith.[48]

In this respect *Consuelo* represents Sand's fertile and salutory encounter with mythology. A novel of initiation by its thematic attention to the process of rebirth in several of the characters, *Consuelo* is also a novel of initiation with regard to the author herself. Its composition made it possible for the writer to articulate some of her deeply buried convictions and, in turn, to come to grips with her own tempestuous psychic life. If *Lélia* was her novel of despair and *Spiridion* her novel of heresy, *Consuelo* is the fiction of Sand's own descent into and return from hell. The writing of this novel was also her cure. *Consuelo* verifies the fact that, as Max Milner has noted, the unconscious is not so much a reservoir of ready-made myths as the site of a toiling of the mind, of a swarming of potential images waiting to be born.

The Metamorphosis of Cyane

Of the novels studied thus far, four—*Indiana, Lélia, Spiridion,* and *Consuelo*—end in a very comparable way, with the silencing of the hero or heroine. Indiana ceases to speak altogether; Lélia is literally made voiceless as she is strangled by the mad priest Magnus (a little man, despite his name); Alexis is stabbed to death in the middle of his speech of revolutionary compassion; and Consuelo loses her voice after her initiation. The four novels, through four images of the broken voice—a mysterious case of muteness, a broken neck, a murder, the mysterious loss of a singing talent—express a central Sandian phobia. We might wonder at the fear of silence in a writer who produced over eighty novels, thirty volumes of letters, numerous plays, critical articles of every description, a significant body of journalistic writings, and approximately three thousand pages of memoirs. And we remember the prophetic words pronounced by her first artist: "My voice is my life" (*Histoire du rêveur*). But perhaps one of Sand's motivating forces is revealed here; the only way not to be silenced was to continue to write. Unlike her dark heroine Lélia, unlike Indiana, Alexis-Aurore, and Consuelo, Sand never ceased to give voice to her inner life through her writing. And the products of that fertile mind are incontestably our gain.

A dark myth, then, lies at the bottom of Sand's mind, a myth of male violence and silencing, the myth of Cyane. Ovid's *Metamorphoses* tells this myth about one of Proserpina's nymphs who was metamorphosed and thereby lost the power of speech. She was the only one to witness Proserpina's abduction by the lord of the underworld. When she came forth to help, Pluto changed her into a fountain so that she would not able to reveal what she had seen. Later, when Ceres came looking for her daughter, Cyane remained silent. Ovid tells us: "Were the nymph not water, she would have told her everything; she tried to, but had no lips, no mouth, no tongue to speak with."[49] This myth, which resonates in four of her novels, suggests that, although George Sand was one of the most prolific women writers we know, her fear of being silenced was nevertheless a powerful and frightening emotion. The melancholic Indiana, the nihilistic Lélia, and the mystical Alexis–Aurore all betrayed their likeness to Cyane's fate. *Consuelo* formulates the myth for a fourth time as it applies to the artist.

There are in fact two variants of the myth in Sand's works, one framed in a pessimistic, the other in an optimistic mode. *Lélia* and *Spiridion* represent the first. In *Lélia*, as the monk squeezes her neck with a rosary, she loses her breath, her voice, and her life. Her symbolic murder represents the attempts of the orthodox religious sphere to suppress the sacrilegious words she utters. In this text, where a feminized figure of Prometheus plays a strong role, the heroine appears to be punished for the unsanctioned knowledge she has wrested from the gods. Similarly, the words of provocation Alexis pronounces causes his death at the hands of the revolutionary soldiers, and thereby their act also represents an emblematic silencing of the heretical word.

Indiana and Consuelo, by contrast, suffer no such fate. Their nar-

ratives end in the mode of "and they lived happily ever after." But the
theme of the strangled voice is nevertheless present. In *Indiana* it underlies the domestic violence that erupts at several points in the text. In
the most violent scene, Indiana's husband, Delmare, expresses his desire to strangle his wife: "Il était tenté de l'étrangler, de la traîner par les
cheveux, de la fouler aux pieds pour la forcer de crier merci, d'implorer
sa grâce" (*Indiana*, 209; "He was tempted to strangle her, to drag her by
the hair, to trample her underfoot in order to force her to cry for mercy,
to beg for his forgiveness"). Contradictory desires are signaled by Delmare as he simultaneously wants to silence his rebellious wife and to
evoke a specific linguistic response from her—words begging for
mercy, imploring his forgiveness.[50] Furthermore, the end of the novel
finds her entirely mute.

Consuelo, after her major initiation and reunion with Albert,
seemingly obtains the impossible—love within marriage, a deep and
abiding respect for her husband, a fulfilling and happy maternity (the
bearing of five children seems to have had no affect on her looks, her
girth, or her disposition). Most important, she had been given the mission of spreading the word of resistance against tyranny and of proclaiming utopian progress, the ideal of brotherhood, and the life of
humanity. But all this comes at the price of her voice. One morning, the
narrator tells us, she had simply lost her voice. Her artistic career as an
operatic soprano came to an abrupt end. And, although she is portrayed composing music in the epilogue, her life as an artist has been
subsumed by that of companion to her husband, who is both a prophet
and a madman.

Critics have consistently been puzzled by Consuelo losing her
voice, because it seems to contradict the picture they imagine Sand to
have created of her heroine, as an ideal woman of talent, intelligence,
and moral fiber. Since the structure of the novel is initiatory and since
the heroine emerges triumphant from her trials, why does her victory
need to be tainted by such unjust punishment? It is true that there are
inconsistencies in the text. Annabelle Rea remarks that Consuelo does
not actually lose her voice, in spite of what the narrator says, and
points to several passages that are clearly problematic.[51] The epilogue,
which gives the full text of Consuelo's musical composition, "La bonne
déesse de la pauvreté," suggests that her voice may in fact have been
dichotomized. She has lost her public voice, which exercized itself in
the illusory sphere of the theater; but she has retained her more private
"voice" for her work among the sect of the Invisibles. By losing her
performing but not her prophetic voice, Consuelo has merely lost the
ability to sing in public, but not to compose music. The text, then, can
be seen as the heroine's moving from the secular realm of the theater,
to the sacred community of her sect.[52]

Sand's four endings are indications that the theme of silencing plays an important role in her personal mythology. Whether the novels end well (*Indiana*, *La Comtesse de Rudolstadt*) or badly (*Lélia*, *Spiridion*), the same punishment is inflicted on the heroines or androgynous hero. This suggests that Sand had a Cyane complex; she needed to speak, to sing, to write, in order to feel that she was alive. The terror that she might be silenced was what incited her to write novel after novel. We know she was not driven by ambition and was convinced that her work would not last into posterity. She derived almost no pride from her past work, claiming that the novel slid into oblivion the moment she had finished it. What drove her to write, therefore, was the *process* of writing itself. She wrote because she needed to talk. Silence for her was the equivalent of death, the loss of a precious right, of a unique talent. If she finished one book during the hours she allotted to writing, she immediately began another in the hope that she would not lose her voice. The important thing was not to be silenced as Cyane and so many other heroines in Greek mythology had been.

In the moving "Notice" of *Jean Zyzska*, written in 1843—that is, between the composition of *Consuelo* and *La Comtesse de Rudolstadt*— Sand directed her anger at the inequity of the social hierarchy and affirmed her need to voice that anger, in a determined effort not to be "degraded":

> . . . c'est pour vous [les femmes] que j'écris. . . . Voilà pourquoi, pauvres femmes, nobles êtres qu'il n'a pas été au pouvoir de l'homme de dégrader, voilà pourquoi l'histoire de l'hérésie doit vous intéresser et vous toucher particulièrement; car vous êtes filles de l'hérésie, vous êtes toutes des hérétiques.[53]

> (It is for you [women] that I write. . . . That is why, unfortunate women, noble beings whom men have not been able to degrade totally, that is why the history of heresy must be of interest to you and touch you deeply; for you are the daughters of heresy, you are all heretics.)

To be a heretic is to be potentially vulnerable to silencing. We have Cyane the heretic, Sand the heretic, Consuelo and Lélia and Indiana and Alexis, all heretics. The fear of being silenced was also, as Sand discovered, the desire to keep on writing for her life.

9

Articulating an Ars Poetica

A Genuine Ars Poetica

The great French writers of the Romantic generation—Hugo, Balzac, Michelet, Dumas—had at least one trait in common: the immensity of their literary output. The "vast nineteenth century," as Hugo called it, created a myth of the Gargantuan male writer, whose voluminous creation was synonymous with the greatness of his inspiration and the magnitude of his writing. To these Frenchmen, "ces formidables bûcherons" ("those masterful woodcutters") to use André Fermigier's words in his excellent preface to *François le champi*,[1] we could add other nineteenth-century European writers—George Eliot, Charles Dickens, Leo Tolstoy, Fyodor Dostoevsky, Ivan Turgenev, Henry James, Anthony Trollope. More than merely the consequence of what has come to be defined as the economics of serialization, their sheer productivity is above all a sign of the exuberance of their century.

Significantly, the very element that marks the greatness of Balzac, the "forçat" condemned to the hard labor of the *Comédie humaine*, or is equated with virility in Hugo, that "force of nature [which] has the sap of trees in his blood," as Flaubert called him,[2] has all too often been offered as a sign of failure in the case of George Sand. Her critics have repeatedly refused to see her astounding productivity as a virtue.[3] Instead her voluminous output is educed to refute her genius, and to deny the seriousness of her writing. In spite of Sand's own comments regarding her staggering capacity for literary work, comments that have largely been ignored, clichés concerning her oeuvre still tend to equate her facility of style with artlessness. The same metaphor of the literary "forçat" applied to Balzac and others can also be found in Sand's writings, as Francine Mallet notes, citing the following images: "un âne," "un pauvre âne," "une bête," "un nègre," "un vieux nègre," "un boeuf du Berry," "un manoeuvre," "un esclave," "un galérien," "un cheval de pressoir" ("a donkey," "a poor donkey," "a beast of burden," "a Negro," "an old Negro," "an ox from the Berry," "a laborer," "a slave," "a galley slave," "a workhorse").[4] In sharp contrast to the resolutely masculine references with which Sand alludes to her craft, critics have preferred to substitute derogatory feminine images of creativity. Noble potency in Balzac or in Hugo is transmuted as bovine fecundity in Sand. The virile ox is metamorphosed into a common cow. Sand as the milking cow of literature certainly constitutes a negative version of the Gargantuan myth of the writer. Nietzsche called her "that terrible writing cow," Jules Renard "the milk cow of literature" ("la vache bretonne de la littérature").[5] Sand's literary production is identified with lactic fluids; her creative mind reduced to a milk-producing organ. If both male myth and female antimyth highlight the phenomenon of writing facility, the former sees in it a true sign of inspiration, divine or at the very least cerebral; the latter associates it with an uncontrollable and slightly repulsive natural body function.

Théophile Gautier expanded on the idea of lack of control in the very process of Sand's writing. He saw her as a kind of monster whose presence unwittingly generated alarming mounds of paper: "She cannot sit down in a room without there popping up quill pens, blue ink, cigarette paper, Turkish tobacco, and lined writing paper."[6] Yet the comic vignette conjured up by Gautier does not do justice to Sand's attested dedication to her craft, a dedication voiced with particular intensity throughout the correspondence. As early as 1831, in a letter to Jules Boucoiran, she describes writing as a "violent and almost indestructible" vocation: "my existence is from now on filled with purpose. I have a goal, a task . . . a *passion*" (*Corr.*, 1:817–818). In 1846 she complains to Pauline Viardot of being "clouée à mon encrier de 7 heures du matin à 5 heures du soir" ("chained to my inkwell from 7 A.M. till 5 P.M."; 3 June 1846; *Corr.*, 7:369). In 1851 she repeats "I am working, I am working day and night" (*Corr.*, 10:381). And the hours pay off: ten chapters of *Consuelo* in eleven days, *La Mare au diable* finished in four nights;[7] the mammoth *Histoire de ma vie* composed in record time. In the memoirs we find the same refrain: "For several years, I allowed myself only four hours of sleep. . . . I fought against atrocious migraines to the point of fainting over my work" (HV, 2:406). But the critical discourse has paid little attention to statements such as these, preferring to describe her writing as an irrepressible, almost physical need. The young Flaubert represents this school of thought in an obscene comment he made to Louise Colet. This was years before he met and came to admire Sand in 1866. Not only did he suggest that Colet could reach the height of her talent only by shedding her gender, but he used Sand as a countermodel: "her writing oozes, and the idea seeps out between the words as from between flabby thighs" (16 Nov. 1852).[8] In our time, the malicious Guillemin has also gone beyond the boundaries of decency when he discusses Sand's style:

> George Sand's style crushes me. . . . I experience a physical repugnance before this outpouring . . . waves and waves of dirty water pushing along . . . handfuls of big words; the whole reminding me much less of the gushing of a mountain torrent than the unstoppable overflow of a septic tank.[9]

Baudelaire's misogynist evaluation of Sand's style emphasizes what he calls her "style coulant" ("flowing style") which is "dear to the bourgeois." Interestingly, the liquid metaphor is counterbalanced by another, since in his opinion only holy water can exorcize the unholy flow of "that woman Sand":

> . . . she is stupid, clumsy, she babbles; she has the same profundity in her opinions on moral issues and the same delicacy of feeling as a concierge or a courtisan. . . . She is above all . . . a stupid goose. . . . I cannot think of this stupid creature without a shiver of horror. If I were to meet her, I would not be able to stop myself from emptying a font of holy water on her head.[10]

The derogatory myth of Sand's writing, then, incorporates three major points of attack. The first is its very liquidity, metonymized by milk or murky water. The second is the dubious nature of this liquid, seen as the very antithesis of pure spring water, that standard image for a divinely inspired prose or poetry. The third is the uncontrollable nature of the writing which emerges without shape or style.

No doubt Sand herself contributed to her own myth. She seemed to enjoy the pretense of dashing things off and made it a point to appear as if she did not take her writing occupation very seriously. Was this modesty or a certain understated elegance? In a letter to Charles Duvernet, for instance, she explained that she really wrote for the money it provided: "For me . . . the writer's trade is an income of three thousand pounds" (*Corr.*, 2:88). She seemed amused by the idea that her writing was just another domestic task: "Ce ne sont pas . . . les travaux de l'esprit qui me fatiguent," she writes to her friend Emile Regnault on 13 August 1832. "J'y suis tellement habituée à présent que j'écris avec autant de facilité que je ferais un ourlet" (*Corr.*, 2:135–136; "It is not the . . . mental exertion that tires me out. I am so used to it now that I write as easily as I would sew a hem"). Rather than taking her statements at face value, I detect an underhanded form of bravado in them, which is remarkable in such a young writer (after all, she had only just finished *Indiana* when she wrote this). Her remark highlights her painless entrance into the literary *cénacle* and reinforces our sense that, already as a young novice, she had mastered her craft and internalized its exigencies so that the discipline of composing for hours on end had become second nature.

This attitude of apparent frivolity toward her work only intensified with the passing of time. During the composition of *Histoire de ma vie*, Sand continued to further her own myth by insisting that she ascribed so little weight to her own literary output that she actually *forgot* what she had written:

cet oubli où mon cerveau enterre immédiatement les produits de
mon travail n'a fait que croître et embellir. Si je n'avais pas mes
ouvrages sur un rayon, j'oublierais jusqu'à leur titre. . . . On peut
me lire un demi-volume de certains romans que je n'ai pas eu à re-
voir en épreuves depuis quelques semaines sans que . . . je de-
vine qu'ils sont de moi.   (HV, 2:168)

(This forgetting where my brain immediately buries what it has
produced has only intensified with time. If I did not have my
works on a shelf, I would forget even their titles. . . . You can read
me half a volume of some novels I have not had to revise in proof
for several weeks . . . without my realizing that they are by me.)

As late as 1867, in a letter to Flaubert, she insisted: "*Consuelo, La Comtesse de Rudolstadt*, qu'est-ce que c'est que ça? Est-ce que c'est de moi? Je
ne m'en rappelle pas un traître mot" ("*Consuelo, La Comtesse de
Rudolstadt*, what is that? Is it by me? I do not remember one blessed
word of it").[11] She also maintained that she never revised: "Excepté un
ou deux [livres] je n'ai jamais pu rien y refaire" ("Except for one or two
[books], I have never been able to rewrite anything"; HV, 2:168). That
Sand deliberately misrepresents her case is made clear in Georges
Lubin's lucid commentary to *Histoire de ma vie* where he notes that
many of Sand's novels were written twice, sometimes in radically different versions (*Indiana, Leone Leoni, Mauprat*, and *Spiridion*) and that at
times she totally reworked her text (*Lettres d'un voyageur* and, as we
know, *Lélia* are striking examples).[12]

Why, we may wonder, did Sand enjoy misrepresenting and
damaging her case? A possible answer lies in a letter she wrote to the
critic Fortoul in 1835, just after he had published a laudatory article
about *Lélia* in *Le Droit*:

les chemins des vallées et les fleurs des montagnes ont plus d'attrait que toute la littérature du monde, et il faut avoir divorcé avec
la nature pour se vouer exclusivement à la muse. . . . Il y a, sur
cette terre, mille choses qui valent mieux, la maternité, l'amour,
l'amitié, le beau temps, les chats et mille autres choses encore.   (late Dec. 1836; *Corr.*, 3:196)

(the paths of the valleys and the wild flowers of the mountains are
more appealing than all the literature in the world, and one has to
be divorced from nature in order to devote oneself exclusively to
the muse. . . . There are on this earth, so many more worthy
things: motherhood, love, friendship, fine weather, cats, and a
thousand other things.)

Sand seems to be articulating her firm sense of priorities here.
Unlike Flaubert, she was never willing to remove herself from life so as

to devote all of her energies to art. Sand, for her part, claimed never to have "buried" herself in literature.[13] In opposition to Flaubert, whom she describes as "confiné dans la solitude en artiste enragé, dédaigneux de tous les plaisirs de ce monde" ("confined in the solitude of a frenzied artist, disdainful of all the pleasures of this world"),[14] she insisted on maintaining an equilibrium between the delights of the world and the exigencies of her art (which she spelled with a small *a*, in opposition to Flaubert's capitalization). When she compared her art to the sewing of a hem, she was not so much reducing the artistic to the domestic as attempting to incorporate it into a vital and rich system in which the values of life were praised, its exuberant flow accepted generously and enjoyed. Not only had she integrated life and art in her massive ten-volume *Histoire de ma vie*, she could not absent herself from her milieu. In the 1851 preface to her complete works, for example, she firmly stated: "Quel est donc l'artiste qui peut s'abstraire des choses divines et humaines, se passer du reflet des croyances de son époque, et vivre étranger au milieu où il respire?" ("What kind of artist can distance him- or herself from divine and human affairs, pay no heed to the aura of beliefs which the period has articulated, and live estranged from the milieu in which he or she lives?")[15] This affirmation of integrating one's writing career into a harmonious whole is a reiterated Sandian principle.

In addition, there is much material in Sand's works themselves to disclaim her own statements. A set of coherent and deeply thought-out reflections on her art can be extracted from a number of texts. Through a careful study of documents relating to the formulation of an ars poetica, the reader becomes firmly convinced that Sand articulated the guidelines for a genuine "prosaics" of the novel. It was not always in agreement with the fashion of the time, and often at a significant remove from what today we so narrowly call nineteenth-century Realism. It corresponded instead to a personal *cri du coeur* and posited the author's responsibility to both the reader and the social order. Sand displayed a fundamentally dialogic attitude vis-à-vis her sphere of readers. Her considerable attention to her *lecteur* or *lectrice* is a sign of her propensity to see in the act of writing a turning outward. Very little of her output was wittingly destined for the drawer. And so the ideal reader occupies a prominent place in her fictional universe—witness the numerous cases of direct address in the novels ("madame la lectrice," *Consuelo*; "messieurs," *Lettres d'un voyageur*; "lecteur bénévole," *Indiana*, orig. ed.; "vous," *Horace*) and outside the novelistic frame itself (the large number of prefaces).

Furthermore, the evidence of genuine reflection on art in Sand's works is extensive and compelling. Over thirty prefaces to her novels; numerous reflections on her craft in her autobiographical works, both *Histoire de ma vie* and *Lettres d'un voyageur*; numerous critical articles about her fellow-writers; a rich correspondence with many of her literary contemporaries in which she does not shy away from discussions of literature and its aims, as the letters to Latouche, Balzac, Fromentin, and Hugo, for example, attest.[16] Her correspondence with Flaubert especially gives the reader a privileged entrance into the novelist's "creative laboratory." Sand took literature seriously but she never used it as a pretext to take herself seriously. As a result, there is never the slightest hint of pomposity or self-satisfaction in any of her literary discussions.

La Mare au diable

One of the fundamental principles of Sand's poetics, already discussed in Chapter 2, is the principle of a spatial imagination, representative of what Albert Sonnenfeld has called "a vision-crazed nineteenth century."[17] The "Notice" and the first two chapters of La mare au diable perhaps constitute the clearest synopsis of Sand's ars poetica in miniature. This text, written in four nights at the end of September 1845, was first published two months later in Leroux's Revue sociale. The simple and slender story, for all its delicate charm, takes on full meaning only when considered in relation to the critical and scholarly metatexts surrounding the core plot. The beginning pages are made up of a "Notice," a first chapter entitled "L'Auteur au lecteur" ("From the Author to the Reader"), and a second chapter "Le Labour" ("Plowing"). The end of the story is rounded out by a four-chapter appendix entitled "Les Noces de campagne" ("A Country Wedding"). The beginning betrays an aesthetic preoccupation just as the ending demonstrates Sand's ethnographic or sociological concerns. Both metatexts, which are situated in the margins of the actual plot, employ similar novelistic devices. The characters remain anonymous for the most part. Chapter 2 describes an "old laborer," "a young man," "a child six or seven years old," who in the actual story will come to be identified as Père Maurice, Germain, and Petit Pierre. The participants in the peasant wedding (of Germain and Marie), described in the appendix, tend to be defined by their function rather than by their name. The dialogue between the two anonymous peasant-poets—the "fossoyeur" (the gravedigger) and the "chanvreur" (the hemp-dresser)—is characteristic in this respect. Furthermore, both metatexts are situated outside history, as well as outside the narrative. Time is portrayed as primitive and cyclical, marked only by the passing of seasons and annual festivities. The laborer's circular vision of time constitutes an agricultural chronotope, where the passage of time is divided up by natural cycles and by the modest festivities of a peasant society—weddings, baptisms, funerals, and religious holidays. Significantly, the beginning of La Mare au diable deploys a specific moment in the agricultural cycle, the plowing of the fields in readiness for planting, while the appendix lingers on the festivities surrounding the wedding feast. Thus a locus—the pastoral landscape—and a class—the peasantry—are privileged. Both figure as exceptions in the predominantly urban and middle-class novel of the nineteenth century. Although in the "Notice" Sand denies any attempt on her part to depict a new subject matter or to propose a new novelistic chronotope—"Je n'ai voulu ni faire une nouvelle langue, ni me chercher une nouvelle manière" (*La Mare*, 27; "I never wanted either to fashion a new language, or to forge for myself a new style")—this is precisely what she does.

Lazarus's Dung Heap

Leaving the appendix to the sociologists, I want to concentrate on the critical texts of the beginning. The epigraph, a quatrain in old French, is the somber commentary to a woodcut by Holbein the younger from the series entitled *Les Simulachres de la mort* (*The Dance of Death*). The woodcut of "Le Laboureur," which Sand describes in detail in the incipit, constitutes plate 38 in Holbein's series:

> La gravure représente un laboureur conduisant sa charrue au milieu d'un champ. Une vaste campagne s'étend au loin, on y voit de pauvres cabanes; le soleil se couche derrière la colline. C'est la fin d'une rude journée de travail. Le paysan est vieux, trapu, couvert de haillons. L'attelage de quatre chevaux qu'il pousse en avant est maigre, exténué; le soc s'enfonce dans un fonds raboteux et rebelle. Un seul être est allègre et ingambe dans cette scène de *sueur et usaige*. C'est un personnage fantastique, un squelette armé d'un fouet, qui court dans le sillon à côté des chevaux effrayés et les frappe, servant ainsi de valet de charrue au vieux laboureur. C'est la mort. . .   (*La Mare*, 29–30)

> (The engraving represents a laborer steering his plow in the middle of a field. A vast countryside stretches out in the distance, dotted by modest cottages; the sun is setting behind the hill. It is the end of a hard day's work. The peasant is old, thick-set, dressed in tatters. The team of four horses he drives in front of him is thin, worn-out. The plowshare catches the coarse and obdurate ground. One single being is lightfooted and carefree in this scene of *sweat and toil*. He is a spectral character, a skeleton armed with a whip, who is running in the furrow next to the frightened horses and whipping them, thereby playing the plowboy to the old plowman. He is death. . .)

She continues to ponder on Holbein's woodcuts, remarking that the figure of death is absent[18] only in the one illustrating the parable from Luke about a rich man and a beggar named Lazarus. This woodcut (no. 47) shows him, as she puts it, lying "on a dung heap" at the rich man's door.[19] Although this is a standard iconographic representation of Lazarus (as it is of Job), this image of the dung heap becomes under Sand's pen a metaphor for a certain kind of contemporary writing, the first element in what will constitute for her an opposition of two different kinds of fictional representation. The series of woodcuts taken together, Sand tells us, constitutes "the painful satire, the true painting of the society that Holbein had before his eyes" (*La Mare*, 30–31). With this pivotal remark Sand turns to concentrate on the present epoch and its representational repertoire: "Mais nous, artistes d'un autre siècle, que peindrons-nous? Chercherons-nous dans la pensée de la mort la rémunération de l'humanité présente?" (*La Mare*, 31; "But we, artists of another century, what will we paint? Will we look for the recompense of contemporary humanity in the meditation of death?") Holbein's woodcut, with its dystopian vision of the world, is used here as an exemplification of certain modern tendencies in art. Some of her contemporaries continue to depict reality through the prism of gloom and decay, and she finds their vision to be wanting: "Certains artistes de notre temps, jetant un regard sérieux sur ce qui les entoure, s'attachent à peindre la douleur, l'abjection de la misère, *le fumier de Lazare*" (emphasis added; *La Mare*, 31; "Certain artists of our time, taking a serious look at what surrounds them, dedicate themselves to painting the pain, the wretchedness of poverty, *the dung heap of Lazarus*").

To counteract this literature of gloom, she proposes a "utopian" vision of literature which denounces the perverse enjoyment of those writers who linger on the misery of Lazarus (Eugène Sue is Sand's main unnamed target). The laborer must no longer be seen through Holbein's eyes as eeking out an existence on the brink of starvation and despair, but must be depicted as an optimistic and productive contributor to the social good. I use the term utopian in the Baudelairian sense of the absolute power of poetry to put the world on its head. In *L'Art romantique*, he had praised the power of literature to "contradict the fact":

> The destiny of poetry is a great one! Joyous or painful, it always bears within it the divine *utopian* character. It endlessly contradicts fact. . . . In the prison cell, it becomes a revolt; at the hospital window, it is the ardent hope of cure; in the broken-down and dirty attic room, it decks itself out, like a fairy, with luxury and elegance; not only does it take notice, it repairs. Everywhere it makes itself the negation of iniquity.[20]

In keeping with Baudelaire's call for literature to transform claustration into liberation and illness into health, Sand proclaims the necessity for Lazarus to get off his dung heap. The will to life must overcome the death instinct so often expressed in modern literature:

nous n'avons plus affaire à la mort, mais à la vie. . . . Il faut que
Lazare quitte son fumier, afin que le pauvre ne se réjouisse plus de
la mort du riche. Il faut que tous soient heureux, afin que le
bonheur de quelques-uns ne soit pas criminel et maudit de Dieu. Il
faut que le laboureur, en semant son blé, sache qu'il travaille à
l'oeuvre de vie, et non qu'il se réjouisse de ce que la mort marche à
ses côtés. (*La Mare*, 31)

(we are no longer dealing with death but with life. . . . Lazarus
must leave his dung heap, so that the poor man no longer rejoices
in the rich man's death. Everyone must be happy, so that the happiness of some is not criminal and accursed by God. The plowman
must know, when sowing his wheat, that he is contributing to the
work of life, and not rejoice that death is walking at his side.)

Counteracting the realists' tendency to insist on the ugly, repug-
nant, filthy aspects of life, Sand proposes the eudaemonistic mission of
art, and its duty to construct the utopian possibilities of the future.
Here, unlike Baudelaire, Sand is not merely content to identify the utopian powers of literature which separate it from real life, she wants literature's direct impact on the quotidian, its aid in bringing about the
metamorphosis of society. As her vision parts ways with Baudelairian
art for art's sake, Sand pronounces her now famous literary credo:

Nous croyons que la mission de l'art est une mission de sentiment
et d'amour, que le roman d'aujourd'hui devrait remplacer la para-
bole et l'apologue des temps naïfs, et que l'artiste a une tâche plus
large et plus poétique que celle de proposer quelques mesures de
prudence et de conciliation pour atténuer l'effroi qu'inspirent ses
peintures. Son but devrait être de faire aimer les objets de sa sol-
licitude, et au besoin, je ne lui ferais pas un reproche de les embellir
un peu. (*La Mare*, 33)

(We believe that the mission of art is one of feeling and of love, that
the novel of today should replace the parable and the fable of a
more primitive time, and that artists have a broader and more poetic task than that of proposing prudent and conciliatory measures
to attenuate the fright that their paintings elicit. Their goal should
be to inspire love for the objects of their concern, and if pressed, I
would not reproach the artists for embellishing them a little.)

The allowance for embellishment, just like the allowance for simplify-
ing, is not purely in the service of making art more attractive or more
accessible. Both are deliberate stratagems in the author's determination to give a meaning to literary representations beyond the narrowly
aesthetic, above the purely entertaining. Literature for Sand is not only
for the consumption of other poets; it must also inspire generalized

audiences to visualize better worlds, to conjure up the utopian parameters of future societies. It is in this light that her famous line— "l'art
n'est pas une étude de la réalité positive; c'est une recherche de la vérité idéale" (*La Mare*, 33; "art is not a study of positive reality; it is a
search for the ideal truth")—must be understood. For Sand art is not
pure escape or reversal of reality, as it is in Baudelaire's quote, nor is it
the systematic search for the most despicable aspects of life as it is for
certain contemporary novelists. It is the quest for a language that can
elevate its readers temporarily and inspire them, as they return to their
daily round, to put the vision into action.

The Fertile Furrow

Having *stated* her position, Sand sets out to *illustrate* her point in
the following chapter. "Le Labour" represents a putting into action of
her theory of literature's quest for "ideal truth." The narrator is transformed from a theoretician to a *promeneur*. The masculine "I" has just
put the Holbein woodcut aside and is now strolling in the fields, medi-
tating on the implications of the German artist's message. Putting in
opposition what Sand calls "the man of leisure," who has both the education and the free time to write but lacks the poetic inclination, and
"the man of the fields," who has neither the time nor the ability to
write, in spite of the poetic atmosphere surrounding him, the narrator
remarks:

> le plus heureux des hommes serait celui qui, possédant la science
> de son labeur, et travaillant de ses mains, puisant le bien-être et la
> liberté dans l'exercice de sa force intelligente, aurait le temps de
> vivre par le coeur et par le cerveau, de comprendre son oeuvre et
> d'aimer celle de Dieu.   (*La Mare*, 36)

> (He would be the happiest of men who, possessing the knowledge
> of his labor, and working with his hands, deriving well-being and
> freedom from the exertion of his intelligent strength, would have
> the time to live according to his heart and his head, to understand
> his work and to love the work of God.)

Sand's dream here is to establish a harmony between manual labor and
poetic toil, between the laborer's privileged knowledge of life and the
artist's deep understanding. In this utopian view of the writer, such a
"holy harmony" would ensure the substitution of life for death: "au
lieu de la piteuse et affreuse mort, marchant dans son sillon, le peintre
d'allégories pourrait placer à ses côtés un ange radieux, semant à
pleines mains le blé béni sur le sillon fumant" (*La Mare*, 36–37; "instead
of pitiful and horrible death, walking in his furrow, the allegorical

painter could place at the laborer's side a radiant angel, sowing with both hands the blessed wheat onto the steaming furrow").

Sand is about to become this painter of allegories. The sinister furrow of Holbein's woodcut, with its rocky and sterile bed, is about to be replaced with a "sillon fumant" which is the metonymic representation of the new writing preconized by the author. Setting up against Holbein's "desolation making"[21] the principle of "ideal truth," she proceeds to create a landscape, a pastoral vision which, by its epiphanic quality, is equivalent to a natural tableau. The narrator constructs a utopian antithesis to the woodcut that quite literally deconstructs the Holbein image in the reader's mind. Her visual counterpoint has poetic ramifications and a central meaning. Moving from the Holbein woodcut to her own privileged landscape, she attempts to paint a master image that will mask the other. Acting like a palimpsest, her own text superimposes itself, thus rubbing out all traces of the woodcut. The panorama, she reminds us, is as vast as Holbein's; the season is the same. But whereas bleakness dominated the woodcut, here a synesthetic sense of well-being permeates the text: "La journée était claire et tiède, et la terre, fraîchement ouverte par le tranchant des charrues, exhalait une vapeur légère" ("The day was clear and warm, and the earth freshly opened by the passage of the plows, exhaled wisps of steam"). Holbein's peasant is replaced by a more prosperous and noble figure:

> Dans le haut du champ un vieillard, dont le dos large et la figure sévère *rappelaient celui d'Holbein, mais dont les vêtements n'annonçaient pas la misère*, poussait gravement son areau de forme antique, traîné par deux boeufs tranquilles, à la robe jaune pâle, véritables patriarches de la prairie.   (emphasis added; *La Mare*, 38)

> (On the high ground, an old man, whose broad back and severe face *recalled that of Holbein, but whose clothes did not suggest wretchedness*, solemnly pushed along his old-fashioned plow, drawn by two quiet yellow-coated oxen, true patriarchs of the prairie.)

Not content to simply replace Holbein's dismal peasant with a more prosperous-looking laborer, Sand turns her attention to the old man's son, who now draws four oxen. And in a movement of apotheosis, she dwells at length on yet another and even younger laborer, whose team is now made up of eight oxen. The amplification from two to eight animals is significant and emphasizes the seme of fertility and *épanouissement* which Sand is purposefully constructing:

> Mais ce qui attira ensuite mon attention était véritablement un beau spectacle, un noble sujet pour un peintre. A l'autre extrémité

> de la plaine labourable, un jeune homme du bonne mine con-
> duisait un attelage magnifique: quatre paires de jeunes animaux à
> robe sombre mêlée de noir fauve à reflets de feu, avec ces têtes
> courtes et frisées qui sentent encore le taureau sauvage.   (La Mare,
> 39)

> (But what then drew my attention was a truly beautiful sight, a
> noble subject for a painter. At the other end of the field, a robust
> young man was driving a magnificent team: four pairs of young
> oxen with dark coats of tawny black mottled with glints of fire,
> their short and curly haired heads recalling wild bulls.)

To deconstruct the hideous allegory of death of Holbein's text, Sand
introduces an angelic child, "his shoulders covered . . . with a sheep-
skin," who is reminiscent of the "little Saint John the Baptist of Renais-
sance painters" (39–40). The small boy who walks alongside the bulls,
encouraging them on with a long pole, thus represents one artistic figuration taking over for another. Finally, the young father's song replaces the sinister quatrain that commented on the Holbein scene.

Thus, the series of substitutions is complete: "Il se trouvait donc
que j'avais sous les yeux un tableau qui contrastait avec celui d'Holbein, quoique ce fut une scène pareille" (42; "And so it happened that I
had before my eyes a painting that contrasted with Holbein's, although
it was the same scene"). The miserable peasant has been replaced by a
young man in the bloom of health; the exhausted and ragged horses
are exchanged for eight robust oxen; a cherubic boy takes the place of
Death; the picture of despair and destruction is canceled out in favor of
a vision of energy and prosperity. Sand has drawn a symbolic landscape in which she rejects naturalistic realism and creates a viable
poetic vision. True to her own credo, in the tableau that she has depicted, life replaces death, beauty and happiness displace the macabre
desperation of the woodcut.

In a final paragraph, Sand proposes a countermetaphor to that of
the realists, in order to displace or banish permanently "Lazarus's
dung heap." Wishing to mark the transition between her theoretical
prologue and the story she wants to tell, she comments that Germain's
tale was "une histoire aussi simple, aussi droite et aussi peu ornée que
le sillon qu'il traçait avec sa charrue" (44; "a story as simple, straightforward, and plain as the furrow he was marking with his plow"). The
word "furrow" takes on metaphoric resonance as it gradually becomes
synonymous with the word "story." The linguistic slide from *sillon*
meaning furrow to *sillon* meaning story is marked by the repetition of
the word:

> L'année prochaine, ce *sillon* sera comblé et couvert par un *sillon*
> nouveau. Ainsi s'imprime et disparaît la trace de la plupart des

hommes dans le champ de l'humanité. Un peu de terre l'efface, et
les *sillons* que nous avons creusés se succèdent les uns aux autres
comme les tombes dans le cimetière. Le *sillon* du laboureur ne
vaut-il pas celui de l'oisif. . . . Eh bien! arrachons, s'il se peut, au
néant de l'oubli, le *sillon* de Germain, le fin laboureur.   (emphasis added; *La Mare*, 44–45)

(Next year, this *furrow* will be filled in and covered by a new *furrow*.
Similarly, the traces of most men in the fields of mankind are laid
down and then disappear. A little earth will cover it, and the *furrows* that we have dug succeed one another like tombs in a ceme-
tery. Is not the plowman's *furrow* worth that of a man of
leisure? . . . Well then! let us pull up, if possible, from the nothingness of oblivion, the *furrow* of Germain, the skillful plowman.)

Using an agricultural code for the act of writing, the "furrow" becomes
the product of Sand's prosaics. "The furrow of Germain" refers to the
story about to be related to us by Sand. The furrow, metonymically associated with fecundity, thus replaces the dung heap of putrid hopelessness and sterility. Germain, as the peasant hero of the tale, is the
new Lazarus who has risen from his dung heap. By associating plowing with writing, and the furrow that results from the laborer's work
with the story issuing from the writer's pen, Sand also reconciles the
link between the laborer and the poet. Her utopian desire that expresses the hope for a peasant-artist ("A day will come when a
plowman can also be an artist," *La Mare*, 37) is not entirely realized. But
the artist, by becoming a kind of laborer, a plower of words, temporarily at least, bridges the gap between "the man of leisure" and "the
man of labor."

Elsewhere Sand proclaimed the right of authors to contemplate
the world and to write about what they saw: "Qu'il soit donc permis à
chacun et à tous de voir avec les yeux qu'ils ont" ("May each one and all
therefore be allowed to see with the eyes they have").[22] That Flaubert
could have accused her of looking at the world "à travers une couleur
d'or" ("through a golden haze") demonstrates that he had not sufficiently understood her propensity not so much for embellishing what
she saw, but for choosing to dwell on and describe the privileged visions she considered to be of inspirational value for her readers.[23]

Creating a New Pastoral Language

The pastoral novel is a fertile vein in Sand's oeuvre, making its early
entrance into her fictional world with her second novel. If *Valentine*, as
a precursor pastoral novel, witnessed the uneasy cohabitation of the
nobility with the peasantry, the *roman champêtre* developed into a veritable *roman paysan*, in which the peasant class came to occupy entirely

and dominate the fictional stage. Sand then concentrated her efforts on the elaboration of a new hero and the articulation of a new language.

We can follow this evolution in Sand's prefaces to her pastoral novels. The margins of these deceptively simple stories have a significant bearing on her vision of literature. In the "Notice" to *Le Compagnon du tour de France* she clarified once and for all her literary position by contrasting it, albeit somewhat schematically, to Balzac's:

> Depuis quand le roman est-il forcément la peinture de ce qui est, la dure et froide réalité des hommes et des choses contemporaines? Il en peut être ainsi, je le sais, et Balzac, un maître devant lequel je me suis toujours incliné, a fait la *Comédie humaine*. Mais, tout en étant lié d'amitié avec cet homme illustre, je voyais les choses humaines sous un tout autre aspect, et je me souviens de lui avoir dit . . . "Vous faites la *Comédie humaine*. Ce titre est modeste; vous pourriez aussi bien dire le *drame*, la *tragédie humaine*. —Oui, me répondit-il, et vous, vous faites l'*épopée humaine*. —Cette fois, repris-je, le titre serait trop relevé. Mais je voudrais faire l'*églogue humaine*, le *poëme*, le *roman humain*. En somme, vous voulez et savez peindre l'homme tel qu'il est sous vos yeux. . . ! Moi, je me sens porté à le peindre tel que je souhaite qu'il soit. . .[24]

> (Since when is the novel necessarily a depiction of what is, the cold and hard reality of contemporary people and things? It may be this, I know; after all Balzac, a master whom I have always greatly esteemed, produced the *Human Comedy*. But even while I had a friendship with this famous man, I saw human concerns from a completely different angle, and I remember telling him . . . —You are writing the *Human Comedy*. Your title is overly modest; you could equally well say the *drama, the human tragedy*. —Yes, he replied, and you are writing the *human epic*. —That title, I said, would be too grand. But I would like to write the *human eclogue*, the *human poem*, the *human novel*. In sum, you want to and know how to paint man as you see him before you. . . ! I feel impelled to paint him as I wish he were. . .)

Thus two antithetical visions are expressed, the idealist and the realist, representing two poles of the nineteenth-century French novel. Sand's idealizing portrayal of characters as she wishes they were, as opposed to Balzac's way of depicting his heroes as they really are, conjures up the traditional antithesis drawn between Racine and Corneille (and subsequently taught to generations of French school children). In opposition to Racine's depiction of human passion and failings, Corneille had constructed a heroic and moral universe in which the character's choice always elevated him or her above baser instincts. If the two novelists repeated the great opposition articulated by the two classical tragedians, then Balzac explored Racine's way, while Sand went the way of Corneille.

It was precisely the pastoral mode that allowed Sand to travel the road of idealization. Sensing her predilection for what she called "bergeries," that is to say, romances in the style of *Daphnis and Chloë*, she identified in them the yearning for the Ideal:

> J'ai vu et j'ai senti par moi-même . . . que la vie primitive était le rêve, l'idéal de tous les hommes et de tous les temps. Depuis les bergers de Longus jusqu'à ceux de Trianon, la vie pastorale est un Eden parfumé où les âmes tourmentées et lassées du tumulte du monde ont essayé de se réfugier. L'art, ce grand flatteur, ce chercheur complaisant de consolations . . . a traversé une suite ininterrompue de *bergeries*. Et sous ce titre: *Histoire des bergeries*, j'ai souvent désiré faire un livre . . . où j'aurais passé en revue tous ces différents rêves champêtres. ("Avant-Propos," *François le Champi*, 48)

> (I have seen and I have myself experienced that the primitive life was the dream, the ideal of all men and of all times. From the shepherds of Longus to those of Trianon, the pastoral life is a perfumed Eden where souls tormented and wearied by the world's tumult have tried to find refuge. Art, that great flatterer, that obliging seeker of consolation . . . has passed through an uninterrupted series of pastorals. And under the title *Histoire des bergeries* I have often wished to write a book . . . wherein I would review all these different pastoral dreams in turn.)

While she never accomplished this desire to make a catalogue of shepherd's tales, she did explore the pastoral dream in several of her novels. In *Jeanne*, for instance, where the visual inspiration for the main character seems to have stepped out of a Holbein painting of the Virgin, Sand's emphasis lies precisely in the exploration of pastoral simplicity in a modern setting, with the resulting clash collapsing into tragedy. "Cette *femme primitive*, cette *vierge de l'âge d'or*, où la trouver dans la société moderne?" ("This *primitive woman*, this *virgin of the golden age*, where is she to be found in modern society?") the narrator asks in the preface. While this model is finally found in a peasant woman of the Berry region, Sand experiences a linguistic discomfort, a kind of gap between the narrative's modern idiom, which is at once literary, urban, and bourgeois, and the world she is trying to depict. Although she wanted to make her reader "forget the modern world and the present life," she senses that her language creates a barrier between form and content: "Mon propre style, ma phrase me gênait . . . il me semblait que je barbouillais d'huile . . . les peintures sèches . . . naïves et plates des maîtres primitifs . . . que je profanais le nu antique avec des draperies modernes" (*Jeanne*, 29; "My own style, my phrasing bothered me . . . it seemed to me that I was dabbing with oils . . . the matte, naive, and flat paintings of the primitive masters . . . that I was profaning the nude of antiquity with modern clothing"). She felt her linguistic repertoire inadequate to the subject she was trying to depict. She likened herself to a primitive painter using the wrong kind of paint; the medium did not suit the message.

The problem of increasing concern to her is language. Several years later, in the preface to *François le champi*, the narrator and François Rollinat are depicted strolling through the countryside, discussing the problem of peasant representation in the nineteenth-century novel. Rollinat asks the writer to identify the missing link between his own overly active intelligence and the peasant's quiescent mind: "quel est le rapport possible . . . entre deux états opposés de l'existence des choses et des êtres, entre le palais et la chaumière, entre l'artiste et la création, entre le poète et le laboureur . . . entre la langue que parlent cette nature, cette vie primitive . . . et [la langue] que parlent l'art, la science, *la connaissance*, en un mot" ("what is the possible relationship . . . between two opposite states of things and of living beings, between the palace and the cottage, between the artist and the creation, between the poet and the plowman . . . between the language of nature, of this primitive life . . . and that spoken by art, science, *knowledge*, in short"). The opposition already articulated in *La Mare au diable* between the laborer and the man of leisure, that is, between primitive life and "la vie factice," appears again here. The architectural gap between the palace and the peasant cottage ("la chaumière") is identical to the linguistic gap between the two antithetical language systems. Rollinat identifies in the novelist's earlier pastoral novels precisely this lack of correspondence between a language that describes and a language that belongs to the world described: "ton langage fait avec [celui des personnages] un effet disparate . . . l'auteur y montre encore de temps en temps le bout de l'oreille" (*François le champi*, 51; "your language clashes with that of the characters . . . traces of the writer still poke through from time to time"). If it is true that the peasants' language necessitates a translation into French so as to be accessible to all, how shall the narrator speak at once "clairement pour le Parisien" and "naïvement pour le paysan" (*François le champi*, 53)? The question is formulated but the answer not provided. The impossible dream for a hybrid language that would incorporate both a popular and a cultivated idiom had already been proposed in *Mauprat* by the peasant-sage, Patience, when he talked about the need for an "idiome mélangé" ("mixed idiom") which would allow each one "sans dégrader sa raison, de peupler l'univers et de l'expliquer avec ses rêves" ("without degrading one's mind, to populate the universe and to make sense of it with one's own dreams").[25] Patience did not specify the way this actually would be realized, but Sand's novels, especially in the pastoral period, can be viewed as a series of attempts to provide such a synthetic language.

Sand by her very interest in language shows her modernity. As we have seen, as early as *Indiana*, she was concerned with the issues concerning literary language. Having exorcized once and for all the temptation of a rhetoric of power such as it was represented by her character, Raymon de Ramière, she never ceased questioning the nature of literary language itself—what kind of discourse entered into literature, which discourse was marginalized, what verbal power could mean. She was very much a believer in the predominance of *parole* (the spoken word) over *mot* (the written word), and considered the former as the basis for any analysis of language. From a Bakhtinian perspective, one could equate Sand's value system with a predominance in her work of dialogical over monological structures. More precisely, her predilection for oral over written language emphasizes the primacy of spontaneity in her writing. This improvisatory quality must not be equated with literary sloppiness or indifference to style on her part, but rather can be ascribed to what she called the "delights of composition." Her friend Flaubert once claimed that art was not a matter of inspiration but of patience. Sand's vision, which she designates as a modern Abbaye de Thélème in *Nouvelles lettres d'un voyageur*, expresses just the opposite opinion. The idealized inhabitants of the Abbaye, most of them artists, have invented a language as rapid as thought ("aussi rapide que la pensée"), which they use to conceive "sublime books."[26] Sand's ideal contradicts Flaubert's credo of artistic patience (etymologically linked with suffering) since it insists that the language of inspiration is essentially im-patient, that is, not linked to pain, but associated with joy and swiftness.

Sand's conviction that such a language must exist is inextricably linked to Corambé, the mythopoeic creation of her childhood psyche. This mysterious and androgynous deity is identified in *Histoire de ma vie* as the Godlike voice that she heard when she improvised her first stories (see HV, 1:809–821). Many years later, when Sand became a novelist, Corambé ceased to exist as a separate autonomous voice (see my discussion in Chapter 3). But by internalizing Corambé's voice and appropriating the deity's essence, Sand came to incorporate into her concept of literary craft certain crucial elements culled from Corambé—namely a privileging of orality and a confident attitude toward the act of creation. In a word, she chose as her model the bigendered discourse of a being who epitomized the elegant ease of literary composition and thus rejected the arduous and painstaking "agonies of style" characteristic of a writer such as Flaubert.

This set of priorities is evident in Sand as early as the autumn of 1831, when she was writing one of her first *ébauches*, *La Marraine*. More important than the actual work was the discovery of her literary temperament, her realization that she wrote very much as Corambé had improvised, with speed and with ease. "Je reconnus," she explains in *Histoire de ma vie*, "que j'écrivais vite, facilement, longtemps sans fatigue; que mes idées, engourdies dans mon cerveau, s'éveillaient et s'enchaînaient . . . au courant de la plume" (2:101; "I realized that I wrote quickly, easily and for long periods without tiring; that my ideas, which were sluggish in my brain, came alive and fell naturally into place under my pen").

What Ann Berger has called Sand's "phonocentrism,"[27] that is, her faith in the voice as instrument and source of truth, explains at once the writer's elevation of language to divine status, and our sense as readers that Sand's fiction is based on a dialogue between her inner voices and an idealized reality. In the novel *André* (1835), for example, the heroine's sudden understanding of the rapport between the inner "impressions of the mind" and the outer "beauties of nature" provokes a moment of epiphany. Geneviève's vertigo upon discovering that the feeling for art is a form of religious experience expresses itself in an image of poetic *sublimatio*: "elle s'éleva au-dessus d'elle-même et de toutes les choses réelles qui l'entouraient pour vouer un culte enthousiaste au nouveau Dieu du nouvel univers déroulé devant elle" ("she rose above herself and all the real things surrounding her in order to declare an enthusiastic cult to the new God and the new universe that unfolded before her").[28] This scene can also be read as the expression of the writer's own artistic fervor. The hearing of voices and the feeling of spiritual elevation are Sand's two preferred metaphors for expressing artistic creation. In this sense, Corambé truly is the Sandian god of language.

Madame Dudevant, homme de lettres[29]

Although it may be disappointing to some that Sand never articulated a *feminine* poetics per se, it is important to understand the extent to which androgyny was the fundamental basis upon which she constructed her fictional universe. Although her artistic theories can often be seen as the *feminization* of a traditionally male canon, up to the end of her long literary life, Sand resolutely refused to restrict herself to a single-gendered vision. When Flaubert wrote to her toward the end of her life that he possessed "both sexes," she promptly and unequivocally retorted that there was only one sex when it came to writing.[30] One can witness the emergence of this androgynous Sandian vision especially in her novels from the 1840s on. But she was not a system maker and her theories were not systematized anywhere. Balzac was right when he claimed that Sand was the great eclectic of the century, eager to explore the divergent paths on the fictional map of possibilities, and daring to probe difficult literary problems and articulate innovative solutions.

With the exception of the black period, there is a basic "serenity of writing" in Sand. She knew that writing does not necessarily issue from indignation, although she acknowledged that *Indiana*, *Valentine*, and *Lélia* had been in part molded by feelings of anger. Her 1842 "Préface" to *Indiana*, for instance, stressed that she had written her novel "avec *le sentiment non raisonné* . . . de l'injustice et de la barbarie des lois qui régissent encore l'existence de la femme . . . j'ai cédé à *un instinct puissant* de plainte et de reproche" (emphasis added; *Indiana*, 46; "with *an overwhelming and almost irrational feeling* . . . of the injustice and barbarity of laws that still rule over women's lives . . . I yielded to *a powerful instinct* of lamentation and reproach"). Subsequently she discovered that one could write outside of the body, from a place of mental composure, beyond feelings of fury.

In the years when Sand was articulating her ars poetica, her writing expresses most a deep sense of equilibrium, whereby she stresses the harmony between the poet and his or her fictional world, and posits the possibility of a synthesis of nature and creativity, of ideology and style. This metaphysical search for a synthesis may appear surprising in a writer with such a diverse oeuvre. On the other hand, this search gives coherence to her eclectic fictional universe. One main theme running through her writings focuses on the bridging of chasms, the synthesis of opposites. How to find the common measure between the ailments of her age and the solutions to those personal and social ills; how to better integrate the individual and society; how to respond to both the demands of physical life and the search for the absolute; how, in a word, to effect the magical reunification of the various fragmented selves—psychological, social, philosophical. With the pastoral period, Sand reached full literary integration and her final words on her deathbed, "Laissez verdure," make clear the culminating force of this androgynous pastoral vision.

This serenity of writing and sense of harmony may in part be due to Sand's own facility of composition—we know that regularly she was capable of writing up to fifty pages a day—and also may stem, essentially, from her rejection of a formalist aesthetic. Whereas her friend Flaubert created highly structured and exhaustively organized texts, she was able to write without a plan, letting inspiration take her where it wished. This capacity for improvisation is especially manifest in her discussion of the Other, as she counteracts Flaubert's notion of "le mot juste" with the concept of multiplicity, of endless possibility. The delights of free-form composition replace his "affres du style:"

> Vous m'étonnez toujours avec votre travail pénible. Est-ce une coquetterie? . . . Ce que je trouve difficile, moi, c'est de choisir entre

mille combinaisons de l'action scénique qui peuvent varier à l'infini, la situation nette et saisissante qui ne soit pas brutale ou
forcée. Quant au style, j'en fais meilleur marché que vous. Le vent
joue de ma vieille harpe comme il lui plaît d'en jouer. Il a ses *haut* et
ses *bas*, ses grosses notes et ses défaillances, au fond ça m'est égal
pourvu que l'émotion vienne, mais je ne peux rien trouver en moi.
C'est *l'autre* qui chante à son gré, mal ou bien. . . . Laissez donc le
vent courir un peu dans vos cordes. Moi je crois que vous prenez
plus de peine qu'il ne faut, et que vous devriez laisser faire *l'autre*
plus souvent.[31]

(You always astonish me with your painstaking work; is it coque-
try? . . . What I find difficult to choose from the thousand com-
binations of scenic action, which can vary infinitely, the clear and
striking situation that is not brutal nor forced. As for style, I attach
less importance to it than you do. The wind plays my old harp as it
wishes. It has its *high notes*, its *low notes*, its heavy notes, and its
faltering notes, in the end it is all the same to me provided the emotion comes, but I can find nothing in myself. It is *the Other* who
sings at will, badly, or well. Let the wind blow a little over your
strings. I think that you take more trouble than you need, and that
you ought to let *the Other* do it more often.)

This is not the first time Sand has conjured up this "Other." Already
in the item of juvenilia, "Nuit d'hiver" (examined in Chapter 1), the
writer had described the sensation of an inner doubling. Remarkably,
Sand can still allude to its existence over forty years later in *Nouvelles
lettres d'un voyageur*, where she gives as clear a definition of "l'autre" as
one could ever hope to find. What artists call the Other, she explains, is
a kind of "troisième âme." In the case of musical inspiration, the third
soul "chante quand le compositeur écoute et . . . vibre quand le vir-
tuose improvise" ("sings when the composer listens and . . . vibrates
when the virtuoso improvises"). In the literary sphere the third soul
"pense quand la main écrit et . . . fait quelquefois qu'on exprime *au-
delà* de ce que l'on songeait à exprimer"[32] ("thinks when the hand
writes and . . . is responsible that the writer sometimes expressed
beyond what he or she tried to express"). The Other, then, designates
in Sand's terms the inner voice of inspiration which she never ceased
to hear.

Sand's remarks regarding the Other may explain her attitude of
modesty about her own genius. She always defined artistic genius as a
natural, unexceptional occurrence. Since genius was part of nature,
there was no need for the writer to sever the bond between the artifice
of the book and its inspirational source. Here is how she put it to
Flaubert:

Nous sommes de la nature, dans la nature, par la nature et pour la
nature. Le talent, la volonté, le génie, sont des phénomènes

naturels comme le lac, le volcan, la montagne, le vent, l'astre, le nuage. Ce que l'homme tripote est gentil ou laid, ingénieux ou bête; ce qu'il reçoit de la nature est bon ou mauvais, mais cela *est*. Cela existe et subsiste. . . . La nature seule sait parler à l'intelligence, une langue impérissable, toujours la même, parce qu'elle ne sort pas du vrai éternel, de beau absolu.[33]

(We are of nature, in nature, by nature, and for nature. Talent, will, genius, are natural phenomena like the lake, the volcano, the mountain, the wind, the star, the cloud. What man dabbles in is pretty or ugly, ingenious or stupid; what he gets from nature is good or bad, but it *is*, it exists and subsists. . . . Nature alone knows how to speak to the intelligence in a language that is imperishable, always the same, because it does not depart from the eternally true, the absolutely beautiful).

This refusal to be alienated from nature, a stance already apparent in the 1835 letter to Fortoul cited earlier in this chapter, marks Sand's entire oeuvre with grace. It points to her extraordinary success in creating a genuinely coherent fictional world that was also socially fluid and free of gender biases.

Significantly, in a mature novel, *Isidora* (1846), Sand would coin a double metaphor, with which to express the trajectory of her own mental development and her increasing sense of harmony with the natural world. She grounded this double image in nature, using two antithetical landscapes to designate the two stages of life, youth and old age. The former, which she compares to "an admirable Alpine landscape," is primarily apprehended as the uneasy cohabitation of opposites, where gentle phenomena struggle against violent forces: "partout le précipice est au bord du sentier fleuri, le vertige et le danger accompagnent tous les pas du voyageur . . . nature . . . sublime aux prises avec d'effroyables cataclysmes"[34] ("Everywhere the precipice stands on the edge of the flowered path, vertigo and danger accompany the voyageur's every step . . . sublime nature . . . in the throes of terrifying cataclysms"). In opposition stands "the beautiful, wellplanted garden" (168) in which one can reap and enjoy the benefits of old age. Isidora's "jardin de vieillesse," stamped with the seal of equilibrium and serenity, perhaps also alludes to Sand's increasing selfdiscovery and psychic integration. The trajectory from the volcanic landscape of *Histoire du rêveur* to the "garden of old age" in *Isidora* can be understood as Sand's path toward harmony with herself. To follow her on her travels is to admire the itinerary from uncertainty and fear to self-assurance and self-knowledge. It is to follow in the footsteps of one of the most open-minded and free-spirited writers of her age.

Notes

INTRODUCTION

1. Honoré de Balzac, *Lettres à Madame Hanska* 4 vols. (Paris: Bibliophiles de l'Originale, 1967), 1:584, 585.

2. Curtis Cate, *George Sand* (New York: Avon, 1975), 254–255. The anecdote comes to us from Paul de Musset's *Lui et elle* (1859).

3. I use here the formula proposed by Béatrice Didier in her book by the same name.

4. Luce Irigaray, "Pouvoir du discours," *Ce Sexe qui n'en est pas un* (Paris: Seuil, 1977), 74.

5. Sandra Gilbert and Susan Gubar, *The Madwoman in the Attic* (New Haven: Yale University Press, 1979), 76.

6. Items of juvenilia include "Voyage en Auvergne" (1827), "Voyage en Espagne" (1829), "Nuit d'hiver" (1829), "Voyage chez M. Blaise" (1829, the signature—"Aurore, plus tard George Sand"—is revealing), "Les Couperies" (1830), "Histoire du rêveur" (1830), "La Marraine" (1830), "Jehan Cauvin" (1831). The collaborative works include "La Prima Donna" (1831), "La Fille d'Albano" (1831), *Rose et Blanche* (1831).

7. I chose the color green with two purposes in mind: one, to insist on Sand's "vegetal imagination," exemplified in her *ultima verba* on her death bed: "Laissez verdure"; and two, to contest the notion that the pastoral imagination is necessarily associated with what critics have often thought to be Sand's sentimental *rose-colored* view of life.

8. At the beginning of 1990, the titles available at the Editions de l'Aurore (in order of their publication) are: *Horace*, 1982 (ed. Nicole Courrier and Thierry Bodin); *Le Péché de Monsieur Antoine*, 1982 (ed. Jean Courrier and Jean-Hervé Donnard); *Contes d'un grand-mère*, 1882–1883, 2 vols. (ed. Philippe Berthier); *Consuelo* and *La Comtesse de Rudolstadt*, 1983, 3 vols. (ed. Simone Vierne and René Bourgeois); *Tamaris*, 1984 (ed. Georges Lubin); *Le Château des désertes*, 1985 (ed. J.-M. Bailbé); *Un Hiver à Majorque*, 1985 (ed. Jean Mallion and Pierre Salomon); *La Ville noire*, 1985 (ed. Jean Courrier); *Jeanne*, 1986 (ed. Simone Vierne); *Elle et lui*, 1986 (ed. Thierry Bodin and Joseph Barry); *Nanon*, 1987 (ed. Nicole Mozet); *André*, 1987 (ed. M. Gilot and H. Burine); *Jean de la Roche*, 1988 (ed. Claude Tricotel); *Lélia*, 1988, 2 vols. (ed. Béatrice Didier); *Valentine*, 1988 (ed. Aline Alquier); *Le Marquis de Villemer*, 1988 (ed. Jean Courrier); *La Filleule*, 1989 (ed. Marie-Paule Rambeau); *Le Meunier d'Angibault*, 1990 (ed. Marielle Caors).

9. Cited by Elaine Showalter, "Feminist Criticism in the Wilderness," *Writing and Sexual Difference*, ed. Elizabeth Abel (Chicago: University of Chicago Press, 1982), 15.

10. See Patricia Meyer Spacks, *The Female Imagination* (New York: Knopf, 1975); Ellen Moers, *Literary Women* (Garden City: Doubleday, 1976); Elaine Showalter, *A Literature of Their Own* (Princeton: Princeton University Press, 1977); Nina Baym, *Women's Fiction* (Ithaca: Cornell University Press, 1978);

Sandra Gilbert and Susan Gubar, *The Madwoman in the Attic* (New Haven: Yale University Press, 1979); Margaret Homans, *Women Writers and Poetic Identity* (Princeton: Princeton University Press, 1980); Alice Jardine, *Gynesis* (Ithaca: Cornell University Press, 1985).

11. For an annotated bibliography on the subject, see the very useful *French Feminist Criticism: Women, Language and Literature*, ed. Elissa D. Gelfand and Virginia Thorndike Hules (New York and London: Garland, 1985).

12. Cited by Roland Barthes, *Michelet* (Paris: Seuil, 1954), 5.

13. Virginia Woolf, *A Room of One's Own* (New York and London: Harvest/HJB Books, 1957), 102.

14. George Sand, *Monsieur Sylvestre*, ed. Simone Vierne (Paris and Geneva: Slatkine, 1980), 330.

15. Ibid., 333.

16. See Charles Baudelaire, "Mon Coeur mis à nu," *Oeuvres complètes*, ed. Claude Pichois, 2 vols. (Paris: Pléiade, 1975–1976), 1:686–687; and Léon Daudet, "L'Aberration romantique et ses conséquences," *Le Stupide XIXe siècle* (Paris: Nouvelle librairie nationale, 1922), 81–149.

17. Henri Guillemin, *La Liaison Musset-Sand* (Paris: Gallimard, 1972).

18. A staggering number of monographs are devoted to Sand and her lovers. Here is a selected bibliography: Charles Maurras, *Les Amants de Venise: George Sand et Musset* (1917); Francis Gribble, *George Sand and Her Lovers* (1907); Casimir Carrère, *George Sand amoureuse: Ses amants, ses amitiés tendres* (1967); Anthony West, *Mortal Wounds* (1973); W. Atwood, *The Lioness and the Little One: The Liaison of George Sand and Frederic Chopin* (1980). Notice the dizzying number of books devoted to the Sand–Musset affair, starting with Paul de Musset's *Lui et elle* and culminating with Henri Guillemin's particularly offensive *La Liaison Musset-Sand*.

19. See Noel B. Gerson, *George Sand: A Biography of the First Modern Liberated Woman* (New York: McKay, 1972); Monique Jambert, ed., *George Sand: Femme de notre temps* (Châteauroux: Mataresse, 1976).

20. Curtis Cate, *George Sand* (New York: Avon, 1975); Joseph Barry, *Infamous Woman: The Life of George Sand* (Garden City: Doubleday, 1976); Ruth Jordan, *George Sand: A Biographical Portrait* (London: Constable, 1976); Francine Mallet, *George Sand* (Paris: Grasset, 1976); Tamara Hovey, *A Mind of Her Own: A Life of the Writer George Sand* (New York: Harper and Row, 1977); Renee Winegarten, *The Double Life of George Sand: Woman and Writer* (New York: Basic Books, 1978). The total number of biographies runs into the dozens.

21. Henry James, "George Sand," in *Literary Criticism: French Writers, Other European Writers, The Prefaces to the New York Edition*, ed. Leon Edel (New York: The Library of America, 1984), 703.

22. The political positions are discussed in Jean Gaultier, *George Sand et la guerre de 1870–1871* (Guéret, Creuse: Presses du Massif Central, 1970); Edouard Dolléans, *Féminisme et mouvement ouvrier: George Sand* (Paris: Editions ouvrières, 1951). For the socialist views, see Henri Bourdet-Guillerault, *George Sand: Ce qu'elle croyait* (Marseille: Editions Rijois, 1979); Jean-Pierre Lacassagne, *Histoire d'une amitié: Pierre Leroux et George Sand* (Paris: Klincksieck, 1973); Pierre Vermeylen, *Les Idées politiques et sociales de George Sand* (Brussels: Editions de l'Université de Bruxelles, 1984).

23. See Claude Tricotel, *Comme deux troubadours: Histoire de l'amitié Flaubert-Sand* (Paris: SEDES, 1978); Linda Kelly, *The Young Romantics: Victor Hugo, Sainte-Beuve, Vigny, Dumas, Musset and George Sand and Their Friendships, Feuds and Loves* (New York: Random House, 1976).

24. Léon Cellier, "Baudelaire et George Sand," "Occultisme dans *Consuelo*," "Le Roman initiatique au temps du romantisme," in *Parcours initiatiques* (Neuchâtel: La Baconnière, 1977); Ellen Moers, *Literary Women* (Garden City: Doubleday, 1976); Jean Pommier, *George Sand et le rêve monastique* (Paris: Nizet, 1966).

25. Gerald Schaeffer, *Espace et temps chez George Sand* (Neuchâtel: La Baconnière, 1981). The volume also contains several essays on Nerval.

26. Natal'ia Trapeznikova, *Romantizm Zhorzh Sand* (Kazan': Izdatel'stvo Kazanskogo universiteta, 1976).

27. The book entitled *George Sand: Colloque de Cerisy,* edited by Simone Vierne, was published by SEDES in 1983. Sixteen articles by international Sand scholars are included.

28. Kathryn J. Crecelius, *Family Romances: George Sand's Early Novels* (Bloomington: Indiana University Press, 1987).

29. André Maurois, *Lélia ou la vie de George Sand* (Paris: Hachette, 1952), 7.

30. Sand herself seems to have suggested that joint writing projects with Jules Sandeau had been predominantly her work, however. Cf. a letter to François Buloz, 26 June 1834: "J'ai fait en grande partie le peu de choses publiées sous le nom de J. Sand" (*Corr.*, 2:642).

31. Georges Lubin speculates that 90 percent of the text of the second edition is Sand's. Cf. a lecture he delivered at the Collège de France, 23 Oct. 1976, "*Rose et Blanche* ou le roman renié," as well as an unpublished article, "Autour de *Rose et Blanche.*" Lubin thinks that if Sand disowned the novel in 1855 and again in 1867 in her correspondence with her editor, it was because Jules Sandeau was still alive at the time. Significantly, neither Sand nor Sandeau included the novel in their respective lists of complete works. I am grateful to Georges Lubin for this invaluable information.

32. "The new edition of this work, which has been completely recast, also differs from the first edition in 12o in numerous and important deletions and additions; in its present format and type-face, it is intended to be a part of the collected works of George Sand" (cited by Lubin in OA, 2:1335).

33. *The French Romantics*, ed. D. G. Charlton, 2 vols. (Cambridge: Cambridge University Press, 1984), 1:173.

34. Cited by Julie Sabiani, "L'Amour universel selon George Sand et Charles Péguy," *Travaux de linguistique et de littérature de l'Université de Strasbourg*, 11/2(1973):213.

35. George Sand, "Préface générale," *Questions d'art et de littérature* (Paris: Calmann-Lévy, 1878), 2.

36. Review in *Le National*, 29 Sept. 1833. Rpt. in Sainte-Beuve, *Portraits contemporains*, 5 vols. (Paris: Calmann-Lévy, 1881), 1:501.

37. James, "George Sand," in *Literary Criticism* 705–706.

38. "Charles de Bernard and Gustave Flaubert," in Ibid., 183. See also Aaron Noland, "Henry James, George Sand and the 'Metaphysical Imagination,'" *George Sand Newsletter*, 5/2 (fall/winter 1982):26–39.

CHAPTER 1: GYNOGRAPHY AND ANDROGYNY

1. Sand herself explains: "The newspapers all spoke of Mr. G. Sand with praise, insinuating that the hand of a woman must have slipped in here and there to reveal to the author a certain delicacy of heart and mind, but declaring that the style and the commentaries had too much virility not to belong to a man" (HV, 2:174).

2. See Georges Lubin, "Chronology," *George Sand Newsletter*, 2/2 (1979):19.

3. For further discussion, see Crecelius, *Family Romances*, 57–59.

4. For a detailed discussion of the theme of the androgyne in French thought, see the fine article by A.J.L. Busst, "The Image of the Androgyne in the Nineteenth Century," in Ian Fletcher, ed., *Romantic Mythologies* (London: Routledge and Kegan Paul, 1967). In keeping with Busst's practice, I consider here the terms "androgyne" and "hermaphrodite" as synonymous, both being defined broadly as designating "a person who unites certain of the essential characteristics of both sexes and who . . . may be considered as both a man and a woman or as neither a man nor a woman, as bisexual or asexual" (1).

5. Honoré de Balzac, *Séraphita*, in *La Comédie humaine*, (Paris: Pléiade, 1980), 11:782.

6. Lucienne Frappier-Mazur, "Balzac et l'androgyne," *L'Année balzacienne* (Paris: Garnier, 1973), 260.

7. Cited by Gaston Bachelard, *La Poétique de la rêverie* (Paris: PUF, 1961), 50.

8. "What eye can see itself?" is a leitmotif of *La Vie de Henry Brulard* (1890).

9. Théophile Gautier, *Mademoiselle de Maupin* (Paris: Charpentier, 1860), 215, 363.

10. George Sand, *L'Uscoque*, (Paris: Calmann-Lévy, 1885), 210.

11. HV, 2:118–119. See also the anecdote in which Emile Paultre calls the young man he takes to be George Sand's brother a "pedant": "Ah! madame . . . je vous demande pardon! Ce jeune homme est votre frère, car vous lui ressemblez extraordinairement. . . . Planet . . . voulut le tranquilliser en lui disant que le frère et la soeur étaient une seule et même personne. Il n'en voulut rien croire et se fâcha presque de ce qu'il prenait pour une mystification" (HV, 2:119–120; "Ah, madame, . . . please excuse me! The young man is your brother, you bear an extraordinary resemblance to him. . . . Planet . . . wanted to calm him by telling him that brother and sister were one and the same person. He didn't want to believe any of it and almost got angry at what he took to be intentional mystification").

12. "Avec un chapeau gris et une grosse cravate de laine, j'étais absolument un petit étudiant de première année. Je ne peux pas dire quel plaisir me firent mes bottes. . . . Avec ces petits talons ferrés, j'étais solide sur le trottoir. Je voltigeais d'un bout de Paris à l'autre. Il me semblait que j'aurais fait le tour du monde" (HV, 2:117; "With a grey hat and a large wool tie, I was the perfect little first year student. I can't express the pleasure my boots gave me. . . . With their low, iron-capped heels, I was steady on the sidewalk. I flew from one end of Paris to the other. I felt as though I could have gone around the world").

13. Note Joan Didion's remark on her own invisibility as a writer: "There used to be a comic strip when I was little . . . called Invisible Scarlet O'Neil. Invisible Scarlet O'Neil was a reporter. She would press a band on her wrist, become invisible and cover the story invisibly. And everybody would be

amazed that she had gotten the story. Well, that is how ideally I would like to be" (cited by Leslie Garis in "Didion and Dunne: The Rewards of a Literary Marriage," *New York Times Magazine*, 8 Feb. 1987).

14. Gilbert and Gubar, *Madwoman in the Attic*, 73.

15. Cited by Patricia Meyer Spacks, *Female Imagination*, 12.

16. Ibid., 282.

17. M. M. Bakhtin, "Forms of Time and Chronotope in the Novel," *The Dialogic Imagination*, ed. M. Holquist (Austin: University of Texas Press, 1982), 231.

18. It is the novel *Lélia* that has generated this kind of critical response to the greatest degree. André Maurois calls Sand Lélia routinely in his biography; indeed his very title uses the character's name to designate the writer. Pierre Reboul cannot resist the temptation of suggesting that an allusion to Lélia's once hairy arms must be "une confidence" on the part of the author.

19. Spacks, *Female Imagination*, 35.

20. Béatrice Didier, *L'Ecriture-Femme* (Paris: PUF, 1981), 206.

21. Wladimir Karénine, *George Sand: Sa vie et ses oeuvres*, 4 vols. (Paris: Plon, 1926), 4:374.

22. Stendahl, *Souvenirs d'égotisme*, in *Oeuvres intimes* (Paris: Pléiade, 1955), 1472–1473.

23. Balzac, "Avant-Propos," *La Comédie humaine*, 12 vols. (Paris: Pléiade, 1976), 1:8. The full reference is as follows: "The differences between a soldier, a worker, an administrator, a lawyer, a man of leisure, a scholar, a statesman, a tradesman, a sailor, a poet, a poor man, a priest are, albeit more difficult to grasp, as considerable as those that differentiate the wolf, the lion, the ass, the crow, the shark, the walrus, the lamb, etc. In short, there have always existed and there always will exist Social Species just as there are Zoological Species".

24. Béatrice Didier, *Stendhal autobiographe* (Paris: PUF, 1983), 45.

25. The pseudonym she gives her lover, Michel de Bourges.

26. Lidiia Ginzburg, *O Psikhologicheskoi proze* (On Psychological Prose) (Leningrad: Nauka, 1971), 315.

27. Cited by Pierre Reboul, "Accueil de *Lélia* en 1833," in George Sand, *Lélia* (Paris: Garnier, 1960), 595. The letter is dated 16 Aug. 1833.

28. I study this instance of intertextuality in my article, "Germaine de Staël among the Romantics," in *Germaine de Staël: Crossing the Borders*, ed. Madelyn Gutwirth, Avriel Goldberger, and Karyna Szmurlo (New Brunswick: Rutgers University Press, 1991).

29. George Sand, "La Fille d'Albano," in *Les Sept Cordes de la lyre*, nouv. ed. (Paris: Michel Lévy, 1869), 287.

30. Emphasis added; OA, 2:547. Also cited by Marie-Jacques Hoog, "*Lettres d'un voyageur*, texte initiatique," in *George Sand: Colloque de Cerisy*, 139.

CHAPTER 2: *HISTOIRE DU RÊVEUR*: THE DREAMER'S PLOT

1. It was first published in book form by her granddaughter, Aurore Sand, in 1931.

2. For a presentation of this text, see Thérèse Marix-Spire, *Les Romantiques et la musique: Le cas George Sand (1804–1838)* (Paris: Nouvelles éditions latines,

1954), 200–203; and Kathryn Crecelius, "Writing a Self: From Aurore Dudevant to George Sand," *Tulsa Studies in Women's Literature* (fall 1985).

3. Tricket is the first of Sand's irreverent and clever narrator-characters who romp through *Lettres d'un voyageur, Teverino,* and several of the pastoral novels.

4. See René's meditation on the top of Mount Etna, in which to he exclaims: "So it is that all my life I have had before my eyes a creation simultaneously immense and imperceptible and a yawning abyss at my feet" (François-René de Chateaubriand, *Atala, René, Le Dernier Abencérage* [Paris: Folio, 1971], 152).

5. See Marjorie Hope Nicolson, *Mountain Gloom and Mountain Glory: The Development of the Aesthetics of the Infinite* (Ithaca: Cornell University Press, 1959), 372.

6. "Whatever is in any sort terrible, or is conversant about terrible objects, or operates in a manner analogous to the terrible is a source of the sublime; that is, it is productive of the strongest emotion the mind is capable of feeling." Cited by Malcolm Ware, *Sublimity in the Novels of Ann Radcliffe* (Uppsala: Lundequistska Bokhandeln, 1963), 5.

7. OA, 2:512. In *Histoire de ma vie,* Sand's "Voyage aux Pyrénées" (1825) conveys similar emotions: "Enfin nous sommes entrés dans les Pyrénées. La surprise et l'admiration m'ont saisie jusqu'à l'étouffement. J'ai toujours rêvé les hautes montagnes. . . . Tout cela m'a paru horrible et délicieux en même temps. J'avais peur . . . une peur de vertige qui n'était pas sans charme" (HV, 2:59–60; "Finally we entered the Pyrenees. Surprise and admiration seized me to the point of suffocation. I have always dreamed of towering mountains. . . All of that appeared horrible and delightful at the same time. I was afraid . . . a fear of heights that was not without charm").

8. Jean-Jacques Rousseau, *La Nouvelle Héloïse* (Paris: Pléiade, 1969), 79. Senancour, *Obermann,* ed. Jean-Maurice Monnoyer (Paris: Folio, 1984), 93.

9. The key passage is as follows: "On the high mountains, where the air is pure and delicate, one feels breathing is easier, the body is lighter, the mind is more serene. . . . There meditations take on somewhat of a grandiose and sublime character. . . . At such elevation above mankind's abode, it seems as though one leaves behind every lowly and earthly feeling and that as one gets closer to the ethereal realm, the soul gets infected with its unchanging purity" (*La Nouvelle Héloïse,* 78).

10. "un mélange de ce qu'il y a de plus harmonieux dans les facultés musicales de chaque sexe" (*Rêveur,* 13; "a blend of the most harmonious features of the musical faculties of each sex").

11. "J'ai souvent éprouvé cette sorte de vertige dans les régions élevées que j'ai parcourues" (*Rêveur,* 16; "I have often experienced that sort of vertigo in the high elevations that I have traversed").

12. "Mon front est rouge encor du baiser de la reine" (Gérard de Nerval, *Oeuvres,* ed. A. Béguin et J. Richer, 2 vols. [Paris: Pléiade, 1952–1956], 1:29; "My forehead is still red from the queen's kiss").

13. See his reference to "les belles pages de *Lélia,*" (in Gérard de Nerval, *Oeuvres* 1:757).

14. George Sand, "La Fille d'Albano," in *Les Sept Cordes de la lyre* (1869), 286.

The story was written in collaboration with Jules Sandeau, although Sand later claimed this tale as her own.

15. Gaston Bachelard, *La Psychanalyse du feu* (Paris: Gallimard/Idées, 1949), 35–38.

16. "Extension is either in length, height, or depth. Of these the length strikes least. . . . I am apt to imagine likewise that height is less grand than depth; and that *we are more struck at looking down from a precipice, than at looking up at an object of equal height*." (Edmund Burke, *A Philosophical Enquiry into the Origin of Our Ideas of the Sublime and Beautiful*, ed. J. T. Boulton [London: Routledge and Kegan Paul, 1958], 72; emphasis added).

17. "L'homme en songeant descend au gouffre universel. / . . . Le spectre m'attendait; l'être sombre et tranquille / Me prit par les cheveux dans sa main qui grandit, / M'emporta sur le haut du rocher . . . " (Victor Hugo, *Oeuvres poétiques*, ed. P. Albouy, 3 vols. [Paris: Pléiade, 1967], 2:801; "Man in his dreams descends into the universal abyss . . . the spectre awaited me; the somber and calm being grabbed me by the hair with its hand which was growing, and carried me to the summit of the rock").

18. See Léon Cellier, "Baudelaire et George Sand," in *Parcours initiatiques*, 221–242.

19. See the episode described in HV, 1:860.

20. George Sand, "Préface" to Maurice Sand, *Le Monde des Papillons*, reprinted in *Questions d'art et de littérature*, 273. Francine Mallet's chapter on "La Recherche de l'absolu" in her *George Sand* also cites this passage.

21. Baudelaire, "Salon de 1859," *Oeuvres complètes*, 2:668.

22. Jacques' last words curiously echo Ralph's final wish in *Indiana*.

23. George Sand, *Jacques*, nouv. ed. (Paris: Michel Lévy, 1866), 353. Interestingly, more *was* heard from him, many years later in *Le Diable aux champs* (written 1851; pub. 1857). Jacques, like Ralph and Indiana, belong to Sand's cast of *resurrected* characters. See Tatiana Greene, "George Sand et le caché dans *Le Diable aux champs*," *George Sand Newsletter*, 6/1–2 (fall/winter 1983): 47–51.

24. Saint-Marc Girardin, *Cours de littérature dramatique*, 5 vols. (Paris: Charpentier, 1861–1868), 1:79.

25. "il faut que je me cache pour mourir. Mon suicide aurait l'air d'un reproche" (343).

26. Arlette Béteille, "Où finit *Indiana*? Problématique d'un dénouement," in *George Sand: Recherches nouvelles*, Françoise van Rossum-Guyon, ed., *Cahiers de Recherches Interuniversitaires Néerlandaises* (CRIN), nos. 6–7 (1983): 65.

27. George Sand, *Le Piccinino*, 2 vols. (Paris: Michel Lévy, 1869), 1:16. Emphasis added.

28. Gigault de la Salle, *Voyage pittoresque en Sicile* (Paris: Didot, 1822).

29. Annarosa Poli, *L'Italie dans la vie et l'oeuvre de George Sand* (Paris: Colin, 1960), 14. The author further assumes that it is this same work Sand alludes to in her "Notice" to *Le Piccinino* some thirty years later.

30. Emphasis added; OA, 2:630. Years later, she reiterates: "Descartes disait: Je pense donc j'existe. Les rêveurs de mon espèce pourraient dire aujourd'hui: je rêve, donc je vois" (in *Questions politiques et sociales* [Paris: Calmann-Lévy, 1879], 25; "Descartes said: I think, therefore I exist. Dreamers like me might say today: I dream, therefore I see").

31. As Poli explains: "The future novelist was particularly struck by 'the image' and these collections of engravings [Gigault de la Salle, *Voyage pittoresque en Sicile*; J. A. de Gourbillon, *Voyage critique à l'Etna en 1818*; Marquis de La Foresta, *Lettres sur la Sicile*] must have fired her imagination" (*L'Italie*, 14).

32. On 29 May 1830, Sand writes: "J'ai été hier au musée. Mais je n'ai pas vu la moitié de ce que je voulais voir. J'y retourne maintenant" (*Corr.*, I, 653; "I was at the museum yesterday. But I didn't see the half of what I wanted to see. I am going back there now"); 5 June 1830: "Je vais encore faire une séance au musée des tableaux" (*Corr.*, I, 656; "I am going to spend another session at the fine arts museum"); 8 June 1830: "Nous avons passé la journée . . . à *muser* au *musée*" (*Corr.*, I, 657; "We spent the day . . . *musing* at the *museum*").

33. See article by Marie-Jacques Hoog, "Du rêve à l'écriture chez George Sand," *George Sand Newsletter*, 5/2 (fall/winter 1982): 47–50.

34. George Sand, "Notice," *Jeanne* (Meylan: Editions de l'Aurore, 1986), 28.

35. Honoré de Balzac, "Etudes sur M. Beyle," *Oeuvres diverses* (1836–1848), ed. Bouteron et Longnon (Paris: Conard, 1940), 3:371. Emphasis added.

36. Ibid., 371.

37. Baudelaire, "Théophile Gautier [I]," *Oeuvres complètes*, 2:117.

38. Baudelaire, "Salon de 1859," Ibid., 2:667.

39. Ibid., 2:668.

Chapter 3: *Indiana* or the Creation of a Literary Voice

1. These statistics are provided by Marguerite Iknayan's invaluable study of the French novel between 1815 and 1848: *The Idea of the Novel in France, 1815–1848* (Geneva: Droz, 1961).

2. Françoise Van Rossum-Guyon, "A propos d'*Indiana*: La préface de 1832, Problèmes du métadiscours," in *George Sand: Recherches nouvelles*, 22–23.

3. Iknayan, *Idea of the Novel*, 52.

4. Louis-Simon Auger, *Mélanges philosophiques et littéraires* (Paris: Ladvocat, 1828), 2:355.

5. Auger writes in 1828: "let them turn out their novels and their clothes!" (*Mélanges*, 2:359). And he continues with a lamentable lack of perspicacity: "the time will come, perhaps very soon, when the man who turns out a novel will be as ridiculous as those whom we see today turning out dresses and bonnets."

6. Eugène Pelletan, review of *Le Meunier d'Angibault* in *La Presse*, 31 Aug. 1845. He continues: "It can capture the world as it was . . . as it should be. . . . It can glimpse into the ideal, throw itself into poetry, touch upon metaphysical or religious problems, descend into the depths of psychology. . . . Not only can the novel capture all of human nature . . . seize the physiognomy of places, peoples, customs, it can also . . . summon before it all of creation, all types of landscape, all animate or inanimate beings."

7. M. M. Bakhtin, "From the Prehistory of Novelistic Discourse," *Dialogic Imagination*, 50.

8. Auguste Barbier, for instance, while acknowledging that the novel "has conquered a secure position in literature," nevertheless saw in the form "a degeneration of the epic," a lowering of the Muse (*RDM*, 14 [4th ser. 1838]: 409).

9. See Gaschon de Molènes's remark: "The most appealing and the most

complete form in which a writer can embody his thought is the novel." ("Simples essais d'histoire littéraire" (*RDM*, 32 [4th ser. 1842]: 390).

10. Van Rossum-Guyon, "A propos d'*Indiana*," 22.

11. Félix Pyat, *L'Artiste*, 3 (27 May 1832).

12. Van Rossum-Guyon, "A propos d'*Indiana*," 23.

13. Gustave Planche, *RDM*, 3 (2d ser. 1833): 367.

14. Cited by Van Rossum-Guyon, 27.

15. Paul Van Tieghem, *Le Romantisme dans la littérature européenne* (Paris: Albin Michel, 1948), 250.

16. Henry James, "George Sand," in *Literary Criticism*, 717.

17. Ibid., 718.

18. From our modern perspective a sense of "déjà-lu" emerges from the opening pages of *Indiana*, since they conjure up in many a reader's mind certain passages from the early part of Chateaubriand's memoirs. But Sand could not have known these pages, since the *Mémoires d'outre-tombe* were not published in toto until 1851. Although these descriptions of Chateaubriand's childhood years had been written by 1826, the text was not available for Sand to have read them by 1832. Small fragments of the so-called Manuscript of 1826 appeared in the "Introduction générale" and in several prefaces to Chateaubriand's *Oeuvres complètes*, published between 1826 and 1831, but they did not dwell on descriptions of family life at Combourg. An astonishing example of pure intertextuality, but not literary influence, exists in two passages from *Indiana* and the *Mémoires*. Chateaubriand's describes autumn and winter evenings at Combourg, during which René and Lucile sit at the fire while their father grimly paces the large hall, casting a spell of Gothic gloom and terror over his family, only to break it when he retires to bed. (See Chateaubriand, *Mémoires d'outre-tombe*, ed. Pierre Moreau, 6 vols. [Paris: Garnier, 1947], 1:115.) Sand's text likewise insists on the atmosphere of hallucination and domestic terror of her tableau vivant (see *Indiana*, 53).

19. *Indiana* uses the events of July 1830 as the backdrop for the heroine's personal drama at the end of the story. In much the same way, Flaubert, in his *Education sentimentale*, would later use this device of a revolution as the backdrop for a hero's personal web of events.

20. See Béatrice Didier's commentary on the word pastiche in her notes to *Indiana* (392–393): "G. Sand uses here one of Latouche's favorite words, who always reproached her for making pastiches of Balzac, and it is all the more amusing that Laure de Nangy is a very Balzacian character, as much by her name as by her personality and social position."

21. At the time of *Indiana* the word pastiche is linked in Sand's mind with Balzac. See in *Histoire de ma vie* the episode in which Latouche reads his protégée's manuscript: "Delatouche grimpa à ma mansarde et trouva le premier exemplaire d'*Indiana*. Il le prit, le flaira, le retourna, curieux, inquiet, railleur surtout ce jour-là. . . . Allons! c'est un *pastiche*; école de Balzac! *Pastiche*, que me veux-tu? Balzac que me veux-tu!" (emphasis added; HV, 2:42; "Delatouche climbed up to my garret and found the first copy of *Indiana*. He took it, sniffed it, and turned it over, curious, troubled, and especially derisive that day. . . . Come on, it's a *pastiche*; in the manner of Balzac! A *pastiche*, what else can I say? It's Balzac, what can I say?").

22. For a remarkably fair and evenhanded analysis of the literary impact of George Sand on Baudelaire, see Léon Cellier, "Baudelaire et George Sand," *Revue d'histoire littéraire de la France*, 67/2 (Apr.–June 1967): 239–259. In a delightful little article, Cellier also traces the fortune of this well-known line. See "La Nature est un temple, ou l'Apprenti-Sourcier," *Revue universitaire*, 64/1 (Jan.–Feb. 1955): 26–28.

23. She writes: "They were really supposed to jump into the cataract. . . . But George Sand . . . changed her mind and added an epilogue in which Indiana and Ralph, just as they are about to jump into the abyss, suddenly make a double discovery—that she is still capable of love; that he has always loved her" (Wladimir Karénine, *George Sand*, 1:370). Cited by Pierre Salomon in his Introduction to *Indiana* (Paris: Garnier, 1983), vi.

24. I am grateful to Georges Lubin for verifying this point for me.

25. See "the primitive hut," frontispiece from the second edition of Laugier's *Essai sur l'architecture*, engraved by Ch. Eisen.

26. A character who reminds the reader of Chateaubriand's narrator at the end of *Atala* or of Bernardin's *Paul et Virginie*.

27. As she explains: "for what I had loved the most . . . up to then was a woman; it was my mother" (HV, 1:813). Such a remark seriously undermines a strictly Freudian interpretation of Sand's psychology according to which *Histoire de ma vie* expresses a classic case of father adulation, perforce accompanied by a brutal rejection of the mother. Sand's remarkably rich mental life in childhood allowed her to experience passionate feelings of love toward both her father and mother—a phenomenon that would inform her professional life when her bisexual imagination allowed her to articulate fully a double-gendered human experience.

28. In Julia Kristeva's system the semiotic order preceeds the symbolic: "The semiotic . . . chronologically antecedent and synchronically transversal to the sign, to syntax, to denotation, to signification" (*Polylogue* [Paris: Seuil, 1977], 14). The curious disappearance of Corambé would suggest the permanent passage from one order to the other. To the reader of Sand, however, it is obvious that the semiotic order of Corambé never really ceased to nourish her imagination. See Simone Vierne, "George Sand et l'imagination," *George Sand Newsletter*, 5/2 (fall/winter 1982).

29. See the three prefaces to *Indiana* for her reflections on the subject.

30. The most distressing evidence of Sand's occasional lack of a feminist perspective is the letter she wrote to the "Comité central de la Gauche" in 1848, in which she stated her opposition to women's suffrage. The letter is reproduced in Marie Collins and Sylvie Weil Sayre, *Les Femmes en France* (New York: Scribner's, 1974), 141–146. It is entitled "A propos de la femme dans la société politique."

31. See Pierre Salomon's Introduction to *Indiana* (Paris: Garnier, 1983) for an illustration of this approach.

32. Gustave Planche, review of *Indiana* and *Valentine* in RDM, (30 Nov. 1832): 695.

33. Review in *La Caricature*, 31 May 1832. See Honoré de Balzac, *Oeuvres complètes*, ed. Marcel Bouteron and Henri Longnon, 40 vols. (Paris: Conard, 1938), 39:539.

34. Kristeva, *Polylogue*, p. 519; emphasis added.

Chapter 4: *Valentine* and the Theory of Spheres

1. See Gustave Planche in the *RDM* and Sainte-Beuve in the *National*.

2. Thierry Bodin's impeccable study provides a thoroughly documented grid for such an enterprise. See his "Balzac et Sand: Histoire d'une amitié," *Présence de George Sand*, 13 (février 1982): 4–21.

3. Pierre Reboul, "Introduction" *Lélia*, lvi.

4. We know that both *Louis Lambert* and *La Peau de chagrin* were read by Sand: "Nous avons commencé hier *La Peau* [*de chagrin*], et comme il est impossible de la lâcher quand on la tient, nous n'avons pas pu lire les autres brochures" (*Corr.*, 1:933–934; "Yesterday we began *Le Peau* [*de chagrin*], and since it is impossible to put it down once it is in your hand, we haven't been able to read the other brochures"). "Vous êtes bien aimable de m'envoyer votre beau et bon livre [*Louis Lambert*]. Je le lis avec enthousiasme" (*Corr.*, 2:253; "You are very kind to have sent me your fine and beautiful book [*Louis Lambert*]. I am reading it with enthusiasm"). We also know that she sent *Valentine* and *Lélia* to her friend in 1833, *Valentine* in February; it is not known when precisely she sent him *Lélia*. See *Corr.*, 2:253. According to Thierry Bodin, Balzac read at least the following works to Sand in these early years: *La Peau de chagrin, L'Enfant maudit, Un Message, La Femme abandonnée, L'Elixir de longue vie, L'Auberge rouge*. Four of the six texts belong to the "Etudes philosophiques."

5. Mirecourt described the *entrevue* in this way: "What happened during her visit was very strange. The philosopher, silent and dignified, waited for her to speak first, in order to answer her. But apparently, Madame Sand never started a conversation when meeting with people for the first time. As for Virginie de Senancourt, she didn't dare break the silence. They all looked at one another for a few minutes. Then they exchanged a ceremonious bow and the caller left without having uttered a single word" (Eugène de Mirecourt, *Madame Clémence Robert* [Paris: G. Havard, 1856], 42). Cited by Georges Lubin in George Sand, *Corr.*, 2:334.

6. HV, 2:154. The term *bon enfant* is a typical Sandian expression.

7. See Madeleine Fargeaud, "Madame Balzac, son mysticisme et ses enfants," *Année balzacienne* (1965): 30.

8. See his "Lettre à Nodier," published in the *Revue de Paris* in 1832: "I have dedicated myself for many years to a few ideas that intersect with yours at the most distant of points from the center of the dazzling and vast circumference which you have so poetically traversed."

9. Honoré de Balzac, *Correspondance*, ed. R. Pierrot (Paris: Garnier, 1966), 4:417–418.

10. "In this way I wish to attest to the true friendship that has continued between us throughout our travels and our absences, in spite of our work and the unkindness of the world. This feeling will certainly never change" (Balzac, *La Comédie humaine*, 1:195).

11. *Correspondance Flaubert-Sand*, ed. Alphonse Jacobs (Paris: Flammarion, 1981), 64; letter dated 16 May 1866.

12. Chateaubriand, *Le Génie du Christianisme*, (Paris: Firmin-Didot, 1865), 1:104 (pt. 1, bk. 5, ch. 2).

13. Cited by Reboul, *Lélia*, 150n.

14. Pierre Simon Ballanche, *La Ville des expiations* (Lyon, Presses universitaires de Lyon, 1981); 17, 32, 150, and 32, respectively.

15. Ibid., 23.

16. Charles Nodier, *Oeuvres complètes* (Geneva: Slatkine Rpts., 1968), rpt. Paris, 1832–1837, 12 vols., 5: *Rêveries*, 354–355. Emphasis added.

17. See J. Matter, *Histoire critique du gnosticisme et de son influence sur les sectes religieuses et philosophiques* (Paris: Levrault, 1828), 2 vols; 2d ed., Strasbourg: Vve Levrault, 1843–1844, 3 vols.

18. In turn, the following year *Lélia*, with its aims at "invisible fiction," would have a similar effect on *Séraphita*.

19. Balzac, *Béatrix*, in *La Comédie humaine*, 2:814.

20. Thierry Bodin, "Du côté de chez Sand," *Année balzacienne* (1972), 252.

21. See Balzac, *Les Proscrits*, in *La Comédie humaine*, 11:540; and *Louis Lambert*, in *La Comédie humaine*, 11:617.

22. Per Nykrog, *Le Pensée de Balzac dans la Comédie humaine* (Copenhagen: Munksgaard, 1965), 187.

23. Max Andréoli, "Une nouvelle de Balzac: "La Maison du Chat-qui-pelote," in *Année balzacienne* (1972), 64.

24. See Foedora: "Neither sinful nor virtuous, this woman lived far from human society, in a sphere of her own, whether hell or paradise" (*La Peau de chagrin*, in *La Comédie humaine*, 10:175; emphasis added.)

25. A good example is *Ivanhoe*.

26. Curiously, in her earlier works, *Rose et Blanche* and *Indiana*, her device is to differentiate her two heroines not so much according to hair color as according to eye or skin color. The melancholy Blanche has blue eyes while the fiery Rose has black eyes. Both Noun and Indiana are brunettes, but Noun is dark-skinned and dark-eyed, while Indiana is pale and has blue eyes.

27. Cf. the description of Mlle de Chartres: "The whiteness of her complexion and her blond hair gave her a brilliance never seen but in her; all her features were regular, and her face and her person were full of grace and charm" (Madame de Lafayette, *Romances et nouvelles*, ed. E. Magne [Paris: Garnier, 1961] 248).

28. The aristocratic ball in *Le Piccinino* allows for the uneasy but actual mixing of aristocrats and artisans.

29. For an exploration of the theme of fatal love in *Valentine*, see Kathryn Crecelius's chapter, "*Valentine*: Tristan and Iseut in the Berry," in *Family Romances*, 81–94.

30. In her 1852 preface to *Jeanne* Sand would again face the linguistic problem of depicting class more fully. Her "Notice" clearly presents a new problematic encountered not on the level of character (since she had already populated her works with different social types) but with respect to language.

31. See article by Micheline Besnard, "Quelques repères structurels, les lieux dans *Valentine*," *Présence de George Sand*, 22 (Mar. 1985).

32. Valentine says of her mother, grandmother, and fiancé: "Moi seule . . . je voulais faire du mariage une obligation réciproque et sacrée. Mais ils riaient de ma simplicité; l'un me parlait d'argent, l'autre de dignité, un troisième de convenances. L'ambition ou le plaisir, c'était là toute la morale de leurs actions, tout le sens de leurs préceptes" (206; "I alone . . . wished to

make the marriage a reciprocal and sacred obligation. But they laughed at my simplicity. One would speak to me of money, another of dignity, and a third of proprieties. Ambition or pleasure were the only moral standards of their actions, the entire substance of their precepts").

33. A fragment of what would become *Gobseck* came out in *La Mode* in March 1830 under the title of *L'Usurier*. One month later the first edition of the novella *Les Dangers de l'inconduite*, which comprised the article in *La Mode*, came out in book form. See Pierre Citron, "Introduction" in Balzac, *La Comédie humaine*, 2:945.

34. Balzac, *César Birotteau*, in *La Comédie humaine*, 6:243.

35. This episode is also a clear allusion to *La Princesse de Clèves*.

36. An obvious reference to *La Princesse de Clèves*.

37. "I found myself between two centuries, *as if I were at the confluence of two rivers*; I plunged into their troubled waters, moving away with regret from the ancient shore where I had been born, swimming with hope toward an unknown shore" (Chateaubriand, *Mémoires d'outre-tombe*, ed. Maurice Levaillant and Georges Moulinier, 2 vols. [Paris: Pléiade, 1946–1951], 2:936; emphasis added).

38. See *Histoire de ma vie*, pt. 2, ch. 15, where Sand talks about the constant struggle between "ces deux mères" (HV, 1:604). Monique Bosco writes: "One could say that George Sand lived that part of her life as a victim in the constant and agonizing struggle between these two implacably possessive and tenacious women who fought over the child" ("George Sand ou la nouvelle Aurore," in *George Sand: Voyage et écriture*, special issue of *Etudes françaises*, 24/1 [1988]:90).

39. In *Les Martyrs ignorés* Balzac writes: "Thinking is the most violent of all the agents of destruction; it is the veritable exterminating angel of humanity" (*La Comédie humaine*, 12:742).

40. "Nous ne sommes pas des freluquets, des *habits noirs*, comme toi" (*Valentine*, 125; "We are not fops like you, decked out in black").

41. *Corr.*, 2:162–163; letter to Ch. Meure, dated 16 Sept. 1832.

42. *Corr.*, 2:288; letter to L. Decerfz, 1 Apr. 1833.

43. *Corr.*, 2:639; letter to E. Paultre, June 1834.

44. See Bernard Guyon, *La Création littéraire chez Balzac* (Paris: Armand Colin, 1951), esp. 202–223.

45. Ibid., 212.

46. Sand writes, with her usual modesty: "J'irai moi-même . . . vous porter *Valentine*, une bien mauvaise chose auprès de tout ce que vous faites." Cited in Balzac, *Correspondance*, 2:247–248; letter dated 8 Feb. 1833 ("I will bring . . . you *Valentine* myself; it's a poor thing compared to everything you produce").

47. Balzac, *Lettres à Madame Hanska*, 1:275.

48. Honoré de Balzac, *Le Médecin de campagne*, ed. E. Le Roy Ladurie, 2d ed. (Paris: Folio, 1974), 253.

49. Balzac "Confession inédite," in Guyon, *La Création*, 247.

50. Louis de Loménie, *Galerie des contemporains illustres* (1840), 35–36: "Nearly all of them [Sand's novels] contain a kind of morality of misfortune in the denouement." Cited by Pierre Salomon, *Indiana*, li.

51. Pierre Barbéris, *Balzac et le mal du siècle*, 2 vols. (Paris: Gallimard, 1970), 2:1856.

52. Barbéris, *Balzac*, 2:1848.

53. "Un type peut se définir la personnification réelle d'un genre parvenu à sa plus haute puissance. . . . Saisir vivement un type . . . le prendre sur nature, l'étreindre, le reproduire avec vigueur, c'est ravir un rayon de plus à ce merveilleux soleil de l'art" (George Sand, "Honoré de Balzac," in Balzac, *Oeuvres complètes* [Paris: Houssiaux, 1855], 1:xv; "A type may be defined as the genuine personification of a general class raised to its greatest power. . . . To capture a type vividly . . . to take hold of it in its natural form, to grasp it, to reproduce it with vigor, is to ravish yet one more ray from the marvelous sun of art").

54. Roger Shattuck, *The Innocent Eye* (New York: Farrar Straus Giroux, 1984), 127.

55. Emphasis added. George Sand, "Honoré de Balzac," 1:xv.

56. Nancy Miller, "Writing (from) the Feminine: George Sand and the Novel of Female Pastoral," *The Representation of Women in Fiction*, ed. C. Heilbrun and M. Higonnet (Baltimore: Johns Hopkins Press, 1981), 124–151.

57. A similar displacement of spheres will take place in *Le Meunier d'Angibault*.

58. Cited by Maurice Regard in *L'Adversaire des romantiques: Gustave Planche*, 2 vols. (Paris: Nouvelles éditions latines, 1955), 2:187–189.

CHAPTER 5: *LÉLIA*: NOVEL OF THE INVISIBLE

1. Jean Cassou, "George Sand et le secret du XIXe siècle," *Mercure de France*, Dec. 1961, 616.

2. "Préface de 1839," *Lélia*, 350.

3. Alfred Desessarts, *La France littéraire* (1833), 211–216. Cited by Reboul, "Accueil de *Lélia* en 1833," in *Lélia*, 588.

4. Baudelaire, *Oeuvres complétes*, 2:282–283.

5. For a lucid examination of the incongruous Reboul–Sand pair, see Marie-Jacques Hoog, "Avez-vous lu Reboul?" in *George Sand Newsletter*, 6/1–2 (fall/winter 1983): 72–74.

6. Pierre Reboul, *Errements littéraires et historiques* (Paris: Presses universitaires de Lille, 1979), 113.

7. Sainte-Beuve, *Correspondance générale*, 19 vols. (Paris: Stock, 1935), 1:374.

8. Sainte-Beuve, *Portraits contemporains*, 5 vols. (Paris: Calmann-Lévy, 1881), 1:497, 501, 502–503. Emphasis added.

9. Sainte-Beuve, *Oeuvres*, ed. Maxime Leroy, 2 vols. (Paris: Pléiade, 1956–1960), 1:383.

10. Cited by Marie-Louise Pailleron, *François Buloz et ses amis: La vie littéraire sous Louis-Philippe* (Paris: Calmann-Lévy, 1919), 385; emphasis added.

11. Hippolyte Fortoul (1811–1856), writer and critic, collaborated with the *Encyclopédie nouvelle* and wrote articles and reviews in several newspapers and literary journals: *Le Droit*, *La Revue de Paris*, *Le National*, *La Revue indépendante*. See Paul Raphaël, "Fortoul journaliste républicain et critique littéraire," *Nouvelle revue*, Dec. 1922 and Jan. 1923. See also the interesting letter Sand

writes him in response to his "éloge dithyrambique" of her in *Le Droit*, 21 Dec. 1835 (*Corr.*, 3:195–197).

12. Hippolyte Fortoul, "De l'art actuel," *Revue encyclopédique*, 59 (July 1833): 126. Subsequent references to this article are given in the text as "De l'art actuel," followed by the page number.

13. "Les Bas bleus," on 9 August; and a feuilleton on *Lélia* on 22 August 1833.

14. See Regard, *L'Adversaire des romantiques*, 2:79–82. Sand was displeased by the duel and remarked to Sainte-Beuve in October of that year, on the occasion of his article of praise for *Lélia*: "Vos paroles valent bien mieux et me sont bien plus utiles que les coups d'épées de mes autres amis" (*Corr.*, 2:431; "Your words are worth much more and are much more useful to me than the sword thrusts of my other friends"). Georges Lubin, in his commentary to the letter, aptly remarks: "Pauvre Gustave!"

15. Honoré de Balzac, "Etudes sur M. Beyle," *Oeuvres diverses*, 3:371.

16. The critic Armand Baschet, for example, called *Séraphita* "this book, incomprehensible when taken as a whole, but admirable as Swedenborgian poetry." Cited by Pauline Bernheim, *Balzac und Swedenborg* (Berlin: Verlag von Emil Ebering, 1914), 110.

17. Balzac writes to Madame Hanska (11 Mar. 1835): "One can write *Goriot* anyday; but one can write *Séraphita* only once in a lifetime" (*Lettres à Madame Hanska*, 1:311).

18. Cited in George Sand, *Journal intime* (Paris: Calmann-Lévy, 1926), 133.

19. Albert Béguin, *Balzac visionnaire* (Paris: Skira, 1946), 95.

20. Balzac, *Correspondance*, 2:654–655.

21. Pauline Bernheim, *Balzac und Swedenborg*, 22.

22. The ending of *Spirite* plays on the same notion of the invisible: "The walls became transparent . . . leaving an immense depth to be seen, not the sky that catches the human eye, but the sky that is penetrable only to the eyes of the clairvoyant" (Théophile Gautier, *Oeuvres complètes* [Geneva: Slatkine, 1978] 4:234).

23. *Quintilia* is the original title of *Le Secrétaire intime* (1834).

24. Cited by Annarosa Poli, "George Sand devant la critique, 1831–1833," in *George Sand: Colloque de Cerisy*, 98.

25. Cited by Reboul, "Accueil de *Lélia* en 1833," in *Lélia*, 589.

26. Jean Pommier, "A propos d'un centenaire romantique: *Lélia*," *Revue des cours et conférences*, 3 (15 Jan. 1934): 234.

27. George Sand, "Romans et nouvelles," in *Questions d'art et de littérature*, 48.

28. Béatrice Didier, "Préface," in *Indiana*, 14.

29. Cf. Chateaubriand, "Préface de 1805," *Atala*.

30. I am deliberately using Barthes's word "readerly" (*lisible*) as a compliment here, since the accusation brought before the text was that it was not readerly, that it was *illisible*.

31. *Lélia*, 45. As Pierre Reboul remarks, "Lélia's costume is therefore that of a man." Two indications of this are "le vêtement austère . . . d'un jeune poète" and "le satin noir de son pourpoint."

32. This scene is based on a contemporary event. A cholera epidemic had

spread through Paris between March and July of the preceding year. See Sand's letter to her mother on the subject, dated 14 Apr. 1832, *Corr.*, 2:65–66.

33. Mikhail Bakhtin, *Problems of Dostoevsky's Poetics*, trans. C. Emerson (Minneapolis: University of Minnesota Press, 1984), 5.

34. See Pierre Barbéris's comment in reference to Balzac's *Le Médecin de campagne*: "Un héros est un héraut" ("A hero is a herald").

35. Emphasis added; *Valentine*, 106. See also Sand's "Invocation," written on her bedroom wall in 1836: "Dans nos nuits d'agonie nous cherchons la Trace de Tes pas au jardin des Olives" (*Corr.*, 3:494–495).

36. *Lélia*, 104. The word "apathie" is from Senancour's repertoire.

37. Francis Bacon, *Meditationes sacrae, De Haeresibus*. Cited by Reboul in *Lélia*, 120n.

38. Reboul's comment comparing *Obermann* and *Lélia* considerably belittles the latter: "It isn't that the two books are identical: on the one hand Sand cannot attain Senancour's depth, on the other her goal is not exactly the same. Senancour writes a phenomenology about the pain of being a man; Sand, a systematic experimentation of morals and systems" ("Introduction" to *Lélia*, lix).

On the subject of Nodier, Reboul reports that Sand had the greatest admiration for the writer and had most certainly read the volumes of his complete works published in 1832, in particular the preface to *Adèle*, and the articles "De la palingénésie," "De la perfectibilité," "De la fin prochaine du genre humain," and "De l'amour et de son influence." Nodier's pessimism and nihilism, as well as his eschatological view of the world, can be discerned in *Lélia*'s speeches.

As for Balzac, Foedora, the "femme froide" of *La Peau de chagrin*, can be seen as a kind of sister of Lélia, although the two heroines are refracted through very different lenses: Sand's sympathy for her heroine contrasts sharply with Balzac's disdain for his. A stylistic analysis of the devices used by each author to convey such an impression would be a fruitful endeavor.

39. See Alfred de Musset's *La Confession d'un enfant du siècle*: "An inexpressible feeling of uneasiness began to ferment in all young hearts. Condemned to inaction by the sovereigns of the world, handed over to pedants of all kinds, to idleness and to boredom, the young people saw the foaming waves, against which they had prepared their strength, pull away" (Paris: Folio, 1973, 27). See also Stendhal, *Mémoires d'un touriste* and Alfred de Vigny, *Servitude et grandeur militaires*.

40. F. M. Dostoevskii, *Polnoe sobranie sochinenii* (Complete Works), 30 vols. (Leningrad: Nauka, 1972–1988), 24:51. A slightly different translation can be found in Dostoevsky, *Diary of a Writer*, trans. Boris Brasol (Santa Barbara: Peregrine Smith, 1974), 543.

41. Senancour, *Obermann*, 61.

Chapter 6: Two Metaphysical Novels: *Spiridion* and the *Lélia* of 1839

1. The *Bibliographie de la France* announced the publication of *Spiridion*, in book form, in February 1839; of *Lélia*, in September of the same year.

2. Citations from the 1839 edition of *Lélia* come from Béatrice Didier's mod-

ern critical edition in two volumes, *Lélia* II. For examples of Sand's more overt feminism in the second version of *Lélia*, see, for instance, the end of Lélia's letter to Valmarina: "Malheur! malheur à cette farouche moitié du genre humain [i.e. les hommes], qui, pour s'approprier l'autre, ne lui a laissé que le choix de l'esclavage ou du suicide!" (*Lélia* II, 2:25; "Woe, woe to that fierce half of the human species [i.e. men] who, for the sake of dominating the other half, has left it only the choice between servitude or suicide!"); and Lélia's words to Sténio: "Les intérêts [des hommes et des femmes] sont opposés; l'homme croit les siens plus précieux et plus importants. . . . Il faut donc que l'existence de la femme disparaisse, absorbée par celle de l'homme; et moi, je voulais exister. Je ne l'ai pas pu, j'ai préféré scinder mon existence et sacrifier ma part de vie humaine à la vie divine, que de perdre l'une et l'autre dans une lutte vaine et funeste" (2:136; "The interests [of men and women] are opposed; men think theirs more precious and important. . . . It follows therefore that the existence of woman must disappear, absorbed by that of man; but I wanted to live. I wasn't able to, I prefered to split my existence in two and sacrifice my share of human life to the divine, rather than lose both in a vain and baleful struggle").

3. Hugo, *William Shakespeare*, (Paris: Charpentier et Fasquelle, n.d.), bk. 2, "XIXe siècle," 299, 304. Similarly, Balzac comments in *Les Illusions perdues*: "The eighteenth century put everything into question. It is the responsibility of the nineteenth to provide the answers" (*La Comédie humaine*, 5:460).

4. Cited by Léon Cellier, *L'Epopée humanitaire et les grands mythes romantiques* (Paris: SEDES, 1971), 53.

5. George Sand, *Nanon*, ed. Nicole Mozet (Meylan: Editions de l'Aurore, 1987), 102–103; emphasis added. *Nanon*, although situated during the Revolution itself, also examines the primary causes for the events. The heroine equates the coming of the Revolution with the excesses of spiritual and worldly domination committed by the Catholic church over centuries. In turn, the violence of the Revolution embodied by the Terror is ascribed to a certain *accoutumance* toward terrorism which the Church made possible: "tout le mal vient du clergé," says Nanon, "qui a entretenu si longtemps le régime de terreur que ses ennemis exercent à présent contre lui. Comment voulez-vous que les victimes de la violence soient de doux élèves reconnaissants? Le mal engendre le mal . . . " (*Nanon*, 103; "All the evil comes from the clergy, which for so long maintained the regime of terror that its enemies are now exercising against it. How can you expect the victims of violence to be docile and grateful pupils? Evil begets evil . . . "). The revolution represents the erecting of a new religious order to counteract the former. Nanon's fear is that it will abuse its power in turn and fall into the same errors and terrorist tactics indulged by the Church before it.

6. Louis Blanc, *Histoire de la Révolution française*, 1842 ed., 1:90–91. Cited by David Owen Evans, *Social Romanticism in France, 1830–1848* (New York: Octagon, 1969), 53. Emphasis added.

7. In this respect it resembles Sand's *Maîtres mosaïstes*.

8. Pierre Leroux, "De la philosophie et du christianisme," *Revue encyclopédique*, 55/164 (Aug. 1832): 282.

9. Jean Pommier, "Autour d'un roman religieux de G. Sand," *Revue d'histoire et de philosophie religieuses* (Strasbourg 1928), 551.

10. M. M. Bakhtin, "Discourse in the Novel," *The Dialogic Imagination*, 347.

11. See Leonid Grossman, *Dostoevskii* (Moskva: Molodaia gvardiia, 1962), 434; Joseph Frank, *Dostoevsky: The Seeds of Revolt, 1821–1849* (Princeton: Princeton University Press, 1976), 130; Isabelle Naginski, "Two Opponents of the Anthill: Dostoevski and George Sand," in *Dostoevski and the Human Condition* (New York: Greenwood Press, 1986), 199–210; Isabelle Naginski, "The Serenity of Influence: The Literary Relationship of George Sand and Dostoevsky," in *George Sand: Collected Essays*, ed. J. Glasgow (Troy, N.Y.: Whitston, 1985), 110–125.

12. Renee Winegarten, *Double Life of George Sand*, 213.

13. "Philosophie de l'histoire. De la loi de continuité qui unit le dix-huitième siècle au dix-septième," *Revue encyclopédique*, 57 (Mar. 1833): 469–470.

14. Sand, "Lamartine utopiste," *Questions d'art et de littérature*, 89.

15. In her 1863 preface to *Mademoiselle la Quintinie*, Sand made her agenda clear. Her novel is an attempt to extricate the reader from the "labyrinthe d'ambiguïtés" in which the official Catholic church has per force plunged him or her: "Longtemps la critique a prononcé que la recherche de l'idéal social ou religieux n'était pas du domaine du roman . . . aujourd'hui . . . elle reconnaît que les lettres de la conscience et l'analyse des idées les plus hautes sont du ressort de l'art littéraire" ("For a long time the critics proclaimed that the search for the social or religious ideal was not the province of the novel . . . today . . . they recognize that articles of conscience and the analysis of the most lofty ideas fall within the scope of literature").

16. Cited David Evans, *Le Socialisme romantique: Pierre Leroux et ses contemporains* (Paris: 1948), 9.

17. Ibid., 63.

18. "I possess," Lovenjoul adds, "this autograph manuscript, which bears the usual marks that the typesetting leaves, and I am referring, of course, to the text of the original edition" (Félix Thomas, *Pierre Leroux—sa vie, son oeuvre, sa doctrine: Contribution à l'histoire des idées au 19e siècle* [Paris: Alcan, 1904], 65–66). Cited by David Evans, "Pierre Leroux and His Philosophy in Relation to Literature," PMLA, 44/1 (March 1929): 286.

19. Evans, *Socialisme romantique*, 41.

20. Thanks to Lubin, Jean Pommier, in his remarkable *George Sand et le rêve monastique*, was able to rectify the mistake he had committed in an earlier article, "Autour d'un roman religieux de G. Sand," 535–559.

21. See Sand's letter to Franz Liszt: "J'ai bien de la peine à tenir ma plume. Le malheureux Piffoël est affligé d'un rhumatisme dans le bras droit qui descend le long du flanc jusqu'au genou. . . . Je n'écris plus du tout quoique je travaille toujours pas mal. C'est Mallefille et Maurice qui écrivent sous ma dictée" (*Corr.*, 4:337; "I have great difficulty holding a pen. The unfortunate Piffoël is afflected with rhumatism in his right arm that extends all the way down his side to the knee. . . . I'm not writing at all although I am still working well enough. Mallefille and Maurice are writing down what I dictate").

22. Cited by Joanna Russ, *How to Suppress Women's Writing* (Austin: University of Texas Press, 1983), 21.

23. See in this respect a provocative article by Carol Delaney, "The Meaning of Paternity and the Virgin Birth," *Man* (N.S.), 21 (Sept. 1986): 494–513.

24. The critic is G. Brandès. Cited by Roger Picard, *Le Romantisme social* (New York: Brentano, 1944), 197.

25. Cited by Jean Pommier, *Les Ecrivains devant la révolution de 1848* (Paris: PUF, 1948), 49.

26. Fourier called himself the "Messiah of Reason" ("Le Messie de la Raison") and claimed that "le règne de l'harmonie sociétaire n'est pas autre chose que le 'Règne du Christ'" (*Le Nouveau monde*, 380). Cited by Henri Desroche, *Dieux d'hommes: Dictionnaire des messianismes* (Paris/The Hague: Mouton, 1969). See also in this context Frank Bowman's "Fouriérismes et christianisme: Du Post-curseur à l'Omniarque amphimondain," *Romantisme*, 1976, 11:28–42.

27. Enfantin called himself "chef suprême de la religion saint-simonienne" and "Christ des Nations."

28. On the three eras of Christianity, see *Spiridion*, 258–259. The era of a new religion is but the continuation of Christianity (259).

29. Cited by Frank Bowman, *Le Christ romantique* (Geneva: Droz, 1973), 13.

30. In one of his "Lettres sur la littérature," Balzac commented on the identical mission of Jesus and Fourier which was to rehabilitate the passions: "Even if Fourier had only invented his theory on the passions, he would deserve to be better studied. In this regard, he continues the doctrine of Jesus. Jesus gave the world a soul . . . he revealed the theory; Fourier is inventing the application." (*Oeuvres diverses*, 3:314).

31. In her article on Lamartine (Dec. 1841), Sand called him "le cygne du christianisme, devenu aigle de la prophétie nouvelle" (*Questions d'art et de littérature*, 83).

32. Jean-Claude Fizaine, "Les Aspects mystiques du romantisme français," *Romantisme*, 1976, 11:10.

33. Ibid.

34. Saint-Martin, "Lettre sur la révolution". Cited by Desroche, *Dieux d'hommes*, 226.

35. Jules Michelet, *Les Soldats de la révolution* (Paris: Calmann Lévy, 1878), 5–7.

36. Quoted in Desroche, *Dieux d'hommes*, 227.

37. George Sand, "La Religion en France, in *Souvenirs de 1848* (Paris: Calmann-Lévy, 1880), 105. See also *Le Compagnon du tour de France*, where a character remarks: "Si le Christ revenait parmi nous et qu'il passât devant cette maison, que ferait-il?" (130; "If Christ returned among us and passed in front of this house, what would he do?").

38. Cited by Léon Cellier, *L'Epopée humanitaire*, 66.

39. As Frank Bowman notes: "From the appearance of the *Nouveau christianisme* on . . . texts which link socialism and Christianity abound" ("Fouriérismes et christianisme," 29).

40. Fizaine, "Les Aspects mystiques du romantisme français," 9.

41. Sand, "Lettre aux riches," *Questions politiques et sociales* (Paris, Calmann-Lévy, 1879), 225–230.

42. "Placé face à face avec le doute, cet esprit sincère et religieux s'épouvanta de son isolement, et se prit à suer l'eau et le sang, comme le Christ sur la montagne, à la vue de son calice" (*Spiridion*, 73; "Standing face to face with doubt, this sincere and religious mind was horrified by his isolation and began to sweat water and blood, like Christ on the Mount at the sight of his chalice").

43. Préface de Jean Gaulmier à Ernest Renan, *Vie de Jésus* (Paris: Folio, 1974),

10. Sand's letters, especially in the 1860s, vigorously argue against Jesus as God.

44. F. M. Dostoevskii, *Dnevnik pisatelia za 1876 god. Mai-oktiabr'* (Diary of a Writer for 1876. May–October), *Polnoe sobranie sochinenii* 23:37; emphasis added.

45. Sand, *Corr.*, 4:613. Letter to François Buloz, 25 (?) Mar. 1839. This remark is made in reference to *Les Sept Cordes de la lyre*, but it applies equally well to the novel in question.

46. Epigraph to Célestin Raillard, *Pierre Leroux et ses oeuvres* (Châteauroux: P. Langlois, 1899).

47. Cited by François André Isambert, *Christianisme et classe ouvrière: Jalons pour une étude de sociologie historique* (Paris: Casterman, 1961), 121.

48. Emphasis added; *Corr.*, 3:576; "échareugné" is a berrichon word for "écorché."

49. These two fragments make up chapters 57 and 58 in Part 6 of the 1839 edition. The first fragment appeared 15 July and the second 1 December 1836 in the *RDM*.

50. Sainte-Beuve, review in *Le National*; rpt. in *Portraits contemporains*, 499.

51. This scene is not unlike Balzac's Raphaël de Valentin peering at Foedora in *La Peau de chagrin*.

52. Francine Mallet, *George Sand*, 52.

53. Review of *Spiridion* in the *RDM*, 15 Sept. 1839.

54. This is from the 1833 text of *Lélia*, 167. Interestingly, Sand removed it from the second version, perhaps because she wanted to minimize the autobiographical and the sexual connotations of her novel. But the reference to "la vie positive" is retained. See Lélia's confession to Pulchérie: "Je n'ai jamais pu me résigner à la vie positive" (*Lélia*, 167; *Lélia* II, 1:165).

55. See Marie-Jacques Hoog, "Le mythe de la Sibylle au temps du romantisme," in *Le Mythe et le mythique (Colloque de Cerisy)* (Paris: Albin Michel, 1987), 165–180.

56. Saint Augustine, *The Confessions* (Baltimore: Penguin Books, 1961), 177, 178.

Chapter 7: From *Desolatio* to *Consolatio*: The Utopian Convalescence of an Enfant du siècle

1. Vissarion Grigorievich Belinskii, *Polnoe sobranie sochinenii* (Complete Works) (Moscow: Akademiia nauk, 1955), 6:279.

2. Maxime Leroy, *Histoire des idées sociales en France*, 3 vols. (Paris: Gallimard, 1950), 3:145. Leroy also suggests that Romantic literature sensitized the French to social issues: "It is through the voice of poetry, novels, plays, literary criticism that the public of the Restoration and the July monarchy became sensitive to the social issues of this time stemming from the inhuman harshness of industry, from the despair of Waterloo, from the fury, the disgrace and the resentment of the White Terror" (130).

3. Cited by S. Makashin in his article on "The Literary Interrelationships of Russia and France," in *Literaturnoe nasledstvo* (Literary Heritage), 1937, 29–30: xxxviii.

4. G. M. Fridlender, *Dostoevskii i mirovaia literatura* (Dostoevsky and World Literature) (Moskva: Khudozhestvennaia literatura, 1979), 142.

5. The critic Natal'ia Trapeznikova, for instance, devotes five chapters to individual texts, *Valentine, Jacques, Horace,* the *Consuelo* saga, the "pastoral trilogy," and *Le Marquis de Villemer.* See her *Romantizm Zhorzh Sand,* 1976.

6. See M. Treskunov, *Zhorzh Sand: Kritiko-biograficheskii ocherk* (George Sand: A Critical and Biographical Sketch) (Leningrad: Khudozhestvennaia literatura, 1976).

7. Article dated 11 Oct. 1830. Rpt. in Sainte-Beuve, *Premiers lundis,* in *Oeuvres,* 1:377.

8. Hugo, *William Shakespeare,* 300.

9. See Lubin's remarks on "George Sand's conversion to ideas of progress" (*Corr.,* 5:547).

10. She writes: "il y a un monde invisible, inconnu, où nous avons vécu et où nous ne faisions qu'un. Nous ne nous en souvenons pas, mais le besoin incessant et l'espoir vague d'y retourner nous attestent l'existence d'un passé où nous étions unis, d'un avenir où nous le serons sans doute. De ce monde invisible, il nous descend encore parfois des avertissements que dans notre langue humaine nous appelons des instincts" (*Corr.,* 3:657–658; "there exists an unknown, invisible world where we have lived and where we were one. We do not remember it, but the incessant need and the vague hope to return there testify to us of the existence of a past where we were united, of a future where we will certainly be united once again. . . . Glimpses of this invisible world, that we, in our human language, call instincts, still sometimes filter down to us").

11. Julie Sabiani, "L'Amour universel," 129, 135.

12. Cited by Jacques Viard, "Pour George Sand et pour Pierre Leroux," *RDM,* Oct. 1975, 247.

13. In a long letter to Guiseppe Mazzini Sand remarks that Leroux was not a materialist philosopher, "au contraire . . . il pèche . . . un peu par excès de l'abstraction, quand il pèche" (23 May 1852; *Corr.,* 11:184).

14. Marie d'Agoult insisted on this point in a letter to George Sand about Leroux: "there is so much poetry in his philosophy . . . that you will find yourself some evening having listened to a complete system and thinking you have heard a harmony by Lamartine" (cited by Hubert Juin, *Lectures du XIXe siècle,* 2 vols. [Paris: Union générale d'éditions, 1977], 2:176).

15. In her *Journal intime,* Sand devotes several pages to a vision of ecstasy which is reminiscent of Leroux: "L'extase est une puissance interdite qui se manifeste chez les hommes livrés aux idées abstraites et qui marque peut-être la borne où l'âme peut toucher dans les régions les plus sublimes, mais au-delà de laquelle un pas de plus la jetterait dans la confusion et la démence" (95; "Ecstasy is a forbidden power that manifests itself in men given to abstract ideas, and that perhaps marks the limit of the most sublime regions a soul can attain, but beyond which one step further would throw a soul into confusion and madness").

16. "When Sainte-Beuve saw me tormented with the despair of *Lélia,* he told me to turn toward the light that [Leroux and Reynaud] could offer," Sand writes (HV, 2:355).

17. Cited by André Maurois, *Lélia,* 477.

18. *Correspondance Flaubert-Sand* (25 Oct. 1871), 357.

19. She writes Flaubert (14 June 1867): "Je sais si bien vivre *hors de moi*! ça n'a pas toujours été comme ça. J'ai été jeune aussi et sujette aux indignations. C'est fini!" (ibid., 143).

20. Daniel Halévy, in *Pages libres*, 182 (25 June 1904): 507. Cited by Julie Sabiani, "L'Amour universel," 126.

21. Emphasis added; *Compagnon*, 313. Compare with Victor Hugo's much later remark in his *Les Misérables*: "When it is a question of probing a wound, of sounding the depths of an abyss or a society, since when is it wrong to descend too far, to go all the way to the bottom? . . . since when does horror preclude study? since when does illness cause the doctor to flee?" (Paris: Gallimard/ Folio, 1973), 3:10.

22. "J'ai fait la magique étude / Du bonheur, qu'aucun n'élude." These verses of Rimbaud are cited by Bailbé in his introduction to *Le Château des Désertes* (Meylan: Editions de l'Aurore, 1985), 23.

23. Published in installments in Louis Blanc's *La Réforme*, 21 Jan. to 19 Mar. 1845.

24. Sand wrote to Flaubert many years later (12 Jan. 1876): "Je crois que l'art, cet art spécial du récit, ne vaut que par l'opposition des caractères; mais, dans leur lutte, *je veux voir triompher le bien*" (emphasis added; *Correspondance Flaubert-Sand*, 519. "I believe that art, this special art of the narrative, is only worth while through the opposition of the characters; but, in their struggle, *I want to see the right prevail*").

25. W. H. Auden, *The Dyer's Hand* (N. Y.: Vintage Books, 1968), 409.

26. Ernest Renan, *Histoire du peuple d'Israël*, in his *Oeuvres complètes*, ed. Henriette Psichari, 10 vols. (Paris: Calmann-Lévy, 1947–1961), 6:1204.

27. *Le Producteur, Journal philosophique de l'industrie, des sciences et des beaux-arts* was a Saint-Simonian journal in the 1820s. Its epigraph was: "L'âge d'or, qu'une aveugle tradition a placé jusqu'ici dans le passé, est devant nous."

28. Saltykov-Shchedrin, *Za rubezhom* (Abroad) (Moskva: Gos. izd. khud. lit., 1950), 148.

29. "Rêver la rêverie est bien, rêver l'utopie est mieux." Cited in Paul Souchon, *Les Prophéties de Victor Hugo* (Paris: Jules Tallandier, 1945), 141.

30. See Leroux's letter to George Sand (16 Sept. 1841): "It is the people, or several writers from the people, who have discovered this name *communism*. . . . I would prefer *communionism*, which expresses a social doctrine founded on brotherhood." Cited by Jean-Pierre Lacassagne, *Histoire d'une amitié: Pierre Leroux et George Sand* (Paris: Klincksieck, 1973), 127.

31. Leroux, "De la doctrine de la perfectibilité," in *Oeuvres de Pierre Leroux (1825–1850)* (Paris: Louis Nétré, 1851), 2:169.

32. *Doctrine Saint-Simonienne. Exposition* (Paris: Librairie nouvelle, 1854), 69.

33. Sand, *Monsieur Sylvestre*, ed. Simone Vierne, reprt. 1866 ed. (Geneva: Slatkine, 1980), 76.

34. Pierre Leroux, *Revue sociale* (1846), 70: cited by Raillard, *Pierre Leroux et ses oeuvres*, 99.

35. Leroux, *Discours aux philosophes*: cited by Raillard, 127.

36. *Monsieur Antoine*, 373–374. The first emphasis is added; the second is in the original.

37. Sand, *Le Meunier d'Angibault*, ed. Béatrice Didier (Paris: Livre de Poche, 1985), 155–156.

38. Sand, "Lettres à Marcie," *Les Sept Cordes de la lyre* (Paris: Michel Lévy, 1869), 209.

39. Sand, "Fragment ou exposé d'une croyance spiritualiste," *Souvenirs et idées* (Paris: Calmann-Lévy, n.d.), 275.

40. Georges Lubin has proposed the following "limited series" in which Sand uses the device of the "retour des personnages:" *Lucrezia Floriani* and *Le Château des Désertes; Monsieur Sylvestre* and *Le Dernier amour; Pierre qui roule* and *Le Beau Laurence; Flamarande* and *Les Deux Frères.* See "George Sand et la révolte des femmes contre les institutions," in *Roman et société*, Colloque 6 nov. 1971 (Publications de l'Histoire littéraire de la France) (Paris: A. Colin, 1973), 43.

41. Emphasis added. Sand, "A propos de botanique," *Nouvelles lettres d'un voyageur* (Plan de la Tour: Editions d'aujourd'hui, 1979), 161; LV, 140.

42. Emphasis added; "A propos de botanique," 162.

43. I am grateful to Georges Lubin for having checked this point for me.

44. See Dostoevsky in *Diary of a Writer*, Dec. 1876 entry: "Ideas go flying about the air . . . ideas are alike and spread according to laws that are too difficult for us to perceive. Ideas are infectious."

45. Sand, *Nouvelles Lettres d'un voyageur*, 160.

CHAPTER 8: *CONSUELO* AND *LA COMTESSE DE RUDOLSTADT*: FROM GOTHIC NOVEL TO NOVEL OF INITIATION

1. For the sake of simplification, I refer to both *Consuelo* and its sequel, *La Comtesse de Rudolstadt*, as *Consuelo* throughout.

2. "Hence the necessity to reconsider the whole of nineteenth-century literature and to emphasize the crucial importance of new "literary genres": the Gothic novel, the serialized novel, the musical novel, the novel of initiation. All these genres . . . are combined in the extraordinary *Consuelo*."

3. See "Musique et musiciens dans *Consuelo*: Répertoire alphabétique," established by Simone Vierne and René Bourgeois in *Consuelo*, vol. 2.

4. Thematic elements: a castle for the Gothic, a descent into hell for the initiation novel. Characters: a virtuous young heroine and her male tormentor for the Gothic, an initiate and a guide for the initiation novel. Formal exigencies: the use of a narrative of nocturnal terror for the Gothic, the use of a double discourse in which the visible always alludes to the invisible in the initiation novel. A traceable tradition: the eighteenth-century English Gothicists; the nineteenth- and twentieth-century French *roman initiatique*.

5. In the text I am citing, 310 pages out of 815.

6. Peter Brooks, *The Melodramatic Imagination* (New Haven: Yale University Press, 1976), 19.

7. Ann Radcliffe, *The Mysteries of Udolpho* (Oxford/New York: Oxford University Press, 1966), 258; henceforth referred to as *Udolpho*.

8. Maurice Lévy, *Le Roman "gothique" anglais, 1764–1824* (Toulouse: Publications de la Faculté des lettres et des sciences humaines de Toulouse, 1968), 621.

9. Gaston Bachelard, *La Terre et les rêveries du repos* (Paris: Corti, 1948), 215.

10. William Patrick Day, *In the Circles of Fear and Desire* (Chicago: University of Chicago Press, 1985), 85.

11. Ibid., 103.

12. Lucienne Frappier-Mazur, "Code romantique et résurgences de fémi-nin dans *La Comtesse de Rudolstadt*," in *Le Récit amoureux: Colloque de Cerisy*, ed. Didier Coste and Michel Zénaffa, (Paris: Editions du Champ Vallon, 1984), 65. See also Julia Kristeva's chapter "Approaching Abjection," in her *Powers of Horror: An Essay on Abjection*, trans. Leon S. Roudiez (New York: Columbia University Press, 1982), 1–31.

13. Day, *In the Circles*, 47.

14. Cf. "Remembering the few books, which even in the hurry of her departure from Udolpho, she had put into her little package" (*Udolpho*, 416).

15. Ann Radcliffe, cited by Day, *In the Circles*, 106.

16. There are also elements of Gothic architecture and mood in other Sand works, most notably in the opening pages of *Mauprat*, in the *Château des Désertes*, in *Spiridion* (especially noteworthy is a descent into the catacombs), and in *Lélia* (the monastery scenes in both versions).

17. Ellen Moers, *Literary Women*, 209.

18. Day, *In the Circles*, 80.

19. Frappier-Mazur, "Code romantique," 65.

20. Day, *In the Circles*, 73–74.

21. Michel Foucault, *Les Mots et les choses* (Paris: Gallimard, 1966), 232.

22. Lowry Nelson, Jr., "Night Thoughts on the Gothic Novel," *Yale Review*, 52 (1963): 249.

23. See Léon Cellier, "Chaos Vaincu: Victor Hugo et le roman initiatique," *Bulletin de la Faculté des lettres de Strasbourg*, 6 (Mar. 1962): 329–339; "Le Grand Meaulnes ou l'Initiation manquée," *Archives des lettres modernes* 5 (1963), no. 51; "Le Roman initiatique en France au temps du Romantisme," in *Parcours initiatiques*, 118–137.

24. Cellier, "Le Roman initiatique," 125. I found it necessary to change Cellier's language so that his remarks could apply to *Consuelo* and to both male and female characters.

25. See Harry Levin, *The Gates of Horn* (New York: Oxford Univ. Press, 1966), for an apology of Realism at the expense of Idealism.

26. Naomi Schor, "Idealism in the Novel: Recanonizing Sand," *Yale French Studies*, 75 (1988): 56–73.

27. Quatremère de Quincy, *Essai sur la nature, le but et les moyens de l'imitation dans les beaux-arts* (Paris: J. Didot l'aîné, 1823), 280; cited by Marguerite Iknayan, *The Concave Mirror* (Stanford: Anma Libri, 1983), 24.

28. *Archives littéraires de l'Europe*, 6 (1805): 404.

29. "La faculté de percevoir par l'imagination," Quatremère de Quincy, *Essai sur l'idéal* (Paris: A. Leclerc, 1837), 273.

30. Cellier, "Le Grand Meaulnes ou l'Initiation manquée," 42.

31. Cellier, "L'Occultisme dans *Consuelo*," *Romantisme*, 16 (1977): 9.

32. For an overview of the role of mythology in Romanticism, see Frank Bowman's invaluable "Illuminism, Utopia, Mythology," in *The French Romantics*, ed. D. G. Charlton, 2 vols. (Cambridge: Cambridge University Press, 1984), 1:76–112.

33. Mircea Eliade, "Avant-Propos," *Images et symboles: Essais sur le symbolisme magico-religieux* (Paris: Gallimard, 1952), 12.

34. Eliade insists: "Modern man is free to be contemptuous of mythologies

and theologies, this does not prevent him from feeding on *forfeited myths and degraded images*" (ibid., 22; emphasis added).

35. Cellier, "Le Roman initiatique," 123.

36. Hélène Laperrousaz, "George Sand et Gustave Moreau: Le Mythe d'Orphée ou l'Expression impossible," in *George Sand: Collected Essays*, 281.

37. Cellier, "Le Roman initiatique," 121.

38. Victor Hugo, *Dieu* (Paris: Hetzel, n.d.), 121.

39. Léon Cellier, *L'Epopée humanitaire*, 365.

40. See Eliade, *Mephistopheles and the Androgyne*; Jung, *The Psychology of Transference*.

41. René Canat, *L'Hellénisme des romantiques*, 2: *Le Romantisme des Grecs, 1826–1840* (Paris: Didier, 1953): 241n, 293–294.

42. Gilbert Durand's discussion of "le régime nocturne" can be found in *Les Structures anthropologiques de l'imaginaire* (Paris: PUF, 1963), 201–298.

43. Canat, *L'Hellénisme*, 294.

44. Edgar Quinet, *Oeuvres complètes*, 8: *Prométhée* (Paris: Pagnerre, 1857), 133.

45. Emphasis added; *Les Sept Cordes de la lyre*, 15–16.

46. See his edition of *Consuelo* (Paris: Garnier, 1959), 3:489. Cellier is citing Mlle Rouget, *George Sand "socialiste"*, 103. For a study of Leroux's impact on *Consuelo*, see Evans's chapter on the subject in his *Socialisme romantique*.

47. Béatrice Didier, "Sexe, société et création: *Consuelo* et *La Comtesse de Rudolstadt*," *Romantisme*, 13–14 (1976): 161–162.

48. Gustave Rudler, "Avant-propos," in H. J. Hunt, *The Epic in Nineteenth-Century France* (Oxford, 1941).

49. Ovid, *Metamorphoses*, trans. R. Humphries, (Bloomington: Indiana University Press, 1955), 121. Interestingly, Demeter finally obtained the information from another nymph, Arethusa. Although *she* had also been changed into a fountain (this time by Diana), she did not seem to need lips or a tongue to speak.

50. She tells him: "N'invoquez pas son nom [celui de Dieu] pour . . . me réduire au silence" (250).

51. Perhaps, further suggests Rea, Consuelo "loses" her voice not as a punishment but as a marker of society's incapacity to understand "the message of equality, liberty, and fraternity brought by the couple" (Annabelle Rea, "Toward a Definition of Women's Voice in Sand's Novels: The Siren and the Witch," *George Sand: Collected Essays*, 231). In other words, the public voice falls silent while the private one endures.

52. Simone Vierne writes that Consuelo loses her cantatrice voice because it is "the only thing . . . which bound her to the secular world." And she quotes a revealing passage from *Les Sept Cordes de la lyre* on the divine essence of the human voice, which further emphasizes that Consuelo has lost her mundane link to a world she has outgrown. She is now free to focus her energies on the sacred realm ("George Sand et le mythe initiatique," *George Sand: Collected Essays*, 293). Eve Sourian's opposite view states that Consuelo has lost her voice "because she is no longer the fiancée of the ideal" ("Les Opinions religieuses de George Sand: Pourquoi Consuelo a-t-elle perdu sa voix?" in *George Sand: Collected Essays*, 135.) Finally, Léon Cellier remarks that Consuelo loses her voice just as Albert loses his mind (*Parcours initiatiques*, 135). All these astute but

somewhat contradictory opinions suggest that some deeper explanation lies buried within Sand's psyche.

53. Cited by Tatiana Greene, "George Sand, hérétique," in *George Sand: Collected Essays*, 146.

Chapter 9: Articulating an Ars Poetica

1. André Fermigier, "Préface" *François le Champi*, 7.

2. Cited by Léopold Mabilleau, *Victor Hugo* (Paris: Hachette, 1925), 145.

3. An important exception is Francine Mallet who aptly remarks: "Her greatest love is perhaps the love of work" (*George Sand*, 12).

4. Ibid., 107.

5. Cited by Fermigier, "Préface," 9. Per Nykrog uses the same image to discuss Balzac: "The current view of Balzac seems to be that he was a sort of brute force of Nature . . . a human machine for painting pictures of contemporary moeurs, rather in the manner that one considers a cow as a machine for producing milk" (*La Pensée de Balzac*, 5). The difference is that Balzac has since been exonerated of this accusation, while critics continue to make it about Sand. Her rehabilitation lags behind Balzac's by at least a generation.

6. Cited by Edmond et Jules de Goncourt, *Journal des Goncourt*, 3 vols. (Paris: Charpentier, 1888), 2:146. The rest of the passage reads: "Well, you know what happened. Something monstrous! One day she finished a novel at one in the morning . . . and she started right in on another that same night . . . churning out text is a function with Mme Sand."

7. Sand writes: "J'ai fini mon petit roman, je l'ai fait en quatre jours . . . et cela m'a remise en goût de travail" (*Corr.*, 7:151).

8. Flaubert, *Correspondance*, ed. Jean Bruneau, 2 vols. (Paris: Pléiade, 1973–1980), 2:177.

9. Henri Guillemin, *La Liaison Musset-Sand*, 10–11.

10. Baudelaire, "Mon Coeur mis à nu," *Oeuvre complètes*, 1:686–687. See also Barbey d'Aurevilly whose misogynistic point of view incorporates all the attacks found in Baudelaire: as a woman who dares to write, Sand is a phenomenon *contre nature*; her "style coulant" makes of her a representative of the nineteenth-century bourgeoisie. She lacks originality; her popularity makes her suspect; her style if vulgar and prosaic. Cf. Philippe Berthier, "L'Inquisiteur et la dépravatrice: Barbey d'Aurevilly et George Sand," Part I (1833–1850), *Revue d'histoire littéraire de la France*, 78 (1978):736–758; followed by Part II (1850–1889), *Revue d'histoire littéraire de la France*, 79 (1979):50–61.

11. 15 Jan. 1867; *Correspondance Flaubert-Sand*, 120.

12. See HV, 2:1342.

13. "Moi qui ne me suis jamais enterrée dans la littérature" (*Correspondance Flaubert-Sand*, 205).

14. Ibid., 212–213.

15. "Préfaces générales," *Questions d'art et de littérature*, 8.

16. The following prefaces are especially noteworthy: the *Préfaces générales* of 1842 and 1851; the prefaces to *Le Château des Désertes*; *Le Compagnon du Tour de France*; *Consuelo*; *François le champi*; *Indiana* (1832, 1842, 1852); *Jacques*; *Jean de la Roche*; *Jeanne*; *Lélia* (1833 and 1839); *Légendes rustiques*; *Lettres á Marcie*; *Lettres d'un voyageur*; *Lucrezia Floriani*; *Mademoiselle la Quintinie*; *Les Maîtres sonneurs*;

Les Maîtres mosaïstes; La Mare au diable; Le Péché de Monsieur Antoine; La Petite Fadette; Valentine.

As for Sand's literary criticism, many articles can be found in three collections: (1) *Questions d'art et de littérature*, vol. 93 of the *Oeuvres complétes* (Paris: Calmann-Lévy, 1878), which includes articles on Senancour's *Obermann*; "popular poets" and proletarian poetry; Lamartine; Victor Hugo; *Hamlet*; Flaubert's *Salammbô* and *L'Education sentimentale*; realism; theater. (2) *Autour de la table*, vol. 5 of the *Oeuvres complétes* (1876). Selected contents: the first two installments are entirely devoted to Hugo's *Contemplations*; also contains articles on "le drame fantastique" in Goethe, Byron, and Mickiewicz; Balzac; Béranger; Fenimore Cooper; Harriet Beecher Stowe; Eugéne Fromentin. (3) *Impressions et souvenirs* (Paris: Calmann-Lévy, 1904) includes many of her prefaces and writings about the theater. See also *Souvenirs de 1848* (Paris: Calmann-Lévy, 1880) and *Souvenirs et idées* (Paris: Calmann-Lévy, 1904).

17. Albert Sonnenfeld, "George Sand: Music and Sexualities," *Nineteenth-Century French Studies*, 16/2–3 (spring/summer 1988): 313.

18. In fact, as Cellier notes, death is absent also from several other woodcuts. It is significant that Sand singles out the woodcut depicting Lazarus as the only one that deploys a "realistic," even naturalistic, set of artistic criteria. The figure of death is absent; only the hideous details of decay and filth are present.

19. See Luke 16:19–31. This Lazarus is not to be confused with the better-known Lazarus whom Jesus rose from the dead and instructed to walk.

20. Emphasis added. Baudelaire, *L'Art romantique*, in *Oeuvres complètes*, 2:35.

21. *Correspondance Flaubert-Sand*, 511 ("faire de la désolation," letter dated 18–19 Dec. 1875).

22. George Sand, "Le réalisme," *Questions d'art et de littérature*, 293.

23. *Correspondance Flaubert-Sand*, 348 (letter dated 8 Sept. 1871).

24. Strangely the "Notice" is not included in the Editions des introuvables which I have used, but is in the old Calmann-Lévy edition (1900).

25. George Sand, *Mauprat*, ed. Claude Sicard (Paris: Garnier-Flammarion, 1969), 119. Cited by Yvette Bozon-Scalzitti, "*Mauprat*, ou la Belle et la Bête," *Nineteenth-Century French Studies*, 10/1–2 (fall/winter 1981–1982): 15.

26. Sand, "De Marseille à Menton," *Nouvelles lettres d'un voyageur*, 156.

27. Ann Berger, "Ce que dit le ruisseau," in *George Sand: Voyage et écriture*, special issue of *Etudes françaises* 24/1 (1988): 102.

28. George Sand, *André*, ed. H. Burine and M. Gilot (Meylan: Editions de l'Aurore, 1987), 99.

29. Thus was George Sand listed in the *Almanach général parisien* in 1837; cited by Georges Lubin, *Corr.*, 3:853.

30. "J'ai les deux sexes." "Il n'y a qu'un sexe." *Correspondance Flaubert-Sand*, 118, 121.

31. *Correspondance Flaubert-Sand*, 102–103, 29 Nov. 1866.

32. George Sand, "A propos de botanique," *Nouvelles Lettres d'un voyageur*, 188.

33. *Correspondance Flaubert-Sand*, 476.

34. George Sand, *Isidora* (Paris: Calmann-Lévy, 1894), 167.

Index